DANGEROUS GUESTS

DANGEROUS GUESTS

ENEMY CAPTIVES AND REVOLUTIONARY COMMUNITIES DURING THE WAR FOR INDEPENDENCE

KEN MILLER

CORNELL UNIVERSITY PRESS

Ithaca and London

First published 2014 by Cornell University Press
First paperback printing 2018

Printed in the United States of America

Library of Congress Cataloging-in-Publication Data

Miller, Ken, 1966– author.
    Dangerous guests : enemy captives and revolutionary communities during the War for Independence / Ken Miller.
        pages cm
    Includes bibliographical references and index.
    ISBN 978-0-8014-5055-6 (cloth : alk. paper)
    ISBN 978-1-5017-2588-3 (pbk. : alk. paper)
    1. Prisoners of war—Pennsylvania—Lancaster—History—18th century. 2. Nationalism—Pennsylvania—Lancaster—History—18th century. 3. Lancaster (Pa.)—History—Revolution, 1775–1783—Prisoners and prisons. 4. United States—History—Revolution, 1775–1783—Prisoners and prisons. I. Title.
    F159.L2M55   2014
    973.3—dc23   2014004487

Cornell University Press strives to use environmentally responsible suppliers and materials to the fullest extent possible in the publishing of its books. Such materials include vegetable-based, low-VOC inks and acid-free papers that are recycled, totally chlorine-free, or partly composed of nonwood fibers. For further information, visit our website at cornellpress.cornell.edu.

CONTENTS

ACKNOWLEDGMENTS

I am deeply indebted to the many institutions, colleagues, friends, and family members whose support and assistance made this book possible. The book began at the University of California at Davis, and I offer my heartfelt gratitude to the following people for their wise counsel, generous support, and continued encouragement. John Smolenski's masterly grasp of early American historiography and Pennsylvania history proved of incalculable value. One of my favorite people, Karen Halttunen, prodded me to answer the important questions and sharpen my prose and analysis with unfailing warmth and humor. I am especially grateful and particularly indebted to Alan "Bread & Water" Taylor who helped me define the project from its origins. Alan's high standards, patient counsel, and wry humor helped make my years in Davis among the most rewarding and memorable of my life. His professionalism and tireless commitment remain a continuing source of inspiration. Lisa Materson offered guidance above and beyond the call. Several colleagues provided welcome friendship and assistance. Andy Young shared valuable suggestions during the project's earliest stages. Robert Chester supplied characteristically pointed and good humored feedback on numerous chapters as the manuscript evolved. Mike Meloy provided pleasant company and accommodations during my research at the Library of Congress. One of my greatest personal and professional debts is to Brett Rushforth, a member of my Davis cohort who has since become like family to me. Brett read every chapter more than once, serving as a sounding board for my often ill-defined ideas while generously contributing brilliant insights of his own. Frustratingly, he frequently had a clearer sense of what I was trying to convey than I did. Most important, he never doubted that the manuscript would become a book, and his faith and friendship sustained me during the most challenging phases of the process. For the kindness and consideration of these valued friends, I remain most grateful.

I owe additional thanks to the many scholars whose contributions made this a better book than it would have been without their generous assistance. For their valuable suggestions during various stages of the book's development, I am grateful to David Waldstreicher, Aaron Fogleman, Ian Steele, Caroline Cox, Wayne Bodle, Holly Mayer, Karen Guenther, and the late William Pencak. A 2007 colloquium at the Omohundro Institute of Early American History and Culture proved especially fruitful by prompting me to refine or rethink key interpretations, and I offer my deepest thanks to Fredrika Teute, Ron Hoffman, Karin Wulf, Chris Grasso, Paul Mapp, Douglas Winiarski, and Robert Parkinson. As the book neared production, Alice Thiede produced beautiful maps with remarkable speed and efficiency.

Generous fellowships from the University of California at Davis, the Library Company of Philadelphia, the Historical Society of Pennsylvania, the German Historical Institute, the Colonial Williamsburg Foundation, the David Library of the American Revolution, and Washington College facilitated the travel, research, and writing required to complete the book. Of critical importance were the vast holdings of the Historical Society of Pennsylvania, and I extend particular thanks to Max Moeller, the former Director of Research Services. James Green of the Library Company proved a gracious host throughout my stay in Philadelphia. I profited from two especially productive and enjoyable residential fellowships at the David Library of the American Revolution, my home away from home. The David Library's astounding collections, wonderful staff, comfortable lodgings, and beautiful surroundings provided ideal conditions for scholarly research. I offer my warmest thanks to current and former staff, particularly Richard Ryerson, Will Tatum, Katherine Ludwig, and Meg McSweeney. I am also grateful to the many courteous and committed archivists and librarians at the Library of Congress, American Philosophical Society, Maryland State Archives, Maryland Historical Society, William L. Clements Library, and Lancaster County Historical Society.

Washington College, my academic home, furnished generous and sustained financial assistance. I benefited from the hard work of several gifted undergraduate research assistants, including Chris Brown, Katherine Thornton, Charles Weisenberger, Daniel Primiani, Amy Shaw, and especially Ann-Katrin Trebitz. My colleagues Carol Wilson, Clayton Black, and Katherine Maynard found time in their busy schedules to contribute helpful feedback on portions of the manuscript. Donald McColl, another colleague, offered valuable insight into the paintings by the Sussel-Washington artist. I owe a substantial debt to Pam Pears and Carol Wilson for their welcome advice and encouragement during the delicate enterprise of producing a book for tenure at an institution where faculty monographs remain rare. A hearty thanks, too, to Miller Library's Cynthia Sutton and Carol VanVeen, who worked wonders procuring the countless volumes needed to finish the book.

A version of chapter 3 appeared previously as "'A Dangerous Set of People': British Captives and the Making of Revolutionary Identity in the Mid-Atlantic Interior," *Journal of the Early Republic* 32, no. 4 (Winter 2012): 565–601. For their thoughtful and constructive feedback on that article, I thank Susan Klepp and the three anonymous reviewers.

Working with Cornell University Press has proved both a pleasure and a privilege. Amanda Heller sharpened my prose during copyediting, producing a more readable book. Ange Romeo-Hall, managing editor, steered the book through production with meticulous care and admirable expertise, fielding my many questions with patience and assurance. I will never be able to repay the debt owed to my editor Michael McGandy, who, since his first inquiry about my project several years ago, has proved both a consummate professional and an unflagging supporter. Understanding, encouraging, and remarkably patient, he expertly shepherded the manuscript through the review, revision, and production process, pushing at all the right moments and providing thoughtful, incisive feedback all along the way. I am also grateful to my two external reviewers for their faith in the manuscript and their insightful suggestions on how to improve it.

Above all, I wish to thank the members of my family, who waited a long time for this book. Though my mother, father, and brother are far from experts on the American Revolution, they contributed more to this volume than they'll ever know. The profession has carried me a long way from home, but my parents, Ken and Linda Miller, have furnished vital support and encouragement every step of the way. Amid our many anguished discussions of Germany's prospects of securing a fourth World Cup title, my brother Ric invariably inquired about the book's progress. With the book finally finished, I look forward to returning home more frequently. Finally, Donna Whicher read the manuscript more times than I care to count. Time and again, with refreshing wit and insight, she clarified my muddled prose and convoluted thinking. More than anyone else, she helped make this book a reality. For that and for so much more, I will remain in her debt.

DANGEROUS GUESTS

Prologue

A Community at War

On a chilly winter day in late 1778, a weary traveler passing through Lancaster, Pennsylvania, en route to a more southerly destination marveled at the inhabitants' "diversity of religions, nations, and languages." Yet even more astonishing to the bemused traveler was the "harmony they live in." Thomas Anburey's observation was hardly novel. Lancaster had long evoked similar reactions from visitors unacquainted with the striking diversity of the mid-Atlantic interior. Centrally located some sixty miles west of Philadelphia and ten miles east of the winding Susquehanna River, Lancaster exemplified the pluralism of the Pennsylvania hinterland. Founded more than four decades earlier, the town was now home to German, English, and Scots Irish settlers whose faiths ranged from Anglican and Presbyterian to Lutheran and Reformed.[1]

What makes Anburey's observation so remarkable is that Lancaster was never more diverse or divided than at the time of his passage. Indeed by 1778, Lancaster was no ordinary community, and Anburey was no ordinary traveler. Thomas Anburey was a British lieutenant in the Twenty-ninth Regiment of Foot, captured by Continental forces at the Battle of Saratoga just fourteen months before. Accompanying the lieutenant through Lancaster were more than four thousand of his British and German comrades, now bound for a long detention in Charlottesville, Virginia. Lancaster, in turn, was very much a community at war. The harmony that so impressed

1

Anburey animated the relations between his English- and German-speaking captors, Lancaster's committed revolutionaries now united in their shared struggle for independence from Great Britain.

As a captive officer in enemy hands, Anburey surveyed the local conditions with an observant eye. He and his fellow officers resented the revolutionaries' treatment of local loyalists, visibly marginalized for their stubborn devotion to the crown. The lieutenant and his compatriots also noted the varied reception awaiting Lancaster's newly arriving British and German prisoners. Often hostile to the British, most residents approached their German captives more favorably. Adding to the dizzying surroundings were the visiting Continentals from neighboring states garrisoned in Lancaster for winter quarters or on hand as escorts for the prisoners as well as the multinational foreign legionnaires, now allied with the Americans and busy recruiting throughout the interior. The steady traffic among supporters of the American resistance encouraged intimate associations between the town's revolutionaries and their once distant allies. For residents and visitors alike, Lancaster operated as an international crossroads buzzing with assorted peoples and cultures. Anburey soon encountered similar scenes in related sites in his ensuing travels throughout the interior.

But what brought Anburey to Lancaster, and why would he return just two and a half years later? By 1778, Lancaster was a routine stop for the Americans' British and German prisoners, who, by turns, became a familiar presence among the town's inhabitants. When Anburey and his compatriots were making their way through Lancaster's streets, local revolutionaries could already look back on three years of hosting prisoners, and most were now thoroughly seasoned in their dealings with the enemy. Although the Saratoga captives continued on their southbound journey, they encountered numbers of their own in Lancaster, fellow prisoners seized in various engagements, some freely wandering the town, others closely confined in the jail or barracks. Thousands of captives preceded the new arrivals to Lancaster and thousands more would follow. After Cornwallis's forces invaded Virginia in mid-1781, Anburey, too, returned to Lancaster, joined by more than a thousand of his captured comrades, now due for an indefinite stay in the Pennsylvania interior. These British and German prisoners—like their local hosts, separated by language and custom and drawn from assorted portions of their distinct empires—multiplied the town's divisions. Lancaster's peculiar wartime conditions help explain the riddle of harmony amidst diversity. Anburey arrived in Lancaster at a critical moment in the community's development, as locals forged a shared American identity in the face of their wartime adversaries.

By the time Anburey arrived for his second visit, Lancaster had become the hub of an elaborate Continental detention network stretching across the vast American interior. Over the course of the war, the revolutionaries would disperse upwards of thirteen thousand prisoners—both British regulars and their so-called Hessian auxiliaries—in scattered communities nestled deep in the Virginia, Maryland, and Pennsylvania hinterlands. In makeshift detention camps, the captives came under the immediate jurisdiction of local officials loosely supervised by civil and military authorities at both the provincial and Continental levels. Concentrating their prisoners in the heart of their communities brought the revolutionaries' enemies to their doorstep. By early 1779, General George Washington, furious over the captives' ongoing attempts to subvert the American war effort, branded them "dangerous guests in the bowels of our Country."[2]

But what "Country" did Washington have in mind? The distinct provinces and peoples that hosted the captives as yet lacked the necessary ingredients for a unified nation, even amidst a grim and brutal war for national liberation. Years after their bold declaration of July 1776, the revolutionaries' national identity remained intensely problematic, and Washington was presuming precisely what he believed needed to be created to seal America's independence from Great Britain. The dilemma of national identity was nowhere more evident than at the Americans' chief detention site in Lancaster, where local revolutionaries negotiated their remarkable diversity among a host of new enemies. Before the Revolution, Lancaster's English and German speakers generally identified and associated with their own, safeguarding their peculiar languages and customs through an ethnocultural politics oriented toward the defense of specific ethnic and religious interests. The Revolutionary War disrupted customary ethnic ties, as locals became locked in a bitter struggle pitting Briton against Briton and German against German, reducing cultural kinsmen to armed antagonists. Hardening battle lines quickly overrode familiar ethnic distinctions, as locals' ethnocultural differences came to matter less than the collective dangers posed by their assorted adversaries. Lancaster's Revolution thus mitigated long-standing cultural divisions in the Pennsylvania interior by uniting English and German speakers in a shared Continental endeavor.

The Revolution posed unusual dangers for locals, whose preoccupations with internal security often trumped broader commitments to cause and country. In constant proximity to their enemies, Lancaster's revolutionaries faced a daily war at home. As early as 1776, with the British actively soliciting Indian aid against their rebellious colonists, the conflict rekindled familiar fears of bloody raids along the Pennsylvania frontier. Within Lancaster

County, the imperial crisis politicized identities and exacerbated divisions as rebels and loyalists split into hostile camps. A troublesome loyalist minority harried revolutionaries throughout the fight by deriding the cause, collaborating with the enemy, and violently resisting the new republican regime. The community's British prisoners, meanwhile, openly defied their hosts, fleeing, plotting, and rebelling, often with the clandestine support of local loyalists. Compounding the danger was the looming specter of enemy incursion, with the British periodically threatening to reclaim the captives by force. The prisoners' volatility merged with the prospect of raids and conspiracies to keep residents on a knife's edge. With a steady stream of Continental prisoners flowing into the town's barracks, the war continued to intrude on the community, even as it shifted to more distant theaters over the course of military operations. For Lancaster, internal and external threats thus converged, ultimately intensifying local divisions while solidifying the ranks of committed revolutionaries—both soldiers and civilians, and both English and German speakers.

Wartime pressures nurtured an emerging patriotism within the ethnically divided, provincially oriented community. For Lancaster's insurgents, the imperial crisis redefined relationships with both near and distant neighbors, generating new friends and enemies. Troubles at home fed broader ties and sensibilities as local patriots distinguished themselves from their adversaries and identified with like-minded revolutionaries within and beyond their community. Even while tending to local security, revolutionaries became invested in the larger common struggle, transcending their particular ethnic and communal attachments to identify with more remote friends and allies in shared patriotic discourse and practice. Revolutionaries found comfort at home in successes abroad, eagerly following the war from afar and celebrating military and diplomatic triumphs with defiant patriotic displays. Revolutionary rites and festivities helped unify local militants while integrating them into a broader Continental enterprise. In ritual and rhetoric, Lancaster's revolutionaries venerated their friends and repudiated their enemies, evincing a bourgeoning patriotism that vied with their stubbornly persistent parochialism.

Within the last decade or so, in hopes of gleaning fresh insight into the revolutionary experience, historians have shown new interest in the problem of captivity during the War for Independence. Recent investigations of the revolutionaries' British and German captives have generally emphasized the broad contours of Continental prisoner policy. Scholars have devoted far less attention to the dynamic interactions of captors and captives within their scattered detention sites. Yet with local conditions influencing Continental policy throughout the hostilities, they remain fundamental to any proper understanding of the captive experience. As the revolutionaries' principal host community, Lancaster merits special attention. A case study of revolutionary Lancaster reveals how the decisions of distant Continental officials affected group relations within a specific locale, and how the day-to-day, face-to-face exchanges between combatants, in turn, reoriented Continental policy. As colonial insurgents initially lacking the well-defined policies and formal administrative apparatus to govern their prisoners, the revolutionaries had to improvise. While the British typically consigned their captives to English prisons or New York's jails, warehouses, and prison ships, the Americans dispersed theirs among scattered cities, towns, and villages across the emerging United States, where locals struggled to control their often disorderly guests, alternately enforcing or contesting Continental policy. Through the earliest years of the war, Lancaster served as a critical testing ground for the Americans' evolving prisoner policy, with local pressures modifying Continental practice and redefining perceptions of the enemy.[3]

This book approaches the local encounters between revolutionaries and their British and German prisoners as a window onto early American identity formation. Lancaster held an unusual—and, for residents, an unwelcome—stake in the war. With so much invested in the conflict locally, residents kept their attention firmly fixed on Continental developments. Home front and battlefront overlapped in Lancaster, with the pressures, perils, and proximity of war sustaining an ongoing dialogue between the local and the national. Throughout the hostilities, residents struggled to reconcile competing personal, communal, and Continental agendas. By locating the seeds of a budding—if ultimately fleeting—wartime nationalism in the collective hopes, fears, and resentments of the community's revolutionaries, the chapters that follow cast light on the local production of American identity. In Lancaster, diverse revolutionaries expressed an ephemeral national consciousness by defining themselves against their enemies rhetorically as well as ideologically, ritually, and spatially.[4]

Framed by a loose chronology, the discussion unfolds in stages. The six chapters investigate how locals interacted with and defined themselves against distinct sets of enemies, ranging from natives and loyalists to British regulars and German mercenaries. My first chapter charts Lancaster's early history from settlement to the eve of the imperial crisis, highlighting residents' diversity and provincialism and situating local politics within Pennsylvania's broader political culture. The Seven Years' War and Pontiac's Rebellion offered a preview of the conflict to come, reconfiguring customary patterns of identification and interaction of English and German speakers as they closed ranks in the face of dreaded enemies along their frontier.

For the local supporters of the American resistance, the struggle with Britain constituted an even greater challenge than the frontier crises of the preceding decades. Imperial tensions redefined local identities and commitments by demanding unprecedented levels of interethnic and intercolonial cooperation. Chapter 2 traces Lancaster's response to the mounting troubles with Britain from the mid-1760s to the declaration of independence, underscoring the implications of the rebels' initial wartime mobilization and the transformation of local political culture. Empowering the supporters and marginalizing the opponents of independence, war and revolution bred new divisions between rebels and loyalists, radicals and moderates.

My third chapter sets the stage for the peculiar dangers facing Lancaster's revolutionaries, examining their hostile interactions with the prisoners seized during the rebels' Canadian expedition of late 1775. Complicating matters for the makers of Continental policy, their earliest captives were fellow Britons seized in a colonial insurgency. Continental officials' feelings of shared kinship with their imperial opposition informed their approach to their new captives, as they pursued a policy designed to promote kindred relations between the prisoners and their local hosts in hopes of eliciting British sympathy for the cause. Instead, locals' contentious dealings with their captives thwarted Continental designs and fostered a distinct revolutionary identity.

Washington's capture of over nine hundred Hessians at the Battle of Trenton in late 1776 brought another set of prisoners and problems to Lancaster, the focus of chapter 4. Initially reviled by the patriots as ruthless, rapacious minions of violence, Britain's German auxiliaries subsequently became the focus of a conflicting propaganda campaign designed to seduce them from the king's service. Approaching the mercenaries as mutual victims of royal oppression, Continental officials tendered them generous offers of land and liberty in exchange for their desertion from imperial ranks. To convert their new German captives, the revolutionaries repeated the experiment that had failed with the British, encouraging hospitable local relations, with more favorable results. Sharing cultural and linguistic ties with Lancaster's German-speaking majority, the mercenaries proved more malleable and cooperative than their British allies, ultimately validating the Continentals' subversion campaign.

Following General William Howe's occupation of Philadelphia in late 1777, Lancaster faced the British Army to the east and Indian and Tory raiders to the north and west, aggravating the smoldering tensions between captors and captives, rebels and loyalists. Meanwhile, the decision for independence, Pennsylvania's radical constitution, and recent military reversals dampened support for the cause, fostering war weariness and exacerbating the tensions between militants and moderates. Spanning the years between Howe's 1777 invasion and the 1781 siege of Yorktown, chapter 5 demonstrates how the converging pressures of war rallied local insurgents by rendering them increasingly assertive of their status as revolutionaries and bolstering their vision of themselves as a distinct American people. Threatened from within and without, Lancaster's hard-liners identified with distant American allies, embracing a larger revolutionary community through patriotic rituals and celebrations while policing more immediate dangers at home.

Highlighting the conflict's concluding years to the peace of 1783, my last chapter provides a broader analysis of American prisoner policy by investigating patterns in related host communities across the United States. Only during the latter half of the war would a full-blown Continental detention system emerge, with Lancaster serving as the continuing center of operations. By 1782, their enemies defeated and peace all but assured, the revolutionaries confronted the dilemma of how best to manage their more than ten thousand remaining prisoners. After a long and costly war, locals and Continental authorities had their own, often conflicting ideas about how to deal with their British and German prisoners. The captives in turn faced their own decision: to return to their ranks and their Old World communities or to begin life anew among their wartime adversaries. Resolving these dilemmas created new problems for captors and captives alike. With local controls slackening after the decisive British defeat at Yorktown, the revolutionaries' detention network unraveled, resulting in more escapes and renewed pressures to bring the captives to heel. As the hostilities drew to a close, the revolutionaries began to reconstitute their communities, either including or excluding erstwhile enemies. Chapter 6 concludes by exploring the degree to which wartime expediency and the Revolution's universalistic ideals facilitated the incorporation of particular prisoners into the new United States.

A brief epilogue brings the study full circle. Returning to Lancaster, the epilogue asks what changed and what remained the same following a long and disruptive war, evaluating the extent to which prerevolutionary patterns of identification and association resumed with the peace. The book concludes with the related question of whether the patriotism of Lancaster's residents survived once their victory had dispelled the demons of war.

CHAPTER 1

"A Colony of Aliens"

Diversity, Politics, and War in Prerevolutionary Lancaster

The provincial assembly carved out Lancaster County from the western portion of Chester County in 1729 amidst a rising tide of German and Scots Irish immigration into the Pennsylvania interior. Drawn to a colony rich in affordable land and free of oppressive taxes, military obligations, and an established church, waves of immigrants disembarked at the bustling ports of the mid-Atlantic seaboard and pushed into the rapidly expanding provincial hinterland to plant their scattered settlements east of the Susquehanna River. As their numbers swelled, the newly arrived backcountry settlers bristled at their remoteness from Chester, the county seat, situated along the Delaware River more than a day's travel to the east. Stressing the inconvenience of residing so far from the center of social, commercial, and administrative affairs, disgruntled residents eagerly petitioned the provincial government for the creation of a new county with a seat closer to the Susquehanna. The provincial assembly dutifully obliged, folding the lands east of the proprietary boundary and north of Octoraro Creek to the Schuykill River into the new county of Lancaster. A steady flood of settlement brought a host of new towns in the decades to follow. By the early 1770s, the county consisted of upwards of two dozen townships and a borough.[1]

Founded in 1730, some sixty miles west of Philadelphia and ten miles east of the Susquehanna, the town of Lancaster became the new county seat, the first in a succession of backcountry seats designed to populate and consolidate the Pennsylvania interior. Later followed by York, Carlisle, Reading, and Easton, Lancaster formed an integral part of the province's interconnected political and economic apparatus. Luring immigrants into the expanding hinterland, these burgeoning market towns soon constituted the nuclei of Pennsylvania's increasingly complex urban geography. In Pennsylvania, the creation of new towns typically fell to the proprietary Penn family. Founded by the Hamilton clan, close associates of the Penns and recent purchasers of the property selected for the new county seat, Lancaster proved an exception to the rule. As Lancaster's legal proprietors, the Hamiltons designed their new town, apportioned lots for purchase, and collected annual ground rents from homeowners through their local agent. The family continued to draw revenues from town rents for the duration of the eighteenth century.[2]

Philadelphia in Miniature

Located in the heart of the county amid tumbling hills, dense woods, and scattered swamps, Lancaster functioned as a commercial and administrative center, boasting a market, courthouse, and jail by the mid-1730s. The town's design conformed to a gridiron system, with a central square flanked by cross streets running east to west and north to south. Dotting the countryside beyond the town limits were prosperous farms, many of them owned by German sectarians, who tended abundant livestock and fertile fields of grain. Like their rural neighbors, these Amish and Mennonites were drawn to the rich limestone soils of the gently sloping Lancaster plain. As a hub of social and economic activity, Lancaster quickly became a magnet for outlying residents, who paid regular visits to seek fellowship among its multiplying denominations and to engage in commercial transactions with its thriving artisans and merchants.[3]

Situated at a well-traveled crossroads, Lancaster soon emerged as a key trading and manufacturing town linking Pennsylvania's coast with its frontier. By 1741, the King's Highway connected Lancaster to the buzzing capital to the east, bringing a persistent stream of travelers making the long trek between Philadelphia and the expanding hinterland. Patronizing Lancaster's assorted inns, taverns, and shops was a diverse clientele of residents and visitors passing through the town en route to more distant destinations. Post riders, meanwhile, arrived with news from Philadelphia, neighboring colonies, and ports overseas. A rapidly expanding community, Lancaster attracted a mix of laborers, craftsmen, merchants, and professionals, encompassing several hundred residents by the early 1740s. During the first decade of settlement, the

Hamiltons deeded more than 130 lots. In 1748, Lancaster's Lutheran minister reported that the town contained "about 400 houses, with more still being built. On account of the good livelihood." Six years later, a visitor described Lancaster as a "growing Town, and making Money." During the earliest years of settlement, the comparatively small population, diversity of local production, and relatively broad distribution of wealth ensured that many inhabitants enjoyed a reasonably comfortable standard of living. Residents' homes reflected their middling status. "The houses for the most part are built and covered with wood," observed one visitor in 1744, "except some few which are built of brick and stone. They are generally low, seldom exceeding two stories." Many town lots included carefully tended gardens and orchards in the Old World fashion.[4]

Within a generation, as Lancaster expanded commercially, the town came to resemble a stratified urban community, with measurable class divisions and disparities of wealth. In 1766, one Pennsylvanian described Lancaster, now the backcountry's major entrepôt for manufacture and exchange, as "Philadelphia in Miniature." The community's rapid development reflected Pennsylvania's steady incorporation into a broader Atlantic economy. Lancaster participated in an extensive trading network linking Pennsylvania, Maryland, and Virginia to more far-flung ports overseas. Leading the community in the accumulation of wealth were members of a small but privileged merchant class, both retailers and wholesalers. According to Jerome Wood, by 1759, merchants constituted at least 8 percent of Lancaster's heads of families and routinely topped the town's annual assessment lists.[5]

Local traders relied on suppliers in Philadelphia, although a few maintained profitable ties with merchants in the more southerly port of Baltimore. Residents' inventories encompassed an impressive range of merchandise, from sugar, textiles, and hardware to coffee, tea, wine, and rum. After receiving their imported goods from Philadelphia, most storekeepers sold them retail to local consumers. A handful of the town's leading traders, however, formed partnerships with neighbors or with merchants in the capital to act as wholesalers to shopkeepers in Lancaster or in outlying towns and villages. The merchants with sufficient financial means extended their operations deeper into the interior, supplying the isolated settlements farther west. A few served as factors for mercantile houses in Philadelphia, furnishing them with a range of commodities from inland regions. Several of Lancaster's most successful merchants carved out a role in the western Indian trade. Without ready access to a navigable river system, local shopkeepers relied on the overland trade. Carrying grain, produce, livestock, skins, and pelts eastward and returning with the precious staples of the Atlantic trade were the famed

Conestoga wagons, which, one observer reported in 1771, "travel in great numbers," occasionally "being about one hundred in a company."[6]

After emigrating from Offenheim during the 1730s, the merchant Sebastian Graff quickly emerged as one of Lancaster County's wealthiest inhabitants. Graff steadily expanded his fortune as a local creditor and land speculator. By the early 1760s, his estate totaled more than £5,000 and included four houses in Lancaster and large holdings in neighboring Manheim. The Lancaster merchant Joseph Simon, by contrast, left England during the early 1740s to establish an elaborate trading network and become one of the backcountry's most respected entrepreneurs. Along with other ventures that included manufacturing and land speculation, Simon played a leading role in the Indian trade, shipping cloth, leather goods, metal tools, silver trinkets, and wampum west in exchange for the prized skins and pelts destined for overseas markets. Like his competitor Sebastian Graff, Simon eventually acquired choice properties in Lancaster and extensive acreage in Manheim. In 1771, only ten of Simon's Lancaster neighbors paid a higher proprietary tax.[7]

Ultimately, however, a diverse collection of industrious craftsmen, some with their own shops, set the tone for the bustling market center. By 1760, craftsmen accounted for more than 50 percent of Lancaster's heads of household. A decade later, the proportion had increased to more than 60 percent. According to Lancaster's 1759 census, residents practiced nearly forty different trades. Roughly 25 percent of Lancaster's artisans worked in the leather trades. For example, the town was home to thirty-four shoemakers and nineteen saddlers. Carpenters and masons, members of the building trades, constituted at least one-fifth of Lancaster's craftsmen by 1760. Forty-four residents, or nearly 20 percent of the town's artisans, practiced textile crafts, while another thirty-seven, or approximately 15 percent, made their living in the metal trades. Ten years later, Lancaster boasted twenty-two tailors and seventeen blacksmiths. Many of their neighbors engaged in food processing. By 1770, for example, fifteen bakers and seventeen butchers plied their trade in Lancaster.[8]

Some of the town's more enterprising artisans diversified their business operations. Lorenz Marquedant served Lancaster County as both a dyer and a stocking weaver after moving to Pennsylvania in 1750. By 1760, he numbered among the uppermost 20 percent on Lancaster's assessment list. Within a generation of emigrating to Penn's province, he had accumulated enough capital to purchase property in distant Northumberland County. Situated in the heart of Pennsylvania's expanding backcountry, Lancaster's gunsmiths found their services in particular demand. After apprenticing in Lancaster prior to the Seven Years' War, the second-generation Irish American William

Henry became one of the province's most esteemed gunsmiths. As the threat of war lifted in 1759, Henry remained one of only four gunsmiths in Lancaster. That same year, he joined with Joseph Simon to open a successful hardware store on the central square. Prospering in his varied enterprises, he paid a slightly higher proprietary tax in 1771 than his fellow craftsman Marquedant.[9]

As the population swelled and a larger proportion of the town's wealth became concentrated in fewer hands, a visible gulf separated the rich and the poor. As early as 1751, the richest 20 percent of Lancaster's household heads controlled nearly 50 percent of the community's taxable assets, while the poorest 50 percent possessed a mere quarter of the town's wealth. By 1756, with steadily rising land values increasing the price of lots, nearly one hundred of the town's 360 listed heads of household were tenants. Just three years later, upwards of 20 percent of Lancaster's taxpayers remained mired in poverty, working as laborers or wagoners and earning more meager incomes than their artisan, merchant, and professional neighbors. As the local notable and Hamilton family agent Edward Shippen reported in 1773, Lancaster contained an "abundance of Poor People," who "very seldom get any employment" and "maintain their Families with great difficulty by day Labour." Given the straitened circumstances of the poorer sort, their situation remained relatively fluid. Short of opportunities in Lancaster, many moved on in hopes of finding better prospects to the south or west. Moreover, while freemen predominated, Lancaster's 1754 assessment list included fifty-five indentured servants, most of them Germans indentured to artisans and traders. During the earliest years of settlement, Lancaster contained only a handful of slaves, the property of the town's wealthier inhabitants. In 1756, thirteen slaves resided in the community, although their numbers more than doubled over the following decade.[10]

Although a member of the local elite like Edward Shippen may have sympathized with Lancaster's underprivileged, by pursuing lives of luxury and refinement in their rapidly developing backcountry environment, he and other wealthy inhabitants accentuated the divide between rich and poor. Born into a prominent provincial family, Shippen had relocated to the backcountry from Philadelphia, where he had served as mayor and prospered as a successful merchant. He moved to Lancaster during the early 1750s after developing a lucrative interest in the fur trade. Placing him among the town's most privileged inhabitants, Shippen's genteel existence came at the expense of several household servants and slaves. The local elites' status consciousness became increasingly evident in patterns of conspicuous consumption and association.[11]

Within a few decades of the town's founding, wealth dictated where locals resided, promoting a trend of residential segregation based on income. While the lower sorts congregated in Lancaster's poorer neighborhoods, literally on the margins of town, the wealthier artisans, merchants, and professionals paid higher ground rents to occupy the most spacious, sumptuous, and lavishly furnished dwellings lining the major thoroughfares. Joseph Simon, for instance, owned a premium lot on the southeast corner of the town square, where he profited from the labors of indentured servants and a slave. Wealthy notables like the Anglo attorney George Ross and the German tavern keeper Wilhelm Bausman distinguished themselves from their poorer neighbors by purchasing such luxurious items as clocks, china, coaches, and mahogany furniture. Dismayed by the tensions within his congregation, in 1760 the Reverend Thomas Barton, Lancaster's newly arrived Anglican minister, bemoaned the fact that some parishioners "puffed up with a notion of their superior knowledge, fortunes and families seem apprehensive of ranking with the meaner sort." Most members of Lancaster's elite were happy to see the rootless poor continue on their way after a brief and disappointing spell in the community.[12]

Palatine Boors

Despite the population's persistent fluidity, Lancaster proceeded to grow apace. Indeed, by 1770, with close to three thousand residents, Lancaster not only was the largest town in a county of more than thirty thousand inhabitants but also ranked as one of the largest inland communities in the British mainland colonies. Lancaster formed part of Greater Pennsylvania, a thickly settled region, defined by cultural pluralism, which stretched from southeastern Pennsylvania into the southern backcountry to the North Carolina Piedmont. Immigration accounted for most of Lancaster's growth during the first decades of settlement as swarms of settlers from northern Ireland and southwestern Germany flocked to the Pennsylvania interior through the early to mid-eighteenth century in search of economic opportunity and religious freedom. By 1750, the Germans made up an estimated 40 percent and the Scots Irish some 25 percent of Pennsylvania's total population. Although Swiss Mennonites first settled the area that would become Lancaster, establishing industrious farms around 1710, Rhineland Germans constituted the county's largest group of initial immigrants, followed by Ulster Scots. Welsh and English settlers arrived in smaller numbers.[13]

Propelled by geographic, cultural, and kinship ties in an accelerating chain migration, distinct sets of Old World emigrants clustered among their own,

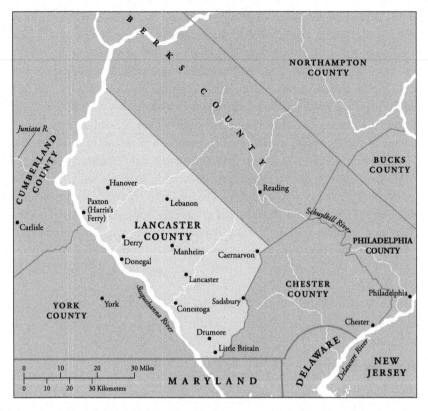

MAP 1.   Lancaster County, Pennsylvania, circa 1770, with a sample of towns and townships. Drawn by Alice Thiede.

forming scattered pockets of ethnic settlement. As early as the 1720s, the provincial secretary, James Logan, noted that Pennsylvania's newly arriving Scots Irish immigrants refused to "mix in their settlements," preferring to congregate "among themselves." Similarly, in 1750, the Lutheran pastor Henry Melchior Mühlenberg observed that the province's multiplying German immigrants "spread out in crowds scattered throughout the country." Lancaster County's German and Scots Irish settlers gravitated to the north and west, the English and Welsh to the south and east. Historians have shown how the names of towns hinted at their settlers' geographic origins, reflecting the world they'd left behind. North of Lancaster, for example, Germans flocked to the newly established towns of Manheim and Heidelberg, while farther west, running along the Susquehanna, Derry and Donegal contained large numbers of Scots Irish. While English settlers predominated in Little Britain, located at the southern tip of Lancaster County, the Welsh preferred to make their homes in Caernarvon, along the eastern border.[14]

Like most of the county's towns, Lancaster was home to an ethnically mixed population. By 1760, German speakers constituted nearly 70 percent of Lancaster's families, while the English and Scots Irish made up most of the remaining population. Lancaster thus boasted a significantly higher proportion of Germans than did the colony as a whole, and assorted German dialects rang out through the community well into the late eighteenth century. Accompanying the town's ethnic diversity was an even wider array of religious faiths that featured Anglicans, Presbyterians, Quakers, Catholics, Jews, Lutherans, Moravians, and German Reformed. Passing through Lancaster in 1744, one traveler marveled at the town's remarkable denominational complexity, noting, "The religions which prevail here are hardly to be numbered." By the mid-1750s, Lancaster contained Anglican, Lutheran, Reformed, Catholic, and Moravian churches. The town's small Quaker population worshipped in neighboring Sadsbury, ten miles to the east, before erecting its own meetinghouse in 1760. Ten years later, Presbyterians opened the doors to their own church.[15]

Settlers' pronounced ethnocultural divisions sparked tensions within the county's newly established communities. Clustered in loose ethnic enclaves, the backcountry's English and German speakers dealt uneasily with their foreign neighbors. During the first half of the eighteenth century, some Anglo observers actually welcomed the Germans as industrious settlers of their budding province. Happy to number Germans among the first settlers of his new town, James Hamilton, Lancaster's proprietor, celebrated their contributions as the "most laborious and by much the best Improvers in the Country." Similarly, during the 1740s, the former indentured servant William Moraley remarked that Pennsylvania's Germans "behave themselves so well, as gains them the Respect of the *English*," adding, "They have many considerable Farms, which they improve to the best Advantage." In fledgling communities like Lancaster, however, where newly settled English and German speakers resided in unaccustomed proximity, diversity bred friction as New World pluralism reinforced Old World particularities. Devoted to their peculiar cultures and interests, Lancaster's competing ethnocultural groups eyed one another with prejudice and suspicion. Surrounded by an alien culture, German newcomers slowly adapted to British laws and institutions while clinging to their own language and customs and limiting their dealings with the town's English-speaking population. Though some close and sustained interactions were inevitable within the confines of a mixed community, patterns of voluntary separation quickly emerged. In the Lancaster suburb of Adamstown, for example, Germans eagerly congregated among their own, to the alternating relief and frustration of their English-speaking neighbors.

For English speakers, such exclusiveness only emphasized the Germans' discomfiting foreignness.[16]

Increasingly, across the province worried Anglo officials lamented the Germans' reluctance to assimilate, branding their continuing ethnic cohesiveness as stubborn clannishness. Concerns mounted from the 1730s on, as German immigrants, aided by elaborate kin, village, and religious networks, continued to flood into the province, threatening to engulf their English-speaking neighbors. From 18,000 in 1700, Pennsylvania's population had climbed to 120,000 by 1750. Largely English and Welsh, the Quakers shrank to a mere quarter of the population, while the Germans, now multiplying annually by the thousands, made up more than a third of the whole. As early as 1727, James Logan had predicted that the growing number of Palatines would produce a "German Colony here." Decades later, alarmed provincial officials warned that the foreign transplants would eventually claim their right to vote, terminating Anglos' political and cultural hegemony. In 1750, an adviser informed Thomas Penn that the "present clamour of a great many people here of all Ranks, Friends as much as others, is that the Dutch, by their numbers and Industry, will soon become Masters of the province, and also a Majority in the Legislature."[17]

The increasingly outspoken Benjamin Franklin found the newcomers' pervasive influence especially unsettling. "Of the six printing houses in the Province," Franklin complained to a colleague in 1753, "two are entirely German, two half German half English, and but two entirely English." Furthermore, "advertisements intended to be general are now printed in Dutch and English," while the "Signs in our Streets," he added, "have inscriptions in both languages, and in some places only German." Meanwhile, in the courts, the "German Business so encreases that there is continual need of Interpreters; and I suppose in a few years they will be also necessary in the Assembly; to tell one half of our Legislators what the other half say." Perhaps worst of all, "those who come hither are generally of the most ignorant Stupid Sort of their own Nation," and "not being used to Liberty, they know not how to make a modest use of it."[18]

In hopes of containing or harnessing the newcomers' increasing political influence, anxious provincial advisers proposed restricting German immigration and anglicizing the growing German population. "Unless the stream of their importation could be turned from this to other Colonies," Franklin predicted, "all the advantages we have will not (in My Opinion) be able to preserve our language, and even our Government will become precarious." Two years later, in a crude racialization of the Germans, an agitated Franklin queried: "Why should the *Palatine Boors* be suffered to swarm into our settlements, and by herding together establish their languages and manners to the exclusion of ours? Why should *Pennsylvania*, founded by the *English*, become a colony of *Aliens*, who will shortly be so numerous as to German-ize us instead of our Anglifying them, and will never adopt our language or customs, any more than they can acquire our complexion." A year earlier, Franklin's nemesis, the acerbic William Smith, had callously lampooned the colony's "uncultivated Race of Germans" as a "Body of ignorant, proud, stubborn Clowns (who are unacquainted with our Language, our Manners, our Laws, and our Interests)." Smith recommended denying the Germans the franchise "till they have a sufficient Knowledge of our Language and Constitution," while Franklin proposed sending the newcomers to English schools planted throughout the interior. The Germans, in turn, spurned Anglo presumptions. During the late 1740s, a new arrival from Germany ascribed Anglos' "supreme contempt for the Germans" to their "exalted opinion of themselves."[19]

The Germans' multiplying numbers and alien origins prompted the pro-vincial assembly to impose a loyalty oath on foreign arrivals to the port of Philadelphia as early as 1725. Several decades later, as war with the French loomed, skeptical provincial authorities continued to doubt the Germans' al-legiance. Dismissing most Germans' Reformed or Lutheran affiliations, their critics damned the foreigners as popish Francophiles who could be lured into a potentially fatal alliance with the enemy. In 1754, one official pessimisti-cally concluded that as the "Generality of these Germans, place all Happiness in a large Farm, they will greedily accept the easy Settlements which the French will be enabled to offer them. Thus vast numbers will be induced to go over to the Enemy." A year later, Deputy Governor Robert Morris warned that the "French by means of the Foreigners in this Province may possibly subject the whole Continent to their Dominion."[20]

In Lancaster, the Germans' heightened political involvement raised the ire of the Anglo minority. With more than three hundred inhabitants in 1742, Lancaster achieved borough status, which afforded locals an unusual degree of self-government. With borough status came residents' right to hold markets and fairs, elect town officials, and convene town meetings. Every fall, eligible voters elected two burgesses, six assistants, a constable, and a town clerk. Possessing an insider's knowledge of British legal and political culture, Lancaster's Anglo minority enjoyed a near monopoly on the offices of burgess and town clerk through the 1740s. As more Germans became in-vested in their community's development, they endorsed German candidates to represent their interests and to govern alongside their English-speaking neighbors. Frustrated by the Germans' exclusion from office, Lancaster's

Lutheran minister Frederick Handschuh complained that the town's government remained in the "hands of the Quakers with whom were associated a
few frivolous and course-minded Englishmen."[21]

As growing numbers of naturalized or second-generation Germans
earned the right to vote, borough elections became more fiercely contested.
Reverend Handschuh rejoiced in 1749 after three of his parishioners won
election to the offices of town constable and chief and assistant burgesses.
The elated minister predicted, "From this new government we can anticipate
much good for our town and congregation." Considerably less sanguine
was Thomas Cookson, the former chief burgess, who blasted the political
participation of the "Lowest Sort of Germans unacquainted with Our Constitution & Laws." Three years later, Dr. Adam Simon Kuhn, Lancaster's chief
burgess, filed suit against the Quaker and the former burgess, Peter Worrall.
Worrall had publicly insulted Kuhn, declaring, "I . . . understand the office
of a burgess better . . . and you . . . being a Dutchman cannot understand
your Duty as well as myself." Similarly, during the mid-1760s, a recent arrival to the community cursed the "shocking Stupidity and Insensibility of
the gaping Dutchmen," who "know so little of good manners, & are so very
selfish, that the Devil himself cannot put them off with a denial when they
fancy themselves (as they generally do) Persons of importance and their business urgent." As late as 1769, Reverend Mühlenberg lamented the persistent
prejudice of the county's English speakers, who "look upon the Germans as
nothing but wig-blocks, which are thick and hard, to be sure, but wanting
brains."[22]

Multitudes of Dissenters

If many of the mid-Atlantic's newly settled English and German speakers
perceived each other as an undifferentiated mass, they remained keenly aware
of the distinctions among themselves. To casual observers, settlers' broadly
shared ethnic and linguistic connections often obscured their more particular
divisions of region, religion, and class. Pennsylvania's English- and German-
speaking populations proved neither static nor seamless but fluid and fragmented, ever evolving and continually redefined by New World conditions
and Old World infusions. Within their distinct communities, English and
German speakers alike juggled competing identities and split along lines of
rich and poor, native and newcomer, church and sect. Those born in Pennsylvania routinely distinguished themselves from the steady stream of immigrants who instinctively identified with their Old World origins. Just as
English speakers claimed descent from England, Scotland, or Ireland, German

arrivals sprang from such diverse locales as Alsace, Swabia, or Hanau, with all of their associated dialects. While distinguishing themselves from their English-speaking neighbors, the Germans drew more particular distinctions between their own churches and sects, identifying as Reformed, Lutheran, Moravian, or Mennonite. Similar divisions separated Pennsylvania's English speakers. In 1761, the Reverend Thomas Barton expressed dismay upon finding his new flock "surrounded by multitudes of Dissenters" who differed as "widely from one another as they differ from us."[23]

Inspired by William Penn's promise of religious toleration, Lancaster's competing denominations eagerly formed congregations, constructed churches, recruited ministers, and established parochial schools for the rising generation. Lancaster's Reformed congregation emerged during the early 1730s and embraced more than five hundred members just two decades later, but was quickly dwarfed by the burgeoning Lutheran congregation. Lacking the numbers and financial resources of their German neighbors, the town's Anglican and Presbyterian congregations languished by comparison. Despite their organizational difficulties, however, the English-speaking parishioners avidly strove for fellowship within their denominations. Numbering fewer than a hundred congregants as late as 1760, the borough's Anglicans embraced itinerant ministers, held services in the county courthouse, and worshipped alongside members of their denomination in neighboring towns before unveiling St. James Church in the early 1750s.[24]

The formation of congregations helped newly arrived settlers impose order and an air of familiarity on their unfamiliar environment. Some of Lancaster's earliest parishioners had migrated from the same or neighboring towns or villages in Germany. Local parishioners identified and associated with their fellow congregants, who provided welcome support in life and death, serving as sponsors for baptisms and executors for wills. With ministers in short supply throughout the province, congregations relied on the generous support and capable leadership of committed lay members. Deacons, elders, and trustees drawn from the more influential ranks of the community helped oversee congregational interests, secure ministers, and finance church improvements. Though qualified instructors remained scarce, Lancaster's Lutheran, Reformed, and Moravian congregations maintained their own elementary schools as early as 1750.[25]

Parishioners' denominational commitments transcended locale, with the faithful cultivating broader provincial connections. The borough's Moravians sustained intimate relations with their brethren to the northeast in the town of Bethlehem. Lancaster's Anglican, Lutheran, and Reformed churches maintained denominational ties with a host of outlying congregations, sharing ministers and contributing funds. Lancaster's Lutheran minister Caspar Stoever, for instance, split his pastoral duties among several county congregations. Members of the Lutheran church raised subscriptions for congregations as far away as Germantown and Philadelphia. Solicitous of their internal interests and suspicious of external authority, Lancaster's Reformed and Lutheran congregations forged more tenuous ties to the provincial Coetus and Ministerium.[26]

Parishioners' fervor disrupted denominational unity, as scandals, disputes over finances, and doctrinal differences related to the Great Awakening periodically rocked Lancaster's congregations. Clergy and laity vied for control of their churches. In 1747, Lancaster's Anglican pastor Richard Locke informed his London superiors that he faced a "great deal of opposition" from his angry communicants for his theological leanings and service to outlying congregations. The borough's Lutheran and Reformed congregations in particular earned reputations for internal discord among eastern ecclesiastical authorities and encountered difficulties maintaining settled ministers. Reverend Mühlenberg repeatedly condemned the "wrangling congregation in Lancaster" made up of "rough and bastardly Lutherans" who forfeited "all discipline and respectability." Pastor Handschuh alienated the more status-minded members of his Lancaster congregation in 1750 when he married his maidservant, a woman of "common origin." The reverend was soon ridiculed by his parishioners, who refused to pay his salary and evicted him from his residence. Mühlenberg feared that his forsaken colleague would ultimately be "either driven out or starved out." A second Lutheran minister, the Reverend Gabriel Wortmann, fell out with the congregation only a few years later by drinking to excess, beating his wife, and assaulting a church deacon.[27]

The bitterest divisions were those separating church and sect. Trouble erupted during the mid-1740s, when Lancaster's new Lutheran minister, Pastor Laurentius Thorstensson Nyberg, betrayed Moravian leanings, winning eager converts and leaving the congregation "split and in a state of mistrust." Ensuing mediation and litigation only exacerbated tensions between the contending factions, which refused to reconcile, creating a permanent schism. Although the controversy cooled after Nyberg's faction left the congregation to establish St. Andrew's Moravian Church in the late 1740s, both the town's Lutheran and Reformed churches dreaded further sectarian inroads. Stung by the recent Moravian conversions, a furious Mühlenberg raged, "We must either drive them out or they us." Nearly two decades later, however, he lamented that Lancaster's troubled Lutheran congregation remained plagued by "every imaginable kind of crafty sect."[28]

Church folk resented the sects not only for their theological differences but also for their impressive wealth and organization. Many sectarians, in turn, delighted in the continuing internal disputes of rival churchgoers. Muted resentments yielded to open contempt and conflict. After adopting the dress and speech of her Lancaster Quaker employer, for example, a young Scots Irish servant found "her Relations much against her." In late 1745, Lancaster's Lutheran and Moravian factions nearly came to blows when they heatedly contested control of their church for a Sunday service. "Some of them went to the church with guns and swords," reported a stunned Mühlenberg, and "even the women took a hand in the fray." More than a decade later, Bernard Hubley, a respected tradesman, burgess, and elder in the borough's Lutheran congregation, narrowly escaped conviction for manslaughter after fatally assaulting a Mennonite during a violent religious dispute. Tensions increased during the Seven Years' War, when the sectarians' pacifist principles clashed with their frightened neighbors' demands for frontier defense.[29]

Among the mid-Atlantic's English and German speakers, New World conditions reinforced Old World distinctions. Whatever their differences, however, Germans, like their Anglo counterparts, embraced a shared language and many common customs. Pennsylvania's jarring diversity highlighted settlers' similarities in the face of their more decidedly foreign neighbors. Within their pluralistic communities, both English and German speakers found comfort and commonality in the broadly familiar, often transcending their more particular divisions to intermingle with their own kind. In their alien and sometimes hostile surroundings, fellow Germans found particular grounds for cooperation.[30]

Although settlers remained solicitous of their denominational interests, they also cooperated across confessional lines. With their pastorates occasionally vacant, some parishioners gratefully attended the services of rival denominations or asked the ministers of competing faiths to perform baptisms, weddings, or funerals. The county's few clergy thus ministered to diverse flocks. Pastor Handschuh, for example, reported that his sermons drew listeners from "many unheard of sects." While most residents remained committed to their congregations, the scarcity of ministers and tolerance for different faiths promoted fluidity among local denominations. As the Moravians' success in attracting Lutheran and Reformed converts demonstrates, experimentation across congregations occurred often enough to prove an ongoing concern for denominational leaders. Some wealthy parishioners made donations or left charitable bequests to churches serving other denominations. Often strapped for funds, denominations occasionally organized joint fund-raisers to build or improve their churches. In 1774, Lancaster's

Lutherans set aside their neighbors' doctrinal differences and invited the Moravian trombone choir to perform at their church.[31]

Within the bustling community, residents' expanding social and commercial networks soon transcended religious affiliations to encompass neighbors of diverging faiths. Lancaster's Germans increasingly secured servants, creditors, sponsors, and executors outside their own denominations. English speakers, too, formed bonds of friendship and kinship that overrode religious distinctions. Local notables such as Edward Shippen, George Ross, and James Burd counted both Anglicans and Presbyterians among their closest associates. The devout Shippen attended both churches. Though most residents married within their faith, others formed enduring cross-confessional unions. Reverend Mühlenberg reported in 1754 that "Lutheran and Reformed people throughout the country are interwoven with each other by marriage." Lancaster's Reformed leader Nicolaus Kendel had a Lutheran wife, for example, and Philipp Rudesill, his Lutheran neighbor, married Susanna Beyer, a communicant in the Reformed Church.[32]

Much rarer were conjugal unions joining English and German speakers, who remained committed to preserving their own languages and customs and minimizing their interactions with their foreign neighbors. By 1760, anglicization had achieved limited inroads among the county's German speakers, and language and ethnicity still accounted for the sharpest divisions in the diverse Pennsylvania interior. Although many of Lancaster's most influential Germans spoke English, the majority of their ethnic kindred faced a divisive language barrier. Lancaster's first newspaper, the bilingual *Lancastersche Zeitung*, published from 1752 to 1753, dramatically underlined the lingering cultural and linguistic divisions between the community's English and German speakers.[33]

Considerations of Interest, Power, and Ascendancy

Ethnocultural considerations structured political activity in Penn's province. After his visit to Pennsylvania during the 1750s, the discerning Anglican minister Andrew Burnaby described a province teeming with "people of different nations, different manners, different religions and different languages," all of whom harbored a "mutual jealousy of each other, fomented by considerations of interest, power, and ascendancy." Pennsylvania's political system alleviated ethnocultural tensions by encouraging political accommodation and containing interest group conflict. In pursuit of shared and peculiar interests, competing factions learned to vent their resentments and to negotiate their differences in the political arena. With no ethnic or religious group able to impose its will as a clear majority of the population, peaceful coexistence became the celebrated ideal. Pennsylvania's political culture thus reinforced ethnocultural divisions while promoting cooperation and mitigating violence. Paradoxically, within the province's pluralistic communities, religious bigotry and ethnic prejudice persisted amidst the grudging tolerance for Protestants.[34]

Presiding over a broad multiethnic coalition committed to mutual and particular interests, Pennsylvania's founding Quaker party dominated provincial politics during the first half of the eighteenth century, largely through the combined support of Anglicans, Presbyterians, and German church folk and sectarians. The Quakers' commitment to nonviolence proved especially appealing to the German sectarians, who shared the Friends' pacifist principles. Among diverse immigrant groups, the Quakers quickly earned a reputation as the custodians of peace and prosperity and the defenders of the people's rights and liberties. During the 1740s, Quaker leaders helped integrate German and Scots Irish settlers into Pennsylvania's political system, securing the newcomers' political allegiance by endorsing liberty of conscience, individual property rights, limited executive power, and freedom from onerous military service and taxation. The Quakers' commitment to the public welfare contrasted sharply with the self-serving proprietary interest, whose unpopular land policy hindered newly arriving settlers' acquisition and control of property. During the 1730s, Thomas Penn raised both quitrents and the price of land, rejected payment in paper money, and threatened delinquent settlers with ejection or foreclosure, alienating many Germans and Scots Irish.[35]

Lancaster County's politics squared with broader provincial patterns, with both the Quaker and proprietary factions represented locally. Despite constituting a small minority, the Quakers exercised undue influence in the county's politics through the initial decades of settlement. Similarly, though German speakers claimed a large share of the franchise, English speakers held a disproportionate share of the local offices. In his posts of clerk of the county commissioners, prothonotary of the Court of Common Pleas, recorder of the Court of Quarter Sessions, and justice of the peace, Edward Shippen quickly emerged as the county's leading spokesman for the proprietary interest. By contrast, Peter Worrall remained Lancaster's most influential representative of the Quaker faction until resigning from the assembly and relocating to Philadelphia in the mid-1750s. A prosperous innkeeper and large landholder, Worrall served as burgess, assistant burgess, and justice of the peace before concluding his long tenure in the assembly.[36]

Lancaster's borough status afforded the community a liberal franchise. Residents' newly awarded charter stipulated that the "Burgesses, Constables, assistants and freeholders, together with such inhabitants, house-keepers," who had lived within the borough for one full year preceding any election and "hired a house and ground" to the "yearly value of *five pounds* or up-wards" could vote in Lancaster's annual elections. One historian suggests that three-fifths or more of the borough's heads of household could vote before the Revolution. In 1768, a local described how one of the candidates for town burgess made the rounds at Lancaster's marketplace and taverns, seeking the "Votes and Interest of the Butchers, Barbers, Taylors, Blacksmiths, &c. which form a Chief Part of our worshipful Corporation." But while grow-ing numbers of residents turned out for the town's elections, they showed less interest in the routine administration of their community. The town meet-ing invited broad participation, but locals remained largely indifferent. Most Germans, for example, still adjusting to the language barrier and the alien political culture, preferred attending to their congregations and commercial pursuits. Preoccupied with settling into their communities and securing their livelihoods, most residents happily deferred to their elected representatives.[37]

The town's magistrates saw to public order, attending to the mundane tasks of civil administration. Drawn from the leading members of the English- and German–speaking communities, they included artisans, merchants, and professionals. The residents selected as burgesses generally served multiple year-long terms and represented the wealthiest portion of Lancaster's popu-lation. The prospering Anglican attorney Thomas Cookson, for example, served six terms as chief burgess before his death in 1753. The wealthy German-born Wilhelm Bausman, by contrast, served twice as burgess, twice as assistant burgess, and once as chief burgess while running his tavern and helping to administer the Reformed congregation between 1760 and 1765. Though Germans made up roughly two-thirds of the population, between 1742 and 1770, Anglos supplied at least 50 percent of Lancaster's burgesses, a percentage that remained relatively stable over time. Three of the six Anglo burgesses elected before 1760 were Quakers, while Germans often accounted for two-thirds or more of the assistants.[38]

Although German votes helped decide elections, Anglo officeholders remained even more predominant at the county and provincial levels. In county elections, voters chose commissioners, assessors, a coroner, and a sher-iff. Commissioners and assessors oversaw the county's finances, levying and collecting taxes and distributing revenues, while the sheriff performed judi-cial and electoral duties. English speakers monopolized the office of sheriff, and only one German, Matthias Slough, served as coroner prior to 1760. Lancaster County elected four representatives to the provincial assembly, as opposed to the eight assemblymen representing each of the three older counties of Philadelphia, Bucks, and Chester, denying residents an equal voice in provincial affairs. Quakers, moreover, claimed an inordinate share of the county's assembly seats. Except for a single year between 1755 and 1776, Lancaster County had one or more Quaker representatives in the assembly. The county's Germans and Scots Irish, by contrast, remained grossly underrepresented in the legislature. Between 1755 and 1773, the county appears to have sent only two German speakers and not a single Scots Irish representative to the assembly. After voters elected four Quaker assemblymen in 1755, the Philadelphia Quaker leader Isaac Norris declared, "It is remarkable . . . That the Frontier County of Lancaster, Composed of all Sorts of Presbyterians & Independents, of all Sorts of Germans, & Some Church of England Electors, have Chosen All Their Representatives Out of ye Quakers, tho' there are Scarcely One Hundred of that Profession in the Whole County." The growing predominance of the backcountry's Germans and Scots Irish foretold their future political influence but failed to translate into a more immediate share of the political spoils. Until the mid-1750s, many of the backcountry's diverse settlers remained content to cast their lot with the time-tested Quaker faction.[39]

During the 1750s and 1760s, war, frontier unrest, and an ill-conceived and poorly timed campaign to embrace royal government threatened the Quakers' long-standing hold on provincial affairs by producing a temporary political realignment and heightened cooperation among the backcountry's German, English, and Scots Irish settlers. The war with the French and their Indian allies dealt a costly blow to Pennsylvania's Quaker faction, whose pacifist leanings and disputes with the proprietor stymied defense measures and infuriated aggrieved settlers on the blood-soaked frontier. As violence raged across the backcountry, endangering settlers' lives and property, growing numbers of Germans, English, and Scots Irish transcended their ethnic differences and made common cause against shared enemies to the east and west. Just as the crisis encouraged interethnic cooperation, it sharpened intra-ethnic conflict, as pacifists committed to restoring peace squared off against non-pacifists determined to protect their families and fortunes. Britain's contest for empire thus briefly reconfigured social and political relations in Lancaster County by uniting newly threatened English and German speakers against deadly raiders to the west and callous politicians to the east.[40]

To Defend Our Country

The Seven Years' War began as Britain and France contested control of the Ohio Country, home to assorted Indian peoples keen to retain or reclaim

their ancestral lands. The conflict with France fractured Pennsylvania's Long
Peace, inaugurated more than half a century before with William Penn's
dream of benevolent relations and peaceful coexistence with the region's Indians. The founder's utopian vision of a "holy experiment" uniting diverse
peoples in harmony and tolerance encompassed his province's indigenous
inhabitants. Mostly scattered bands reduced in size and strength by decades of
colonial warfare and disease, the surrounding natives welcomed Penn's sincere
commitment to peace and his policy of paying a fair price for their lands. Yet
the sustained pressure on a rapidly expanding frontier strained the peace, as
waves of immigrants flooded into the Susquehanna Valley in search of unoc-
cupied lands, crowding and abusing their new Indian neighbors. As the colonial population surged, so too did acts of violence against native towns, leading
one Delaware Indian to complain to provincial officials that his people had
"great reason to believe you intend to drive us away, and settle the country."
Indeed, eager to acquire more land and expand the provincial domain, Penn's
successors departed from his policies in order to defraud and dispossess the Indians, pushing many farther west. By the early 1750s, France found receptive
native allies keen to repay British deceit and land hunger. In 1755, the Shawnee and western Delaware took up the hatchet to stem the steadily advancing
tide of British settlement. That summer, Pennsylvania homesteaders reeled
from the first retaliatory incursions of France's determined Indian allies.[41]

The residents of Lancaster were no strangers to the neighboring Indian
peoples, observing with curious fascination the Conestoga, Shawnee, Delaware, and Iroquois who passed through the borough for the informal exchange of trade goods or the formal treaty conferences of 1744 and 1748.
Wonder turned to dread when Pennsylvania's new Indian enemies launched
their deadly raids on the poorly prepared inhabitants of the provincial interior. Without a militia to defend their exposed frontier, alarmed settlers
began clamoring for protection well before the first blows fell. As early as
the summer of 1754, worried residents of Lancaster County sent anxious
petitions to eastern officials emphasizing their vulnerability to the "French
and French Indians." One year later, during the summer harvest, the first
small war parties struck at the scattered homesteads west of the Susquehanna
River. Provincial prospects dimmed in July 1755, when General Edward
Braddock's unexpected defeat en route to engaging the French garrison at
Fort Duquesne opened Pennsylvania to potential invasion.[42]

Through the fall of 1755, the enemy laid siege to the provincial backcountry. Although some of the most determined settlers defiantly stood their
ground to protect their homes, hundreds of others took flight. Threatening to roll back the advancing frontier by driving terrified settlers eastward

across the Susquehanna, the incursions sowed panic in Lancaster. A disruptive stream of disoriented refugees, bearing grisly if often exaggerated accounts of frontier atrocities, brought the dangers home to the borough's frightened inhabitants. Accumulating reports of settlers massacred and homes, crops, and livestock destroyed confirmed residents' worst fears and forecast what lay in store for Lancaster County should the frontier continue to recede. In early November 1755, Edward Shippen, the official tasked with organizing the locals' defense, informed the deputy governor that he hoped for the "assemblies assistance" following more "melancholly news of the murder of many families, and the burning of their houses."[43]

The Indians' raiding parties were merely defending or avenging their own embattled communities, long exposed to the dislocations of colonial settlement. Yet the frightened and infuriated inhabitants of Lancaster County saw only bloodthirsty enemies. As Lancaster buzzed with fresh reports of the enemy's proximity, residents braced for violence. In October 1755, rumors falsely warned that fifteen hundred French and Indians were due to invade the lower Susquehanna Valley. During late fall, small native war parties breached the county by crossing the Susquehanna and striking at Swatara and Tulpehocken. Afraid that their enemies had fixed their sights on Lancaster, locals raised a night watch and mounted a makeshift defense. "Ever Since the Defeat of General Braddock . . . we have been in great Confusion," an alarmed Shippen reported. "The Enemy have destroyed numbers of our back Settlers within 35 Miles of this Town & have threatened to come quite here," he added, "so that we are obliged to be upon our Guard night and day."[44]

Shippen warned the deputy governor that residents were willing to defend the town but remained disorganized and poorly equipped. In late November, Shippen proposed that a "sufficient quantity of men . . . be Sent immediately to guard the Frontiers and at least 100 to this Burrough, for whenever we are attackt I doubt not but the Number of Men will be much greater than we can possibly make up for our defence, and if the enemy Shou'd take possession of this town and destroy the People, who can dare to Stay on their Plantations betwixt here and Philadelphia." Just days later, following a midnight alarm, some three hundred panicked residents assembled in the town square only to discover that they remained woefully short of arms and ammunition. Afterward, Shippen informed James Hamilton of locals' plans for a blockhouse protected by a broad ditch and a drawbridge to "place our wives, girls and children within, that they may be in safety." He concluded, "These are fearful times," adding, "God only knows how they will end."[45]

To mobilize the backcountry's diverse communities, local officials emphasized their shared plight in the face of an unprecedented crisis. The initial efforts to organize a common defense underscored the problems ahead for Lancaster County's ethnically diverse and parochially oriented inhabitants. The extent of local divisions and the difficulties of quickly surmounting them became painfully evident in the fall of 1755, following the first wave of attacks. In October, Lancaster's English and German speakers had to convene separate meetings to formulate plans for their town's defense after failing to come to terms during their earlier joint session. That same month, at the height of the invasion scare, a few hundred of the county's English and German speakers assembled from their separate townships and raced westward to meet the anticipated incursion and shield their families from attack, eventually halting in the largely Scots Irish settlement of Paxton, along the Susquehanna. After seeing no sign of the rumored fifteen hundred invaders, the motley marchers beat a hasty retreat to their own communities, insisting that they had "not come up to serve as Guards to Paxton people." Even faced with the growing dangers to the provincial interior, some residents balked at supporting the broader war effort. In the summer of 1755, for example, Shippen complained, after he had trouble procuring a wagon for troops sent to protect the frontier, of "people alledging that they had done enough already."[46]

As the raids intensified and British setbacks underscored the magnitude of the crisis, locals more willingly contributed to the provincial defense. In addition to providing a temporary haven for hundreds of desperate refugees fleeing the chaotic violence on the frontier, Lancaster served as a supply center and staging ground for western military operations, with county residents furnishing food, wagons, and horses for the major British expeditions. Throughout the hostilities, borough residents quartered and provisioned the imperial and provincial forces sent against the enemy. The war brought new business to local merchants and craftsmen in the form of lucrative military contracts. The trader Joseph Simon and his business partner William Henry, for instance, provided arms for British forces.[47]

In conjunction with neighboring communities, Lancaster furnished volunteers for the newly formed Pennsylvania Regiment, and provincial officers vigorously recruited in the borough. Edward Shippen's son-in-law Colonel James Burd commanded one of the regiment's three battalions, while his son Joseph Shippen served as a captain. With Shippen's encouragement, Lancaster also fielded a German company in response to locals' language differences. Though some residents joined the provincial forces in the west, others preferred to serve close to home, as scouts or rangers patrolling the surrounding woods. The escalating violence also generated widespread sympathy for the war's victims, and Lancaster's assorted denominations graciously collected donations for the relief of their suffering neighbors, both English and German speakers, to the north and west.[48]

Uniting the backcountry's aggrieved communities were shared anxieties of a besieged west and a negligent east. By late 1756, more than a year's worth of frontier violence had taken a devastating toll on the province. In December, in a letter to his father in Scotland, James Burd calculated the war's shocking cost. "Our country which was a few years ago the most pleasant, peaceable country in the World is now become a Land of Murder and Rapine," he wrote, with the "most unheard of barbarities . . . daily comitted upon our inhabitants by our merciless Savage Enemies the Indians and their most Christian Allies the French." Earlier that spring, Shippen had estimated that "our perfidious Delawares" alone had taken "about two hundred scalps." In long-suffering Hanover, a mixed German and Scots Irish settlement in northern Lancaster County, Indian raids soon claimed more than 130 residents. Following the capture of several British forts in the summer of 1756, one local lamented that "there is now a door open to let the French & their Indians into the heart of this Province," adding, "God preserve and unite us to defend our Country."[49]

Emboldened by French victories, Indian war parties pressed deeper into the province. With the enemy frequently in striking distance, the war assumed a terrifying immediacy for Lancaster's distressed inhabitants. Despite an outlying chain of fortifications and blockhouses designed to screen the Susquehanna Valley from the worst enemy depredations, small bands continued to prey on the county's most exposed residents. During the summer of 1756, Shippen cautioned his son and son-in-law to the west to be "very cautious of venturing to come to see us, lest you should both be waylaid," for the "Indians are said to be so thick about." Nine months later, he sent word of families scalped "within 10 miles of this place." As the frontier reeled from relentless raids and inadequate defenses, locals issued increasingly frantic pleas for protection to eastern officials. By the spring of 1757, a despondent Shippen prophesied that without prompt assistance, "we of this borough shall, in less than a month, become the frontiers."[50]

The focus of local frustration now fluctuated between elusive Indians and meddlesome pacifists. The most vulnerable backcountry residents proved especially hostile to Pennsylvania's Quaker-dominated assembly. Although most Quakers acknowledged the need for defense, an influential minority in the assembly opposed military appropriations. The assembly eventually passed a militia law in late 1755 in the face of mounting frontier violence and settler discontent, but legions of disgruntled inhabitants never forgave the delay. Determined to preserve their provincial influence, Quaker leaders also sought to control the appropriations process, leading to a continued struggle with the proprietary faction, to additional delays in defense, and to renewed protests from the interior. As Quakers wrangled with the proprietor over military expenditures, the Indians' incursions threatened to consume the frontier. The seeming indifference of Quaker assemblymen to the plight of their western neighbors alienated many of their German and Scots Irish constituents, who bore the brunt of the enemy's attacks and were crying out for military protection.

The Quakers made more enemies by refusing to take up arms and conducting unauthorized negotiations with the natives. After Deputy Governor Morris declared war on the Delaware and Shawnee, and principled pacifists withdrew from the assembly in early 1756, the Quakers continued to work toward peaceful reconciliation with France's native allies outside of formal government channels via their "Friendly Association for Regaining and Preserving Peace with the Indians by Pacific Measures." As the Quakers' Friendly Association courted the Indians, lavishing them with expensive gifts in hopes of restoring peace, whole frontier families were butchered in their homes. As late as September 1757, Captain Daniel Clark reported from Lancaster that the residents remained desperate for a stronger militia law, for only days before, "no less than twenty-two were killed and captivated in Hanover township."[51]

When locals' pleas for assistance met with delays or went unheeded, many blamed Pennsylvania's Quaker leadership. After natives killed or carried off dozens of their neighbors during the bloodiest attacks of late 1755 and early 1756, scores of distraught inhabitants assembled in Lancaster and prepared to march on Philadelphia to demand relief from the assembly. Only Deputy Governor Morris's timely declaration of war forestalled the march. Just over a year later, following more attacks in northern Lancaster County, Indian leaders, the deputy governor, and Quaker representatives of the Friendly Association convened in the borough for treaty deliberations. Observers recoiled in horror as survivors of the latest raids disrupted the proceedings by displaying four freshly scalped corpses "as a spectacle" for the pacifists, whom they blamed for "these Horrid Cruelties." The locals had merely followed the grisly example of several hundred of their Berks County neighbors, who, more than a year before, had descended on Philadelphia's State House bearing a number of their slain kinsmen to convey the urgent need for defense. "Cursing the Quakers Principles," and bidding the assemblymen to "behold the Fruits of their Obstinacy," the German marchers promised that "if they should come down on a like Errand again, and find nothing done for their Protection, the Consequences should be fatal." The backcountry's rising regional animus reinforced the locals' parochialism, fears of isolation and underrepresentation, and dependence on their diverse neighbors.[52]

Peace finally returned to the province in late 1758, following successful negotiations with the Indians and repeated French defeats to the west. The fall of Montreal two years later effectively ended the war in North America, although hostilities only formally concluded with the 1763 Treaty of Paris. Pennsylvania's wartime resentments simmered through the early 1760s, however, when the deadly Indian uprising dubbed Pontiac's Rebellion suddenly visited more misery on the war-weary frontier and dealt a fresh blow to Quaker authority. The Indians of the Ohio Country had come to rue the French withdrawal that triggered renewed settler encroachment, new trade disadvantages, and an end to gift giving. In mid-1763, just two months after the peace settlement ending the Seven Years' War, Delaware and Shawnee warriors joined the rebellion against Britain and resumed their raids on the Pennsylvania frontier. The renewed hostilities exacerbated lingering racial and regional tensions by reuniting besieged backcountry settlers against familiar antagonists to the east and west. Like the Seven Years' War, Pontiac's Rebellion overrode ethnic divisions as English and German speakers huddled and bled together in Pennsylvania's war-ravaged communities and jointly protested government Indian policy.[53]

An Unrelenting Quaker Faction

Within Lancaster County, the uprising revived the dreaded cycle of raids, rumors, and panicked appeals and preparations. Lancaster again provided refuge to scores of displaced families desperate to escape the slaughter to the west, while hauntingly familiar accounts of atrocities, of settlers scalped and homesteads burned, echoed in their wake. Inevitably there came newly terrifying rumors—this time unfounded—of native war parties sweeping into the heart of the county to murder the defenseless inhabitants. With the Pennsylvania Regiment demobilized in 1758, provincials lacked an armed force to counter the new incursions. Under pressure from backcountry settlers and the deputy governor but short of funds following the Seven Years' War, the assembly authorized the formation of a small frontier militia in the summer of 1763. By fall, however, came the familiar bickering over appropriations that had stymied frontier defense years before. Fearing more delays from the assembly, and drawing on the hard lessons of the Seven Years' War, backcountry residents formed volunteer companies for their own defense, including Lancaster County's Paxton Rangers. In late summer 1763, the volunteers commenced offensive operations, launching unauthorized expeditions against scattered Indian settlements to the north and west. Still seething from memories of the war, most rangers, like many of their backcountry neighbors, now ignored the customary distinctions between friendly and hostile Indians. Indeed, the most hardened inhabitants harbored long-standing suspicions of the province's peaceful Indians as so many spies and conspirators in secret alliance with the enemy.[54]

County militants' simmering hatred of their Indian neighbors boiled over in late 1763, with deadly consequences for a small settlement of peaceful Indians long under government protection at Conestoga Manor, several miles southwest of Lancaster. Early in the morning of December 14, some fifty volunteers from the northern portion of the county, armed with rifles, hatchets, and scalping knives, fell on the unsuspecting village and massacred six of the sleeping inhabitants. In grim emulation of the native scalping parties to the west, the raiders butchered their hapless victims and torched their homes. Although shocked county authorities promptly sheltered the village's fourteen remaining Indian inhabitants in Lancaster's workhouse, the rangers finished their deadly work just two weeks later. On December 27, upwards of fifty riders swooped into Lancaster during the early afternoon, broke open the workhouse, and slaughtered every surviving Conestoga man, woman, and child, departing as quickly as they came. Horrified authorities found the lifeless victims littering the open workhouse yard, "shot, scalped, hacked and cut to pieces." Before galloping out of town, the murderers allegedly swore to kill Pennsylvania's remaining friendly Indians, now under government protection in Philadelphia. Having sent a terrifying message to their western enemies, the so-called Paxton Boys turned their fury eastward.[55]

When the rangers heard that eastern officials had condemned the murders and urged that the perpetrators be brought to justice, they threatened to confront both Philadelphia's refugee Indians and their provincial defenders. Learning that the militants had bolstered their numbers and planned to march on the capital, the alarmed government invoked the riot act and mounted an improvised defense, with swarms of civilians, including a few hundred Friends, taking up arms in tense anticipation of a violent showdown with their western neighbors. In early February 1764, more than two hundred predominantly Scots Irish frontiersmen headed eastward, stopping in Germantown, six miles shy of the capital, where they commenced impromptu negotiations with provincial officials after learning of Philadelphia's heightened defenses. Insisting that they had intended only to protest the government's Indian policy and expel the remaining refugee Indians from the province, the marchers averted a bloody confrontation with the city's forces by agreeing to submit their grievances in writing and return peacefully to their homes. Among the marchers' principal grievances were the backcountry's underrepresentation in the assembly and the Friends' continued neglect of the interior and coddling of Indians.[56]

The Conestoga massacre fractured opinion in Lancaster County. When the Quaker faction launched a vitriolic print campaign reviling the murderers for their savage brutality, Lancaster's Anglican minister Thomas Barton quickly sprang to his neighbors' defense in the widely circulated pamphlet *Conduct of the Paxton-Men, Impartially Represented.* A supporter of the proprietary interest, Barton was hardly impartial. Turning the tables on the political opposition, the reverend cast the murders as the unhappy culmination of nearly a decade spent at the "Mercy of a cruel Savage Enemy and an unrelenting Quaker Faction." Barton reserved his special ire for the Friends, who, he claimed, cared more for Pennsylvania's natives than for their own "distressed Countrymen and Fellow subjects." While the Friends catered to the Indians and ignored frontier defense, Barton raged, the "Dutch and Irish are murder'd without Pity."[57]

But the county's most influential proprietary representative, the venerable Edward Shippen, found the "riotous behavior" that flew "in the Face of the Government" a graver cause for concern. Following the resumption of hostilities in 1763, Shippen once again featured prominently in the backcountry's military mobilization. Though he supported resuming the scalp bounties of the Seven Years' War to raise as many volunteers as possible, and he shared his neighbors' distrust of the Susquehanna Valley's friendly Indians, he deplored the unrestrained ferocity of the Conestoga slayings. As a member of the local elite, Shippen looked to channel militants' resentments for the better defense of their communities but recoiled when their fury assumed subversively destructive dimensions. Driven by shared animus, once-divided neighbors could become a frighteningly unpredictable and undifferentiated mass.[58]

During the spring of 1764, exasperated by their continuing battles with the proprietor and worried about the growing influence of the province's Scots Irish Presbyterians, the Quaker faction seized upon the prevailing disorder to launch a campaign to replace the Penn proprietorship with royal government. The Quakers' endorsement of royal governance undercut their reputation as the defenders of the people's rights and privileges. Many backcountry inhabitants, stinging from a decade of violence, considered the campaign for royal government a cynical Quaker ploy to avoid providing for frontier defense. Frustrated by the Quakers' defense policy and fearful that royal control would jeopardize the freedoms protected under Pennsylvania's Charter of Rights and Privileges, growing numbers of church Germans and Scots Irish threw their support behind the proprietary faction. During the election of 1764, the Quaker faction suffered surprising defeats in both the city and county of Philadelphia, where proprietary candidates secured eight of the ten contested seats in the assembly. Although the Friends' faction maintained its majority in the assembly, chastened leaders eventually abandoned their push for royal government. In the election of 1765, the Quaker party reclaimed enough German support to recapture the Philadelphia seats lost the year before.[59]

Despite their faction's continued dominance in the assembly, the upheavals of the 1750s and 1760s had shaken the Quakers' authority. Even though many Pennsylvanians still considered Friends the best guarantors of their civil and religious freedoms, for backcountry residents, the lessons of the previous decade remained very clear: whatever their virtues in peace, the Quakers proved poor servants in times of war. During the late 1750s, the rival proprietary faction picked up increasing support from disgruntled German and Scots Irish settlers in Northampton and Cumberland counties. By contrast, the proprietary faction's determined and increasingly organized efforts to attract political support yielded mixed results in Lancaster County, where the Quakers retained much of their influence into the early 1770s through careful maneuvering and the combined votes of German sectarians and church folk. Even in the interior communities where Quakers' political control held relatively firm, however, the intermittent frontier violence heightened regional tensions by feeding resentment of the perceived negligence of eastern officials.[60]

Although the Quakers remained a potent presence in local politics, the proprietary interest made new inroads in Lancaster County through the 1760s owing to enhanced support from Scots Irish Presbyterians and German Lutherans and Reformed. The county's proprietary operatives had seized on the growing dissatisfaction with the assembly in hopes of luring away the Quakers' disaffected German supporters as early as the Seven Years' War. In September 1756, Edward Shippen Jr. counseled his father from Philadelphia to put together an appealing ticket for the looming assembly election. "We are pushing for a change in all the counties," he concluded optimistically, and "shall certainly carry it in some." Yet "the chief thing," he added, "is to split the Dutch." Years later, before the 1764 assembly election, one of the county's proprietary supporters enthusiastically noted, "We have on our side all the Lutherin & Calvanists Dutch with many others of the Germains."[61]

Hoping to exploit the Quakers' vulnerability amid the controversial campaign for royal government, proprietary organizers made a more concerted push for German and Scots Irish support by diversifying their party's tickets. Ahead of the 1764 assembly election, Samuel Purviance, one of Philadelphia's key proprietary operatives, advised his Lancaster County lieutenants to consider fielding German and Scots Irish candidates to "turn the scale in our favor." Adam Simon Kuhn, a Lutheran and a respected member of Lancaster's German-speaking community, emerged as a leading proprietary activist. Purviance urged James Burd to run Dr. Kuhn, "or some other popular Lutheran or Calvinist" for the 1765 assembly election. In 1769, local proprietary party operatives objected to a slate for county assessors that explicitly favored the Germans, proposing instead a more diverse ticket that included "leading men among the Presbyterians" to entice "others of the same persuasion to join the party." The stratagem helped the proprietary faction sweep that year's elections for county commissioners and assessors. While Lancaster County's Quakers continued to wield political influence disproportionate to their small numbers, proprietary representatives managed to dominate the board of commissioners and assessors into the early 1770s.[62]

As the county's proprietary interest grew more competitive, local politics became more heated. To ensure success against the Quaker faction during the 1765 assembly election, Purviance urged county activists to arm every proprietary supporter "with a good shillelah" and warn the opposition that at the first hint of electoral tampering, "you will thrash the sheriff, every inspector, Quaker and Mennonist to a jelly." Purviance saw "no danger in the scheme but that of a riot, which would require great prudence to avoid." Party animus persisted through the years ahead. In September 1768, a Lancaster proprietary supporter updated a friend on the "politics of the town," reporting that "both Presbyterians and Quakers" remained as "hot as party feuds and disappointed rage can make them." A year later he observed, "Electioneering goes on with Vigour on all Sides & both Parties are eager to shew their Generalship, by every Manoeuvre in the Art of Parliamenteering."[63]

Heightened ethnic intermingling accompanied locals' increasing political cooperation. Through time and proximity, residents became better acquainted—if not always entirely comfortable—with the distinct groups who made up their pluralistic community. Despite enduring strains of ethnic prejudice, the shared dangers of the 1750s and 1760s had helped pave the way for future cooperation among the county's diverse inhabitants. The decades' wartime crises had confirmed the Germans' allegiance and underscored what locals shared in common as the besieged inhabitants of an isolated backcountry environment. Whatever their differences, growing numbers recognized that they were close neighbors in what all hoped would remain a peaceful and smoothly functioning community. Residents' capacity for compromise yielded general harmony amidst a stubborn undercurrent of persistent prejudice.[64]

King and Country

Lancaster's English and German speakers fashioned new friendships, business associations, and family connections. Residents mingled in the square, jostled in the streets, shared toasts in the taverns, and haggled in the marketplace during market and fair days and elections and court sessions. To ensure their community's safety, dozens of English and German speakers volunteered for the three competing fire companies formed by the early 1760s. As the borough developed, the most prominent Anglo and German clans sought each other's company at the key events on their expanding social calendar. Recently arrived from Philadelphia to serve as clerk to Edward Shippen, the budding attorney Jasper Yeates eagerly attended a 1765 engagement party for the daughter of one of Lancaster's wealthiest German families. For ambitious young men like Yeates, such occasions provided welcome forums for socializing and cultivating new business. Yeates soon counted the influential German tavern keeper Matthias Slough and the thriving German shopkeeper Paul Zantzinger among his closest acquaintances. The trio regularly convened for games of whist at Slough's tavern, the White Swan.[65]

Growing numbers of residents procured goods and services, obtained credit, rented homes, or purchased land from their English- and German-speaking neighbors alike, while expanding commercial networks linked the town's diverse merchants and craftsmen. Yeates dealt with German clients in his daily business operations, assisting them with a host of routine legal transactions. To enhance his business prospects, Yeates had learned German shortly after relocating to Lancaster, and he insisted that his young nephew do the same, including the boy's fluency in the language among his qualifications when recommending him for an apprenticeship to Philadelphia's leading merchants. The brothers John and Jacob Hubley, from one of Lancaster's leading German families, were soon studying law under Yeates. Some of the borough's wealthiest English speakers increased their daily dealings with Germans by indenturing newly arrived immigrants. Young Edward Burd purchased German servants in Philadelphia for his father, James, and his grandfather Edward Shippen. After securing one German laborer in the fall of 1770, Burd assured his father that the "young man has been used to farming, so that he will be of immediate service to you." Two years later, writing to a relative, Shippen reported being "well pleased with my Dutch boy, and so," he added, "is Mr. Burd with his." A handful of enterprising inhabitants successfully merged their business operations, forging productive partnerships. John Miller, a German blacksmith, formed close commercial ties with the gunsmith William Henry and the merchant Joseph Simon. In another joint venture, Miller, Simon, and Moses Mordecai manufactured "distill'd Liquors."[66]

Residents also collaborated in more solemn enterprises and sealed more formal unions. Frequently without a minister of their own during the first decades of settlement, Anglicans sometimes attended services in Lancaster's Lutheran church. Following his arrival in Lancaster during the early 1760s, the Reverend Thomas Barton returned the favor, ministering to the Germans who understood English when they had "no service of their own." Barton joined several German pastors in delivering a sermon at the 1766 public dedication ceremony of Lancaster's new Holy Trinity Lutheran Church. Eight years later, assorted mourners assembled for the funeral of Barton's wife, with the town's Lutheran minister officiating. Even after their churches became more firmly established, Lancaster's English- and German-speaking communities found occasions for interdenominational cooperation. With funds scarce, competing denominations sometimes pooled resources to finance church improvements. In much rarer instances, English and German speakers formally joined each other's congregations. By the early 1770s, for example, the increasingly anglicized Slough, Kuhn, and Zantzinger attended both St. James Anglican and Trinity Lutheran churches.[67]

As in the case of Jasper Yeates, residents' willingness to mingle across ethnic lines sprang not only from prolonged exposure but also from calculated personal or family interests. Some of the borough's more influential German families eagerly embraced anglicization and cultivated ties with their most respectable English-speaking neighbors. Anglicization offered tangible rewards to the Germans who craved polite company and new prospects for social, economic, and political advancement. Indeed, for a growing portion of the local elite, status trumped ethnicity, as both English and German speakers pursued lives of genteel refinement in their rough-hewn but rapidly developing hinterland environment. A few of the borough's leading Anglo and German clans formalized their social and professional connections through intermarriage. Jacob Hubley, for example, married into the prominent Burd and Shippen families. Yeates's two whist partners, Slough and Zantzinger—like Hubley, native Pennsylvanians—both had English wives.[68]

As late as the 1770s, however, Lancaster remained an ethnically divided community. For all their heightened interaction, most of the borough's diverse inhabitants identified first and foremost with their own kind, English or German speaking, church or sect, Anglican, Lutheran, or Presbyterian, traversing multiple layers of identity. Upon arriving in Lancaster, Reverend Barton remained cautiously optimistic about eventually luring a healthy portion of the Germans into St. James Church. The minister was ultimately disappointed, for during his pastorate he won few converts among the German-speaking population. Although several prominent German families had taken the first steps toward anglicization, most of their ethnic kindred remained more withdrawn from their English neighbors and jealously safeguarded their cherished language and customs.[69]

Even those who embraced anglicization retained much of their German identity and remained audibly and often visibly distinguishable from their Anglo associates. After joining St. James, for example, Kuhn remained a trustee and Slough a deacon at Trinity Lutheran. The German language prevailed throughout the town, mingling with a blend of competing languages and dialects. Inspired by efforts to anglicize Pennsylvania's Germans, a free school committed to English-language instruction appeared in Lancaster in 1755 but soon languished, as most Germans opted to support their own church schools. With educational facilities in short supply, some English parents reluctantly sent their children to one of the borough's several German-run schools. Part of the value of the few local slaves who spoke both English and German derived from their marketable capacity to bridge and negotiate the community's distinct cultural worlds.[70]

At home and in church, locals preferred the company of their own. Though denominations often cooperated and confessional lines occasionally blurred, most residents remained staunchly devoted to their particular faith and few formally joined one another's churches. On the eve of the revolutionary crisis, all but a handful of Lancaster's Germans belonged to the Lutheran, Reformed, or Moravian congregations. Conversely, most English speakers worshipped as Anglicans, Presbyterians, or Quakers. Similarly, those residents who married across ethnic lines proved exceptions to the rule, most still favoring unions with fellow English or German speakers within their specific denomination. For all of his profitable connections to Lancaster's German-speaking community, Yeates concealed a lingering prejudice, even privately parroting Franklin's crudely racialized characterization of the Germans as *"Boors."* The rising attorney remained determined to marry into a distinguished Anglo family, preferring the county's "fair" English girls, whom he judged "not so far removed from those of Philadelphia in the Article of Beauty," to his neighborhood's *"Tawny Dutch Squaws."* Yeates eventually sealed a very lucrative match with the granddaughter of his former employer Edward Shippen.[71]

Yet even if locals continued to identify as Englishmen, Germans, or Scots Irish, they also considered themselves British subjects. Though residents had remained chiefly preoccupied with their own defense through the decade following the first rumblings of war in the Ohio Country, Britain's victory had increased their pride in the newly expansive empire. Throughout the Seven Years' War, Lancaster's Anglo leaders had defiantly celebrated their ties to "King and Country" while vilifying "his Majesties' perverse Enemys," the "copper-colored cannibals and French savages, equally cruel and perfidious in their natures." Solidifying the besieged settlers' ranks a world away from the seat of empire were these intrusive alien enemies they now shared with their king. More than any dimly felt imperial affiliation, the native "dogs and their brothers, the French" had bound locals to broader British interests. In their diverse communities, settlers had lamented British defeats and applauded British triumphs. In subtle and unforeseen ways, as residents supplied, hosted, and fought alongside the king's troops, the hostilities slowly reinforced their connection to Great Britain. The visiting royal forces added to the stresses and strains of war but also provided welcome protection from Lancaster's foreign enemies. Even as the decade's violence underlined settlers' reliance on the mother country, however, most remained mentally rooted to their locale, their concerns rarely straying beyond county or province. Moreover, the war with France reaffirmed Pennsylvanians' allegiance to Britain just before a graver imperial crisis rocked the empire anew.[72]

Through the upheavals of the 1750s and early 1760s, the backcountry's English and German speakers forged makeshift alliances to protect their communities. In Lancaster County, the frontier turmoil reconfigured social relations, heightening local tensions and spurring new cooperation across ethnic lines. The imperial crisis of the 1760s and 1770s would determine whether Pennsylvania's diverse ethnocultural groups could transcend their ethnic, communal, and provincial attachments when faced with new British and German adversaries in a struggle of more sweeping proportions. Could Lancaster's English and German speakers find common ground when they squared off against their own ethnic kinsmen amidst civil war and revolution?

The imperial crisis that embroiled Britain and its American colonies posed a fundamental challenge to Lancaster's ethnically diverse and locally oriented inhabitants. Indeed, when war next came to Lancaster, it mobilized the borough's English and German speakers in novel ways by challenging them to look beyond ethnicity, community, and province and embrace a common cause and a shared identity. The war with Britain disrupted customary modes of identification, forcing residents to rethink their imperial relationship and their subordinate status in the empire. Confronted by new enemies, both British and German, Lancaster's Whigs found new friends in fellow supporters of the intercolonial resistance, cultivating a tenuous military and ideological alliance that strained their more particular ethnic and regional commitments.

CHAPTER 2

"Divided We Must Inevitably Fall"

War Comes to Lancaster

In early June 1774, news of Parliament's passage of the Coercive Acts roused the residents of Lancaster to action. The legislation came in response to the Boston Tea Party, where, on the night of December 16, 1773, American rebels dumped 342 chests of taxed tea into Boston Harbor in defiance of the recently implemented Tea Act. Soon reviled throughout the colonies as the Intolerable Acts, the measures closed the port of Boston until residents paid for the lost tea, restricted Boston's town meetings to once a year, transformed the Massachusetts Council from an elective to an appointive body, and barred local courts from trying British soldiers and officials for offenses committed against the rebelling colonists. Lancaster's residents deemed the acts a violation of the rights of British subjects and the principle of local autonomy, taking particular offense at the Boston Port Bill. By identifying with the plight of distant New Englanders, the community's disgruntled inhabitants embraced a burgeoning intercolonial controversy.[1]

On June 15, at the request of borough officials, local residents assembled at the county courthouse to discuss the escalating imperial crisis. The agitated participants vigorously denounced the Boston Port Bill as a clear violation of the constitutional rights of British subjects and urged that the colonies unite to secure its repeal. To that end, they endorsed halting all imports and exports to and from Great Britain until Parliament repealed the act, pledging to join the "patriotic Merchants, Manufacturers, Tradesmen, and Freeholders, of the City and County of Philadelphia, and other Parts of this Province, in an Association or solemn Agreement to this purpose." Locals then appointed ten of the borough's leading citizens to a new Committee of Correspondence to keep the county's inhabitants apprised of developments. At the request of Philadelphia's Committee of Correspondence, Lancaster's committee agreed to convene a general meeting of the county's principal inhabitants on July 9 to discuss the "alarming and critical situation of the American colonies."[2]

At two o'clock in the afternoon of July 9, county residents crowded into Lancaster's courthouse, where George Ross, chairman of Lancaster's committee, appealed for unanimity and cooperation in defense of the "Common Interest of America." Thundered Ross, "The Hand of Power has been stretched forth," and "every Liberty and Privilege which we justly pride and value . . . has been invaded in the Proceedings of the Mother Country towards the Town of Boston," where the distressed inhabitants "receive the supplies of Nature from the Points of Bayonets." Even "tho' the Blow seems aimed at the Bostonians only," he continued, the Coercive Acts threatened all colonists. To combat the danger, he insisted, the advocates of resistance must stand firm and united. Ross implored his listeners: "May we never in this Time of Danger, know Party Feuds or political animosities amongst each other. May we consider the Town of Boston as suffering in our own Cause, paying Tribute for our Liberty and the Preservation of our just Rights." For "divided," he warned, "we must inevitably fall an easy Prey to our Enemies."[3]

Spurred on by borough authorities, hundreds of local residents eagerly joined the intercolonial effort, embracing commitments beyond their province and identifying with a larger community of resistance. Following the lead of Philadelphia's Whig resistance, locals passed a resolution branding Parliament's efforts to tax the colonies "unconstitutional, unjust, and oppressive" and recommended a "close Union of the Colonies" and adherence to the dictates of a general congress as the best means to redress their grievances and safeguard American rights. They then nominated eight county delegates to confer with other provincial representatives in the capital about appointing deputies for their newly proposed Continental Congress. As a gesture of sympathy and support, residents also began raising subscriptions to relieve their "Brethren of Boston, who are suffering in the American Cause." More than 180 inhabitants generously contributed over £150 in aid. Committing to a larger contest, residents began to associate their local interests with a broader American agenda.[4]

But local authorities had no intention of promoting a revolution. Steering a cautious course, moderates led Lancaster's emerging resistance. Professionals, merchants, and officials, they had prospered under the imperial regime. Fearful of disorder, they harbored no desires for independence but longed for a peaceful reconciliation with the mother country. Lancaster's two most prominent committeemen and outspoken advocates of intercolonial cooperation, George Ross and Edward Shippen, shared a fundamental conservatism. Shippen and Ross had both resided in Lancaster since the early 1750s, attending the borough's Anglican church and accruing considerable wealth and influence. A supporter of the proprietary faction, Shippen had long numbered among the county's most influential inhabitants. After settling in Lancaster, he dutifully occupied the offices of clerk of the county commissioners, prothonotary of the Court of Common Pleas, recorder of the Court of Quarter Sessions, and justice of the peace. Ross, a successful attorney affiliated with the Quaker party, had served as both a prosecutor for the king and a county representative in the assembly.[5]

At the general meeting on July 9, Ross reassured his audience that the Whig resistance sought to avoid a "Rupture with England." For "under her fostering wing we have attained to this flourishing State," Ross explained, adding: "She has protected and I trust she will still protect us from our Enemies. She justly may require the most grateful acknowledgments from us." Lancaster's Whig representatives blamed the crisis on Parliament and a corrupt ministry, casting the king as the victim of "evil and designing Men." The members of Lancaster's committee accordingly offered their "warmest expressions of Loyalty to his Majesty," acknowledging him as their "rightful and lawful Sovereign" and pledging to defend him with their "lives and fortunes against his Enemies." But by mobilizing the multitude, local Whig officials had unleashed forces that would eventually prove beyond their control. Residents' heightened political consciousness sparked a growing engagement with public affairs that drastically altered the local political culture.[6]

The Revolution came slowly to Lancaster but soon transformed the community, redefining local identities and commitments by demanding unprecedented levels of interethnic and intercolonial cooperation. By inciting mass resistance and rallying the community, the imperial crisis intensified public activism, spurring Lancaster's diverse residents to embrace new public roles and responsibilities. Unencumbered by the pacifist principles of their sectarian neighbors, church Germans flocked to the rebellion, wielding new influence as military officers and civilian authorities. At the same time, the war with Britain exacerbated the community's social and political fissures as embattled residents divided in their allegiance and commitments. Like the preceding Seven Years' War, the conflict widened the rift between the county's church groups and pacifist sectarians as Scots Irish Presbyterians and

German Lutherans and Reformed converged to protect their shared interests against common enemies.

By joining an intercolonial rebellion that finally sundered the bonds of empire, however, local Whigs broke new ground. As Lancaster committed men and matériel to the contest, the borough's ethnically diverse and locally oriented inhabitants embraced a common cause that transcended ethnicity, community, and province by pitting Briton against American and patriot against loyalist. In the process, the rebellion empowered a new class of armed associators, Pennsylvania's volunteer militiamen mobilized in defense of American rights and liberties. The county's spirited associators policed their communities by marginalizing those who shrank from the cause or wavered in their enthusiasm. Lancaster's rising militants vied for control with more established and cautious Whigs who looked to curb their neighbors' radicalism and preserve America's ties to the empire. Flexing their growing influence at the expense of their more moderate and conservative rivals, the county's hard-line insurgents soon placed Lancaster on the road to revolution.[7]

Military Discipline and the Art of War

The troubles with Britain had been brewing for nearly a decade before they resonated throughout the diverse Pennsylvania interior. The earliest and most vocal colonial resistance surfaced far to the north and south, in Massachusetts and Virginia, where provincial elites, soon known as Whigs, angrily protested the new imperial legislation. From Virginia and Massachusetts, the resistance spread to neighboring colonies as colonial newspapers broadcast the latest ministerial transgressions. During the mid-1760s, protests spilled from the halls of colonial assemblies to the streets of the major seaports, taking a decidedly radical turn as emerging activists, Stamp Act riots, and consumer boycotts sparked the interests and passions of the middle and lower ranks. Lagging behind the seaports were the hundreds of towns and villages scattered throughout the vast American interior, where redcoats, stamp agents, and violent protests were more removed from the locals' everyday experience.

In Pennsylvania, where imperial policies gradually alienated ever-broader proportions of the populace, the resistance movement embraced an increasingly diverse base of support. Conservative eastern merchants exercised disproportionate influence through the 1760s, spearheading a provincial resistance that encompassed supporters of both the proprietary and Quaker factions. As conservatives mobilized growing support, they undercut their own influence, inviting competition from more radical but younger men of

more limited financial means and political experience. Among the first political casualties of Pennsylvania's resistance were many of the east's Quaker
and proprietary leaders who had vied for control of the province during the
decades preceding the Revolution. Quakers, long the masters of provincial
politics, reluctantly withdrew from their positions of influence as the breach
widened with Britain and Pennsylvanians mobilized for war.

Replacing the colony's more established, conservative, and prosperous officials through the mid-1770s were the east's moderate-to-radical Whigs,
now orchestrating the provincial resistance from seats in the newly divided
assembly and increasingly influential committee system. The east's rising
Whig leadership included and drew support from Philadelphia's middling
artisans and shopkeepers, eager to exercise their new voice in provincial affairs. Additional support came from the working-class radicals filling the
city's newly organized militia battalions. Philadelphia's emergent radicals
brought their own agenda to the imperial controversy, pushing for separation from Britain and a slate of domestic reforms designed to curb the influence of the provincial elite and enhance their own political and economic
prospects. By late spring 1776, the moderates and radicals manning the east's
committee system had eclipsed the more conservative assembly, sealing independence from Britain and confirming Pennsylvania's internal political
revolution. Only during the summer of 1774, however, when imperial affairs
reached a crisis in faraway Massachusetts, did the resistance movement begin
to encompass Pennsylvania's vast hinterland majority.[8]

In Lancaster, the passage of the Stamp Act in 1765 first aroused locals'
concern with Britain's shifting imperial policies. By levying a double tax
on foreign-language documents and newspapers, the act placed a special
burden on Pennsylvania's Germans. Many German Americans opposed the
Stamp Act and measures like the Proclamation of 1763 and the Currency
Act of 1764, which hindered their efforts to acquire or secure property.
Through spring 1765, Jasper Yeates reported "great Murmurings" over the
"damned Stamp-Act Resolves" and "fervent Curses on the venal rascal Disposition of the present Ministry." When the borough's residents learned of
the Stamp Act's repeal in 1766, they joyfully illuminated their windows and
took to the streets in celebration, ringing the town bells and firing their rifles
into the heavens. George Ross gleefully contributed several barrels of beer
for the festivities. "What a brilliant figure we cut here with our illuminations," observed one resident, "how many flowing glasses we guzzled down,
(excuse the expression) for the sake of our country."[9]

With the resolution of the Stamp Act controversy, locals followed the
unfolding imperial crisis with wavering interest, occasionally weighing in on

events. Through the mid-1760s, debates over imperial policy between residents and the town's British visitors proceeded along civil lines. Jasper Yeates, for example, struck up a friendship with a British recruiting officer. "Ever & anon in a drunken bout," he noted, "we settle the powers of Parliament & the rights of the Colonies." As support grew for nonimportation during the late 1760s, however, the local elite indulged in the heated rhetoric that came to define the colonial resistance. One county Whig, shamed by the concerted patriotism of the northern seaports, wrote the *Pennsylvania Gazette* in May 1768 bemoaning Philadelphians' languid support of the colonial resistance and exhorting the city's merchants to join their Boston and New York counterparts in the boycotting of British goods. Urging the merchants to act "like Americans," he admonished them: "Let it not be a scandal to be a Philadelphian—a Pennsylvanian. . . . UNION makes the weak STRONG, and STRENGTH makes them SAFE." Indeed, "the skin of a son of liberty," he proclaimed, "will not feel the sparseness of a homespun shirt!" Two years later, in June 1770, local petitioners branded the Townshend Acts "unconstitutional and oppressive." Declaring their unwillingness to "sit unmoved at the Attempts made to deprive us of the Liberty we and our Ancestors have so highly esteemed and gloried in," they pledged their support for nonimportation. "We should deem ourselves unworthy of the Blessings of Freedom," they insisted, "could we tamely view our Situation, as calm Spectators, when we are threatened with the loss of Freedom and Property." They disdained the violators of nonimportation as "Traitors to the true Interests of this Country."[10]

Not until mid-1774, however, with the colonists' visceral reaction to the Coercive Acts, would Lancaster begin to mobilize as a community. On the heels of the Coercive Acts came the Quebec Act, which embittered many German residents by extending freedom of religion to French Catholics. Pennsylvania's German Protestants, nursing Old World grievances, deemed Catholicism a threat to their political and religious liberty. "The ax of the Catholics Shall oppress us now," lamented a locally printed German-language broadside before adding defiantly, "The rosary is shown to us, Who will not willingly bend to it." The broadside conjured up powerful imagery among locals determined to shield their faith and newfound freedoms from menacing Old World rivals. As late as the winter of 1774–75, however, as the British reinforced Boston with several men-of-war, Lancaster's leading Whigs remained hopeful of avoiding general hostilities, with Shippen confidently denying that any English admiral would "ever draw sword or trigger against the defenders of Great Britain."[11]

In late April 1775, following word of the British attacks on rebel militia at Lexington and Concord, events assumed a new urgency. News of the bloodshed in Massachusetts, combined with rumors that a "formidable fleet and Army" were "preparing to invade the Colonies," inflamed the community. On May 1, local Whigs proclaimed their commitment to unified armed resistance:

> Whereas, the Enemies of Great Britain and America have resolved by force of arms to carry into execution the most Unjust, Tyrannical, Cruel Edicts of the British Parliament, and reduce the Freeborn Sons of America to a State of Vassalage, and have flattered themselves, from our unacquaintance with military discipline, that we should become an easy prey to them, or tamely submit and bend our necks to the Yoke prepared for us: We do most solemnly agree and associate under the deepest Sense of our Duty to God, our Country, ourselves and Posterity, to defend and protect the Religious and Civil Rights of this and our sister colonies, with our lives and fortunes, to the utmost of our abilities, against any power whatsoever that shall attempt to deprive us of them.

Locals then resolved to acquaint themselves with "military discipline and the art of war."[12]

On Sunday, June 4, 1775, before a packed audience at Lancaster's Presbyterian church, the visiting Reverend John Carmichael delivered a stinging sermon justifying the resort to arms. "When a body of wicked people join together" to "destroy without any just cause an innocent people," Carmichael railed, the "insulted, or invaded people" must then "unite together, to oppose, expel and punish the guilty invaders." The reverend judged it "both lawful and a duty to arm ourselves and use our arms for our own preservation." Despite his fiery rhetoric, Carmichael drew a careful distinction between the king and his conniving ministers, urging continued allegiance to the crown. "Your drawing the sword now must not be against the person of his Majesty," the reverend counseled, "but the mal-administration of his government, by designing, mischief-making ministers." By so vigorously endorsing armed rebellion, however, Carmichael and other leading Whigs validated the expanding intercolonial insurgency, making the cause of Massachusetts their own.[13]

Just as they had donated generous sums for Boston's relief, locals now contributed enthusiastically to the fledgling war effort. In May, at the urging of the county committee, residents began producing and stockpiling supplies, arms, and ammunition. On May 4, nearly a dozen merchants tendered lead and over thirty casks of gunpowder to county authorities. Paul Zantzinger and Adam Simon Kuhn, two of the borough's leading German residents, began processing saltpeter for gunpowder. The German tradesman

Bernard Hubley gave generously to the war effort, even contributing his stock of pewterware to be "moulded into bullets for the cause." In late May, the Lancaster gunsmith John Henry helped manufacture cartridge casings for American troops. Home to makers of the Pennsylvania rifle, Lancaster boasted at least a dozen gunsmiths in the early 1770s. During the fall of 1775, Pennsylvania's assembly ordered six hundred stand of arms from Lancaster County, where gunsmiths busily fashioned rifles, muskets, and bayonets for the provincial forces. With the conflict escalating through early 1776, Lancaster's committee asked the townswomen to contribute linen for bandages for American troops "so unfortunate as to be wounded in defending the Liberties of their Country." Local women had begun contributing to the intercolonial resistance years before, fashioning homespun in support of non-importation. One Lancaster resident boasted in 1770, "We have not a house in this town, where the spinning wheel remains inactive." Nearly six years later, Lancaster's tailors were converting locally spun fabric into uniforms for the new Continental Army.[14]

Residents matched their matériel contributions with manpower. On May 1, 1775, armed volunteers agreed to combine into companies under a general military association, dividing the county into six military districts. Representatives of the borough's leading families promptly enrolled as officers. George Ross, for example, became a colonel in the county militia, while his son James dutifully enlisted as a captain. The call to arms also spurred formerly inactive or obscure members of the community to public service. Men of more limited means and influence, who had operated on the margins of provincial affairs, now eagerly appeared on the public stage, rifle in hand. The resistance movement decidedly enhanced the influence of the county's church Germans, who spurned the principled pacifism of their divergent sectarian neighbors. Indeed, members of the local Lutheran and Reformed congregations soon swelled the ranks of the county's hastily organized militia battalions, with dozens of Lancaster's German artisans and shopkeepers numbering among the first recruits. By early May, one resident estimated that some three hundred men were under arms. Several months later, Lancaster's Lutheran minister Heinrich Helmuth observed: "The zeal which finds expression in these troubled conditions is not to be described. Where a hundred men are called for, many more than that number report immediately, who are rejected–to their great dissatisfaction, because one does not need them all."[15]

By early summer, the county's newly formed militia regularly mustered and drilled on the town common. The county ultimately fielded eleven battalions of volunteers. Many of these troops later joined the regiments incorporated into the Pennsylvania Line. In June 1775, to harness the special prowess of backcountry associators, Congress ordered Lancaster County to raise a company of volunteers for a new battalion of riflemen hailing from Pennsylvania, Maryland, and Virginia. By midsummer, the county had raised not one but two companies. To rally more Germans to the armed resistance, in May 1776, Congress began recruiting an exclusively German regiment. Originally composed of German speakers from Maryland and Pennsylvania, the regiment featured one company from Lancaster County. The county also furnished a handful of recruits for the Marechausee Corps, an elite German unit charged with policing and enforcing discipline in the American ranks.[16]

To Defend Their Inherited Liberty

Military mobilization gave the county's Germans greater access to positions of public authority. The leaders of the local German-speaking community had long governed in conjunction with their English-speaking neighbors, serving as borough or, less often, as county representatives. War and revolution, however, created both increasing opportunities and fresh avenues to power for the Germans as military officers or civil administrators. Some of Lancaster's most prominent German residents officered the county's militia companies or received commissions in the Pennsylvania Line. In addition to serving on Lancaster's committee, the well-to-do Lutheran tavern keeper and longtime county officeholder Matthias Slough held the rank of colonel in the provincial militia and the Continental Flying Camp. Another committeeman, the wealthy merchant and Reformed Church member Wilhelm Bausman, enlisted as a lieutenant in the militia before claiming the more coveted and remunerative post of county forage master. The local physician Christian Rheinick served as a surgeon's mate in Pennsylvania's Rifle Battalion and the Continental Line before his death at the Battle of Paoli on September 20, 1777. Military service also enabled less influential members of the community to enhance their standing. The local shopkeeper Michael App enlisted as a corporal in 1775 but quickly rose to the rank of ensign in Pennsylvania's Musketry Battalion. Captured at the Battle of Long Island, he eventually returned to service as a captain in the county militia following his exchange in December 1776. Marcus Jung, a youth who had served with distinction in one of Lancaster's rifle companies, earned an ensign's commission in the German Regiment in late 1776 on the recommendation of local officials. In less than a year, he had achieved the rank of lieutenant.[17]

German speakers also gained increasing representation on the county's high-profile extralegal committees, convening regularly and sharing power with their English and Scots Irish associates. During the summer of 1774, Germans filled only three of the ten seats on the borough's first Committee of Correspondence. That winter, the borough elected twelve members for the county's new Committee of Observation, created to enforce the Continental Association. Half of the borough's dozen representatives were German Americans. A year later, eight Germans sat on Lancaster's eleven-member committee. Only two members of the borough's original Committee of Correspondence, Charles Hall and Jasper Yeates, had no prior experience as civil officeholders. By contrast, four of the committeemen elected in November 1775 were new to civil office. Three of the four, Michael Musser, Jacob Krug, and Jacob Glatz, were German tradesmen and congregants in either Lancaster's Lutheran or Reformed church. The seven-member delegation representing Lancaster County at Pennsylvania's provincial convention in January 1775 included two Germans, the wealthy Adam Simon Kuhn and Sebastian Graff.[18]

By 1776, Lancaster County's Germans had become increasingly visible in the burgeoning American resistance. As the borough's German speakers contributed to the war effort, furnishing supplies, enlisting in American ranks, or staffing extralegal committees, they exercised mounting influence in provincial public affairs. Many of the hinterland's Germans and Scots Irish had ascended to new heights of political consciousness during the preceding decades' frontier crises, as they strove for greater representation for their interior counties. For the Germans especially, however, the Revolution triggered an even broader and more sustained mobilization. The Germans' heightened activism reflected an intensified public commitment, a growing willingness to embrace new public roles and responsibilities in defense of their customary rights and liberties. Given most Germans' more selective engagement with public affairs prior to the imperial crisis, provincial observers found their new enthusiasm surprising. "Regions, of which one must have believed it would take years before the people would voluntarily take arms," marveled Pastor Helmuth in late summer 1775, "have become quite martial in a few weeks." Indeed, "The rough turmoil of war is heard hourly in the streets."[19]

The mobilization of Lancaster's Germans mirrored broader provincial trends. Wherever he traveled during the summer of 1775, the Lutheran Reverend Henry Mühlenberg "found the male inhabitants under arms." In the towns, he reported, "one sees boys, who are still quite small, marching in companies with little drums and wooden flints to defend their inherited liberty." By the mid-1760s, Pennsylvania's German speakers had become increasingly protective of both their liberty and their property and surprisingly adept at navigating Anglo-American political culture. Like their

English-speaking neighbors, Germans feared the impositions of arbitrary authorities acting on behalf of a powerfully intrusive state. Generations of German emigrants had fled state coercion in search of the promised freedom and opportunity of Britain's North American colonies. For the tens of thousands of newly uprooted Germans who swarmed into Pennsylvania through the mid-eighteenth century, freedom generally implied the absence of constraint. Growing numbers of German settlers, however, gradually adapted customary conceptions of liberty to their new circumstances. By the early 1770s, to secure their hard-won material gains, many of the province's Germans had formulated a more positive understanding of liberty that entailed greater public responsibility and the active defense of property rights.[20]

The Germans' evolving conception of liberty and their determination to defend their rights and interests as British subjects led thousands to resist imperial encroachments and take up arms against the king's troops. Captain Alexander Graydon of the Pennsylvania Line later recalled how the "great body of German farmers, extremely tenacious of property," eagerly embraced the cause. After Lexington and Concord, even the onetime loyalist Henry Mühlenberg acknowledged each man's duty to "defend the liberty and rights vouchsafed" by God and government. More pointedly, the reverend conceded, he was obliged to "protect his house and property against thieves who may be presumed to come not only to steal but also to slay and destroy." A German-language broadside circulating through Lancaster queried, "On which side does disgrace fall, America or England?" England, came the reply, while "America gains peace Of Tyrants, and remains free."[21]

The longtime Lancaster resident Bernard Hubley personified Germans' budding public-spiritedness. Born in Maulbronn, Germany, in 1719, Hubley headed one of Lancaster's most distinguished families. His persecuted Huguenot forebears had fled France during the late seventeenth century. After his family suffered renewed hardships in southern Germany, Hubley embarked for Pennsylvania in 1732 in the company of his father, brother, and sister. His father died shortly after the family's arrival in Philadelphia, leaving Bernard and his siblings in the care of their uncle. Hubley settled in Lancaster in the early 1740s, taking the naturalization oath in 1743 and becoming a prominent member of the borough's expanding Lutheran congregation. By the 1750s, he had won the respect of his English- and German-speaking neighbors, operating a flourishing tanning trade and serving as burgess, county treasurer, and county commissioner.

During the early 1770s, Hubley emerged as a warm advocate of resistance to imperial policy. Too old for military service, he assisted the war effort as the county's barracks master. With his business partner Ludwick Lauman, he faithfully contributed funds and supplies. "I am giving my means, and am willing to give my life," Hubley testified, "for my beloved country and the liberty of my brethren." Sharing the old patriot's enthusiasm, at least a half dozen of his sons and nephews enrolled as officers in the German Regiment or the Pennsylvania Militia or Line. Hubley's son Bernard Junior, for example, followed his brothers Adam and Frederick into the American service, enlisting in 1776 before receiving commissions as a lieutenant and later a captain in the German Regiment. Years after mustering out of the army in 1781, Hubley joined fellow veterans in the Society of the Cincinnati, a patriotic organization founded by former officers of the Continental Army, and penned one of the earliest histories of the American Revolution.[22]

The leading members of Pennsylvania's diverse and far-flung German-speaking communities helped their ethnic kindred decipher the specific issues and grasp their personal stake in the broader imperial controversy. In Lancaster, the German businessmen Adam Reigart and Matthias Slough both sat on the local Committee of Correspondence, where they helped mobilize their German-speaking neighbors. Slough and Reigart spoke English, attended the Anglican church, and maintained long-standing commercial ties with the borough's Anglo community. Both men had occupied the influential offices of assistant burgess, county coroner, and county treasurer. A moderate Whig, Slough achieved the additional distinction in 1773 of becoming one of only three of the county's German speakers to serve in the provincial assembly. Working closely with the county's English and Scots Irish Whigs, the pair operated as cultural intermediaries, using their local influence to enlist the support of fellow Germans by translating the ideology of the American resistance. Lancaster's predominantly German-speaking committee began issuing bilingual broadsides as early as May 1775. Moreover, both Slough and Reigart owned taverns, where locals of all backgrounds routinely gathered to receive and discuss the latest news.[23]

German Americans also kept abreast of the unfolding imperial crisis via the German-language press. Through the 1760s, two prominent German printers, Heinrich Miller, publisher of *Der Wochentliche Philadelphische Staatsbote*, and Christopher Sauer, publisher of the *Germantowner Zeitung*, encouraged their subscribers to resist imperial policy. Miller and Sauer were based in Philadelphia and Germantown, respectively, but with agents in the heavily German-speaking communities of Lancaster, York, and Reading, their circulation stretched deep into the Pennsylvania hinterland. In addition to their own material, the printers translated and reprinted news and editorials from competing English-language newspapers, pointedly informing their German readers how British policy affected their peculiar interests. But by defining their audience as Americans and situating German interests within an evolving Anglo-American political culture, they also helped their readers transcend their particular ethnic identities.[24]

Even before the Stamp Act crisis, followers of the German-language press could imbibe Whig principles by reading of their natural and constitutional rights as British subjects. In a 1764 broadside opposing the Quaker-backed campaign for royal government, Sauer declared, "Liberty, my dear compatriots, is our natural right, a right, which the God of nature and of virtue demands you to assert and which he will help you to preserve." Indeed, "by your living here and by the law of the land," he concluded, "you are free men, not slaves. You have a right to all liberties of a native-born Englishman, and you have a share in the fundamental laws of the land." In September 1765, Sauer denounced the Stamp Act as a "heavy, unbearable burden." Miller's *Staatsbote* provided detailed coverage of the Stamp Act crisis. Decrying the act as the "most unconstitutional law these colonies have ever seen," Miller urged his subscribers to pressure their political representatives to renounce the measure. He then joined Anglo printers in defying the act by publishing his newspaper on unstamped paper. On May 19, 1766, the *Staatsbote* described Philadelphians' joyous celebrations of the act's repeal.[25]

Continuing reports of the growing American resistance, both formal and informal protests, helped radicalize public opinion in Pennsylvania. Miller's *Staatsbote*, for example, faithfully chronicled the ongoing exploits of the "Sohne der Freiheit," along with the rising incidence of mob violence in neighboring colonies. In his account of Boston's Stamp Act riots, Miller gleefully provided a translation of the menacing verse adorning the stamp agent's effigy: "A goodlier sight who e'er did see? A Stamp-Man hanging on a tree!" After describing the mob's razing of the agent's residence, he wryly observed, "Would it not be better if all stamp agents took out insurance on their houses?" In early 1774, Miller linked the escalating violence in Massachusetts to the people's distrust of imperial governance, urging their continued resistance.[26]

The German-language press helped integrate agitated readers into the expanding American resistance. By emphasizing the intercolonial dimensions of the crisis and the need for American unity, printers encouraged their subscribers to look beyond ethnic and communal attachments, even as they appealed to Germans in their own language. Miller preached the simple philosophy that "unity makes for power." In March 1769, the *Staatsbote* marked the third anniversary of the Stamp Act's repeal and reminded readers, "United we stand, divided we fall." By describing the effects of British policy on neighboring colonies, Pennsylvania's German-language press gave readers a sense of the common burdens borne by their fellow Americans. On December 8, 1768, Sauer's *Germantowner Zeitung* came out in support of nonimportation, announcing that "America's freedom depends on it."[27]

By urging readers to identify with their fellow colonists and acknowledge their shared American experience, German printers, like their Anglo counterparts, helped lay the foundation for a budding conception of American nationhood. By 1775, in a broadside bewailing the hostilities in Massachusetts, German speakers could see America described as their "dear fatherland." In 1776, one month after the publication of a German translation of Thomas Paine's *Common Sense*, an English-speaking Whig reported that the tract "works on the minds of those people amazingly." Paine's clever boast that "Europe, and not England, is the parent country of America" surely won Germans' enthusiastic approval. As Paine astutely observed, "This new World hath been the asylum for the persecuted lovers of civil and religious liberty from EVERY PART of Europe." Provincial and Continental officials worked closely with German printers to reach the German-speaking public, publishing their resolves in German. Miller, for example, translated and published the full proceedings of the First and Second Continental Congress. On July 6, 1776, German printers circulated a translation of the Declaration of Independence.[28]

By early 1776, many of Pennsylvania's Germans had eagerly embraced the American rebellion, becoming devoted defenders of revolutionary republicanism. Increasingly schooled in Whig ideology, the German insurgents hoped to make the most of the new opportunities associated with their support of the resistance. En route to camp, Pennsylvania's German volunteers sang as they marched:

> Kleine Georgel, Kaiser, Koenig,
> Ist fer Gott un uns zu wennich.
> Little Georgie, emperor, king,
> Is for God and us too little a thing.

Pennsylvania eventually supplied five of the German Regiment's nine companies. By July 1776, two months after recruitment began, the regiment had over a thousand enlistees. First-generation Germans constituted approximately a quarter of Pennsylvania's men under arms. Hailing mostly from Lancaster County or adjacent central Pennsylvania counties, these troops proved indispensable to the American war effort.[29]

Military service empowered the Germans, affording them new rights and privileges. Heavily influenced by Quakers who increasingly opposed the armed resistance, Pennsylvania's three original eastern counties—Philadelphia,

Bucks, and Chester—had long dominated provincial affairs. Eastern political control left the province's interior counties at a noticeable disadvantage,
particularly during the 1750s and 1760s, when war erupted on the frontier
and Pennsylvania's Quaker-dominated assembly stymied defense measures.
The power and perceived callousness of eastern interests embittered vulnerable backcountry inhabitants eager to redress the political imbalance by
increasing their representation in the assembly. In early spring 1776, to offset
the political influence of their more conservative legislature, Philadelphia's
radicals helped secure greater representation for the province's eight interior
counties, where the resistance movement found growing support among
Scots Irish Presbyterians and German Lutherans and Reformed keen to enhance their voice in provincial affairs. A month later, English- and German-
speaking militiamen pressured the assembly to grant foreign-born associators
the "Rights and Privileges" of "natural-born Subjects." Facilitating the naturalization of alien associators promised to strengthen Pennsylvania's radical
faction and bolster support for independence.[30]

German militants made their influence felt in June 1776 at the provincial
conference to organize a new constitutional convention. Delegates resolved
that associators who were over twenty-one and had paid taxes or resided in
the province for more than a year could vote for representatives to Pennsylvania's upcoming convention. In September, the state's new radical constitution eased naturalization restrictions, granting citizenship to aliens who
declared their allegiance to the state and met the one-year residency require-
ment. The measure sought to strengthen Germans' ties to Pennsylvania's new
revolutionary government by appealing to foreign-born emigrants hopeful
of securing citizenship and the franchise. Though many Germans brought
their own motives to the contest, their avid participation in the resistance
altered relations with their near and distant neighbors.[31]

The Sole Denomination of Americans

Heightened German activism transformed the provincial political culture
by fostering new levels of interethnic cooperation as Pennsylvania's sun-
dry insurgents strove to subordinate their ethnic divisions to a broader
revolutionary agenda. The imperial crisis slowly redefined customary patterns of ethnocultural association, altering the ways in which English- and
German-speaking Whigs identified and interacted. A May 1776 broadside
circulated by English-speaking proponents of a constitutional convention,
for instance, celebrated "those German inhabitants . . . who are now incorporated with us in one common stock." The revolutionaries' armed struggle

generated new alliances and allegiances, as novel patriotic attachments vied with long-established ethnic and linguistic bonds. In Philadelphia, reported Pastor Helmuth in August 1775, "English and German pupils" joined military units, donned uniforms, and paraded "like regular troops." Similarly, Lancaster's German associators mustered and marched and soon fought and bled alongside their English and Scots Irish neighbors in their county's new ethnically integrated units. English speakers dominated the county's rifle battalions, while most Germans preferred militia service. The roster of Colonel Matthias Slough's First Battalion of Lancaster County Militia featured names ranging from Cornelius Taylor and William McCormick to Ulrich Fissel and Jacob Landmesser. Eventually, even the German Regiment incorporated English-speaking recruits.[32]

To be sure, the interior's diverse ethnic groups had cooperated during previous crises. Two decades before, clusters of Lancaster County's most vulnerable English- and German-speaking inhabitants had jointly taken up arms during the dislocating Seven Years' War. During the 1750s and 1760s, however, the county's residents had armed chiefly for local defense, even as they defended broader British interests within the familiar confines of the Anglo imperial system. By contrast, during their conflict with Britain, the province's English and German speakers mobilized in much greater numbers and identified and interacted in new ways, not as colonial subjects defending imperial interests but as American insurgents armed against British and German invaders in defense of their shared rights and liberties.[33]

The call to arms invited local troops to look beyond town, county, and province and identify with a larger American community. During the summer of 1775, prior to the British evacuation of Boston, Lancaster's riflemen marched to Cambridge, Massachusetts, where they joined volunteers from neighboring colonies, becoming part of a broader American fold defined by martial spirit and selfless activism in defense of the common cause. Only a year before, few Pennsylvanians could have envisioned the hinterland's diverse German and Scots Irish inhabitants, long noted for their clannish parochialism, venturing north together to protect the rights of aggrieved New Englanders. In June 1775, however, at a time "when all the other colonies in North-America, like the true children of *a free-born family*," were "taking each other as by the hand, and uniting by the invincible chains of love, friendship, and interest," the Reverend John Carmichael celebrated the county's associators in a sermon at Lancaster's Presbyterian church. The reverend concluded his sermon with the hope that God would bless their "very laudable and grand undertaking, in connection with all the Militia of North-America."[34]

Lancaster's motley insurgents found the common cause more easily embraced in the abstract, however, with long-standing ethnic and provincial
attachments proving stubbornly persistent during the war's early months.
As the county's English- and German-speaking associators mingled in un-
comfortable proximity and with unaccustomed regularity, familiar ethnic
antagonisms flared. In September 1775, soldiers from one of the local militia
battalions reported that their corps was so badly divided that "some parts of it
threaten to disarm other parts by force," pitting "one Society against another"
and "one Nation against another." Among the county's assorted volunteers,
claims to Americanness remained deeply contested.[35]

To curb conflict and promote cooperation in the ranks, local and provincial
leaders worked to minimize the ethnic friction among Pennsylvania's associators. In his June 1775 sermon at Lancaster's Presbyterian church, Reverend
Carmichael exhorted the county's militia to "guard against every thing that has
the least or remotest tendency, to jar the blessed unison of the whole American
harpsichord, as now set to the tune of liberty, by the honourable great artists
the CONTINENTAL CONGRESS." He urged, "Let every denomination
of Christians treat each other with love and respect," as "brethren engaged in,
and struggling for the one and same common cause." Promulgated in August
1775, Article 20 of the rules governing Pennsylvania's associators required
that "all National distinctions in dress or name . . . be avoided, it being proper
that we should now be united in this general Association for defending our
liberties and properties under the sole denomination of Americans."[36]

The escapades of the county's riflemen reveal the lingering tensions and
competing allegiances hindering a unified American war effort. Winding
through the towns of Pennsylvania en route to joining the growing American force assembling in Cambridge, the riflemen met with enthusiastic
crowds eager to see them showcase their reputed skills. Clothed in hunting
frocks, leggings, and moccasins, and armed with long rifles, tomahawks, and
hunting knives, the frontiersmen readily obliged their hosts, staging elaborate
demonstrations of their military prowess and thrilling audiences with daz-
zling feats of marksmanship. In Lancaster, an awestruck admirer recalled how
a visiting company of riflemen kindled a great fire "around a pole planted
in the courthouse square." Then, "with the captain at their head, all naked to
the waist, and painted like savages," the soldiers "indulged a vast concourse
of people with a perfect exhibition of a war-dance, and all the manoeuvres
of Indians, holding council, going to war, circumventing their enemies by
defiles, ambuscades, attacking, scalping, &c."[37]

Arriving in New England as strangers, with their rough backcountry
dress and demeanor, some of Pennsylvania's riflemen weathered a colder

reception after clashing with northern soldiers and civilians. While passing through Hartford, Connecticut, a company of Lancaster County riflemen became embroiled in a heated dispute with the town's Whigs. Only the timely intervention of Captain James Ross averted potential bloodshed. The condition of the New England troops left the riflemen similarly unimpressed. Major Robert Magaw of Cumberland County, Pennsylvania, for example, observed in August 1775 that the "Massachusetts bay Troops are Numerous but the least Respectable of any," consisting of "Small & Great old & Young some Neagros and Molattas . . . Some with long Coats Almost Trailing the Ground the Next Naked to their Middle," and "in General but ill officered." With General Washington's new Continental Army still in its fledgling stages, divisions among the troops from different colonies sparked predictable tensions in the ranks. In late 1775, the exasperated officers of a Pennsylvania rifle battalion demanded that "all distinctions of colonies . . . be laid aside, so that one and the same spirit may animate the whole."[38]

The riflemen's arrival in Massachusetts produced some equally ambivalent and volatile encounters with the enemy. Burning to test their skills in combat, the marksmen regularly slipped away from camp to snipe at their British enemies from afar. "The Riflemen go where they please," reported one of their officers in early August, and "keep the regulars in continual hot water." Another American officer found them "remarkably stout and hardy men," adding that their deadly accuracy with a rifle "frequently proved fatal to British officers and soldiers who expose themselves to view, even at more than double the distance of common musket-shot." British officers, the riflemen's preferred target, quickly came to dread the marksmen, dubbing them "widow makers." Whenever possible, the riflemen menaced their enemies at close range. In Hartford, a paroled British prisoner of war, Ensign Christopher French, had an unfortunate run-in with a Lancaster County rifleman who, he grimly recounted, "wanted much to shoot me." Indeed, for all their enthusiasm, the county's riflemen fought on their own terms and exhibited a shocking lack of discipline. In Cambridge, the riflemen promptly acquired a reputation for misconduct. In early September 1775, over thirty of Captain James Ross's men mutinied and were fortunate to escape serious punishment. Fellow Pennsylvanians and New England militia helped suppress the rebellion. Fed up with the restrictions of camp life, some riflemen deserted to the enemy. For these soldiers, through the months ahead, battle lines and allegiances remained especially fluid.[39]

Only in the crucible of war, after sustained clashes with their British adversaries, would Lancaster's troops begin to forge broader but still brittle bonds of union beyond their more parochial attachments to kin and community.

Mortally wounded by British cannon fire in late August 1775, the young Lancaster County rifleman William Simpson became one of Pennsylvania's first military casualties. According to fellow rifleman James Wilkinson, the dying man was "visited and consoled" by General Washington and "most of the officers of rank belonging to the American Army." Mourned by his compatriots, Simpson's death, Wilkinson noted, became a "theme of common sorrow in an army of twelve or fourteen thousand men."[40]

During late 1775, a local rifle company joined Colonel Benedict Arnold's ill-fated Canadian expedition, eventually participating in the disastrous assault on Quebec. Taken captive by the British, dozens of the county's riflemen languished in prison alongside the troops from neighboring colonies. Their captivity now reinforcing the bonds forged in camp and combat, many of the prisoners later returned to Pennsylvania with a broader yet more refined sense of American identity. After his release from captivity, the Lancaster rifleman John Henry fondly reminisced of his northern and southern compatriots, the Virginians and New Englanders under Arnold's command who fought alongside him and his fellow Pennsylvanians. "Of as rude and hardy a race as ourselves . . . and as fearless as we were," he recalled, "they were an excellent body of men, formed by nature as the stamina of an army, fitted for the tough and tight defence of the *liberties* of their country." Even while subtly distinguishing among his compatriots, Henry envisioned them as part of a larger American collective. Despite their lingering prejudice and parochialism, Lancaster's diverse insurgents slowly came to identify with like-minded patriot neighbors and distant American allies.[41]

The Want of Confidence and Union amongst Us

Just as the imperial crisis generated new alliances, it bred new divisions, progressively drawing the county's insurgents into an emerging revolutionary community while marginalizing nonconformists. In a process that continued throughout the war, Lancaster's militants measured their virtue and defined their identities against their opposition. Risking their lives and fortunes in the manly defense of kin and country, armed associators vented an increasingly belligerent patriotism that vilified and circumscribed dissenters who withheld their support from the growing resistance. From Lancaster in late summer 1775, Pastor Helmuth reported: "The people are for the most part all in a veritable enthusiasm regarding freedom. . . . Those few who think otherwise dare not speak otherwise. If, indeed, a few have been so incautious, they fare so badly that others have no desire to show the least opposition to the course entered upon."[42]

From their newly formed extralegal committees, local Whigs enforced conformity by proscribing dissent. On December 15, 1774, the county elected a new Committee of Observation to uphold the Continental Association's program of domestic frugality, industry, and nonimportation by publicly condemning violators as "enemies of American liberty." Days later, the committee closed a recently opened dancing school that violated the association's standards by encouraging "extravagance and dissipation." Committeemen routinely inspected the shops of merchants suspected of breaking the boycott on British tea. In November 1775, after local gunsmiths balked at filling orders at prices set by Congress, Lancaster's committee threatened to confiscate their tools, close their shops, confine them to their residences, and proclaim them "enemies of this Country." A dozen gunsmiths quickly fell into line, humbly appearing before the committee to submit to Congress's terms.[43]

Whigs took particular pains to root out loyalists who actively resisted the cause. County loyalists risked censure, punishment, and stigmatization by local officials. Lancaster's committee received a report in early January 1776 that the onetime county resident John Connolly, a former Indian trader and associate of Virginia's royal governor John Murray, Lord Dunmore, had been detained in Frederick County, Maryland, for allegedly conspiring with the British to raise a mixed corps of loyalists and Indians. After learning that Alexander McKee, a Paxton resident, fur trader, and long-serving agent in Britain's Department of Indian Affairs, might be implicated in the plot, the committee summoned him to the borough to answer the charge. "In these calamitous Times," wrote acting committee chairman Jasper Yeates, "no good Man would wish his Character to be under an Imputation of disaffection to the Interests of his Country." Months later, another resident came before the committee after boldly proclaiming that should the king's standard ever be "set up in this country he would soon go and join it," and subversively predicting that he would shortly "see it erected in Lancaster."[44]

Whigs also encountered difficulties with the sectarians who passively resisted the cause. During late spring 1775, relations soured between the county's militant associators and religious pacifists, mostly German-speaking Amish, Mennonites, and Moravians who claimed neutral status and formal exemption from military service, rekindling in the process tensions smoldering since the 1760s. Having flourished under the imperial system, many sectarians were loath to challenge royal authority, fearing the inevitable uncertainty attending a permanent break with Great Britain. Opposed to war on moral and religious grounds, the sects had claimed similar exemption from military service during the Seven Years' War. In 1755, as the first native war parties struck along the provincial frontier, Pennsylvania's Mennonites proclaimed it their "fixed principle rather than take up Arms in order to defend our King, our Country or our Selves, to Suffer all that is dear to us to be rend from us, even Life it Self." That same year, to demonstrate their allegiance to the crown, Lancaster County Mennonites offered to pay "whatever duty, Tax, &c., that the Laws of Great Britain and this province requires." They adamantly refused, however, to defend the crown with "Sword in hand." Adhering to the dictates of conscience poisoned relations with the sects' furious English- and German-speaking neighbors, who remained desperate to shore up local defense.[45]

Their troubles during the 1750s and 1760s had taught the sects to fear the worst from war. A month after the bloodshed at Lexington and Concord, a local Moravian rued his neighborhood's "warlike appearance." Complicating matters for the sects, in mobilizing men for military service, Pennsylvania's Whig officials made no provisions for pacifists. Penn's Charter of Privileges and decades of Quaker dominance had long safeguarded the sects' peculiar interests. As Quakers' authority waned amid the escalating hostilities, pacifists became vulnerable to militant supporters of the resistance, whose growing influence came at the expense of their sectarian rivals. Many families scarred by the Indian troubles of earlier decades now looked to settle old scores with sectarian neighbors who had invoked their pacifist principles while the frontier burned. Lancaster County's sectarians soon faced pressure from militant insurgents to enlist. "We have a very uneasy and restless time here," complained one Moravian in late spring 1775. "Nearly all adult men are obliged to exercise," he added, for "Money will not give exemption." When the sectarians refused to enlist, they infuriated the county's newly enrolled associators. Resentful associators charged that the sectarians refused to support the cause even though they stood to profit from the gains won by the resistance. From Lebanon, Moravians now expressed their daily horror at the "open malice of our enemies."[46]

The factional strife erupted in violence during May 1775, when associators from neighboring townships informed Lancaster's committee that sectarians had berated them as "Black-Guards, Fellows who are lazy, & follow the Drum from an idle Disposition." Local Mennonites, in turn, asked for the committee's protection, claiming that the county's soldiers routinely threatened and abused members of their sect for refusing to enlist. The Mennonites offered "chearfully" to "co-operate in the Common Cause except in such Acts as were repugnant to their Consciences." On May 29 the committee, chaired by Edward Shippen, promised protection for sectarian dissenters but sternly rebuked the petitioners, noting that men whose consciences forbade them from bearing arms "ought to be satisfied that they are permitted to sit quietly." They should not "insult or behave with Impertinence towards those who have Virtue to stand forth & risque their Lives in Defense of the Rights & Liberties of their Country." Otherwise, the committee concluded, "they must expect such Treatment, as may perhaps be disagreeable to them."[47]

To conciliate the disputing factions and restore peace to the county, the committee printed broadsides urging the county's residents to refrain from "future Violence, Threats, or Animosities" and to "cultivate that Harmony and Union so absolutely necessary in the present alarming Crisis of Publick Affairs." Like many of Pennsylvania's moderate Whigs, the members of Lancaster's committee grudgingly accepted the sectarians' pacifism. They saw sectarians' neutrality, while regrettable, as posing no visible dangers to their cause. As Reverend Carmichael surmised, "If they will not in these terrible times, draw the sword *for* Liberty and their Country, surely they will not *against* Liberty and their Country." Above all, local officials sought to preserve the peace and stability that had customarily governed the county's social relations. As the established leaders of their community, they naturally assumed that the county's associators would defer to their authority. The committee gravely miscalculated, for the local militia reacted fiercely to official tolerance of the pacifists.[48]

On the afternoon of June 1, after learning of the committee's actions, armed associators descended on the printer's office to confiscate the broadsides, announcing that they "would not muster, if any People whatever were excused from bearing arms & associating." Pinning one of the handbills to Lancaster's whipping post, a party of soldiers took careful aim and blew it to shreds. The soldiers then marched menacingly through the town, insulting and threatening the members of Lancaster's committee. Later that evening, angry associators tarred and feathered the door of a committeeman's home. Fearful of the soldiers' intentions, Lancaster's entire committee resigned the following morning after arranging for the election of a new slate of committeemen. In a letter to Congress announcing their resignation, the deposed officials deprecated the "fatal Consequences of public Anarchy & Confusion," venting their new fears of an armed rabble. "We wish never to see the Day," they lamented, "when the patriotic spirit of our Countrymen shall be the source of our greatest Misfortunes, when the Vigour of Government shall be relaxed, & the Arms put into the Hands of People for the noblest Purposes, shall be perverted to Instruments of Ruin."[49]

The next day, the borough elected a new committee amid fresh allegations that the county's sectarians had bribed the displaced committeemen to gain exemption from militia duty. "The Mennonites," observed an alarmed resident, "are very much hated by the people." One of Lancaster's moderate Whigs, meanwhile, bemoaned the county's growing divisions, complaining that "something ought to be done to prevent our murdering each other." Another added despairingly, "I cannot but sincerely lament the Want of Confidence and Union amongst us, which so obviously retards our public Deliberations." Facing sustained pressure from local associators, Lancaster's newly elected committee adopted a harder line toward pacifist dissenters. In mid-June, the committee recommended that the county's pacifists contribute £3.10 to the public interest on top of an additional sum equivalent to their annual provincial tax. Those who failed to comply were to be reported to the committee.[50]

To preserve order in the province, Congress and Pennsylvania's assembly likewise appealed to the sectarians to subscribe financial support for the associators. On June 30, the assembly recommended that the pacifists "chearfully assist" the public cause in "Proportion to their Abilities." Weeks later, Congress urged the sectarians to *"Contribute Liberally*, in this time of universal calamity" and to render "all other services to their oppressed country, which they can consistently with their Religious principles." Meanwhile, in Lancaster, hard-line insurgents turned up the pressure on their sectarian opposition. By late summer, Lancaster's committee demanded formal lists of the locals who refused to furnish military or financial support to the resistance. A distressed Moravian noted on August 19 that the "Committee went from house to house this week to make a list of everybody. No one exempt from 16 to 50 years. They must all exercise or pay a fine." Several months later, officers of the county militia urged that non-associators be declared ineligible for public office, insisting that the posts be reserved for "such as have shewn themselves spirited in the glorious cause of American liberty (and no other)."[51]

By late 1775, radicals throughout the province had increased the pressure on Pennsylvania's assembly by demanding financial sanctions to compensate for non-associators' refusal to bear arms. Concluding that "where the Liberty of all is at Stake, every Man should assist in its Support," Pennsylvania's newly formed Committee of Safety recommended in September 1775 that non-associators pay an estate tax "equivalent to the Expence and Loss of Time incurred by the Associators." Two months later, the assembly yielded to radical pressure by approving a fine of £2.10 for each non-associator. In April 1776, bowing to renewed appeals for heavier fines, the assembly raised the tax by a pound. To provide the province's associators with adequate arms, assemblymen also approved the disarming of non-associators.[52]

By marginalizing dissenters, Pennsylvania's radicals solidified their own ranks. In Lancaster, the lines of wartime dissent overrode ethnic attachments, with Whigs encountering enemies both within and across their particular ethnic camps. Their disputes with non-associators reinforced the emerging bonds among the county's diverse insurgents, as English- and German-speaking militants squared off against English- and German-speaking pacifists. Before the crisis with Britain, religious differences and a decade of frontier violence had strained relations between the interior's German sectarians and church folk. Although their religions varied, however, the Germans still shared a common language. For these German speakers, maligned as aliens and approached with suspicion by many of their English-speaking neighbors, this linguistic connection mattered. Yet for a growing number of radical German associators, language and custom soon came to matter less than the degree to which their fellow residents supported the American resistance. Correspondingly, most of the county's Scots Irish associators could learn to overlook a German neighbor's ethnic origin if he willingly shared the burden of military service. They would scarcely be so forgiving of an English- or German-speaking pacifist who shunned his military obligations for matters of conscience. Depending on locals' levels of commitment to the cause, the war could alternately blur or magnify existing ethnocultural distinctions, with pacifist sectarians coming under particular scrutiny from their militant neighbors.

Yet the dispute with the pacifists also revealed troubling cracks in the Whig coalition. Local authorities now faced challenges from below from the newly empowered members of their community, the armed associators who demanded a common sacrifice and resented any lapse of patriotic zeal. After Lexington and Concord, a new revolutionary community began to emerge in which a selfless commitment to the common cause rather than economic status or ethnic orientation became the principal measure of merit. In late 1775, Lancaster County's militant associators redefined local patriotism, establishing the acceptable level of public participation in the resistance. In these hard-liners' view, self-sacrificing patriots hazarded their blood and treasure for the public good. By failing fully to endorse the associators' radical position, the borough's more conservative-minded committeemen had called their own patriotism into question. The committee's resignation underscored the declining influence of Lancaster's conservative leaders and the growing power of the county's increasingly politicized militia.

In Lancaster, the war with Britain destabilized customary social relations by enhancing the influence of armed militants inclined to revolution. Initially, the local resistance was led by more established figures who wished to secure American rights within the empire and reconcile with the mother country. By early 1776, however, founding committee members like Edward Shippen and the influential Quaker tradesman James Webb, who deplored the resistance movement's growing radicalism and the looming prospect of independence, withdrew from public life or declined in public favor. Taking their place were such newly elected committeemen as the Scot John Henry and the German John Hubley, both zealous Whigs and junior officers in the county militia. The pair came to office with less administrative experience than their more seasoned predecessors, but they supported both Congress and the mounting calls for independence. Lancaster's new representatives, moreover, now served under the vigilant eyes of the county's increasingly partisan associators.[53]

As chairman of the borough's first Committee of Correspondence, the elderly Shippen had brought a long and distinguished record of public service to the Whig resistance. A vocal critic of the new imperial legislation, he was elected to the county's Committee of Observation in December 1774. But while endorsing America's resort to arms, Shippen longed for a quick peace, dreading a permanent rupture with Great Britain. Like many of Pennsylvania's other long-serving officials, he had obtained wealth and position under British rule. Deeply attached to the empire, he worried that independence and a protracted war would unleash years of social and economic turmoil. A month after Lexington and Concord, Shippen prayed that "not another drop of blood may be spilt," for "both England and America may expect nothing but desolation and Ruin," he forecast, "unless our dispute be speedily ended." Losing favor with the county's radicals during the dispute with non-associators, he resigned from the committee in June 1775, never reclaiming his former influence. A year later, a mournful Shippen despaired as "great numbers of sensible good men as well as others" embraced "that pernicious theme of Independence." On June 8, 1776, as Shippen watched powerlessly from the political sidelines, "a great Majority" of the county's committee formally endorsed the convention to form a new provincial government. Members of the county militia, in turn, applauded the decision of their "patriotic Committee." When the committee nominated representatives for the county's nine-member convention delegation, Shippen informed relatives that he was not "sent for," adding, "Nor do I now expect it." Instead, among the delegates selected in Shippen's absence was the militant Scots Irish Whig Alexander Lowrey. A prosperous landholder, fur trader, and longtime resident of neighboring Donegal Township, Lowrey proudly served as a colonel in the county militia. His inclusion in the delegation reflected the county's radical turn.[54]

By mid-1776, Lancaster's more conservative-leaning officials found themselves effectively muzzled by the county's radical insurgents. Shorn of their former influence, they could do little to avert revolution. Jasper Yeates, now a moderate committeeman and family relation of the Shippens, shared his relative's aversion to independence. "Our present glorious Struggle is for the Preservation of our Privileges, not for an Independence," insisted Yeates in August 1775. "It will become a horrid War, indeed," he prophesied, "if an Independence is aimed at." Ten months later, a Philadelphia correspondent informed Yeates that the news from Lancaster had given him "a full Insight into the politics of your County" and shown him "the hard necessity you were under disguising your Sentiments." With the partisan push for independence now gaining momentum, he rued that "every moderate thinking Man must remain silent and inactive."[55]

Political developments in Lancaster followed trends to the east. Shippen and Yeates shared the misgivings of a larger community of moderates and conservatives progressively marginalized during Pennsylvania's contentious debates over independence. Eager to preserve their political influence and avoid a permanent rupture with Britain, these cautious figures faced growing and often bitter competition from radical outsiders long excluded from the halls of power. In Philadelphia, shopkeepers, master craftsmen, journeymen, and apprentices of diverse ethnic and religious backgrounds joined the province's newly organized militia companies or extralegal committees, bearing arms and casting ballots for the cause. By early 1776, Philadelphia's artisans had assumed an increasingly influential role in the provincial resistance, eventually supplementing their calls for independence with new appeals for radical internal reform.

With demands for greater political and economic equality now harnessed to the drive for independence, radical inroads soon came at the expense of the province's reconciliationist assembly and conservative merchant elite. Outmaneuvered by their partisan rivals in the provincial committee system and the Continental Congress, their hopes of reconciliation dashed by Britain's grim determination to subdue the rebellion by force, many of Pennsylvania's former leaders soon stood on the political margins, unable to prevent the march to independence or the adoption of a revolutionary state government. During the early summer of 1776, Philadelphia's extralegal committees effectively displaced the provincial assembly by organizing a constitutional convention. Dominated by radicals, Pennsylvania's summer convention fashioned the most democratic government in the newly independent United States. Among their chief innovations, the provincial framers introduced a unicameral legislature and eliminated the property requirements for voting and officeholding. In late July, Shippen drew cold consolation from his younger brother's renunciation of Pennsylvania's old order and ringing endorsement of independence. A fiery Philadelphia Whig, Dr. William Shippen reassured his sibling, "We now have in our power what never happened to any People before in the world . . . an opportunity of forming a plan

FIGURE 1. The Sussel-Washington artist's depiction of the initial confrontation between British and American troops, Lancaster County, Pennsylvania, circa 1776. The unknown German itinerant's painting captures both the intimacy and the threatened violence of the encounter. Courtesy, Winterthur Museum, cutwork picture, Sussel-Washington Artist, Lancaster County, Pennsylvania, 1775–1780. Paper (laid), watercolor, ink. Museum purchase with funds provided by Nicholas and Jo Helen Wilson, Thomas K. Johnson II, Bridget and Al Ritter, and the Henry Francis du Pont Collectors Circle, 2013.0031.102A.

of Government, upon the most just, rational, and equal principles," adding, "I dont wonder to see more of our friends offended and full of resentment upon the change, who have heretofore been at ye head of affairs," only "now to be ousted, or at least brought down to a level with their fellow-citizens."[56]

Three weeks earlier, on July 8, 1776, some sixty miles west of the events unfolding in the capital, Lancaster's militants had celebrated their newly declared independence. Shopkeepers shut down at noon and residents flocked to the borough's central square, where the sheriff read Congress's formal declaration before the assembled crowd. After defiantly stripping the king's coat of arms from their courthouse, frenzied associators flung the relic onto a bonfire. Only days before, in hopeful anticipation of the news from Philadelphia, the county's troops had pledged to march to the "assistance of all or any of the FREE AND INDEPENDENT STATES OF AMERICA." Most of the committeemen forced from office the previous summer had by now returned to revolutionary service. They resumed their duties, however, chastened by their militant neighbors who for the time being dictated Lancaster's engagement with the rebellion. Indeed, Lancaster's associators had found a new and powerful voice since the summer of 1775, as their war against Britain intensified and they policed new enemies at home.[57]

Foes of Freedom

By late 1775, with military operations still largely confined to the North, the war had yet to seriously threaten Pennsylvania. During December 1775, however, the war came to Lancaster in unexpected fashion. Three months earlier, the rebel forces had launched their Canadian campaign, a two-pronged preemptive strike designed to forestall a British invasion from the north. During late fall, Continental troops under the command of Brigadier General Richard Montgomery captured the British garrisons manning Forts Chambly and St. Johns, located on the west bank of the Richelieu River just southeast of Montreal. Claiming few American lives and netting nearly seven hundred prisoners, the victories raised Whigs' spirits, adding to their surprising early successes against the imperial forces charged with subduing the rebellion. After taking possession of St. Johns, a Continental officer celebrated this "most fortunate event," which, he boldly predicted, "will be a most fatal stab to the hellish machinations of the foes of freedom."[58]

Yet the surrender of the British garrisons posed a serious problem for the new Continental Congress. Having just commenced hostilities with Britain, the Whigs lacked both a coherent prisoner policy and the necessary institutions to hold hundreds of enemy captives. In the years ahead,

Continental officials would devise a formal administrative apparatus to manage their prisoners, consisting of a commissary general at the national level and deputy commissaries at the state level, all theoretically under the authority of Congress. In late 1775, however, the prisoners remained under the informal control of particular colonies, Congress, and General Washington. Eighteenth-century European military conventions provided Continental officials with several precedents for managing their new captives. Belligerents customarily bore the expense of maintaining their own soldiers in captivity. To reclaim their troops, nations negotiated formal cartels, exchanging rank for rank, with officers receiving priority over the enlisted men. Captured officers were paroled on their honor as gentlemen, a distinction that afforded them more freedom than their men, who were often confined pending their exchange. To reduce the costs and burdens of a long confinement, the combatants occasionally permitted their rank-and-file prisoners to hire out their labor locally until they were exchanged. These conventions had informed the treatment of European captives as recently as the Seven Years' War.[59]

North America's latest conflict was no ordinary war, however, but a colonial revolt against imperial authority. Complicating matters for Continental officials, their prisoners were fellow Britons seized in an unlawful rebellion. British officials refused to bow to conventions in a war against domestic rebels, fearing that any recognition of the Americans' belligerent status might legitimize the insurgency. The Americans also briefly enjoyed a favorable balance of prisoners following their initial success in Canada and felt little urgency to press for a general exchange, particularly with their new captives providing potential leverage in future deliberations. After carefully weighing their options, Continental officials elected to detain their captives pending negotiations with the British. Officials hoped their new prisoners would ensure both the recognition of Continentals' status as formal combatants and the good treatment and safe return of Americans held by the British.[60]

To ensure the prisoners' safekeeping, Congress dispatched them to York, Carlisle, Reading, and Lancaster, Pennsylvania, all inland towns well removed from potentially threatening military operations along the coast. Long connected within a broader commercial and administrative apparatus linking the province's county seats, Pennsylvania's newly designated host towns soon joined related detention sites farther south in an expanding Continental network slicing across the vast American interior. In the years ahead, the revolutionaries would disperse upwards of thirteen thousand prisoners—both British regulars and their so-called Hessian auxiliaries—in over a dozen hinterland communities in Virginia, Maryland, and Pennsylvania. The captives fell under the immediate jurisdiction of local officials in makeshift detention camps loosely supervised by state and national authorities. Boasting some three thousand inhabitants through the War for Independence, Lancaster soon became the Continentals' chief detention center for enemy prisoners. Nestled in Pennsylvania's bountiful agricultural hinterland and equipped with a large barracks constructed during the Seven Years' War, Lancaster offered especially fitting accommodations. The town's Whig inhabitants had already demonstrated their enthusiasm for the cause by mobilizing both men and matériel, and congressional officials now trusted them faithfully to execute Continental policy.[61]

But for Lancaster's insurgents, the new prisoners constituted an unwelcome addition to an already anxious and divided community. In late 1775, amid the growing frictions with Britain and the mounting vicissitudes of war, locals retained vivid memories of the brutal frontier violence of the 1750s and 1760s, when vicious encounters between natives and settlers had scarred the Pennsylvania backcountry. Years after the bloodshed, residents continued to dread the "horrors of an Indian War," and local security remained a primary concern. The region's Indians maintained a precarious neutrality in the escalating conflict with Britain, but the uncertainties surrounding their future commitments placed Lancaster at the crossroads of a potentially explosive frontier. The captives also added a volatile ingredient to the community's simmering wartime divisions and dizzying cultural diversity. As both imperial kinsmen and enemy combatants, the British prisoners threatened to exacerbate local tensions. In the years ahead, Lancaster's assorted captives simultaneously magnified local divisions while solidifying the ranks of militant insurgents who were slowly and painstakingly learning to manage their ethnic differences in war. Faced with new threats to their cause and community, Lancaster's English- and German-speaking revolutionaries gradually found their own ethnic differences of smaller significance.[62]

The escalating imperial crisis forced Lancaster's insurgents to rethink their prevailing patterns of allegiance by reevaluating their status in the community, the province, and the empire. The burgeoning American resistance heightened local political activism, expanding the county's public sphere. Demanding new levels of public cooperation, the rebellion transformed the local political culture, as members of the borough's diverse ethnocultural groups began to identify along new political and ideological lines. By mid-1776, local authorities shared the political stage with a new cast of characters, men inexperienced in administrative matters, who demanded an enhanced voice in public affairs and embraced revolution. Identifying with a broader community of resistance, local Whigs began cautiously venturing beyond the narrower constraints of ethnicity, town, and province. In the borough and on the battlefield, Lancaster's English- and German-speaking revolutionaries now cultivated ties with fellow insurgents immersed in an intercolonial and soon a national endeavor. Entering the fray as colonists and provincials, the most militant patriots increasingly identified as revolutionaries and Americans—the creators of an independent nation.

CHAPTER 3

"A Dangerous Set of People"

British Captives and the Sundering of Empire

Lancaster's first British captives arrived during early December 1775. On Saturday, December 9, 250 members of the British Seventh Regiment of Foot, Royal Fusiliers, marched into the borough under military escort, accompanied by sixty women and children. Another 130 prisoners, members of the Twenty-sixth Regiment of Foot, followed two days later. Lancaster's new Committee of Observation faced an immediate crisis when Egbert Dumond, commander of the American escort, announced that the prisoners had only two days' provisions. Dumond added that he had received no specific orders concerning the captives and could offer local officials no more guidance than to "take such measures . . . as they may think most conducive to the Publick Service."[1]

Lacking instructions from Philadelphia, Lancaster's committee had to determine how to house and provision the prisoners while ensuring their safekeeping and the security of the inhabitants. Local officials moved the British enlisted men and their families into the empty barracks, just a few blocks northeast of the courthouse and central square, but permitted the officers to rent private lodgings at their own expense. The German innkeeper and committeeman Matthias Slough volunteered to supply the captives until Congress appointed a permanent provisioning agent. Congress quickly sent word that the captives should draw their provisions from David Franks, a prominent Philadelphia-based merchant contracted to supply Pennsylvania's

British prisoners "at the expence of the crown." Having resolved the matters of lodging and subsistence, local officials soon found themselves saddled with new responsibilities.[2]

The captives stood in dire need of warm clothing after arriving without their baggage, and with the winter season threatening. Moved by the prisoners' plight and eager to please the Congress, Lancaster's officials furnished their visitors with blankets and linen "on the Public Account." The committee encountered a more serious problem in early January, when the new provisioning agent, David Franks, refused to provide food for the prisoners' wives and children. The wives implored the committee for assistance, arguing that "they must inevitably perish, unless relieved from their present distress." Local officials arranged to supply the families at the public expense until Congress issued orders for their future subsistence.[3]

As the committee's chairman, Jasper Yeates, explained to Congress, "Being mindful that humanity ought ever to distinguish the sons of America, and that cruelty should find no admission amongst a free people, we could not avoid considering the situation of their women and children as pitiable, indeed." Thus, "we were strongly inclined . . . to assist them in their distress." The captive officers thanked the committee and the town for "raising a subscription for the women and children, and, likewise, for other civilities." Congress, too, voiced its warm approval of the "civility" and "humane sentiments" displayed by the town's inhabitants. Locals' generosity mirrored Continental officials' broader concerns for their British captives.[4]

But the Whigs' magnanimity deviated sharply from Britain's treatment of American prisoners. After Lexington and Concord, the British approached their captives as treasonous rebels unworthy of the privileges of formal combatants. Disregarding conventions, they refused to distinguish between American officers and enlisted men, and subjected both to a rigorous confinement. Washington rebuked General Thomas Gage as early as August 1775 for detaining captured American officers in "a common jail appropriated for felons" without consideration for the "most respectable rank." Many British officials felt that a more fitting punishment awaited their prisoners on the scaffold. Authorities admonished the rebels captured at Quebec during December 1775 that "they deserved nothing but death; for they had taken up arms against their own country." The British ultimately consigned most of their American prisoners to a long and severe confinement in cramped and dingy jails, churches, warehouses, sugar refineries, and transport ships.[5]

Even after receiving reports of the harsh treatment meted out to American prisoners, however, Washington and Congress urged Whigs to avoid Britain's "unworthy example" by treating their captives with civility and compassion. In September 1775, Washington issued instructions for the care of British prisoners held by the Hartford, Connecticut, Committee of Correspondence: "Allow me to recommend a gentleness, even to forbearance, with persons so entirely in our power. We know not what the chance of war may be; but . . . the duties of humanity and kindness will demand from us such a treatment as we should expect from others, the case being reversed."[6]

Influencing early Continental policy were the informal conventions governing the humane treatment of European prisoners of war. Washington and leading Continental officials recognized that American prisoner policy needed to remain above reproach. The neglect or abuse of British prisoners could discredit the American resistance and alienate potential supporters. By contrast, a policy of humane treatment could enable Whigs to seize the moral high ground by bolstering their image as injured innocents, particularly in light of Britain's continuing neglect of American captives. Indeed, pursuing a humanitarian policy could legitimize, even sanctify, the American rebellion, while potentially alleviating the distress of rebel prisoners.

Along with such practical considerations, early Continental policy sprang from a persistent cultural affinity toward Great Britain. In late 1775, when envisioning their British adversaries, many Continental officials still felt the faint tug of kinship born of a sense of common identity. After nearly a year of hostilities, the colonies had yet to declare their independence, and reconciliation with the mother country remained the hope of many Americans. Mindful of their shared British heritage and their enduring cultural affiliation with their overseas brethren, authorities on both sides continued to situate their opponents within a collective imperial identity. This feeling of common kinship informed Continental officials' approach to their British captives.[7]

Major General Philip Schuyler, the commander of the Americans' Canadian expedition, articulated this sense of shared identity rooted in a common past in his instructions to the prisoners' military escort. "You will be particularly attentive," he directed, "that no person, who may have forgotten the rights of mankind, and the principles of Englishmen, offer the least insult to any of the gentlemen, their soldiers, their wives, or children." Similarly, in August 1775, Washington assured General Gage that despite the many abuses American prisoners suffered under the British, the colonists treated their captives "with a tenderness due to fellow-citizens and brethren." John Hancock observed of Lancaster's prisoners in January 1776, "As men, they have a claim to all the rights of humanity," and "as countrymen, though enemies," he added, "they claim something more."[8]

Even the British found occasion to praise American policy. A British officer captured at Fort Chambly reported shortly after surrendering that he and his fellow prisoners had "been treated with the greatest civility and politeness." Everywhere he went, his hosts faithfully adhered to the "benevolent principles on which they wish this unnatural contest may be conducted." Impressed by the Whigs' charitableness, he concluded it was "the sincere sentiment of the generality of the Americans, that a happy and honourable accommodation between Great Britain and her colonies may speedily take place." Although the officer misjudged his hosts' commitment to a hasty reconciliation, he astutely grasped the persistent ties of affection binding many Britons and Americans.[9]

Some of Lancaster's leading moderates, hopeful of eventually reconciling with the mother country, continued to envision the British as reluctant antagonists loath to wage a fratricidal war against their American cousins. Weeks after Lexington and Concord, the elderly Edward Shippen sharply distinguished between the British and American troops while acknowledging their common bond. Pondering the distinct motives that brought combatants to the field, Shippen concluded, "The Americans fight for every thing that are most dear to them–their lives Liberty and fortunes; whereas the Regulars, poor fellows, fight for six pence a day, and with reluctancy against their own brethren." In early spring 1776, the wealthy German shopkeeper Eberhart Michael, secretary of Lancaster's committee, informed Lieutenant John André, one of the British officers captured at Fort St. Johns, of his sincere hope that "peace will again reign and inhabitants and soldiers will again enjoy brotherly association. These colonies and Great Britain—a people mighty and famous in the world." Even after a year of armed conflict, such sentiments continued to shape American prisoner policy.[10]

By mid-1776, however, Pennsylvania's diversity, the escalating hostilities, and the mounting antagonisms between local insurgents and their British captives combined to complicate and frustrate Continental policy. In Lancaster, English and German speakers' tense face-to-face, day-to-day encounters with their captives facilitated the break with Britain and nurtured an emerging revolutionary identity. For locals, the prisoners magnified dangers both real and imagined. Lancaster's peculiar vulnerability raised the stakes for local militants and fueled their growing enmity for the British. The continuing infusion of prisoners reaffirmed residents' status as revolutionaries embroiled in an irreconcilable conflict with their imperial antagonists. As Lancaster's prisoners grew in number and became more difficult to control, pressures radiated outward into the diverse Pennsylvania hinterland. Local pressures helped to redefine Continental perceptions of the British and transform American prisoner policy.

As historians have shown, the Revolutionary War rendered the combatants' identities ambiguous and contested. At the onset of hostilities, the British and their colonial adversaries faced each other ambivalently across ill-defined lines. Captivity initially muddled but later clarified identities by widening the breach between the combatants and heightening their sense of difference. In Lancaster, captors and captives met as mutually diverse communities bound by cords of empire. The prisoners, for example, formed a motley assortment of officers and enlisted men, raw recruits and disciplined veterans, English, Irish, Welsh, and Scots. Collectively they contributed to the bewildering blend of languages and dialects resounding through the Pennsylvania interior. Hardening battle lines overrode divisions within the warring camps by underscoring their shared military and political commitments. For most British prisoners, their captivity reinforced perceptions of their enemies as renegades threatening the stability and sanctity of empire. For their American hosts, it exposed the British as devoted agents of tyranny sent to trample cherished rights and liberties. The escalating military crisis fractured and reconfigured prevailing identities and allegiances, slowly transforming the combatants' views of themselves and of their enemies.[11]

In Lancaster, the British prisoners promptly inflamed emerging wartime divisions while consolidating the ranks of hard-line insurgents. Through 1776, locals came to know their prisoners intimately as hard-boiled combatants devoid of sympathy for their erstwhile kindred. Embittered by the enemy's disdain for their cause, militants developed a corresponding revulsion for the imperial fold. As the captives defied their hosts and cultivated subversive associations, militants policed the community, sorting friend from foe. The new dangers rallied Lancaster's English- and German-speaking insurgents, encouraging them to transcend their cultural differences as they distinguished themselves from their British enemies and identified with a broader revolutionary community. But the prisoners also exposed the limits of residents' patriotism by revealing competing communal and Continental agendas.[12]

Prisoners to the Rebels

With no well-defined policy or established apparatus with which to administer their prisoners, Americans had to improvise, and Lancaster soon became a veritable laboratory for the revolutionaries' evolving prisoner policy. When the first British captives arrived in Lancaster, the local committee asked Congress whether their prisoners should "be kept constantly confined to the Barracks under a Guard." Local officials hoped to preserve the "peace of the Borough" and to ensure residents' security by fencing in the barracks and restricting the prisoners' movement. Congress instead preferred a policy of enlargement that would enable the British captives to mix freely with their local hosts. As the Lancaster committeeman and recent congressional representative George Ross indicated, by encouraging fluid interactions between the town's inhabitants and prisoners, Congress hoped to cultivate kindred relations and elicit the captives' sympathy for Americans and their cause. To render the British enlisted prisoners more amenable to Whig influence, Congress ordered their officers relocated to neighboring towns. Congress also insisted the officers sign paroles that prohibited them from traveling more than six miles from their residence and from engaging in any correspondence concerning the dispute between Great Britain and the colonies.[13]

Initially, the Whigs' lax management yielded some encouraging, even surprising, results. Shortly after arriving in Lancaster, the British rank and file demonstrated their malleability by making "frequent applications" to enlist with American recruiting parties. Washington and the Congress opposed the prisoners' enlistment, fearing that it would legitimate Britain's practice of coercing American captives into the British service. Yet during early 1776, the prisoners' eagerness to enlist offered Whig officials deceptive evidence that an indulgent prisoner policy could win British converts to their cause. Events, however, soon indicated that the vast majority of the British prisoners felt neither sympathy nor affection for their rebelling hosts.[14]

Continental policy posed immediate problems, as the proximity between captors and captives bred not mutual understanding but antipathy and mistrust. Nine months of hostilities had frayed whatever bonds remained between the combatants. Indeed, if most Americans continued to see themselves as equal British subjects, invested with the same rights and privileges as their imperial cousins, their enemies disagreed. As the British demonstrated their determination to humble the colonies and to suppress the rebellion by force of arms, growing numbers of Americans began earnestly contemplating independence. Thus, whatever the expectations of Continental officials, in their daily encounters in American host communities, captors and captives eyed each other with suspicion.

Most British regulars bitterly resented the indignities of captivity under colonial insurgents. Paroled officers routinely derided Whigs as "rascals" and "vagabonds," whose unnatural rebellion, railed one lieutenant, "branded the name of America with an odium, that no time can obliterate, no merit expunge." After he and his men surrendered during the summer of 1776,

Captain Alexander Campbell lamented, "I cannot well express how my Soul is affected at the disagreeable manner by which my Friends and other trusty Associates have fallen into the hands of a rebellious and tumultuous enemy." From London, British officials vented similar frustrations. In February 1776, Lord George Germain, the British Secretary of State for America, bemoaned the plight of "his Majesty's officers and loyal subjects" now "in the disgraceful situation of being prisoners to the Rebels."[15]

Many locals approached their British guests with similar disdain. Lancaster's older residents recalled their troubles with the British troops who had garrisoned the community years earlier, when the Seven Years' War left Pennsylvania's backcountry vulnerable to the French and their Indian allies. Though locals had initially welcomed their defenders, the pressures of quartering soldiers in private homes soon brought mounting protests from disgruntled inhabitants, while the royal forces who lingered during the 1760s stirred latent fears of standing armies. Worse troubles loomed a decade later, when the king's troops returned not as custodians of the frontier but as captives in an increasingly bitter colonial rebellion, with the very barracks that had housed imperial forces during the 1760s now serving as quarters for hundreds of restlessly defiant British prisoners. Roving the streets in their scarlet regimentals, the regulars offered locals a grim daily reminder of their escalating difficulties with the mother country and their corresponding insecurity at home.[16]

Indeed, by 1776, the county's troops had already traded blows with the British. In December 1775, local riflemen had participated in the disastrous assault on Quebec, numbering among the more than four hundred Americans killed or captured during the engagement. Several dozen of the county's riflemen still languished in captivity with the approach of spring. Nursing bitter grievances sharpened on the battlefield, local volunteers returned home only to find their enemies haunting their neighborhoods. British officers reaped the particular scorn of local militiamen, who despised their enemies' privileged status and haughty demeanor. One paroled officer testified that he and his colleagues "were not only insulted but threat'ned," while another reportedly felt "in Danger of his Life."[17]

Continental policy faced particular challenges in the diverse Pennsylvania hinterland, where Germans intermingled with their English and Scots Irish neighbors, multiplying and complicating identities. Immigrants from northern Ireland and southwestern Germany had accounted for most of Lancaster County's growth since the 1730s. Although members of Lancaster's English minority might identify their British guests as cultural kinsmen, the Germans and Scots Irish were more inclined to see them as menacing intruders. Many of the county's German clans had traded the chronic warfare and cumbersome military obligations of central Europe for the promised peace and prosperity of Pennsylvania. Legions of Scots Irish emigrants, meanwhile, had borne their long-standing grievances against the English to the Pennsylvania backcountry. In the wake of Lexington and Concord, they supplied many of the county's most zealous recruits. Lancaster's Presbyterian minister John Woodhull, for instance, helped recruit militia and volunteered as a field chaplain.[18]

In June 1775, a full six months before the first prisoners arrived in Pennsylvania, Woodhull's fellow parson, the visiting Presbyterian minister John Carmichael, vilified British regulars, registering the rebels' disdain for standing armies in a sermon before Lancaster's Whigs. "As standing armies are too frequently made up of the scowerings of gaols, and the refuse and filth of the people," declaimed the reverend, "they are but too often found destitute of either good principles or education, and sunk into every species of dissoluteness and debauchery." Thus the "very name of a *Red-Coat*," he concluded, "*stinks in our nostrils*." After relocating with several of his fellow officers to Carlisle, across the Susquehanna in neighboring Cumberland County, Lieutenant André derided the town's inhabitants as "a stubborn, illiberal crew call'd the Scotchirish." Most regulars felt even more repulsed by Pennsylvania's German speakers, with whom they found nothing in common.[19]

In Lancaster, trouble followed within a few weeks of the prisoners' arrival when the British officers balked at Congress's order to separate them from their men. The officers complained that the order violated the terms of their capitulation and that the absence of their baggage, combined with their poor health during the severe winter season, required them to remain in Lancaster. The officers insisted that they had signed their paroles believing that Congress would honor the terms of their surrender and permit them to remain with their troops. They then issued a thinly veiled threat, hinting that they would regret having to break their paroles.[20]

Congress agreed to postpone the officers' relocation but denied their claim that separating them from their men constituted a breach of the capitulation agreement. As the president of Congress, John Hancock, explained, while "all the stipulations of a capitulation ought, undoubtedly, to be held sacred, and faithfully fulfilled . . . no such stipulation is to be found in the capitulation upon which those gentlemen surrendered." Then Hancock issued a warning of his own, promising that Congress would "be extremely sorry to be reduced to the necessity of confining them in prison, if they cancel their parole." The officers' obstinacy fed local anxiety. In late January, committee chairman Jasper Yeates informed a friend, "We fear something disagreeable will happen before those gentlemen leave their privates."[21]

Most troubling to local authorities, however, were the hundreds of rank-and-file prisoners, whose wanderings bred tensions with the town's leery inhabitants. The visibly stratified community already contained a conspicuous number of laboring poor, and many anxious residents now dreaded mingling with the volatile dregs of a conventional standing army. Lancaster's committee promptly established formal regulations to govern the prisoners' conduct along with a night watch consisting of a dozen associators to guard the public magazine, patrol the streets, and preserve the peace. A half measure, the night watch proved unequal to the task of curbing disorder. One resident grumbled on January 10 that the "many soldiers here, more than four hundred, create disturbances." Tensions escalated during early February, following the arrival of several dozen fresh enlisted prisoners from New Jersey. On February 10, Lancaster's committee received complaints of captives roaming the town and antagonizing the residents. The prisoner John Wilson, for instance, ran afoul of local authorities for voicing inflammatory sentiments, which led to his confinement in the town jail.[22]

Lancaster's prisoners had become so unmanageable by late February that Pennsylvania's Council of Safety petitioned Congress for their relocation. The situation in Lancaster had become increasingly precarious, warned the council, with the captives growing more insolent by the day. According to the council's chairman, John Nixon: "The kind treatment given them meets with very improper and indecent return. . . . They often express themselves in most disrespectful and offensive terms, and openly threaten revenge whenever opportunity shall present." Current conditions also furnished opportunities for escape. As Nixon warned, with Lancaster "but a day's march from navigable water, and their prisoners stout and numerous, there may be a danger that should the enemy effect a landing on the upper part of Chesapeake-Bay, a daring spirit might lead them off." The council therefore recommended dispersing the captives throughout the Pennsylvania interior, "in different towns, or . . . among the farmers in the country, where their opportunities of doing mischief will less correspond with their inclinations."[23]

Congress preferred to consolidate the enlisted prisoners in Lancaster, but ordered their officers immediately relocated to York and Carlisle, across the Susquehanna River, "for the greater safety of the publick." Congress authorized local authorities to closely confine officers who refused to comply. On March 22, the officers, accompanied by their servants and a small military escort, bade farewell to their men and set off for York and Carlisle. While Lancaster's insurgents welcomed the officers' departure, their enlisted prisoners remained a source of continuing anxiety. Borough officials notified Pennsylvania's Council of Safety on March 29 of their "utmost Concern" at the small "Number of good Arms in the Hands" of local associators. "The fatal Consequences which may arrive from the Want of arms amongst us are too obvious to be insisted on," warned Jasper Yeates, "particularly in this Town, where we have about four hundred Prisoners, and most of them of active, restless and uneasy Spirits."[24]

County officials faced new pressures in mid-April following the arrival of nearly a half-dozen paroled British officers to the small town of Lebanon, more than twenty miles north of Lancaster. British officers found captivity especially onerous, chafing under the resentments and restrictions of their grudging hosts. Ever solicitous of their honor and the customary privileges of their rank and status, they registered a gentleman's contempt for the provincial upstarts who flouted imperial authority and abused their newfound influence. From York, parolees protested the "ill treatment which our characters as British officers . . . has not merited." The officers complained, "outrage hath succeeded insult," with "a violation of every law of humanity" crudely "dignified by the name of authority." Lieutenant André, in turn, damned Carlisle's "greasy committee of worsted stocking knaves," who took pains to "humiliate us and exalt themselves."[25]

Lebanon's newly arrived parolees, frustrated by their poor accommodations, promptly petitioned provincial officials for relocation. Obtaining no redress despite several appeals, the officers took matters into their own hands. On the night of June 15, Lancaster's committee received alarming news that the officers had escaped. Lebanon authorities reported that the fugitives had left town the day before to go fishing but never returned to their lodgings. The county committee quickly dispatched riders to "alarm the Country" and to warn officials in York and Carlisle to take immediate precautions lest their prisoners attempt a similar escape. "It cannot but be obvious that the public is intimately interested to prevent practices of this nature," exhorted committee chairman Adam Reigart, "as well as to apprehend the Prisoners who have meditated their escape." But dismayed authorities failed to recapture the fugitives, who fled north through Northumberland County, later arriving in British-held New York City.[26]

The officers' escape confirmed locals' suspicions that their prisoners required closer supervision. Officials were especially vexed that the fugitives had violated their sworn parole. Though the officers had been openly critical of the American resistance, county officials trusted them to behave like gentlemen. Instead, the officers rejected the Whigs' authority as illegitimate and underlined their contempt by breaking their parole. Most distressing, however, was how they had managed their escape. Evidence indicated that the fugitives had shed their regimentals and donned American dress, assuming the guise of "Virginia gentlemen" to avoid suspicion and elude their captors. This particular detail alarmed residents of Lancaster, some of whose enlisted prisoners had recently taken to dressing like American riflemen.[27]

Months before, the sight of British prisoners in American dress might have seemed an encouraging sign to local insurgents eager to win British converts to their cause. Now, however, with the war intensifying and relations between the belligerents growing increasingly strained, anxious militants worried that the prisoners' novel choice of apparel revealed less an affinity for their hosts than a cleverly disguised but sinister intent. During late spring 1776, the lines separating Britons and Americans remained ambiguous and ill-defined. Cultural and linguistic ties blurred the divisions between friend and foe, creating a permeable boundary between the combatants. Consequently, though the riflemen's garb vividly distinguished the Americans from their enemies, it readily obscured distinctions when appropriated by the British. The British captives shared enough in common with their English-speaking hosts that they could conceal their Britishness beneath a veneer of American dress. Most British enlisted prisoners, lacking the polish of their officers, could scarcely pass as Virginia gentlemen. Cloaked in the homespun attire of the riflemen, however, they might easily pose as backcountry associators. If so inclined, they could exploit this fluidity for subversive ends, assuming a friendly guise to mask hostile aims.[28]

Celebrated by members of the resistance but notoriously short of discipline, the riflemen provided the perfect cover for British fugitives clandestinely negotiating American lines. Specially recruited from the Pennsylvania, Maryland, and Virginia backcountry for their deadly accuracy with a rifle, they formed an elite corps in the Continental ranks. For many of their compatriots, they embodied the American cause. In their distinctive hunting shirts and leggings, the riflemen breezed through American checkpoints. Pennsylvania's poorly supplied British prisoners mainly donned frontier dress to replace their badly worn uniforms. But Lancaster's insurgents feared that the rifleman's garb provided their captives a virtual "passport," enabling them to move about the country undetected, with the presumable design of thwarting American interests.[29]

The sharpening hostilities and Pennsylvanians' conflicting allegiances afforded the captives fertile ground for subversion. By spring 1776, the deepening crisis had eroded Whigs' hopes for an early end to the conflict. Parliament's Prohibitory Act of December 1775 sealed the colonies' ports and declared open war on American shipping. Ominous overseas intelligence warned that the British had launched a massive military mobilization to crush the rebellion, even commencing negotiations with German princes to enlist the aid of thousands of foreign auxiliaries. Throughout the back-country, rumors hinted that British agents were busy recruiting Indian allies. As early as 1774, a worried Edward Shippen had speculated that the region's vengeful Indians would gladly "put us out of our pain with their toma-hawks." Now, the increasingly disillusioned Shippen fumed that while Lord North lulled the "ignorant people of Great Britain to sleep," the "MON-STEROUS MURDERER is ordering our throats to be cut." Thomas Paine's *Common Sense* and King George III's spurning of the conciliatory Olive Branch Petition, meanwhile, further undercut the provincial proponents of reconciliation.[30]

Staunch Pennsylvania Whigs now realized that they faced the likelihood of a long and bitter struggle. In mid-May 1776, Shippen exchanged corre-spondence with the Reading committeeman James Read, who sternly ruled out any possibility of a peaceful return to the imperial fold. "There is too much Hatred and Bitterness towards us in the Court of Britain," he con-cluded, "to leave us any Hopes of Reconciliation. The Devil is in them and with them wherever they or their murderous Agents go." But Read remained assured of the Whigs' eventual triumph. "Murders, indeed, we shall hear of in great number. But they will rouse us out of our Supineness," he predicted, "and we shall unite and disperse our Enemies."[31]

Read's optimistic forecast of a unified resistance discounted the deep divi-sions polarizing Pennsylvanians. British resolve fueled the radical advocates of independence. The push for independence, in turn, fractured the fragile provincial resistance, as despairing conservatives abandoned the cause to join the ranks of the disaffected. With divisions multiplying daily, Pennsylvania's militants struggled to curb dissent. Insurgents in Lancaster and neighbor-ing host communities faced not only these mounting pressures but also the machinations of their British prisoners, who threatened to exacerbate the province's growing internal fissures. Soon, embattled Whigs suspected their prisoners of actively conspiring against American arms.[32]

Dangerous to the Commonwealth

If congressional officials had hoped to seduce their captives, their enemies promptly turned the tables by tempting the wavering and rallying support for the crown. Persistent rumors warned of captives gathering intelligence, fomenting dissent, and inciting violence. As early as December 1775, Con-gress had received complaints of paroled officers "endeavouring to debauch the minds of the people." In April 1776, Cumberland County's committee accused Lancaster's prisoners of carrying illicit correspondence between local loyalists and the British officers in Carlisle. Committee chairman John Mont-gomery later cautioned Congress that the paroled officers had corrupted "many weak and ignorant persons." Their servants, moreover, were "dressed with hunting-shirts and trousers, the uniform of our people," warned Mont-gomery, "which might facilitate their escape." By summer, locals feared that their captives harbored deadly intentions. The Paxton resident John Harris, for example, who had borne gruesome witness to the murderous frontier violence of previous decades, now reckoned that the fleeing officers from Lebanon were eagerly inciting the Indians to "take up the Hatchet agt us." Potential saboteurs, the prisoners inflamed local suspicions and insecurities.[33]

As stray prisoners prowled the interior, locals labored to curtail subversive activity within their neighborhoods. Lancaster's enlisted prisoners soon re-quired passes for travel outside the borough, and county committees began inspecting the paroled officers' correspondence. In York and Carlisle, the officers fell under an evening curfew, with a handful eventually winding up in the Cumberland County jail. Tempers flared during early summer, when militants accused local loyalists of assisting the officers' escape from Lebanon. Days before the escape, Lancaster's committee had detained the suspected loyalist Thomas Tomlins Prichard for mingling with the rank-and-file pris-oners in the barracks. Even friends of the resistance in Pennsylvania's newly designated host communities risked censure for their casual associations with the enemy. American Major Edward Burd, for instance, antagonized Read-ing's militants by dining with paroled officers and refusing to impose a cur-few. "I feared that the people . . . were possessed of the idea of my being that monster a tory," Burd reported.[34]

The mounting complaints from provincial officials and the widening rift with the British soon prompted Continental authorities to rethink their policies and introduce a more rigorous system of controls. In late Febru-ary, Congress empowered local committees to superintend their prisoners' "conduct, and, in cases of gross misbehaviour, to confine them." A month later, Congress gave provincial officials discretion to relocate their captives "from place to place" within their particular provinces as often as "shall seem proper." With this new authority, however, came new responsibilities. Provincial officials now had to furnish Congress with general returns of their captives. Congress also recirculated all the previously enacted resolves concerning the prisoners to ensure their uniform management.[35]

Not until summer, however, after persistent pressure from provincial au-thorities and British officials' continuing neglect of American prisoners, would Congress finally embrace a policy of confinement in Lancaster. The town's exasperated officials renewed their pleas for stricter controls following the officers' escape from Lebanon. Adding to locals' sense of urgency was an order from Philadelphia summoning the town's militia for service in New Jersey. Residents feared that the militia's absence would place them at the mercy of their vengeful prisoners. Lancaster's committee complained to Congress on July 7, emphasizing the shortcomings of Continental policy and the need for enhanced security. Committee chairman George Ross stressed the "dangerous situation of the town," which stood "exposed to the fury and ravages of near four hundred" prisoners who roamed at will because of the "open state of our barracks."[36]

Ross reminded Congress that it had refused the committee's earlier request to enclose the barracks and post a guard over the captives, assuming that by their "mixing and working with the inhabitants, they would learn and be convinced of the justness of our cause, and become rather the friends than enemies of the rights of America." Instead, "by their mixing with the people they have done much mischief," as they "adhere, with an extraordinary degree of firmness, to their tyrannical master and his cause, and every action and expression convinces us that they would seize every opportunity to promote it and distress us." The committee therefore recommended having the prisoners "in some manner secured, so as to prevent their straggling, carrying intelligence, or insulting or injuring the inhabitants." For "while at liberty, they are a dangerous set of people."[37]

Much to the locals' relief, on July 10, Congress ordered Lancaster's committee to confine and guard the captives and to enclose their barracks with a stockade. The committee quickly rounded up the prisoners under its jurisdiction, issuing a circular to neighboring towns to assemble and forward all their British captives under armed guard for confinement in Lancaster's barracks. Meanwhile, officials raised a town guard of 150 men and began construction of the stockade. "They say it is to be boarded fifty feet high," reported one relieved resident. Developments in Lancaster had far-reaching implications. The town's newly stockaded barracks became the working Continental model, literally furnishing the blueprint for corresponding wartime detention facilities throughout the states. With the new emphasis on confinement, Whig policy also became a closer approximation of British prisoner policy.[38]

But Congress's revamped security measures came with unexpected consequences for Lancaster. The residents of Reading who had quartered enlisted prisoners in their homes since early 1776 now recommended their confinement so "they may be more easily restrained from mischief." Continental officials obligingly relocated the bulk of Reading's loosely supervised prisoners to Lancaster's freshly secured barracks, placing new pressures on the borough

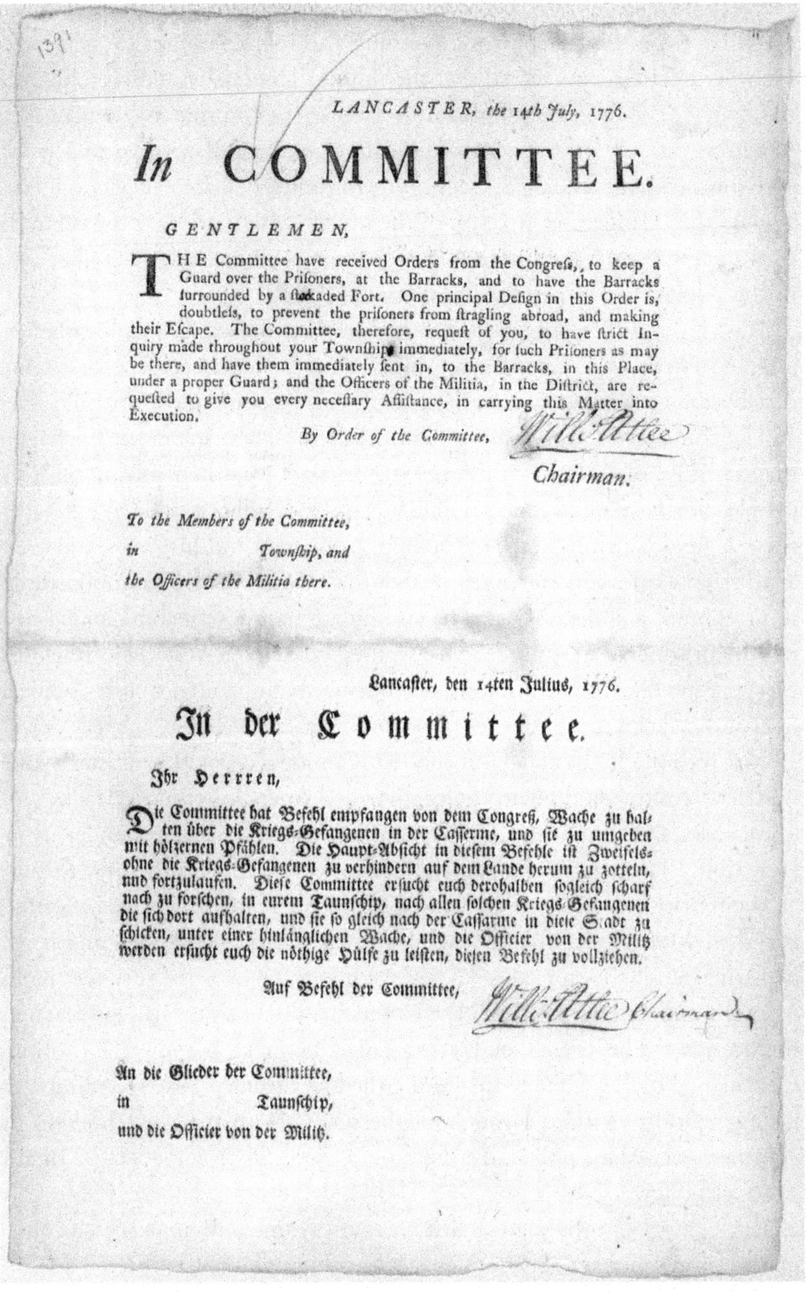

LANCASTER, the 14th July, 1776.

In COMMITTEE.

GENTLEMEN,

THE Committee have received Orders from the Congress, to keep a Guard over the Prisoners, at the Barracks, and to have the Barracks furrounded by a ftockaded Fort. One principal Defign in this Order is, doubtlefs, to prevent the prifoners from ftragling abroad, and making their Efcape. The Committee, therefore, requeft of you, to have ftrict Inquiry made throughout your Townfhip immediately, for fuch Prifoners as may be there, and have them immediately fent in, to the Barracks, in this Place, under a proper Guard; and the Officers of the Militia, in the Diftrict, are requefted to give you every neceffary Affiftance, in carrying this Matter into Execution.

By Order of the Committee, *Will. Atlee*

Chairman.

To the Members of the Committee,

in   Townfhip, and

the Officers of the Militia there.

Lancafter, ben 14ten Julius, 1776.

In der Committee.

Ihr Herren,

Die Committee hat Befehl empfangen von dem Congreß, Wache zu halten über die Kriegs-Gefangenen in der Cafferne, und fie zu umgeben mit hölzernen Pfählen. Die Haupt-Abficht in diefem Befehle ift zweifelsohne die Kriegs-Gefangenen zu verhindern auf dem Lande herum zu zotteln, und fortzulaufen. Diefe Committee erfucht euch derohalben fogleich fcharf nach zu forfchen, in eurem Taunfchip, nach allen folchen Kriegs-Gefangenen die fich dort aufhalten, und fie fo gleich nach der Caffarme in diefe Stadt zu fchicken, unter einer hinlänglichen Wache, und die Officier von der Militz werden erfucht euch die nöthige Hülfe zu leiften, diefen Befehl zu vollziehen.

Auf Befehl der Committee, *Will. Atlee* Chairman

An die Glieder der Committee,

in   Taunfchip,

und die Officier von der Militz.

FIGURE 2.   Bilingual broadside from the Lancaster County Committee, July 14, 1776, announcing Congress's order to confine the British prisoners in Lancaster's stockaded barracks. Courtesy Library of Congress, Rare Book and Special Collections Division.

and raising local anxiety. The sight of one of Reading's newly relocated captives arriving in Lancaster under armed guard, "damning the Congress all the way," only affirmed locals' misgivings. By July 18, the number of British prisoners in Lancaster had nearly doubled, with close to seven hundred occupying the barracks. Days later a resident put the total near a thousand, and local officials realized that they would have to expand the facility.[39]

Lancaster's officials reduced the pressure on their rapidly overcrowding barracks by hiring out skilled captives to local employers as wage laborers. The hiring of prisoners was a familiar wartime practice which offered authorities the dual benefit of mobilizing laborers for local needs while reducing the risks and burdens of consolidating hundreds of enemy captives. Keen to capitalize on their prisoners' labor, provincial officials had considered putting them to work as early as spring 1776. Pennsylvania's Council of Safety asked Lancaster's committee in early March to inquire whether any of their prisoners wished to come to Philadelphia to "work, upon wages, at their respective Occupations." Taking a quick inventory of the prisoners' skills, the committee compiled a list of ninety-eight craftsmen with trades ranging from mason and weaver to tailor and cordwainer.[40]

In a bustling manufacturing town full of tradesmen struggling to meet the demands of a booming wartime economy, the hiring of prisoners answered a pressing local need. With many of Lancaster County's able-bodied males committed to distant military service, and with labor increasingly scarce, the prisoners readily found employers. A small proportion of the captives, in turn, welcomed the opportunity to escape the constraints of the barracks, ply their particular trades, and supplement their meager wages. The local committee's records suggest that upwards of one hundred prisoners hired out through the summer and fall of 1776. On July 25, for example, Samuel Eaton hired out as a stocking weaver. That same month, Daniel Allen and William Sutherland of the Twenty-sixth Regiment entered the employ of the Lancaster tailor Michael Shirdle. William Frenniman hired out twice, first with the Lancaster apothecary Christian Voght and subsequently with the gunsmith Jacob Graeff. As a member of Lancaster's committee explained, because "hands were scarce," many of the tradesmen commanded handsome wages, often assisting local craftsmen who routinely juggled their own militia obligations with the demands of wartime production.[41]

Hiring out the captives not only reduced the costs of their upkeep but also promised to enhance local security. With the prisoners privately employed and earning generous wages, provincial officials hoped they would prove less inclined to flee or to endanger residents' lives and property. Lancaster's

committee held employers responsible for the safekeeping and prompt return of the prisoners, demanding bonds as security for their good behavior.
Contrary to the expectations of provincial authorities, however, hiring out
created additional problems.[42]

Freed from the confines of the barracks, laborers found occasion to roam.
Those inclined to cause trouble made the most of their opportunities, with
offenses ranging from theft and burglary to public intoxication and attempted
escape. The county's military obligations simultaneously increased both the
demands for prisoners' labor and the dangers for unarmed civilians. The
Donegal resident James Work alerted Lancaster's committee in late summer
when a prisoner employed in his neighborhood "got in Drink" and "behav'd
ill," adding, "Most of our men is gone to the army," and "the poor women
and children is afraid to see such . . . men amongst them and going at large."
With security concerns on the rise, prospective employers soon encountered
resistance from local officials. In mid-September, when the county ironmaster Peter Grubb applied for captive laborers for his Cornwall Furnace,
Congress reckoned the "Committee of Lancaster would object to it."[43]

Lancaster's newly confined prisoners compounded the pressures by harry-
ing residents or attempting to escape. During the construction of the stockade, restless captives routinely eluded their guards to stray from the barracks.
On September 11, locals discovered Sergeant Major Wood of the Seventh
Regiment "in the Stable of Henry Waggoner." Just weeks later, authorities
apprehended another prisoner four miles from the borough. Two other fugitives ventured as far as Northumberland County, some fifty miles to the
north, where they were seized by local authorities after "providing themselves with arms, and making other preparations, which appeared to indicate
some ill design." Northumberland officials promptly returned the pair to
Lancaster's committee with a warning that the schemes of such "evil-minded
persons, either to instigate the Indians to acts of hostility, or to raise dis-
sensions among the inhabitants, may be attended with the most pernicious
consequences." As their prisoners fed growing fears, determined militants
feverishly cracked down on the offenders.[44]

After the colonies declared their independence, local patriots became increasingly intolerant of slights to American honor. In late September, for
example, Lancaster's committee instructed the British sergeant majors of the
Seventh and Twenty-sixth regiments to draw up returns of their men and
account for any missing captives. When the sergeant majors had the "im-
pudence to set down in writing . . . that some of the men had inlisted with
the Rebels," the committeemen flew into a rage, branding the pair's conduct
"insulting and designed to affront them" and immediately confining them

to the town jail on a diet of bread and water. Local officials refused to see themselves and their fellow patriots disparaged as "Rebels."[45]

Between June and December, at least forty-eight prisoners landed in the county jail. On August 12, authorities jailed John Allen of the Twenty-sixth Regiment for "insulting the centereys." That same month, Lancaster's committee interrogated several prisoners caught stealing linen from the townspeople. Thomas Roparts earned a spell behind bars in late September after fleeing from the barracks. Weeks later, sentries detained two prisoners caught stealing wine from a resident's cellar. Occasionally, even the jail failed to contain the worst offenders. James Parker, one of the two fugitives recently apprehended in Northumberland County, broke out of jail with a pair of civilian prisoners on the night of October 19. Days later, the trio allegedly burglarized a home in nearby Colerain Township. Promising a £10 reward for the fugitives' apprehension, an October 30 advertisement in the *Pennsylvania Gazette* urged "all honest inhabitants" to "intercept such villains, as they are very dangerous to the Commonwealth."[46]

Even if Whigs exaggerated the dangers posed by their captives, their concerns were genuine. To be sure, many of Lancaster's prisoners refrained from misconduct, passing their captivity in dutiful compliance with local authorities. The borough's captives remained a diverse collection of ethnicities drawn into the king's service and subject to the poor pay and rigorous discipline of the British Army. Some of the prisoners who hired out felt slight affinity for the imperial enterprise and proved eager and reliable laborers. Yet with the war intensifying and many of Lancaster's men away performing military service, the offending prisoners posed a threat disproportionate to their numbers. In a community shaken by the accumulated costs and uncertainties of war, the slightest infraction suddenly carried the hint of rebellion. After months of experimentation, the hosting of enemy prisoners had become a thankless and frustrating task for Lancaster's Whigs.[47]

Shorn of any hopes of converting their British prisoners, Continental officials now shared the locals' exasperation and instituted even stiffer controls. In early October, Congress ordered the appointment of state commissaries to superintend and collect monthly returns of the prisoners. Congress also forbade the prisoners to leave their designated residences without permission from the newly created Continental Board of War. On November 15, the Board of War reminded Lancaster's committee of the need to keep their captives under close surveillance. The prisoners "are not only extremely insolent," warned the board, but also "guilty of Practices of a very dangerous tendency." Specifically, "not satisfied with procuring and conveying intelligence," they circulated "false rumours with the design of damping the spirit of the friends to this country." The board instructed the committee to closely confine "any British prisoner" suspected of "spreading false news, speaking in derogation or otherwise injuring the credit of the Continental currency or conveying any intelligence whatsoever."[48]

Disillusioned officials now approached their captives as sinister conspirators bent on subverting the revolution. In a province populated by untold numbers of Indians and loyalists, the patriots' ability to identify and neutralize their prisoners assumed special urgency. To safeguard their cause and communities, Pennsylvania's Whigs now sought carefully to contain and demarcate their British captives. On July 3, 1776, Pennsylvania's Council of Safety ordered all paroled British officers to "wear their Uniforms whenever they go abroad." Transgressors would be seized and confined. The revolutionaries' newly instituted security measures sharpened the boundaries between friend and foe. Now more than ever before, the British redcoat symbolized an enemy of the cause. Thus, if the colonial insurgency had initially blurred the combatants' identities, the contentious encounters between captors and captives sped their estrangement. For Pennsylvania's embattled Whigs, their British captives proved to be brethren no more. Spurned by their imperial kinsmen, revolutionaries had begun cultivating new identities and allegiances in fierce opposition to their British adversaries.[49]

Spirited Sons of America

Among Lancaster's militants, trouble with the prisoners had combined with the climbing costs of war to erase any lingering affection for the British. Local officials echoed the sentiments of Pennsylvania's Council of Safety in spring 1776 by damning the British as "cruel and inveterate foes." Developments on remote battlefields fed fury and frustration at home. Each battle waged and each ounce of blood shed drove another wedge between Whigs and their imperial relations, while drawing the combatants closer to their compatriots in arms. Even the cautious moderates who had long opposed independence soon felt hopelessly alienated from the British. By midsummer, Edward Shippen, who but a year before had waxed eloquent about the persistent bonds joining Britons and Americans, instead prayed for the "Defeat of our Murdering Enemys."[50]

The war had quickly become an intensely personal affair for both Lancaster's soldiers and its civilians. By fall 1776, the county's troops numbered among the thousands of American casualties suffered during the devastating defeats in New York. Embittered survivors wrote home recalling their savage encounters with the enemy. Captain Peter Grubb Jr. of the State Rifle

Regiment reassured relatives after the rebels' mauling at Long Island that "our men behaved with the greatest courage and stood their ground like heroes" against the British "Butchers." Locals felt the losses acutely as reports told of spiraling numbers of neighbors, friends, and family killed or captured by the enemy. "Our loss," Major Jasper Ewing somberly informed his uncle Jasper Yeates after the Battle of Long Island, "amounts to 500 men and upwards." The Lancaster committeeman William Atlee learned in September 1776 that his brother Samuel, the colonel of Pennsylvania's musketry battalion, had been captured on Long Island. Major Edward Burd, grandson of Edward Shippen, likewise numbered among the prisoners seized in New York.[51]

Tales of the mistreatment of American captives resonated locally, conjuring up an increasingly foreign and well-defined enemy. Burd's family received the chilling news in October that he was confined aboard one of the enemy's dreaded prison ships. Former transport vessels anchored off New York, Britain's infamous harbor hulks soon swarmed with thousands of Americans captured during the battles of late 1776. Dark, dank, filthy, and overcrowded, fertile breeding grounds for typhus, dysentery, smallpox, and yellow fever, the prison ships quickly became floating coffins. In early January 1777, Shippen mourned an acquaintance who "was taken Prisoner . . . used very ill, and is since dead." Moderates like Shippen found British abuses especially repugnant because they issued from erstwhile kindred. Enraged militants, meanwhile, identified with their languishing compatriots to the north. One local captured the sentiments of a growing portion of the county's patriots when he decried the plight of "our Brave, poor Country-men" who perished at the hands of "English tyrants." Residents of Lancaster began subscribing aid to the families of local volunteers imprisoned by the enemy as early as December 1776.[52]

Patriots vented their frustrations at the enemies who remained most vulnerable and near at hand, the prisoners in their midst. Long-smoldering tensions threatened to erupt when locals reeled from losses that hit close to home. After Cumberland County residents received word of their troops killed in Canada, Carlisle's paroled British officers were "pelted and reviled in the streets." Insurgents fumed as British officers exploited liberal paroles while American captives by comparison expired under deplorable conditions. Lieutenant André grimly described how he and his fellow officers had been "invited to smell a brandished hatchet and reminded of its agreeable effects on the skull," adding, "Several of us have been fired at, and we have more than once been waylaid by men determined to assassinate us." Incensed by Whigs' hypocrisy, he concluded, "Such is the brotherly love they, in our capitulation, promised us."[53]

Some of André's backcountry antagonists had traded similar threats with their provincial Indian neighbors scarcely a decade before. Indeed, for locals, the war with Britain revived an anxiety and animus not felt since the terrifying frontier raids of the 1750s and 1760s, though featuring new villains in their former kinsmen. Locals' resentments found familiar expression in the remembered violence of the American backcountry. Rumors in early August 1776 hinted that a company of Cumberland County militia aimed to retaliate against Lancaster's captives for the alleged atrocities perpetrated against prisoners from Pennsylvania. Only a dozen years after the Paxton rioters had massacred the defenseless Conestoga Indians in Lancaster's workhouse, the rumors carried a chilling resonance. Fearing for their lives, the prisoners huddled in their barracks, armed with makeshift clubs. Although the rumors proved unfounded, they indicated the depth of hostility that backcountry associators now harbored toward their British foes. The militants' enmity sprang from locally oriented grievances—as the British stalked their neighborhoods or bloodied their recruits—but slowly drew them into an expanding revolutionary community.[54]

As views of the British changed, so did the revolutionaries' perceptions of themselves. Following the declaration of independence, locals took pains to distinguish themselves from the British, identifying more readily with distant friends of the common cause, the "spirited sons of America," joint members of the revolutionary fold. The conflict's first formal prisoner exchange in late 1776 illuminates the supplanting of older attachments for new. In mid-November, the Board of War ordered Lancaster's committee to forward their British captives under armed escorts to New Jersey's Fort Lee for immediate exchange. General Washington insisted that the prisoners remain under close guard during their march lest they stray to gather intelligence.[55]

Local revolutionaries embraced the opportunity to return their captives and reclaim their compatriots. On November 22, Lancaster's committee exhorted residents to liberate "their distressed fellow-citizens from bondage, and restore them to their country and friends" by helping to forward the British for exchange. The prisoners began their long march to New Jersey a week later, accompanied by nearly sixty wagons and an escort of Lancaster militia. The captives' long-awaited departure brought sighs of relief from anxious residents eager to be rid of their enemies and to return to the familiar rhythms and routines of town life. To locals' mounting consternation, the prisoners' unexpected arrival the year before had placed an increasingly dreaded foe in perilous proximity.[56]

Since early 1776, the prisoners' volatility and the intensifying hostilities had reinforced the budding connections among Lancaster's diverse insurgents.

While the community's English and German speakers remained fully conscious of their cultural differences, the new dangers mitigated militants' ethnic divisions by underscoring their similarities. Prior to the war, many Anglo residents had identified more closely with the distant denizens of Britain, who shared their language and heritage, than with their more inscrutably clannish German neighbors. English speakers' disorienting encounters with their British captives eroded their transatlantic connections while underlining what they shared at stake with their German compatriots. By the summer of 1776, Lancaster's militants identified collectively against the mutual enemies who endangered their cause and community.[57]

The war with Britain thus helped temporarily supersede long-standing cultural divisions in Pennsylvania's hinterland by immersing English- and German-speaking insurgents in a shared Continental endeavor. Negotiating layers of identity, Lancaster's militants subsumed their familiar cultural attachments within a more broadly encompassing revolutionary identity rooted in common enemies and interests. Just as the insurgents squared off against their enemies in the field, they cooperated in policing their captives and community. Locals' clashes with the British, both at home and abroad, nurtured tentative ties to an emerging revolutionary fold with novel commitments to cause and country. But Lancaster's prisoners also exposed the limits of the insurgents' patriotism by revealing conflicting local and Continental agendas.[58]

The prisoners fueled simmering tensions between residents and Continental authorities. The members of Congress who had ordered the British captives to Lancaster were asking residents to perform Continental service by deferring to broader military and diplomatic objectives. Locals remained solicitous of their own interests, however, and claimed a more personal stake in the enterprise. As a chartered corporation, Lancaster had come to enjoy an enviable measure of autonomy. Most residents had grown accustomed to the demands of provincial government, but resented the intrusions of meddling Continental officials who saddled them with their enemies at the risk of their community. Torn between countervailing pressures—the demands of the resistance and their own security—they anxiously awaited the prisoners' departure. Others eagerly capitalized on the prisoners' skills by exploiting their labor. With the captives in private employ, some Whig officials worried that locals would put personal interests before public interests and resist their exchange. Lancaster's committee warned in mid-November that residents who refused to return the prisoners would meet with swift retribution from Continental authorities.[59]

The flagging American resistance gave officials ample reason to doubt local commitments. Patriots had waited in nervous anticipation during the summer of 1776 as a massive expeditionary force consisting of twenty-four thousand British regulars and upwards of eight thousand German auxiliaries assembled on the shores of New York. A series of costly defeats soon sent Washington's battered, exhausted army tumbling in panicked flight through New Jersey and across the Delaware River into Pennsylvania. A despondent George Ross informed a colleague in late November of the "distress of our Soldiers who I have met almost naked and hardly able to walk," adding, "I shudder to tell you that they fall dead on the road with their packs on their backs." As staggering losses and expiring enlistments thinned American ranks, Continental officials questioned their capacity to sustain a viable fighting force.[60]

The British force that pushed toward Pennsylvania now threatened to descend on a deeply divided and dispirited populace. The decision for independence and Pennsylvania's new constitution had badly fragmented the provincial resistance, magnifying Whigs' lingering factional divisions. The cautious moderates who had conceded to independence months before now recoiled from Pennsylvania's newly instituted radical government. After serving as the vice president of Pennsylvania's constitutional convention, George Ross opposed the final document, along with a few dozen of his disgruntled fellow delegates. From Lancaster, Jasper Yeates soon lamented the "confusion and disorder" arising from the new constitution, noting that "many are determined to oppose it at all events, and many to support it at all hazards." Recent military setbacks, meanwhile, tested the commitments of the most spirited insurgents. Many of Lancaster County's associators hesitated to march when summoned to impede the British advance on Philadelphia, preferring to remain near their homes and families. Through the closing days of 1776, patriots' zeal gave way to nagging doubts and despair. Only months after boldly declaring their independence, revolutionaries found themselves at the mercy of an uncompromising foe for whom they had lost all affection.[61]

The fortunes of the revolutionaries suddenly improved in late December 1776, however, when Washington's surprising victory at Trenton resurrected fading hopes for their cause. In Lancaster, the patriots' elation mingled with relief at the long-awaited departure of their British captives. But locals' relief would prove short lived. Washington's victory had unforeseen consequences for Lancaster after Pennsylvania's Council of Safety ordered more than eight hundred of the Trenton captives to the borough's recently vacated barracks. Only weeks after disposing of their British prisoners, locals would play host to an even more ominous set of captives, the much-dreaded Hessians.[62]

Developments in Lancaster provide a case study of the local production of revolutionary identity. More broadly, Lancaster's story illustrates how the Revolution evolved from a civil conflict grounded within a shared sense of imperial belonging to a contest between disparate British and American nationalities. In the diverse Pennsylvania interior, war and revolution disrupted customary modes of identification and association by overriding established bonds of culture and empire. When congressional officials dispatched their British captives to Lancaster in late 1775, they gambled that close interactions between locals and their prisoners would help mend the breach between combatants. Instead, captors and captives squared off as adversaries, approaching each other with mounting suspicion. By early summer 1776, Lancaster's hard-liners felt locked in an irreconcilable conflict with an implacable foe. The struggle with Britain and the dangers posed by their prisoners reinforced militants' preoccupation with internal security while cultivating tenuous attachments to the revolutionary resistance. As the war came home to Lancaster and locals bore the costs of the conflict, militants closed ranks and found support in the company of fellow patriots. Increasingly alienated from the British, the insurgents embraced a revolutionary identity all their own. While the forging of American identity remained an ongoing and deeply contested process, Pennsylvania's revolutionaries had begun fashioning themselves anew—into something quite apart from their transatlantic cousins.

CHAPTER 4

"'Tis Britain Alone That Is Our Enemy"

German Captives and the Promise of America

On the evening of December 30, 1776, Lancaster received heartening news of Washington's surprising victory at the Battle of Trenton. The Americans' unexpected triumph in New Jersey restored faith in the beleaguered resistance by ending a string of demoralizing military setbacks suffered since the beginning of their disastrous campaign for New York. In Lancaster, ecstatic Whigs celebrated the victory, little realizing that the battle carried serious consequences for their community. When Washington's triumphant troops recrossed the Delaware into Pennsylvania, they had more than eight hundred Hessian prisoners in tow. In early January, elation turned to dread when the locals learned that Continental officials had decided to detain their new German prisoners in Lancaster. Only weeks after seeing off their troublesome British captives, residents found themselves faced with yet another set of prisoners. And for the second time in just over a year, Lancaster became the site for Continental experimentation in the formation of Americans' rapidly evolving prisoner policy.[1]

As the Whigs' principal detention center, Lancaster served as a logical site for housing the German prisoners. The borough's recently expanded and vacated barracks could accommodate a large number of captives, while the newly completed stockade furnished additional security. But Continental authorities also had a more specific purpose in mind. Indeed, sending the Hessians to Lancaster formed part of an ongoing American campaign to subvert Britain's German auxiliaries. Continental officials reckoned that as soldiers sold into service by distant princes, the Hessians had at best a dubious commitment to their British employers. By detaining their new prisoners in prosperous German American communities, Continental authorities hoped to incite Hessian desertions and weaken British arms. Whig officials assumed that solicitous care, generous enticements of liberty and property, and familiar interactions with German-speaking residents might induce the captives to quit the British service and embrace the American cause. Ideally, they hoped to recruit the auxiliaries as potential allies in their bitterly contested struggle for independence. Animating these objectives were the universalistic ideals at the core of the Whigs' revolutionary ideology. By late 1776, the revolutionaries saw themselves engaged in a global struggle between republican liberty and monarchical exploitation. That belief, along with the revolutionaries' more pragmatic military objectives, drove the Continental campaign to redeem the Hessians.[2]

In theory, the Whigs' plan made perfect sense. Practically, it posed some problems. To succeed, the campaign had to overcome potent American fears and resentments of the dreaded German auxiliaries. Continental policy stood to encounter stubborn resistance in Pennsylvania, where news of the Hessians' imminent arrival in mid-1776 had helped seal the decision for independence. Subsequent Hessian depredations in New York and New Jersey further inflamed the revolutionary resistance. In the diverse Pennsylvania interior, Britain's employment of the Hessians overrode ethnic associations and solidified revolutionary ranks, as English- and German-speaking insurgents defined themselves against the new invaders. By December 1776, it remained highly questionable whether Lancaster's Whigs could embrace their new enemies as potential friends, particularly after their bitterly disappointing experiences with the recently departed British captives. When locals learned of the German prisoners' impending arrival, most anticipated the worst.[3]

But if their encounters with the British had quickly disillusioned the Whigs, their dealings with the Hessians yielded more favorable results—for both captors and captives. Whigs' success owed as much to the German prisoners' orderly conduct as it did to patriotic imperatives or strategic considerations. Whereas many British regulars felt betrayed by the rebels' repudiation of king and country, their German allies remained more emotionally detached from their new enemies. Thus, compared to the British, the German captives proved more inclined to cooperate with their American hosts. Granted the privilege of hiring out to Whig employers, hundreds of Hessians were soon laboring for the revolutionary resistance. The decision to place the Hessians within largely German-speaking surroundings paid particular dividends. Lancaster's British captives may have found Pennsylvania's Germans unsettlingly alien, but many Hessians found them reassuringly familiar. Residents' productive relations with their German prisoners validated the Continental gamble to befriend the auxiliaries. And growing numbers of locals—both English and German speakers—soon joined Continental officials in welcoming the Hessians as worthy allies in their shared struggle against Old World tyranny. By late 1777, the most optimistic Whigs could boast that they were slowly converting their German captives to revolutionary republicanism. Their favorable interactions with their German prisoners deepened the revolutionaries' estrangement from the British while reinforcing their attachment to an emerging American identity.

These Warlike Transports

Although Whigs roundly deplored Britain's hiring of foreign auxiliaries to quash the domestic rebellion, the decision squared with conventional practice and sprang from a realistic assessment of the military situation. Unable to match the troop strength of their larger European rivals, the British had long resorted to augmenting their domestic forces with trained auxiliary contingents obtained through subsidy treaties with foreign suppliers. For nearly a century, Britain's chief foreign supplier remained a scattered collection of petty principalities in central Germany, long home to a flourishing soldier trade. George I, for example, had contracted the services of some twelve thousand Hessians a half century before the American rebellion. More recently, during the Seven Years' War, the British had again drawn on thousands of German reinforcements. Though they had employed subsidy troops in both Britain and continental Europe, however, they had yet to deploy them in North America.[4]

Lacking the forces required to suppress the insurgency quickly, Britain now opted for the long-established practice of hiring foreign auxiliaries. General Gage had recommended contracting subsidy troops to quell the growing protests in Massachusetts as early as October 1774. Gage's successor, General Howe, seconded the appeal upon assuming command of British forces one year later. Negotiations with several central German principalities commenced in late 1775. By early 1776, Britain had concluded subsidy treaties with Hessen-Kassel, Hessen-Hanau, Brunswick, and Waldeck for upwards of seventeen thousand troops, then secured an additional two thousand reinforcements from the principalities of Ansbach-Bayreuth and Anhalt-Zerbst a year later. Because the majority of the German troops hailed from Hesse, the auxiliaries were collectively dubbed the Hessians. Justified

in terms of expediency and encountering minimal opposition, the subsidy
treaties passed with Parliament's overwhelming support.[5]

Wrongly labeled mercenaries by their American enemies, the Germans
operated not as individuals contracted to the highest bidder but as formal
auxiliaries hired in full contingents. The soldiers earned more in foreign than
in domestic employ, but they served at the pleasure of their German prince,
whose treasury profited from their labors. German sovereigns received compensation per head for supplying the troops, along with generous annual
subsidy payments for the duration of their North American service. The
suppliers maintained troop strength by annually replenishing losses with new
recruits. While in British employ, the soldiers owed dual allegiance to King
George III and to the German sovereign who had enlisted their service. The
auxiliaries fought under their own officers but remained subordinate to the
British high command. Generally, the German detachments consisted of a
blend of professional and nonprofessional soldiers, including regulars, militia,
and fresh conscripts raised for service in North American field and garrison
regiments. The six separate German contingents encompassed both natives
and foreigners recruited from neighboring principalities. A diverse lot, the
soldiers included farmers, artisans, and transients. Most were young peasants
drawn from the countryside.[6]

By mid-1776, some seventeen thousand Germans had boarded British
transports bound for the rebellious colonies. Though the Germans promised
to augment the King's forces substantially, British commanders remained
anxious about how they would perform in the field. While both civil and
military authorities supported the contracting of auxiliaries, some had recommended hiring Russians, fearing that the Germans would be tempted
to desert and settle among their ethnic kindred, now dispersed by the tens
of thousands in scores of flourishing communities from New Jersey to the
Carolinas. During Parliament's debate on the subsidy treaties, a British Whig
had warned the ministry of the danger of sending German troops to America, predicting that they would be "offered lands and protection." As a result,
"these warlike transports" would serve as well as the "Palatine ships for
peopling America with Germans." The warning went unheeded but proved
prophetic.[7]

Alerted by friends abroad to the Germans' potential for desertion, American Whigs soon launched a concerted effort to entice the mercenaries from
their British employers. As early as August 1775, Heinrich Miller's *Staatsbote*
featured a letter from a supporter in Germany who observed that Americans
had an "extensive country for Germans to cultivate, and no people love
profitable labour better, or are better adapted for the purpose." Consequently,

he predicted, if German troops arrived to subdue the American rebellion, they would soon "drop their fire-arms" and start farming. Eight months later, agents in London sent similar reports of the unreliability of the German troops, noting that "if proper offers" were made to the auxiliaries, they would "desert in great numbers." Sparked by the earliest intelligence of Britain's employment of the foreign auxiliaries, the Whig campaign to seduce the Hessians was under way before the first Germans set foot on American soil.[8]

By May 1776, with the auxiliaries expected to arrive shortly, Whigs began formulating their strategy to promote Hessian desertions. Washington astutely recommended that Whigs exploit the foreign troops' ethnic associations with the German speakers in the colonies. In a May 11 letter to Congress, he proposed sending some of "our Germans" among the Hessians to excite a "spirit of disaffection and desertion," counseling, "If a few sensible trusty fellows could get with them, I should think they would have great weight and influence with the common soldiery, who certainly have no enmity towards us, having received no injury nor cause of quarrell from us." In early August, Congress sprang into action, appointing a new three-member committee to "devise a plan for encouraging the Hessians and other Foreigners, employed by the King of Great Britain, and sent to America for the purpose of subjugating these States, to quit that iniquitous service."[9]

During mid-August, Congress drafted a formal appeal to the auxiliaries. Designed to disarm the enemy, the Continental plea underscored the American republic's benevolence and inclusiveness. Congress declared it the policy of the new United States to "extend the protection of their laws to all those who should settle among them," regardless of their national or religious origin, and to grant them the "benefits of civil and religious freedom." Congress offered to invest Hessian deserters with the "rights, privileges and immunities of natives" and, as an additional incentive, to award each deserter fifty acres of land. These were generous terms indeed, particularly for those now in arms against the United States. Significantly, Congress declined to extend the offer to British troops.[10]

Emphasizing the righteousness of the American cause, Congress insisted that the Germans had no legitimate grounds for bearing arms against a "people guilty of no other crime than that of refusing to exchange freedom for slavery." In a clever interpretive ploy, Congress cast the auxiliaries as aggrieved brethren, injured innocents bedeviled by royal despots who wagered the "blood of their people for money." By accepting the Americans' offer, the Germans could exchange the shackles of tyranny and the "toils and dangers of a long and bloody war" for "lands, liberty, safety, and a communion of good laws, and mild Government, in a country where many of their friends and relations are already happily settled." By contrast, Germans who spurned the offer and lent their assistance to Britain's treacherous design faced grimmer prospects. As Congress warned, "By invading and attempting to destroy those who have never injured them or their country, their only reward, if they escape death and captivity, will be a return to the despotism of their Prince, to be by him again sold to do the drudgery of some other enemy to the rights of mankind."[11]

After translating the resolve into German, Congress sent copies to Washington for immediate circulation. Under cover of night, American operatives prowled Staten Island, scattering their propaganda leaflets near the Hessian camp. German-speaking agents reportedly frequented the Hessian encampments to fraternize with the newly arrived troops and acquaint them with the freedoms and opportunities available to foreigners in the new United States. Hoping to broaden their audience, congressional officials soon drafted a second appeal offering "additional rewards to officers in proportion to their rank and pay." Henceforth, German colonels would receive one thousand acres for deserting, majors six hundred acres, and captains four hundred acres.[12]

Whigs had good reason to believe that their efforts would resonate among the auxiliaries. The allegiance of the Germans, as foreign troops staking their lives in the British employ, remained uncertain at best. A blend of nobles and commoners typically better educated than the men they commanded in the field, German officers generally sympathized with the objectives of the British, dismissing their American enemies as spoiled upstarts engaged in a violent rebellion against their rightful sovereign. Career soldiers deeply invested in their profession and determined to advance through the ranks, they had everything to lose by deserting. The average enlisted man, by contrast, who as yet harbored no compelling grievance against the rebels or principled objection to their cause, was more apt to entertain Congress's appeals. As well-drilled contracted auxiliaries, however, most of the German troops dutifully deferred to their British employers. Rebellion on the American scale remained scarcely conceivable to the typical German recruit, who refused to inquire too deeply into the roots of the imperial controversy.[13]

If the German rank and file remained decidedly unimpressed by the revolutionaries' republican ideology, however, they found much to admire in the rebellious colonies' breathtaking material abundance. One of the newly arrived auxiliaries marveled at the lushness of Staten Island, where "peaches, chestnuts, nuts, apples, pears, and grapes grow wild in between rose and blackberry bushes," and "the climate and the soil," he observed, "are surely the most beautiful, healthy, and the most pleasant in the world." Months later, another German praised New Jersey as "one of the most fertile and pleasant provinces in North America," musing, "There are many fine farms here," but too few inhabitants to "cultivate the land sufficiently." The soldier speculated that "it could feed at least four times the number it now feeds."[14]

If many of the nearly twenty thousand Germans first dispatched to North America were loyal, seasoned professionals serving lengthy terms of service for their native principalities, thousands of others were fresh conscripts recruited under duress and unaccustomed to the demands of the soldiers' trade. One of the Americans' first German captives, for example, complained that "he had been torn out of bed, away from his wife and children, and forced into the service." Hessen-Kassel's Lossberg Regiment included a disproportionate share of recruits from neighboring principalities, who shared a tenuous connection with the remote sovereigns who sold or paid for their service. The commanders of the regiment documented discouragingly high desertion rates during the march to their European ports of embarkation.[15]

Mostly poor, propertyless peasants with little hope of acquiring farms of their own in Germany, the Hessian rank and file stood to profit handsomely from Congress's overtures. They knew that thousands of Germans had already found a comfortable haven in North America, making the most of their new opportunities by establishing prosperous settlements throughout Britain's middle and southern colonies. The officials spearheading the Whigs' subversion campaign logically assumed that the German auxiliaries would find America similarly attractive. Whigs soon drew additional encouragement from the growing reports of the Germans' dissatisfaction with the British service. By deserting, the disaffected troops could escape the risks and rigors of military service and join their flourishing, freedom-loving kindred in the German settlements of North America.[16]

A Barbarous, Mercenary People

To the Whigs' dismay, through late 1776, despite their best efforts to convert the Hessians, the project yielded discouraging results. Though Continental officials could point encouragingly to the desertions of dozens of Brunswick troops in Canada, the Hessians in New York, soon numbering more than twelve thousand, showed little inclination to follow their example. Desertion, after all, entailed considerable risk, leaving the fugitive vulnerable to capture and punishment by his superiors. Anticipating the Americans' efforts, the British also took precautions to inoculate their German allies against patriot appeals with carefully measured doses of their own propaganda. Prior to the clash at Long Island, the British indoctrinated the Hessians with gruesome tales of their enemies' brutality. Grafting onto their rebellious colonists the Indians' reputation for savagery, British officers warned the Germans that the Americans were "savage cannibals . . . whom they must exterminate . . . if they were not to be tortured and eaten alive by them." To shield their men from the revolutionaries' subversive designs, Hessian officers had them restricted to their encampments and remained vigilant of circulating American propaganda.[17]

A string of humiliating defeats during their disastrous campaign for New York similarly undermined Americans' appeals to the Hessians by highlighting the weakness and disorganization of Washington's raw and undisciplined army. At the very moment when Continental authorities began soliciting Hessian desertions, their own battered, exhausted, and disillusioned troops were fleeing their ranks in record numbers. With the resistance left reeling from mounting casualties and desertions, British and loyalist observers cheerfully forecast a speedy American collapse. The revolutionaries' lopsided defeats at the battles of Long Island and Fort Washington left the Americans' German enemies less than impressed and provided little incentive to prospective deserters. Even those few Germans tempted by the Whigs' generous solicitations recognized the grave implications of a failed colonial rebellion. Guilty of treason against their king, the American rebels could scarcely honor their promises to German deserters from the gallows, which is where their harshest critics felt sure the insurgency's leaders must inevitably answer for their crimes.[18]

Moreover, as long as the revolutionaries squared off against the Hessians as armed combatants, their calculated professions of friendship would ring hollow. Having failed to earn the Germans' trust or respect, the Whigs desperately required an opportunity to showcase their goodwill firsthand. Ironically, that opportunity came during late December 1776, with Washington's morale-boosting victory over an isolated Hessian garrison at Trenton. To salvage American hopes and reinvigorate the flagging resistance, Washington boldly led his troops from Pennsylvania across the icy Delaware River on the morning of December 26 to surprise a Hessian brigade consisting of the Rall, Lossberg, and Knyphausen regiments. Claiming more than eight hundred prisoners in one decisive stroke, the Americans quickly withdrew before the scrambling British could mount a counterattack. On January 3, 1777, Washington's rejuvenated force netted another hundred or so German captives at the Battle of Princeton.[19]

To make the most of their victories, Continental authorities devised a clever strategy of using their German captives to subvert the British war machine from within. On December 28, an elated Congress recommended delaying the prisoners' exchange to acquaint them with the "situation and circumstances of many of their countrymen, who came here without a farthing of property, and have, by care and industry, acquired plentiful fortunes." To maximize the effects of Whig propaganda, Congress separated the Hessian officers from their men. Washington then instructed Pennsylvania's Council of Safety to transfer the prisoners to the German counties in the state's interior. Once the captives saw "how preferable the Situation of their Countrymen . . . is to theirs," he reasoned, they could be returned "so fraught with a love of Liberty and property" that they would "create a disgust to the Service among the remainder of the foreign Troops."[20]

To prepare Pennsylvania's populace for the captives' arrival, Washington advised the Council of Safety to issue a special public address. On December 31, the council instructed the public that the prisoners should be "well treated, and have such principles instilled into them" that upon their future exchange, they might "fully open the Eyes of their Countrymen in the service of the king of Great Britain." Officials chose Lancaster, now an established Continental detention site with a freshly vacated barracks, as the most appropriate location for the prisoners' detention. In late December, the Council of Safety wrote Lancaster's committee concerning the prisoners' impending arrival and future management. As the captives seemed "perfectly ignorant of the nature of our present contest," the council urged the committee to have "them well informed of the reasons of the war." With hundreds of Hessians now safely in American hands, council members hoped to "sow the seeds of dissension" between them and the British. To this end, Lancaster's Germans, by treating the captives as "brethren and friends," could "do the most essential service to our cause."[21]

While strategically sound, Continental policy remained somewhat surprising, given the long history of anti-German sentiment in Britain's North American colonies. Now helping to orchestrate the campaign to subvert the Hessians was Pennsylvania's Benjamin Franklin, who only a generation before had loudly lamented the threat Germans posed to a uniform anglicization. During the preceding decades, tens of thousands of eager and industrious German immigrants had flocked to Penn's province. As diverse ethnocultural groups maintained their preferred languages and customs in Pennsylvania's pluralistic communities, a grudging tolerance competed with a lingering prejudice. Dismayed by the Germans' perceived clannishness and reluctance to assimilate, many Anglos opposed their continued immigration. Through the mid-eighteenth century, Germans found themselves crudely racialized and stereotyped by their most vocal provincial critics. Whig officials' carefully calculated appeals to the Hessians reminded the most determined opponents of German immigration of their provincial neighbors' unsettling distinctiveness. As the war escalated, however, the need for unity in the face of common enemies, along with many Germans' enthusiastic support for the revolutionary resistance, encouraged growing numbers of English speakers to overlook their long-standing prejudice. Then, too, with the revolutionaries desperately struggling to secure their independence, simple expediency dictated that they do everything possible to undermine British military operations, even if that meant augmenting the German American population with Hessian deserters.[22]

Expedient or not, to succeed, the Continental campaign had to win over a hostile public. For most Whigs, after all, the proposed recipients of Continental beneficence were not merely Germans but mercenaries, professional killers contracted by Britain to extinguish American liberties. Reputed for their savagery and rapaciousness, the Hessians stirred visceral fears and resentments among friends of the resistance. During the early summer of 1776, John Hancock somberly prophesied that the German hirelings, from "their want of connections and those feelings of sympathy which frequently bind together the different parts of the same empire, will be more likely to do the business of their masters without remorse or compunction." Nearly two months before the first Hessians landed at Staten Island, Americans could ponder the advice of a British Whig, who urged that every mercenary captured "be put to death, officers and men, without distinction." Such men were "invaders of the worst kind," he raged, and "should be treated accordingly." Two weeks before the Battle of Long Island, an American colonel, William Douglas, voiced similar sentiments, declaring, "If the Hesiens troops are so Luckey as to Fall into our hands, I am in hopes they will meat with Such Treatment as Properly belongs to their Bloody Crime." For while "we have had no Dispute with them," he argued, they have "turn'd them Selves out as murderours of the Inosent." Indeed, if American troops proudly styled themselves virtuous citizen soldiers who fought for love of cause and country, and in defense of liberty, family, and property, their German opponents seemed the very antithesis—depraved, unprincipled mercenaries animated by the promise of spoils.[23]

That the Americans had broken irrevocably from the mother country by midsummer of 1776 owed much to Britain's employment of foreign auxiliaries. Some Britons had predicted as much. Days before the British unleashed their German allies at the Battle of Long Island, Ambrose Serle, secretary to Lord Richard Howe, ventured that Britain's use of this "most odious kind of Force" would "irritate and inflame the Americans infinitely more than two or three British armies." Months earlier, even the conservative-leaning

Whigs opposed to independence had reluctantly conceded that the employment of foreign troops must inevitably sunder the bonds of empire. Furious
radicals, meanwhile, loudly condemned Britain's unholy alliance. To embittered Whigs, the subsidy treaties confirmed that Britons preferred coercion
to compromise and deemed their colonists an alien, inferior people, unworthy of being treated as fellow citizens. By betraying a long-cherished cultural connection, Britain's employment of the Hessians left English-speaking
Whigs even further estranged from their imperial kindred. Disillusioned
insurgents ultimately concluded that a government which enlisted foreign
mercenaries to subdue its own subjects forfeited all claims to allegiance.[24]

Vindicating the radicals' claim that the mother country was hell-bent
on humiliating its rebellious colonies, news of the subsidy treaties sealed
Pennsylvania's decision for independence. Rumors of Britain's negotiations
reached Philadelphia as early as January 1776, enraging the provincial resistance. In mid-January, a despondent Edward Shippen learned from his son
in the capital that Congress now considered independence "indispensably
necessary" should Britain "employ foreign troops to reduce us." Radicals
in the Congress had already insisted that the fledgling American resistance
would require foreign allies to withstand a British force augmented by thousands of auxiliaries. The negotiations necessary to secure a foreign alliance, in
turn, would require a formal declaration of independence. By inflaming the
populace, the news of the auxiliaries' impending arrival facilitated the radicals' determined efforts to replace Pennsylvania's more conservative assembly
with a government friendly to independence. In late May, after final con-
firmation of the subsidy treaties ended Pennsylvanians' anxious speculation,
an outraged Philadelphian concluded, "This, I think gives the *Coup de Grace*
to the British and American connection," adding, "It has already wrought
wonders in this city," where "conversions have been more rapid than ever
happen'd under Mr. Whitfield." On June 24, the members of Pennsylvania's
Provincial Conference voted unanimously for independence, citing among
their accumulated grievances Britain's contracting of foreign auxiliaries.[25]

Pennsylvania's militants considered the enlistment of foreign troops the
last in a string of unpardonable offenses that shattered all hopes of reconciliation. Benjamin Franklin spoke for growing numbers of his provincial par-
tisans when he informed Lord Howe in late July, "It is impossible we should
think of submission to a Government that has, with the most wanton barbarity and cruelty, burned our defenceless towns in the midst of winter, excited
the savages to massacre our peaceful farmers, instigated our slaves to murder their masters, and is even now bringing foreign mercenaries to deluge
our settlements with blood." Such "atrocious injuries," Franklin concluded,

"have extinguished every spark of affection for that parent country we once held so dear." Following the example of the Declaration of Independence, the radical framers of Pennsylvania's new constitution condemned George III for unleashing not merely the "troops of Great Britain, but foreign mercenaries, savages, and slaves" against his aggrieved subjects. That militants ranked the Hessians among Africans and Indians proved damning testimony of their contempt for the auxiliaries.[26]

Patriot indignation only intensified following the auxiliaries' arrival on American shores. Indeed, a paradox characterized the Whigs' dealings with their German adversaries, as the Continental campaign to reinvent the Hessians clashed with ongoing propaganda reviling them as a "barbarous, mercenary people" who would "cut your throats for the small reward of six-pence." Through late 1776, the Germans supplied abundant grist for their critics' propaganda mill, cementing their reputation as a fierce, marauding soldiery who butchered and plundered with virtual impunity. The ferocity of their earliest encounters with their new enemies confirmed the rebels' worst fears, as the Hessians, eager to impress their British allies, inflicted shocking losses on the unseasoned American opposition. Amidst the first skirmishes in New York, Pennsylvania riflemen proudly returned to camp bearing the bodies of several slain German auxiliaries for display as crude trophies of war. Days later, at the Battle of Long Island, the Hessians took their revenge, as American troops attempting to surrender were savagely cut down where they stood. Chilling accounts of defenseless riflemen unceremoniously spitted to trees on the ends of Hessian bayonets soon swept through the American ranks, sowing terror among Washington's raw recruits. As early as October 1776, Americans complained that the mercenaries refused to distinguish between friend and foe but "plunder all indiscriminately," Whig and Tory alike. A month later, in a circular to the commanding officers of the state militia, Pennsylvania's Council of Safety condemned the "rapacious, ungovernable, and cruel mercenaries" who "spread desolation through our country." Even more than the British, the newly arrived Hessians instilled dread in their American opposition.[27]

Reports of Hessian depredations grew in frequency and alarming detail during the enemy's campaign through New Jersey, as furious propagandists spun grossly exaggerated accounts of mercenary atrocities to rally support for the beleaguered resistance. On December 18, just three weeks before the German prisoners arrived in Lancaster, the *Pennsylvania Packet* complained that the Hessians' march through New Jersey yielded "such scenes of desolation and outrage, as would disgrace the most barbarous nations." The newspaper furnished a tale of ravished maidens, plundered dwellings, and despoiled property, of families "reduced from comfort and affluence to poverty and ruin." A week later, with Howe's forces now hovering in menacing proximity, the *Packet* declared that only the "virtue and determined spirit" of the state militia could "save this once happy province from the ravages of a most cruel, base and inhuman enemy." A member of both the Council of Safety and the Continental Congress, Robert Morris aired Philadelphians' fears. Should the mercenaries "get this fine city," he warned, they will be "satiated, if the ruin of thousands of worthy citizens can satisfy their avarice." For frightened Pennsylvanians, any allusion to the German hirelings now conjured up nightmare visions of monsters who fed on American spoils.[28]

The continued accounts of Hessian brutality fed both fear and fury in Lancaster County, where locals nursed their own grievances against the auxiliaries following demoralizing reports from their battered kindred to the north. Only months before, the Hessians had mauled local troops at the Battle of Long Island. A friend wrote Jasper Yeates in September that the mercenaries had "behaved with great Inhumanity" during the engagement, even bashing the heads of wounded men. Yeates's nephew Major Jasper Ewing furnished a similar account of the battle, recalling how the "inhuman wretches thrust their bayonets through our wounded men, and refused that Mercy to us which we granted to them." Thus "sad experience," Ewing concluded, "convinces our people that they are an enemy not to be despised." Amidst the chaos of the engagement, a party of Colonel Samuel Atlee's musketry battalion was nearly surrounded by a detachment of Hessians. "The opinion we had formed of these troops," Atlee later reported, "determined us to run any risk rather than fall into their hands." Reports from the front stoked a burning antipathy among county residents, English and German speakers alike. Provincial and Continental officials could therefore expect to encounter considerable resistance when they urged Lancaster's Germans to embrace their Trenton captives as brethren and friends.[29]

Reduce by Clemency, and Reform by Mercy

Their common language initially made it no easier for German Americans to identify with the invaders. Indeed, by proposing that residents welcome the Hessians as kindred, Whig officials ignored the Germans' cultural and regional differences. With Germany still a collection of distinct principalities, German speakers lacked a sense of national awareness or attachment, instead identifying with their particular region or locale. Whereas Lancaster County's German speakers descended mostly from Switzerland or the Rhineland Palatinate, most of Britain's auxiliaries hailed from the central German principalities and spoke peculiar dialects. Unlike the Anglos seated in Congress, German revolutionaries and their Hessian adversaries were quick to recognize their differences.[30]

Thousands of Pennsylvania's Germans, moreover, were native-born Americans whose families now stood a generation or more removed from immigration. The children or grandchildren of immigrants, they had never seen Germany and remained more naturally attuned to their New World communities than to their families' ever-receding Old World origins. The Hessians' arrival further eroded many German speakers' Old World sympathies by bolstering their attachment to the freedoms and opportunities enjoyed in their newly imperiled communities. They or their families had emigrated to North American to escape the interminable conflicts ravaging central Europe. For these German speakers—both church and sect—the hirelings conjured up painful reminders of the chronic violence and instability they or their forebears had gratefully left behind. Now the accumulating reports of Hessian marauding scarcely found Pennsylvania's Germans in a forgiving mood.

The Hessians received a hostile reception from many German-speaking civilians, who berated the invaders for endangering their lives and property. An elderly German woman scolded a Hessian officer in Germantown, for instance, asking: "What harm have we people done to you, that you Germans come over here to suck us dry and drive us out of house and home? We have heard enough here of your murderous burning. Will you do the same here as in New York and in the Jerseys?" She angrily promised, "You shall get your pay yet!" The auxiliaries who had family in North America invited reproach for callously and greedily preying on their own kindred. In Philadelphia, a Hessian captive encountered his aunt, who bitterly inquired "what had made him come here to do violence to his own flesh and blood?"[31]

Welcoming the invaders would prove especially difficult for the state's German insurgents. Nearly two years of war had redefined the relations between Pennsylvania's English- and German-speaking revolutionaries. As the British moved to crush the American rebellion, increasingly rigid battle lines slowly eclipsed the Whigs' familiar ethnic attachments by reconfiguring prevailing patterns of cultural association. Within the confines of a brutal insurgency, growing numbers of Pennsylvania's English and German speakers embraced a broader American identity animated by their shared wartime sacrifices and novel republican commitments. Many of the state's most defiant insurgents now fashioned themselves less as Germans than as American patriots, identifying first and foremost with fellow revolutionaries, regardless of their ethnicity.

By late 1776, German Whigs could no more readily identify with Hessian auxiliaries than their Anglo compatriots could identify with British regulars. Like their English-speaking brethren, the German revolutionaries openly spurned the hirelings as debased minions of violence. In mid-August of that year, as the auxiliaries disembarked at Staten Island, Lancaster's John Hubley, a staunch German patriot and member of Pennsylvania's Council of Safety, decried the arrival of the "foreign troops." One Hessian noted his surprise upon encountering a German Whig who seemed "quite indifferent about seeing his countrymen and spoke with contempt of the German nation and of Germany." On the front lines, German American troops registered particular disdain for the auxiliaries, showering abuse on the invaders from their entrenchments. The rebels "insult and berate us with the vilest words," a Hessian captain complained during late summer 1776. "There are many Germans among them," he added, "who especially distinguish themselves in this insolence." After the Battle of Long Island, Captain Caspar Weitzel of Colonel Samuel Miles's rifle regiment vilified the "damned savage Hessians" who cold-bloodedly bayoneted his wounded comrades.[32]

In late December, the Whigs' new Hessian prisoners reaped a bitter reception in Philadelphia. Following the captives' arrival in Pennsylvania, state officials saw that they were "well provided for" and had the "opportunity of hearing God's Word in both the English and German languages." To bolster revolutionary morale, however, Washington also paraded his prisoners through the capital. Fascinated residents turned out in droves to catch a glimpse of the dreaded mercenaries. Lining Philadelphia's crowded streets expecting to encounter savage brutes, the curious spectators instead found a ragged, humbled force marched under a strong guard. According to one witness, "most people seemed very angry they should ever think of running away from such a set of vagabonds." The alarmed military escort frantically shielded their prisoners from the frenzied mob of English and German speakers.[33]

In the wake of Philadelphians' furious reaction to their captives, state officials took pains to elicit public sympathy for the Hessians by drawing a sharp distinction between the auxiliaries and their employers and blaming the British for the Germans' misdeeds. In the skilled hands of state propagandists, the once reviled hirelings now became the unwitting agents of their manipulative British masters. Borrowing a page from earlier congressional propaganda, Pennsylvania's Council of Safety recast the Hessians as exploited brethren—like Whigs, the innocent victims of royal oppression. On December 31, the council declared:

> These miserable creatures now justly excite our Compassion. . . . According to the arbitrary customs of the tyrannical German Princes, they were dragg'd from their native Country and sold to a foreign Monarch. . . . Their pay a mere pittance, they were necessitated and encouraged to plunder. It is therefore nothing strange that they have been guilty of great irregularities, tho' inferior to the brutal behaviour of the British Troops. But from the moment they are rescued from the authority of the British Officers, we ought no longer to regard them as our Enemies. . . . 'Tis Britain alone that is our Enemy.

The council urged the inhabitants to curb their anger and treat the "much injured and deceived Hessians now in our power in the most friendly manner, as a people we would wish to unite with ourselves in improving the fertile forrests of America, extending its manufacture & Commerce, and maintaining its Liberty and independency against all attacks of forreign & Arbitrary Power." By embracing their captives, ordinary citizens could perform revolutionary service and advance the global cause of freedom. The embattled insurgents now had a unique opportunity to deliver their hapless foes from tyranny by sharing the blessings of their emerging republic. By seizing that opportunity, the revolutionaries could secure potential allies in their bitterly contested struggle for independence.[34]

Despite the determined advocacy of provincial and Continental officials, during the months ahead, a divided public continued to debate the prisoners' appropriate fate. In March, for example, a disgruntled patriot complained in the *Pennsylvania Journal* that Americans should exact retribution from the captives for their crimes. In reply, another Whig recommended that Pennsylvanians should instead showcase their magnanimity and "render those our friends, whom our inveterate enemy has endeavoured to use as tools of oppression, and instruments to perpetrate their horrid plan." He urged, "Let the poor deluded wretches, who, ignorant of the Cause against which they are engaged, and the People against whom they fought, be taught, by our courage in conquering, and our kindness to the vanquished, to fear the resentment of such a People when in arms, and to revere and love them, for their kind treatment to those in captivity." He concluded with an impassioned plea to "reduce by clemency, and reform by mercy! Let these ever be part of the American armour." This generous appeal brought an angry response from an embittered Pennsylvania associator recently returned from New Jersey, who drew a stark contrast between the "slavish subjects of Arbitrary Princes, & men born free & happy." Although the captives could now attest to the virtues of the American republic, he warned that it would "prove of the most fatal consequence to take these people to our bosoms." Steeped in tyranny and corruption, the Hessians could not be trusted to relinquish "principals they have imbid'd from their infancy" and would inevitably turn on their hosts. Ultimately, the captives presented both a challenge and an opportunity for Whigs, eliciting a curious mixture of dread and fascination.[35]

The Whigs' initial handling of their prisoners reflected their continuing ambivalence, as their lingering suspicions clashed with the new imperative to seduce the Germans away from their British employers. Eager to avoid trouble with their prisoners, provincial and Continental authorities proceeded cautiously, initially denying the Hessians the liberties earlier enjoyed by Pennsylvania's first British captives. Recalling Pennsylvanians' difficulties with the British, the Board of War ordered Lancaster's committee to keep the Hessians "strictly confined," for they "may be of great Disservice to our Cause if suffered to have Communication with the People of the Country." To avert another turbulent reception for the Hessians, Pennsylvania's Council of Safety instructed the committee to prevent "our weak and over-zealous friends" from abusing the captives, who should be restricted to the barracks, where "persons of discretion" could acquaint them with the merits of the American cause. Finally, the council asked local officials to search the prisoners' baggage for plundered goods from New Jersey so the stolen property could be "restored to the proper owners."[36]

The prisoners' arrival sparked predictable anxiety among Lancaster's wary inhabitants. Fresh from their disillusioning experience with the British and fearful of the Hessians' reputation, local authorities raised a sixty-man guard and relocated the community's powder and stores to the outskirts of town, a safe distance from the barracks. In accordance with instructions, officials restricted access to the prisoners, limiting visits to members of the committee and to the ministers of Lancaster's German denominations. To isolate the Hessians from the contaminating influence of the borough's few remaining British prisoners, the committee confined the new arrivals to a separate wing of the barracks. Reassuring the captives that they would not meet with "any rigour or cruelty," the committee asked that they reflect on the "iniquity" of "killing and plundering the innocent Inhabitants of this Country" who "entered into this Warr only for the preservation of their Liberties & properties." With the prisoners now safely secured, Lancaster's relieved committee proudly informed state officials that the Hessians had "not received the least insult" and that the "inhabitants seem disposed to treat them with civility." Given their recent troubles with the British, however, locals nursed grave doubts about the prospect of successfully subverting their new German prisoners.[37]

Yet in contrast to their contentious dealings with the British, Lancaster's insurgents soon enjoyed relatively stable and productive relations with the Hessians. Residents' interactions with their German captives, however, were shaped as much by calculated local interests as by broader strategic, ideological, or humanitarian imperatives. After ordering the Hessians confined, state and Continental authorities quickly heard from residents eager to relieve pressure on the barracks and to capitalize on their prisoners' labor. And for the second time in barely more than a year, provincial pressures tipped the scales in Continental prisoner administration, forcing Congress to revisit the question of enlargement. Only months after their relocation to the Pennsylvania interior, most of the Hessians found themselves diligently laboring in the Americans' employ. More compliant than their British counterparts, they made a comparatively favorable impression on their local hosts.

Very Usefully Employed

The sudden influx of nearly a thousand prisoners posed immediate problems for Lancaster's committee, as the new arrivals stretched the capacity of the barracks and found themselves crowded seventeen to a room. During the harsh winter, Lancaster officials faced difficulty furnishing their captives with fresh provisions, a shortage that simultaneously lowered morale and heightened the risk of infectious illness. Both the British and German prisoners had access to town physicians and even occasionally to their own regimental surgeons or surgeon's mates, but Lancaster's overcrowded barracks were prone to deadly outbreaks. By late January, with sickness rapidly spreading through the captives' ranks, local officials feared the onset of an epidemic that could spill beyond the barracks and infect the town's inhabitants. To alleviate the dangerous overcrowding in the barracks, Lancaster's committee considered dispersing the Hessian tradesmen among local employers. After compiling an inventory of the prisoners' trades, officials discovered that they had acquired an invaluable source of labor. Over three hundred of the captives, or roughly one-third of the total, claimed to be skilled craftsmen representing upwards of thirty distinct trades. With the hostilities continuing to deplete the county's labor supply by drawing men into military service, these artisans promised to make a welcome contribution to the local wartime economy.[38]

Having already exploited the skills of their British captives, residents now hoped to tap an even larger source of labor. On January 13, committee chairman William Atlee apprised Pennsylvania's Council of Safety of the large number of craftsmen among the prisoners, adding that many would "gladly" work for "small wages rather than be confined in the Barracks." Weeks later, Lancaster officials notified the Board of War that the "Prisoners may be very usefully employed," as they included between "three and four Hundred Tradesmen of different kinds." The committee stressed that tanners, weavers, and smiths were "much wanted in the Town," while the Hessian tailors and shoemakers could work in the barracks in rooms "fitted up for them." Given the rising demands of wartime production, the committee indicated that the potential benefits of employing the captives outweighed the risks.[39]

Christopher Ludwick, an avid Philadelphia Whig and onetime committeeman who had assisted earlier Continental efforts to induce Hessian desertions, agreed. A native of Hessen-Darmstadt, Ludwick could legitimately claim to know the minds of the auxiliaries better than most Whigs and astutely tied their prospective employment to broader Continental objectives. Ludwick wrote Congress in early March to say that many of the German "Prisoners of War especially single men are so well pleased with this Country and the Way of its Inhabitants" that they would "prefer to settle here than to return to the dreary abodes of Bondage from whence they came." Employing the prisoners, Ludwick added, would "relieve the public of the Burthern of maintaining them" and aid the "Inhabitants who are greatly in want of Journeymen and Labourers." Finally, permitting "these unhappy Strangers" to "breathe in the open fragrancy of American freedom" would give them a "renewed Instance of American public Benevolence and lay them under further Obligation to a Generous & Merciful Enemy."[40]

Swayed by the mounting pressure on Lancaster's barracks and their tempting supply of skilled labor, state and Continental authorities sanctioned the German prisoners' employment under strict terms. On March 3, the Council of Safety instructed Lancaster officials to release as many of the "Hessian Prisoners as can be usefully employed" to reduce the crowding in the barracks. In exchange for their labor, the captives would receive a small wage as well as food and lodging. To prevent the prisoners from forging potentially subversive associations with the disaffected, authorities ordered Lancaster's committee to entrust them only to employers "well attached to our cause," who would keep them "comfortable and safe." As with locals' earlier hiring of the British, the employers had to post a bond as security upon the prisoners' release from confinement, guard against escapes, and return them on demand. As a further precaution, the council advised the committee to keep scrupulous records of both the prisoners and their employers. The captives employed in construction had to return to the barracks nightly, while the remaining laborers had to attend weekly roll calls. The prisoners who failed to obtain employment were to remain confined in the barracks.[41]

Whigs quickly profited from their decision to employ the Hessians, as hundreds of skilled and unskilled captives gratefully embraced the opportunity to leave the barracks and supplement their meager pay. Though many of the Hessians had performed civilian wage labor in Europe, they were pleasantly surprised by the generous wages offered by their American employers. While visiting Lancaster in May 1777, Edward Burd reported that the committee eventually had to limit the Hessians' wages to one shilling per day to "prevent Peoples out bidding each other." Employed by scores of English- and German-speaking officials, professionals, craftsmen, and farmers in Lancaster, York, Berks, Chester, and Cumberland counties, the captives performed a multitude of tasks, serving both public and private interests. The Lancaster provisioning agent Joseph Simon estimated on April 6 that nearly three hundred prisoners had left the barracks to meet the growing demand for their labor. Just two weeks later, he reported that "upwards of 600" Hessians were in the Americans' employ.[42]

For state and Continental officials, public business naturally took priority over private interests. Many of the captives found employment as manual laborers or within their specific trades in the state's war-related industries. Lancaster's John Hubley, commissary of the Continental stores, contracted Hessian laborers to build several public storehouses and Hessian cordwainers to make shoes for American troops. Dozens of German prisoners toiled in mills, furnaces, or workshops, where they busily produced arms and munitions for the Continental Army. On May 10, the Board of War directed Lancaster's committee to furnish Colonel Thomas Marbray with between "twenty & thirty Hessian Prisoners" to supply the public with "One hundred Ton of Shot." Two weeks later, the board contracted another forty Hessians to cast "Cannon for the States." Nearly two dozen prisoners, mostly cannoniers in the Hessian artillery corps, worked for Colonel Peter Grubb, forging cannons for the cause at Lancaster County's Cornwall Iron Furnace.[43]

With the approach of summer, the demand for Hessian laborers increased, as local farmers sought additional hands to bring in their crops. Edward Burd wrote his father from Lancaster in late May to report that as "almost every Body" had Hessians for servants, he would try to send him "two clever fellows" to assist with the harvest. That same month, when the Hessian paymaster of the Knyphausen Regiment arrived in Lancaster on a pass with supplies for the captives, he was dismayed to discover that most had hired out on local farms. Outside of town, he came across Hessians on horseback who claimed they had their captors' permission to work for employers within a fifty-mile radius. As envisioned by Continental propagandists, in their travels through the interior, many of the Hessians labored on farms larger than any they had known in Europe.[44]

The German laborers' experiences varied widely, depending on their particular skills, employers, and tasks. Most worked for fellow Germans in Lancaster or in the other largely German-speaking townships of the Pennsylvania interior. Private Justus Heikenroad of the Knyphausen Regiment, for example, took employment with the Lancaster turner Peter Heilman. Joined in captivity by his wife and child and eager to supplement his wages, Private Johannes Goeritz hired out with Lebanon's Francis Zerman. The German residents of neighboring Heidelberg and Tulpenhocken secured the services of more than three dozen Hessians. But Pennsylvania's English speakers were frequently just as eager to make use of their German prisoners' labor. More than fifteen miles northwest of Lancaster in the town of Londonderry, Samuel Broadley, William Hunter, Jacob Cook, and Robert Jamison collectively hired five Hessians from the Knyphausen and Lossberg regiments.[45]

Some of the prisoners found employment among the very Americans they had faced in the field only months before. George Leber of the Rall Regiment worked alongside Lancaster's Henry Hock, who had only recently returned from service with Colonel Samuel Atlee's musketry battalion during the dismal campaign for New York. Having led a detachment of Washington's force at the Battle of Trenton, Brigadier General James Ewing of the Pennsylvania militia now employed several Hessians in Hellam, York County. To the east in Berks County, Mark Bird, a wealthy entrepreneur, committeeman, and lieutenant colonel in the state militia, applied for several dozen "Artificers and Labourers" to speed wartime production in his assorted mills, forges, and furnaces. During February 1777, Colonel Thomas Hartley sought to procure one of the members of the captured Hessian military band for his own regiment's "Band of Musick."[46]

Given the substantial bond required as security for the laborers, most employers hired only one captive to assist on their farm or in their workshop. As the demand for German laborers increased, however, more affluent Whigs hired them in batches. Lancaster's George Ross and Wilhelm Bausman each employed at least a half dozen of the prisoners. Shuffled between employers from different towns, a handful of the captives experienced unusual mobility. The Lossberg private Wilhelm Buchmeyer, for example, worked for Bethel Township's David Miller before eventually hiring out to William Young of neighboring Hanover. For Pennsylvania's insurgents, the sight of Hessians strolling through both town and countryside soon became almost commonplace. By contributing to the local economy and to the Continental war effort, the Hessian laborers provided valuable service to the state's revolutionary community.[47]

Our Prisoners and the Hessians

Although the employment of the Hessians relieved pressure on the borough and fostered refreshingly stable relations between the German captives and their local hosts, new troubles arose with the arrival of a fresh batch of British prisoners from Philadelphia. In mid-April 1777, as the capital was threatened anew by invasion, state authorities relocated the city's British prisoners to more secure sites in the interior. Holding fewer than forty British prisoners in March, Lancaster absorbed more than two hundred during the weeks to come. Continental officials apologized for burdening the town with additional captives, offering to have them "dispersed thro' the Country" should they prove "too troublesome." Preoccupied, however, with the continuing threat to Philadelphia, the authorities instead dispatched another hundred British prisoners to Lancaster in the months that followed. The unwelcome influx of the state's British prisoners stirred fresh anxieties and lingering antipathies. Within days of their arrival, Lancaster's provisioning agent complained that the British had "behav'd exceeding bad coming from Philadelphia" and by all accounts "Do behave Ill here." The Hessians, he was quick to add, "behave well." The Hessians' welcome cooperativeness, combined with their allies' stubborn defiance, deepened locals' distrust of their British captives.[48]

Taking no risks with their British prisoners, Lancaster officials kept the newcomers under close surveillance. To prevent the British from corrupting their German comrades, Lancaster's committee confined the new arrivals to the town jail or to a segregated wing of the barracks. Thus, while hundreds of Hessian captives roamed the county enjoying the privileges of hired laborers, the vast majority of Lancaster's British prisoners remained under strict confinement. Their contrasting treatment was scarcely lost on the resentful British, who aired their frustrations to local authorities. On May 3, for example, several British captives petitioned Lancaster's committee to inquire why, as prisoners of war, they were "Confin'd to gaol as Criminals." The disgruntled prisoners soon channeled their discontent in more alarming directions. On the night of May 16, over a dozen British captives escaped from the barracks, only to be retaken some fourteen miles from Lancaster. The American officer who returned the fugitives cautioned the committee to keep them under close guard, as they seemed "fully Bent in Making their Escape." Authorities had no sooner secured the offenders when another British prisoner escaped from Lancaster's jail.[49]

With most of the Hessians now dispersed throughout the interior to answer locals' insatiable demand for labor, they placed less strain on the barracks and remained less likely to harry the borough's inhabitants. Even the few hundred Hessians still confined within the barracks proved more manageable than their British comrades, who posed continuing dangers to Lancaster's Whigs. In early June, the British captives mounted their most serious challenge yet by staging an uprising in Lancaster's barracks. On June 4, the town's British prisoners dutifully celebrated King George's birthday. Asked to join in the celebrations, the Hessians politely declined. That evening, when the revelers grew overly boisterous, sentries abruptly intervened to halt the festivities, only to be disarmed by the enraged British. While the rioters threatened to breach the stockade, the Hessians remained peacefully secluded within their lodgings. To contain the uprising before it spilled into the streets, reinforcements hastily assembled and fired on the British, killing one prisoner and wounding three others, as the remaining rioters retreated to the safety of their quarters. Concluding that the British had orchestrated the rebellion to facilitate their escape, Lancaster's committee rounded up the suspected ringleaders, clapped them in jail, and slashed their rations. By refusing to join in the violence, the Hessians earned both the respect of their grateful American hosts and the resentment of their bemused British allies.[50]

Following the uprising, town major Christian Wirtz warned Pennsylvania's Council of Safety that the British captives now "threatened the destruction of Lancaster." Gravely alarmed by their British prisoners' "unruly & threatening conduct," townsfolk petitioned the Board of War for their immediate removal. The British "have been troublesome," William Atlee, chair of Lancaster's committee, complained, and as "we cannot avoid placing them in the Barracks among the Hessians," he reported, the town's residents remain "apprehensive they will debauch those people who have hitherto behaved pretty well." As locals anxiously awaited relief from state and Continental authorities, Lancaster's committee bolstered the prisoners' guard.[51]

Exasperated by their British captives' continued misbehavior, Continental authorities sympathized with residents' frustration. Only weeks before, the Board of War had complained of the British prisoners' persistently "flagrant & dangerous Abuses." While some fled from "Prison or from their Paroles," others spread "every Production tending to Disaffection." Elias Boudinot, the newly appointed Continental commissary general of prisoners, aired the Whigs' frustrations with their former imperial kindred when he admonished a notoriously troublesome pair of paroled British officers in midsummer. While "humanity to Prisoners of War has ever been the peculiar Characteristic of the american Army," he declared, Whig officials would no longer hesitate to "prevent the abuse of that Liberty, with which the Prisoners have been indulged." On July 17, the Board of War instructed local authorities to "watch the Conduct of all british Prisoners & punish every Delinquent by immediate Confinement," as nothing but a uniform "Determination to curb the Insolence of the Prisoners will keep them in any tolerable Order." Yet to Lancaster's dismay, Continental officials remained reluctant to relocate their British captives, with the town's barracks still the preferred site for their detention.[52]

Before summer's end, however, the movements of Howe's army prompted the emergency evacuation of both Lancaster's British and German captives. During early 1777, following the rebel forces' narrow escape from New York and unexpected triumphs in New Jersey, the British command formulated a bold but poorly executed strategy to subdue the American rebellion. During early summer, as General John Burgoyne led nine thousand troops south from Canada down the Lake Champlain–Hudson River corridor to Albany with the aim of strangling the New England resistance, Howe abruptly moved to capture Philadelphia so as to defuse the insurgency in the mid-Atlantic. Leaving over eight thousand men under General Henry Clinton in New York to rendezvous with the British force descending from Canada, Howe loaded another fifteen thousand on transports near the end of July and made for Pennsylvania via the Chesapeake Bay. During early August, with a large fleet shadowing the coast and the enemy's destination unknown, Continental officials speculated that Howe might have designs on Lancaster. Warning Atlee on August 11 that Howe may "make an Attempt to deliver the Prisoners with you," Boudinot ordered that both the British and Hessian captives be removed to safer locations upon the first intelligence of the enemy's advancing on the borough. Meanwhile, the Council of Safety instructed Lancaster authorities to double the prisoners' guard.[53]

Two weeks later, word arrived from Philadelphia that the British would soon land at the head of Chesapeake Bay, some thirty-five miles and only a few days' march from Lancaster. An alarmed Atlee promptly recalled most of the German prisoners in Whig employ for immediate evacuation with the town's public stores, excluding the laborers engaged in "distant publick useful Work." On August 24, nervous Lancaster residents watched their "English, Scotch and Irish prisoners, to the number of two hundred," march east for Reading "under a strong guard." During the several days that followed, Lancaster officials sent more than seven hundred Hessians north to neighboring Lebanon. By the end of August, the borough retained only a handful of Hessians and some forty to fifty British troops too ill to travel. Continental authorities began relocating all of Pennsylvania's British prisoners and more than three hundred of the Germans to Virginia through early September. Even after Howe's massive force invaded Pennsylvania en route to the capital, however, more than four hundred Hessian prisoners remained in the state's interior, where many continued to find employment in "Continental Work."[54]

Following the British occupation of Philadelphia on September 26, Continental officials placed new restrictions on the hiring out of their German captives to discourage laborers from fleeing to the enemy. During early October, the Board of War restricted employment to the prisoners engaged in military production. Local officials could release eligible German captives only to tradesmen who remained under contract with the American army and had sworn allegiance to Pennsylvania's new revolutionary regime. Deeming noncommissioned officers and married prisoners at greatest risk for escape, the board insisted that they remain confined.[55]

Despite these new restrictions, hiring of the Hessian prisoners proceeded apace. During December, William Atlee, now one of Pennsylvania's newly appointed deputy commissaries of prisoners, reported that all but about a hundred of the Hessians remained "out at work, some in the publick employ at different Works in York, Cumberland, Berks and this County & the residue in the same County's with Tradesmen & others." At least a dozen, for instance, remained employed in the mills, forges, or furnaces of the Berks County ironmaster Mark Bird. Whig officials proved considerably less indulgent of their British captives, approaching them as a continuing security risk. The Board of War ordered Atlee in early October immediately to forward to Virginia any British prisoners passing through Lancaster, "it not being thought prudent to detain them." As they filed through the borough, British prisoners now met with stinging barbs from their enraged hosts.[56]

One year after the Battle of Trenton, an unresolved tension continued to define Whigs' dealings with their German captives. As early as the summer of 1777, the Hessians had come to occupy a special status in the local imagination. During the preceding months, the Hessians had become a valued wartime resource and a decidedly more compliant set of prisoners than their more truculent British allies. Indeed, some of Lancaster's Whigs now drew a telling distinction between "our Prisoners (soldiers) & the Hessians." When William Atlee suddenly recalled the Hessian laborers prior to their late August evacuation, many of their local employers, sorry to part with such reliable hands, earnestly hoped for their return. Continental officials now trusted their German captives enough to amass some three hundred within eighty miles of British lines for the duration of Philadelphia's occupation. Through the winter following Howe's invasion, Lancaster's leading families hosted elaborate balls featuring the captured Hessian band.[57]

Yet for the jaded patriots who remained haunted by tales of the Hessians' depravity or had witnessed their violence firsthand, Congress's generous solicitations only confirmed the auxiliaries' sordid image as unscrupulous hirelings driven by greed. Months after the Germans' capture, an embittered Pennsylvania associator reminded his countrymen of the mercenaries' insatiable appetite for plunder, graphically recalling their march through New Jersey, where the invaders had ruthlessly fattened off American spoils and littered the depleted landscape with their foul "Hessian puddings." Unwilling to forgive their enemies for murdering and pillaging their patriot brethren, many of Lancaster County's militants spurned their German captives as faithless transients with no allegiance to cause or country. With thousands of Hessian reinforcements bracing Howe's invading army at the battles of Brandywine and Germantown, and through the long Philadelphia occupation, the fury of Pennsylvania's aggrieved only intensified. During late October 1777, vengeful patriots gleefully celebrated the Hessians' devastating losses at the Battle of Redbank. Yet even amid the revolutionaries' lingering hostility, their German captives found new friends.[58]

With Lancaster ultimately well suited for the detention of German prisoners, the efforts of Continental officials to curry favor with the Hessians yielded more promising results than their earlier, more ill-conceived experiment with the British. Congress's expectation that Lancaster's German speakers would embrace their captives as ethnic kindred at least entailed a reasonable leap of the imagination. Envisioned as foreigners by Congress, the Hessians arrived in Pennsylvania's diverse interior as less than wholly alien. Stripped of their menacing military apparatus, they proved more predictable and approachable to Pennsylvania's Germans than their more mercurial British allies. For all their peculiarities, the Hessians shared an unmistakable ethnic and linguistic connection with the state's German preachers, artisans, and farmers. For the Hessian prisoners—only recently uprooted from their homes in Europe to wage a war in an alien land with strange institutions, customs, and languages—friendly interactions with local German speakers offered comforting glimpses of continuity in an otherwise disorienting experience.

Lancaster's captives even found common ground with some of the county's English speakers, who had long since grown accustomed to their daily interactions with German neighbors. Whatever their prejudices, they admired the Germans' industry and avidly contracted Hessian laborers. For older and wealthier Whigs like James Burd, the hiring of Hessian captives resembled the earlier indenturing of German servants. Wandering the interior in the Americans' employ, the Hessians slowly merged with the familiar sights and sounds of Pennsylvania's diverse and bustling wartime communities. Local observers soon concluded that growing numbers of their German prisoners preferred American captivity to British campaigning. Thousands of miles from home, disaffected Hessians often found more in common with their assorted American hosts than with their more inscrutable British comrades.[59]

Similarly, for many of Pennsylvania's insurgents, the defeat of the Hessians at Trenton and their eager compliance in captivity rendered them less menacing as enemies and more appealing as potential converts. By behaving like model prisoners, the Germans earned the sympathy of their local hosts, who, at the urging of Continental propagandists, slowly came to reenvision their captives as ideological brethren in a shared struggle against Old World tyranny. To their American sympathizers, the Hessians' mauling at Redbank, like their earlier humbling at Trenton, underscored their sorry plight as the hapless minions of their British employers, cynically sacrificed in a foreign war. Even before Trenton, Pennsylvania's Pastor Mühlenberg lamented how the Hessians had been forced to prey "upon men of their own race and blood, for the crafty British would rather fill the graves with hired, foreign fascines than with their own native and lordly flesh." By late 1777, with hundreds of Hessians now laboring in the Continental interest, even the aggrieved patriots who remained overtly hostile to the captives preferred them to their more incorrigible British counterparts. As skilled and unskilled laborers, the German prisoners had ably assisted the American resistance. Through the contracting of employer and employed, both Whigs and Hessians came to value their adversaries, forging an opportunistic marriage of convenience at British expense. The Whigs' favorable dealings with their German captives helped erode the Hessians' reputation as depraved butchers while confirming that they were more tractable than their British allies. As the Hessians won trust, they compounded Whigs' distrust of the British.[60]

Pennsylvania's forced evacuation of some six hundred British and German prisoners to Winchester, Virginia, during Howe's invasion highlights the revolutionaries' contrasting experiences with their captives. Within two weeks of their departure, the prisoners and their escort of Pennsylvania associators arrived at the Virginia border, where they expected to rendezvous with a relief guard of local militia who would complete the journey to Winchester. When the Virginians failed to materialize, the agitated Pennsylvanians, anxious to protect their families from the British invaders, instructed their prisoners to proceed alone to Winchester and quickly turned for home. Suddenly deprived of their military escort a few days' march from their destination, the bemused prisoners pondered their options. Days later, stunned observers watched in amazement as the weary detachment filed into

Winchester. When the town's worried officials took a quick head count from the prisoners' accompanying muster lists, they discovered that many of the unguarded British captives had fled north for newly occupied Philadelphia. The roughly three hundred Hessians, by contrast, had arrived to a man. After confining their remaining British prisoners, Winchester's grateful Whigs granted the Hessians the freedom of their town. As one Hessian recalled, the locals approached their new German captives not as enemies but as "friends of the Americans" who would sooner remain in captivity than return to British service.[61]

But what of Continental officials' plans for their German captives after Howe's invasion of Pennsylvania? With thousands of American prisoners now rotting in the British jails and prison ships of New York, Washington and Congress earmarked the Hessians for eventual exchange. Officials hoped that their newly exchanged prisoners would then slowly undermine the British war machine from within by confirming the Americans' good intentions, sowing dissent among the German ranks, and inciting mass desertions. Despite the Hessians' compliance in captivity, however, relatively few contemplated deserting during the year after Trenton. Most preferred to remain with their units and await the end of hostilities in hopes of eventually returning home to Germany. Held captive for less than a year, many continued to feel like strangers in an alien land, still leery of their rebelling hosts.[62]

By late 1777, the war was far from won for either side. Though Howe's occupation of Philadelphia dealt a bitter blow to the American resistance, Burgoyne surrendered his trapped army at Saratoga just weeks later. The capture of Burgoyne's army deposited another two thousand German prisoners—both Brunswickers and Hessians—into American hands. Like the Hessians taken at Trenton nearly a year before, these prisoners would soon discover the prospering German communities and inviting range of opportunities on offer in the expansive American hinterland. The years ahead would determine how the auxiliaries would respond as the war stretched on, casualties rose, morale sank, and thousands more entered a long American captivity disillusioned with the British service and newly tempted by the Continentals' untiring solicitations.[63]

Both ideology and pragmatism governed the revolutionaries' relations with their German captives. Efforts to convert the Hessians squared with the Whigs' self-interest and flattered their self-image. By redeeming the hirelings from tyranny and vice, the Americans could deliver a blow to their true enemies, the British, and perhaps even turn the tide of war, while advancing the global cause of freedom. Less than a year after their victory at Trenton, the Whigs found that their efforts to seduce the Germans had yielded encouraging results. In Lancaster County, residents had forged surprisingly civil relations with their prisoners. Whigs had profited from the Hessians' labor, distanced them from their British allies, and exposed them to the promise of the young republic. Paradoxically, by employing their German captives, locals had effectively harnessed them to the patriot cause, co-opting them as potential allies in their crusade for revolutionary republicanism.

Within the diverse Pennsylvania hinterland, Britain's initial hiring and Americans' subsequent reinvention of the German auxiliaries challenged prevailing cultural assumptions, accentuated the rift with England, and solidified the ranks of militant Whigs. While cautiously embracing the Hessians, growing numbers of Lancaster's insurgents aggressively spurned the British, who continued to plague their community. By finding potential friends in their German prisoners and decided enemies in the British, local revolutionaries claimed common ground in their shared communal and Continental commitments. By late 1777, many of Lancaster's English- and German-speaking insurgents looked to promote their private interests while undermining their British enemies by folding their Hessian captives into their fledgling revolutionary community.

CHAPTER 5

"Enemies of Our Peace"

Captives, the Disaffected, and the Refinement of American Patriotism

Late summer 1777 found Lancaster's revolutionaries in a mounting state of distress. Sobered by two years of war, with prospects of military success bleak and the future of the cause in doubt, local Whigs had lost much of their initial enthusiasm. Independence and Pennsylvania's radical constitution had fueled long-simmering divisions between the community's militants and moderates. Recent military setbacks, meanwhile, had slowly eroded support for the cause, fostering war weariness, exacerbating internal tensions, and increasing the pressure on Pennsylvania's beleaguered revolutionary government. In 1775 and 1776, locals had watched the war unfold from afar. Now, to their horror, the enemy had brought the fight to Pennsylvania. Alarm rang through the community in August 1777 as Howe's army approached from the south and terrifying rumors warned of the invaders' imminent arrival in Lancaster. As local officials evacuated their public stores and all but a handful of their remaining British and Hessian prisoners, scores of frightened inhabitants hastily packed up their belongings and fled the borough. "We are beginning to feel the Calamities of War in our Country," lamented Jasper Yeates. "God grant they may be of short Continuance."[1]

British intentions became only too clear on September 26, when Howe marched his army into Philadelphia to occupy the capital. The British occupation posed special problems for Lancaster as a swarm of eastern refugees descended on the borough. The state government soon followed, shifting its operations to Lancaster and elevating the community's strategic importance. The flood of strangers placed new pressures on Lancaster, taxing the community's already strained resources. Adding to local concerns was the news that Washington, following his defeat at the Battle of Germantown on October 4, 1777, intended to concede Philadelphia to the enemy and take his army into winter quarters. Enraged by mounting reports of British depredations and fearful of the enemy's proximity, Lancaster's Whigs hoped that Washington would expel the invaders from the state and vigorously protested when American forces instead dug in at Valley Forge. Insulated by the American army, local Whigs were spared the trauma and indignities inflicted on their revolutionary brethren in the newly occupied territories to the east. But while Washington's encampment shielded Lancaster from attack, it failed to prevent British agents from infiltrating the county. During the Philadelphia occupation, the county was alternately set upon by a motley assortment of spies, counterfeiters, and horse thieves. Compounding the danger were internal enemies of the Revolution, Pennsylvania's disaffected, galvanized by Howe's invasion and hungry for reprisals.[2]

Emboldened by British success, Pennsylvania's loyalists seized the opportunity to assert their true allegiance and defy their adversaries, to the fury of local Whigs. Months after the British invasion, Christopher Marshall, a radical Philadelphia Whig newly arrived in Lancaster, expressed his wish that the "Enemies of our peace the private as well as publick . . . may be soon remov'd from our borders." To the Whigs' relief, the British complied in June 1778, evacuating Philadelphia and retiring to New York City. Fearing patriot reprisals, over three thousand of Pennsylvania's disaffected fled with the British Army, many never to return. Countless others, however, chose to remain and risk the wrath of their militant neighbors, pinning their hopes on an eventual British victory. Some of the loyalists who remained behind presented an ongoing challenge to the state's revolutionaries through their determined support of the enemy. In the years ahead, as Pennsylvania's Whigs negotiated a myriad of military and economic crises and revolutionary enthusiasm waxed and waned, loyalists derided the cause, collaborated with the British, and obstinately spurned the republican regime.[3]

In Lancaster County, loyalists posed particular problems through their subversive associations with the borough's fluid and expansive prisoner population, occasionally even facilitating their allies' escape. By 1778, Lancaster had housed some two thousand British and Hessian prisoners, with thousands more to follow during the ensuing hostilities. Thus, long after Howe's withdrawal from the province, the war grimly cast its shadow over Lancaster.

Wherever the principal theater of military operations, the steady influx of captives kept the enemy dangerously close at hand, feeding seething wartime divisions. Between 1777 and 1781, the prisoners' volatility, fears of Tory collaboration, and the lingering specter of British invasion heightened local anxiety, aggravating tensions between captors and captives, rebels and loyalists, and reinforcing residents' deep-seated preoccupation with internal security. The revolutionaries' peculiar vulnerability left them increasingly conscious of their shared stake in a broader common struggle, nurturing tenuous ties to cause and country. In venerating friends and repudiating enemies, in celebrating military victories and commemorating American nationhood, Lancaster's militants vented an aggressive patriotism that coexisted uneasily with their stubbornly persistent parochialism.[4]

Alarm and Uneasiness

A year after the Whigs' formal declaration of independence, Pennsylvania's revolutionary resistance remained plagued by flagging commitments and fractious infighting, with thousands resentful of the state's emerging radical government and the continuing costs of war. Amidst these troubles, late 1777 found many of Lancaster's Whigs enrolled in the provincial or Continental service. During March 1777, the state assembly passed a Militia Act mandating compulsory military service for all able-bodied white men between the ages of eighteen and fifty-three under a rotation system. The act imposed a stiff fine for neglect of duty but provided the option of furnishing a substitute. Faced with compelling personal interests, an ever volatile frontier, an undetermined number of loyalists, and the continuous arrival of hundreds of resentful and unpredictable captives, most locals preferred to remain close to home, choosing short stints in the provincial militia over lengthy tours in the Continental Army.[5]

When summoned for distant service, the county's militiamen often proved reluctant to march, to the growing frustration of civil and military authorities. With many farmers in the ranks, the county's militia proved especially unreliable during the hinterland's seasonal summer harvest. Occasionally, local troops refused to march until they were compensated for prior service. Often inadequately supplied and short of arms, locals frequently complained that they were too poorly equipped to face their enemies. Even as the British closed in on the province during late summer 1777, Colonel Bartram Galbraith, the newly appointed Lancaster County lieutenant tasked with forwarding the militia, continued to run up against the "obstinacy of the Inhabitants." As Howe's objectives remained uncertain, many militiamen hesitated to abandon their communities and march eastward at the risk of their families and property. The shifting of military operations to more distant theaters following the British evacuation of June 1778 only reinforced the reluctance of troops to serve beyond their immediate locale.[6]

Howe's arrival in late 1777 also found locals at odds over the newly implemented loyalty oath to the radical state government. Between 1777 and 1779, Pennsylvania's assembly passed several Test Acts requiring adult white males to abjure the king and subscribe an oath of allegiance or affirmation to the state. Designed to enhance state security by proscribing and punishing the disaffected, the first Test Act passed in June 1777. Effectively forfeiting their civil rights, residents who declined the oath could no longer vote, hold office, or serve on juries. Those who refused to comply also risked an indefinite period of detention without bond. From Lancaster, the radical John Hubley predicted a "loud cry against this Tiranical Oath, that it was intended for naught, but to hinder substantial good disposed People to ellect or be ellected, depriving them of the Rights of Freemen." When the borough's militants organized a "Civil Society" during the summer to enforce compliance with the act, their moderate rivals urged defiance. Reluctant to legitimize and forever bind themselves to a radical frame of government that they earnestly hoped to reform, moderates forecast that the compulsory oath would merely aggravate provincial divisions. Radicals, in turn, embraced the Test Act as a convenient means for identifying and censuring their internal enemies. Soon exacerbating local political divisions was the unanticipated influx of eastern moderates and radicals freshly displaced by the British occupation.[7]

In the wake of Howe's invasion and the flood of strangers from the east, Lancaster's militants vigorously enforced the act by jailing visitors who refused to comply. A worried Jasper Yeates reported in early September 1777 that newcomers "who have not taken the Oath, are clapped up immediately, if they refuse swearing. Short work with the Dissenters!" Similarly, a newly arrived Philadelphia Whig cautioned his children, "It will not be safe for any of you to come here" unless "you can produce a certyficate of your having taken the Test." Dismayed by the state's punitive measures and arbitrary policing, the moderate Edward Burd expressed alarm that "upon bare suspicion, for no Crimes even supposed to be committed, & for not taking an Oath," a "man is to lose his Liberty & his Estate & be treated as an Alien & an Enemy by the executive part of Government." If "so little Regard is paid to the Laws," Burd cynically mused, "perhaps I might be apprehended on suspicion & confined in Gaol If I travel to Lancaster this winter." Conversely, hard-liners like the fiery Christopher Marshall urged prompt compliance, counseling his conservative-leaning sons to endorse "our common cause" and declare themselves "subjects and faithfull friends to the Independant States of America." For by refusing, he warned, "you and your familys will be intirely ruined." Coolly calculating the costs of defiance, many of Lancaster's moderates reluctantly obliged.[8]

Militants' uncompromising enforcement of the state's new Test Act exacerbated their already tumultuous relations with the county's pacifist sectarian minority, who opposed the oath on moral and religious grounds. The troubles between the Whigs and the pacifists began brewing as early as spring 1775, when the county's insurgents started mobilizing men and matériel for their armed resistance and the sectarians determinedly withheld their military and financial support. Tensions increased when the radicals began consolidating their political power by circumscribing their domestic opposition. Although the sectarians' resistance arose less from a heartfelt attachment to Great Britain than from a principled objection to war and revolution, Pennsylvania's militants had little tolerance for neutrals. To the minds of the most radical insurgents, one was either a friend or an enemy of the Revolution. From Lebanon in June 1778, an anguished Moravian reported that the county's militants "are greatly enraged at those who will not take the oath." While some sectarians reluctantly complied with the radicals' demands, others continued to resist. Classified as non-jurors, the pacifists paid for their resistance, suffering stiff fines, forfeiture of property, disfranchisement, and occasionally imprisonment. Although the assembly softened the penalties for non-jurors by late 1778, suspicion and animosity lingered throughout Lancaster County. By defying the wartime resistance, the pacifists posed continuing problems for Lancaster's Whigs. Because the sectarians preferred to maintain their neutrality, however, relatively few endangered the cause.[9]

Far more worrisome to Whigs were the Tories who openly endorsed Great Britain and actively opposed the Revolution. A diverse lot, Pennsylvania's loyalists represented a range of ethnicities, religions, and occupations, including English and German speakers, church members and sectarians, merchants and professionals, tradesmen and yeomen. Many loyalists maintained a deep and abiding attachment to their mother country, dismissing the resistance movement as a treasonous challenge to lawful authority. Others shared the Whigs' opposition to imperial policy but stopped short of supporting independence, preferring to reclaim their privileges within the empire and reconcile with Britain. By mid-1776, the ranks of the disaffected also included onetime Whigs who abhorred the radicalizing and democratizing impulses of the Revolution and the breakdown of law and order. Alienated by angry mobs and coercive committees that endangered life and liberty, they branded revolutionary leaders tyrants and usurpers who manipulated the passions of the ignorant masses for their own selfish ends. Following the Whigs' declaration of independence, some loyalists chose to flee the state, seeking an early refuge with the British. The number who chose to stay in Pennsylvania remains impossible to determine. Fearful of rebel persecution, most opted for discretion and preserved their anonymity by avoiding open declarations of allegiance. A minority, however, stood more determined in its opposition and actively worked to undermine the state's new revolutionary regime.[10]

Through 1775 and 1776, as Whigs extended their control over the province and stifled internal dissent, loyalists found themselves increasingly marginalized. Once the stakes increased with their formal declaration of independence, the revolutionaries considered Tories an especially insidious foe, a fifth column in league with the enemy. Throughout the hostilities, loyalists suffered informal harassment and persecution. In late 1776, Lancaster's longtime Anglican minister Thomas Barton reluctantly shut the doors of St. James Church. Barton had incited the "fury of the populace" by refusing to dispense with the liturgical rituals for the king and royal family. The dispirited minister informed his London superiors that Anglican clergymen "who dared to act upon proper principles" now found themselves "obliged to flee for their lives, driven from their habitations & families, laid under arrest & imprisoned!" For his own safety, Barton remained carefully secluded behind closed doors. During the early months of the war, in the absence of formal courts, newly empowered militants eagerly hauled suspected loyalists before their extralegal committees to answer for alleged transgressions. After suffering a rebuke from Lancaster's committee for damning the Congress, the Quaker Elijah Wickersham railed against his partisan neighbors who, he said, "have so industriously & with so much cruelty endeavored to ruin me" from the "most rancorous and implacable motives, and cloaked by the specious name of *Liberty* and the *publick* cause." Wickersham shared many Quakers' disdain for the vengeful rabble who vented their long-simmering resentments against the province's peaceful sectarians.[11]

With every major revolutionary setback, Pennsylvania's Tories assumed greater menace. During early 1777, with the British in close proximity, known and suspected loyalists came under intense scrutiny, facing new punishments and restrictions. The perception of dangers at home drew some militants into revolutionary service. George Simmers, for instance, enlisted in the Lancaster County militia with the professed intention of "keeping down the Tories." Fears escalated after the British occupation of Philadelphia, when thousands of loyalists rallied round the invaders. The occupation revitalized Pennsylvania loyalists, who embraced Howe's arrival as an invitation to chastise their Whig oppressors. To encourage his provincial supporters, Howe extended military protection to the disaffected on October 11, 1777, bringing thousands into the capital. Lancaster's Isaac Gray, for example, fled to British lines after "suffering much from the tyranny of the rebels." Under the protection of Howe's army, loyalists avenged earlier abuses by retaliating against their Whig adversaries. On March 18, 1778, six months into the British occupation, the *Pennsylvania Evening Post* announced that friends of the crown had begun forming loyalist units "to have satisfaction for the unprovoked injuries and cruelties they have sustained." Ultimately, some fourteen hundred loyalists joined volunteer companies during Howe's nine-month sojourn in the capital.[12]

Only days after Philadelphia fell to the British, Lancaster received distressing reports of Tory abuses to the east. On October 4, Christopher Marshall learned that some four to five hundred Tories had recently paraded through the capital, "taking, securing and sending to prison" all whom they considered "friends to the Free States of America." Months later, news continued to arrive telling of the "inhuman behavior of the Tory crew in that City." Marshall and other eastern refugees routinely bemoaned the plight of their poor friends and relations who went without "fuel and other necessaries, while our internal enemies, under the protection of that savage monster Howe, are revelling in luxury, dissipation and drunkenness, without any feelings for the distress of their (once happy) bleeding country."[13]

Newly emboldened in the east, loyalists were soon terrorizing the far north and west by allying with hostile Indians. Eventually situated between British-occupied Philadelphia and their dangerously unstable frontier, Lancaster County's revolutionaries straddled a knife's edge. From as early as January 1776, local Whigs had been haunted by reports of loyalists' soliciting Indian aid. Residents radiated "alarm and uneasiness" in late summer 1776 because of the "Tories and Indians, who are threatening an invasion upon the land." A year later, amid fears of British operations to the east, Lancaster's Whigs learned of loyalist and Indian depredations beyond the northern Pennsylvania border. As the British prepared to invade the province, rumors circulated of the Indians' "breaking in on the frontiers." Within months came disturbing reports from the west of Tories "joining the Savages in murdering and scalping their neighbours." As the violence escalated, Lancaster's anxious residents anticipated the inevitable trains of desperate refugees who would flock to the county for safe haven like their terrified frontier predecessors decades before. The revolutionaries grossly exaggerated their tales of Tories' frontier atrocities, embellishing the raiders' brutality. To the minds of Whigs, by allying with the Indians, these "white savages" had ventured beyond mere political transgression to outright betrayal of their race. Such treachery placed the loyalists beyond the fringe of civilized society, encouraging Pennsylvania's revolutionaries to purge them physically from their communities and ideologically from the emerging American nation.[14]

Aggravating matters for Lancaster's Whigs, their authority at home was now being brazenly challenged by the disaffected. Newly confident of British victory, some loyalists openly defamed the revolutionaries while publicly affirming their allegiance to Great Britain. In late August 1777, in anticipation of Howe's invasion, James Webb, a Lancaster Quaker and former assemblyman, declared Pennsylvania's Whig representatives illegitimate, boldly proclaiming that "they were voted in by a parcel of soldiery and apprentice boys" and that "their laws were not worth regarding." Some loyalists urged locals to enlist in the British service, while others took a more active role in undermining the resistance by engaging in traitorous correspondence or criminal trafficking with the enemy. In November 1777, one suspected loyalist found himself under lock and key for allegedly conspiring with the British to betray the "United States into their hands." Following Howe's invasion, a handful of Tories created particular problems by violently resisting the state's new revolutionary regime.[15]

In September 1777, Whigs seized a county resident, Daniel Shelley, for plotting to destroy the public stores and magazines at York, Carlisle, and Lancaster. Shelley had run afoul of local authorities the year before after attempting to raise loyalist reinforcements for the British Army and taunting his neighbors by claiming that the "King was only playing with them now, and correcting them as he would his child." This left county residents no less stunned by his latest betrayal. While acknowledging that Shelley was a "great Tory," Edward Burd was amazed that "he could be guilty of so villainous a Design." Locals' fears intensified when Shelley implicated numerous York County co-conspirators. The conspiracy came as a chilling reminder that Whigs remained at the mercy of hidden assailants bent on their destruction. After exposing the plot, Pennsylvania's Supreme Executive Council heightened internal security, promising to apprehend these "villains who have been scheming the public ruin" and posting guards throughout Lancaster to identify and secure potential enemies. Increasingly menacing and anonymous, the county's disaffected now posed a threat disproportionate to their limited numbers.[16]

In the years preceding and following the nine-month Philadelphia occupation, however, loyalists raised the most serious alarms through their troubling associations with Lancaster's British prisoners. By mid-1776, local Whigs had become increasingly conscious of the need to avert potential conspiracies by restricting their prisoners' interactions with the disaffected. This proved especially difficult after 1777, when British captives arrived in growing numbers, filling Lancaster's jail and barracks, and local authorities encountered problems mounting an adequate guard. As the number of disaffected grew and the town's militia answered calls for service outside the borough, the balance of allegiance shifted precariously, and internal enemies loomed even larger in the local imagination. Whigs' suspicions increased when they detected a dramatic rise in escapes. Documenting nearly a dozen escapes involving some 130 prisoners between 1778 and 1781, residents soon concluded that the fugitives were receiving welcome assistance from the disaffected.[17]

As early as midsummer 1776, two locals were jailed on suspicion of aiding the flight of several of the county's paroled British officers. Nearly a year later, a neighboring official warned Lancaster's committee to reinforce the prisoners' guard, as they could now count on "friends in the country" to assist their escape. Borough residents Michael Immel and Caleb Johnson suffered imprisonment in October 1777 for allegedly helping a pair of prisoners escape from the town jail. After a party of sixteen prisoners fled during August 1780, William Atlee worried that they would "find such harbour & assistance among the disaffected that they will get off." Several months later, county authorities arrested John Thompson for urging his neighbors to help liberate Lancaster's prisoners. Feeding Whigs' anxiety was the relentless influx of enemy captives. During the Philadelphia occupation, scores of prisoners were streaming into Lancaster at the precise moment when escapes were most tempting because of the proximity of British lines. As local authorities struggled to maintain a reliable guard, more and more of their prisoners took flight. As late as August 1781, Atlee reiterated the importance of "keeping in order a set of artful fellows" who exploited every opportunity to straggle "into the Country & with the assistance of the disaffected make their escape."[18]

The British prisoners' threatening machinations with their new local emissaries inflamed wartime enmities and hardened battle lines within the borough. Increasingly, militants feared that the prisoners and the disaffected had struck up a dangerous alliance that imperiled their community. In March 1781, with men and arms in short supply and with chilling rumors circulating, alluding to a fresh loyalist plot to blow up Lancaster's magazine, locals petitioned Pennsylvania's Supreme Executive Council for a guard for the town's public stores and munitions. "The number of disaffected (which is too notorious) in this Country, and the many strangers who daily pass thro' this place," reasoned Lancaster County's Lieutenant Adam Hubley Jr., "makes it absolutely necessary for the security of the publick property." Nor was the danger purely imagined. Exploiting the borough's lax security, Lancaster's approximately eight hundred British prisoners grew increasingly bold.[19]

In May, a British prisoner of the Seventy-first Regiment informed borough officials that his associates in the barracks were busy hatching an insurrection with the aid of an unidentified loyalist. The informant confided that the prisoners intended to take their hosts by surprise by tunneling "from one of the cellars under the barrack yard and stockades, about 100 yards," to emerge from the graveyard. They then planned to "seize the magazine" which they assumed contained "a large quantity of ammunition and firelocks." There they would arm themselves, rendezvous with a "strong party of tories, set fire to the town, and so proceed to form a junction with the English army." As Hubley later explained to state officials, the conspirators aimed to "fight their way thro' the Country and effect their escape." Instead, local authorities collared the conspirators, "marched them down to the jail and put them in close confinement." Seizing upon the foiled conspiracy to plead for a reinforced supply of arms, Hubley warned that should the prisoners ever successfully breach the stockade, their poorly equipped guards "would not be able to stop them." Moreover, he cautioned, the "well disposed Inhabitants who would be willing to lend their aid & assistance *for want of arms*" could "only be idle spectators and perhaps see their own & neighbours' property destroyed without being able to give the least opposition." Weeks later, Whigs averted another potential rebellion when they caught the prisoners attempting to undermine the stockade. Affairs soon approached a graver crisis following the arrival of several hundred of the British captives taken more than three years before at the Battle of Saratoga in fall 1777. These latest arrivals raised the number of Lancaster's prisoners to the unprecedented high of some fifteen hundred.[20]

Events came to a head during late summer, when internal and external threats converged. Whigs had long feared that loyalists would seize the opportunity to arm and assist their captives in the event of a successful incursion by British troops. In early August, locals learned that a large British force was approaching via the Chesapeake Bay with the potential aim of freeing Lancaster's captives. The Supreme Executive Council advised local officials to ready four battalions of the county militia to march against the advancing enemy and to prepare to evacuate their prisoners and public stores to safer locales. After posting a chain of sentries to the south to monitor the enemy's movements, a frantic Hubley implored the council for reinforcements, hinting that the inadequately supplied militia were now threatening to flee. Hubley grimly predicted that should the British march on Lancaster, they "must carry their point, as our opposition could be but faint, owing to the want of Arms." Although the feared incursion never materialized, Lancaster's alarmed residents soon petitioned state authorities to relocate their newly arrived prisoners, insisting that "there are too many disaffected Persons in the vicinity of this Borough who would count it meritorious to be instrumental in their Escape." State officials obligingly transferred the Saratoga captives to York. To keep Lancaster's disaffected residents and seven hundred remaining prisoners at bay, they secured the services of a seasoned Continental regiment as guards, thereby increasing locals' daily interactions with their visiting Continental brethren.[21]

A Notorious and Avowed Enemy

As Lancaster's hard-liners struggled to police their community, executing their politics at musket point, dissenters became increasingly excluded from the state's emerging political order. The Revolution politicized local identities, rupturing the community and splitting patriots and loyalists into mutually antagonistic camps. Loyalists routinely incurred the wrath of their fiercely partisan neighbors, with divided allegiances even fracturing families. After his father-in-law joined the British during the Philadelphia occupation, Albert Helfenstein, the pastor of Lancaster's German Reformed congregation, denounced him for "assisting the Enemys of his Country, in their unjust attempt to enslave it," and petitioned for a portion of his estate. Confronted with the state's demand that he take the oath of allegiance and abjure loyalty to the king, the Reverend Thomas Barton finally deserted his Lancaster congregation, obtaining the Supreme Executive Council's permission in 1778 to depart for British-occupied New York City. For years Barton had endured the unrelenting abuse of local Whigs. He assured his London superiors, "Altho' I used every prudent step to give no offense even to those who usurped authority & Rule & exercised the severest Tyranny over us, yet my life and property have been threatened upon mere suspicion of being unfriendly to what is called the American cause." Though joined by his wife, Barton left over half a dozen of his children in Pennsylvania. Barred from ever returning, he died in 1780, shortly before his scheduled departure for England.[22]

Initially targeted by extralegal committees, loyalists eventually faced prosecution in the courts and formal civil sanctions as revolutionaries brought the weight of the law down upon their adversaries. Serious offenders risked prosecution under the state's new treason laws or bills of attainder. As early as October 1775, Congress empowered provincial assemblies and committees of safety to seize and imprison residents who threatened the security of the colonies or the "liberties of America." In September 1776, the Pennsylvania convention enacted an ordinance establishing new penalties for high treason. Residents convicted of aiding the enemy or of waging war against the state would now suffer forfeiture and imprisonment. During early 1777, the state's radicals began to take a harder line with their domestic enemies, implementing a stricter treason law that increased the number of offenses constituting high treason and instituted the death penalty for offenders. On March 6, 1778, the assembly passed a confiscation bill authorizing the seizure and sale of the personal property of residents attainted of high treason for taking refuge with the newly occupying British Army. A month later, militants made their intentions plain, commencing the state's spring court session to the "great terror of the disaffected, and the comfort and security of the good people thereof."[23]

New treason laws brought severe consequences for many loyalists and their families. The former Lancaster committeeman Christian Voght left his wife to join the British during their Philadelphia occupation upon growing disillusioned with the cause. After seeing her attainted husband's property seized and sold at public auction, Mrs. Voght found herself "reduced to great Poverty and Distress," having "no Relation or Friend capable of affording her the least assistance." Michael Witman, another onetime committee member, was similarly attainted after fleeing to the enemy, to the shame of his "distressed family." The Lancaster radical John Hubley later secured a sizable portion of his forfeited estate. Convicted of sedition in 1780 for defending the British and maligning the cause, Peter Gotshalk and George Weidell lost half their estates and suffered incarceration for the duration of the war. In 1781, at least three others answered charges of endorsing the enemy and advocating enlistment in the British Army, suffering imprisonment and fines ranging from £250 to £750.[24]

Whigs bore a special animus toward the loyalists who aided enemy captives. After several paroled British officers escaped while boarding at his Lebanon residence, the suspected loyalist Matthew McHugh received threats from his vengeful neighbors, prompting the intervention of Lancaster officials, who decried the dispensing of vigilante justice. Accused of assisting the fugitives, McHugh soon faced criminal charges. Boldly baiting local authorities following his arrest, McHugh sinisterly intimated that he expected Howe's arrival shortly, whereupon his accusers would be jailed in his stead. "The Eyes of all Persons in this part of the Country," observed one local committeeman, "watch over the Proceedings relative to Such a Notorious & avowed Enemy to the Liberties of America." Similarly accused of aiding the fugitives, John White was clapped in irons and thrown into Lancaster's jail, where he languished for over a year. Imprisoned in 1782 on suspicion of facilitating a rash of escapes, the Lancaster resident John Maguire "experienced a variety of Losses & Misfortunes . . . almost to the Ruin of himself & Family."[25]

The British captives sympathized with their allies. The paroled officer Thomas Hughes remarked in September 1777, "I cannot help lamenting the deplorable situation of the Loyalists, who because they will not violate their oath of allegiance, by taking the test tendered them by their upstart rulers, are turn'd out of their houses, their estates sold, and themselves and families reduced (some from affluent and all from easy circumstances) to beggary and want," sourly concluding, "Such is the Land of Liberty." Similarly, after traveling through Lancaster with Burgoyne's captured army in December 1778, Lieutenant Thomas Anburey avowed, "The Loyalists of Pennsylvania are greatly to be pitied, for they have been much persecuted." Even the occasional German captive bemoaned the "harsh treatment" endured by the loyalists.[26]

Despite the manifold risks, some loyalists persistently defied their Whig neighbors. A successful craftsman and former town burgess, the Quaker Caleb Cope had once enjoyed the respect and patronage of his community. After the declaration of independence, however, Cope made no secret of his political leanings and routinely welcomed paroled enemy officers into his home. During early 1776, the Quaker hosted the young Lieutenant John André "on the most intimate & familiar footing." André then maintained an active correspondence with the family between his relocation to Carlisle and subsequent exchange. From his doorstep, Cope joined his British guests in taunting passing Whigs, drawing the ire of Lancaster's militant patriots. Quick to circulate news of British victories, he was eventually censured by local authorities for "raising reports prejudicial to the United States." Unlike several of his fellow Quakers, Cope remained in Lancaster throughout the war, never escaping the shadow of revolution. Cope's casual defiance put him at odds with the town's Whigs, marking him as an enemy of their revolutionary fold.[27]

By identifying and marginalizing their internal enemies, Lancaster's revolutionaries enforced the boundaries of a properly patriotic community and refined their evolving American identity. As the community's hard-liners closed ranks, even committed Whigs learned to shun informal associations with their captives, lest they invite the suspicion and fury of their overzealous neighbors. In May 1779, after failing to procure lodging in Lancaster, a disgruntled Thomas Hughes complained: "The inhabitants say they are afraid to take in British officers, as they shall be accounted Tories. A blessed state of liberty, where people cannot do what they please with their own houses." With the costs of conspiracy climbing, most loyalists wisely chose to avoid or conceal dealings with the prisoners, rendering it more difficult for Whigs to flush out potential enemies.[28]

Menaced internally and externally by Tories, captives, and the British Army, Lancaster's Whigs remained plagued by insecurity. Locals' fears intensified when they suffered military setbacks. Given Lancaster's precarious status as a detention center for prisoners, military reversals could expose Whigs to their enemies, inviting potential subversion from within or incursion from without. After 1776, the war's mounting uncertainties sorely tested the residents' patriotic commitments, sapping morale and aggravating tensions with provincial and Continental authorities. Faced with the very real prospect of failure, disheartened Whigs feared for their safety and wavered in their support. Paradoxically, however, Lancaster's insecurity simultaneously fed broader ties and sensibilities among local militants, even as they policed dangers at home. The revolutionaries' nagging vulnerability left them especially invested in military victory and the success of the resistance. Locals coped with their uncertainty by taking heart in victories both large and small and by clinging to the hope that they could vanquish their enemies and seal their independence. Military and diplomatic triumphs, patriotic celebrations of landmark events, and a growing realization that they were launched in a historic struggle with their Continental compatriots eased residents' misgivings, restored faith in the cause, and nurtured emotional bonds with America's larger revolutionary community.

Friends and Neighbors throughout the Continent

Even for the civilians who stood shielded from the hostilities, the war came obligingly and unrelentingly to Lancaster. Local Whigs paid keen attention to the war's progress, following events from afar via newspapers and correspondence and assembling in inns and taverns to discuss the latest military and diplomatic developments. Military setbacks, which proved a recurrent theme through the war's early years, sowed anxiety and despair. As Howe's army pushed into Pennsylvania during early September 1777, Edward Burd bemoaned the times "when a Day may bring Ruin & Destruction to any of us." Three months later, with Philadelphia "in the hands of cruel taskmasters, the country around ravaged, stripped, and destroyed," and "houses, barns, &c., burnt and levelled with the ground," another Lancaster Whig somberly concluded, "Our affairs wear a very gloomy aspect." In late 1779, a British captive observed that his hosts seemed "heartily tired of this war—even those who a few months ago hated the name of an Englishman now openly court our friendship and tell us they wish a reconciliation could take place." But, he quickly added, "this turn of affairs is not owing to any latent friendship for Great Britain—for the rebels in general have not the least spark of gratitude." Rather, bad news "affects their coward hearts, and they fawn like beaten spaniels." Conversely, at the "receipt of good news their insolence is insufferable." Word of military triumphs imbued Lancaster's war-weary Whigs with renewed hopes for success. Emboldened by victory, they exuded a defiant patriotism.[29]

Predictably, Whigs' accounts of military actions underlined both British villainy and American gallantry to bolster support for the cause. Even in the wake of military defeats, during the darkest hours of the war, despairing residents found reason for muted optimism in defiant reports from the front. In September 1776, days after the slaughter at Long Island, a local volunteer proclaimed: "We are now strong and determined to sacrifice our lives before we'll submit to the villians. . . . I expect we'll all return to Pennsylvania crown'd with victory." Encouraging missives arrived from officers impressed by their new recruits' courage under fire as they weathered the trials of close combat. Following the Continentals' frustrating loss at Brandywine in late summer 1777, the York County colonel Thomas Hartley informed friends in Lancaster that but for bad luck, the British "would have been defeated in every quarter." Though granting "they are kind enough to say the Rebels behaved well," Hartley pledged, "We will let them know upon a proper occasion that the American Bravery is equal to that of Britain."[30]

Lieutenant Colonel Adam Hubley of the Tenth Pennsylvania Regiment echoed his comrade's enthusiasm, reassuring worried friends and family in Lancaster that American forces were "in fine spirits and panting to have at the Enemy again, Confident of their abilities in giving them a total defeat." Days later, as thousands of enemy troops descended triumphantly on the capital, Hubley boldly prophesied, "depend on it, Howes ruin is working fast." Late in the war, Whig officials still saw military setbacks as opportunities to galvanize the resistance. In June 1780, after the fall of Charleston, Congressman Thomas McKean assured William Atlee that the defeat "may be all for the best," as "nothing but this, or something as striking, would draw off the general attention to the accumulation of property, and fix it upon the general cause."[31]

Over the course of the hostilities, as Whigs achieved greater success in the field and reports grew more encouraging, locals reveled in their prospects. Heartened by General Burgoyne's troubles in New York during early

October 1777, Hubley ventured to state that "Providence seems to begin to smile on our Army, and thro his assistance I hope shortly to congratulate those people worthy of freedom on their happy delivery." Following the Whigs' victory at Stony Point, New York, in mid-1779, a brooding British captive derided his hosts' supercilious rejoicing: "This success as usual has rais'd their spirits and they say it's folly for Britain to attempt a war with America." Locals also welcomed news of increasing enemy desertions as evidence that their opponents were tiring of the fight. During the fall of 1777, Hubley sent word that the "Enemy desert in great numbers & come over to us thirty & forty at a time." That same fall, a local celebrated the Continentals' encouraging inroads against the natives. "The Indians to the Northward are intirely humbled by their most unpresidented losses," he noted, with many coming "over from the Enemy Lines." Two years later, Captain John Steele of the Tenth Pennsylvania Regiment informed his Lancaster family, "Yesterday a captain from the British army deserted to us." Although "he is, beyond a doubt, a damn'd rascal," Steele surmised, "it all conspires to make glorious the once dreaded (though now ignominious) arms of Britain." These incoming reports soon mirrored developments at home, where growing numbers of the Whigs' British and German prisoners, having spent months or even years in American captivity, were now choosing to quit their ranks.[32]

By repudiating the opposition, Whigs continued to reinvent themselves. Following their declaration of independence, avid patriots like the recently transplanted Christopher Marshall eagerly distinguished between "our people," citizens of the "rising States of America," and "our enemies, the English." A longtime resident of Philadelphia, Marshall relocated to Lancaster shortly before the British occupation and quickly became a valued member of the local Whig community. Throughout the conflict, Marshall vilified his enemies as "Cruel Monsters in Human Shape," a "band of banditti worse than savages," unleashed on American soil to "steal, kill, and murder." Ruing how "good & faithful Subjects" were suddenly branded with the "Name of Rebels" and "hunted from place to place by English . . . Scotch, Dutch & Savage Nations," Marshall demanded that virtuous freemen purge the "Cursed Motley Crew" from the "Land of liberty."[33]

The revolutionaries' stubborn resilience sprang in part from the support of distant friends and allies, foreign and domestic. News of military developments enabled locals to roam imaginatively beyond the narrow confines of their community and identify with the anonymous members of a broader revolutionary fold. While distinguishing among the New Englanders, Virginians, and Jersey men who, along with Pennsylvanians, fought and bled for their cause, Lancaster's revolutionaries now included them within a unified American community. A popular Continental sermon published in Lancaster in early 1778 attributed the American victory at Saratoga to the "happy union" prevailing among the "troops of the different states" and the "internal animosities and discord" of the "German and British troops." Rejoicing in the "good effects of that perfect harmony" stemming from "courage, friendship, and the united love of our country," the reverend counseled, "Let us cultivate it more and more." In a 1779 Fourth of July toast, Lancaster's Whigs honored the "Memory of the Officers and Soldiers who have fallen in defense of America." Through the sacrifices of their revolutionary brethren, many residents became increasingly conscious of their own role in a shared Continental endeavor. Accounts of battles in neighboring states fostered similar feelings of common suffering and sacrifice. During difficult times, locals empathized with "our afflicted Friends and Neighbours through out the Continent."[34]

A member of one of Lancaster's most prominent German-speaking families, Adam Hubley was sufficiently anglicized to pass for a British officer after falling into enemy hands during the chaotic Battle of Paoli in mid-September 1777. Seized by a group of British soldiers amidst the confused panic of the surprise evening assault, the crafty Hubley "damned them for a parcel of scoundrels" and demanded "what they meant by taking one of their own Officers." His mortified captors promptly released him, enabling him to make a narrow escape to his own hastily re-forming ranks. As a respected officer in the Pennsylvania line, Hubley became an eloquent defender of independence, proud of his ties to the new nation. In late summer 1777, as the British advanced on Philadelphia, Hubley exhorted Lancaster's wavering associators to "follow the brave example of the Militia to the Northward," who "have fought most resolutely, and conquer'd most manly," demanding, "Can you forbear to emulate their noble spirit?" Hubley asked, "Have you not the least ambition, to share with them the applause of not only your Country, but of the whole world?" "Let it be said in future History," he concluded, that the people of "Lancaster . . . amongst the rest of the Americans, step'd forth in their Countrys cause, and nobly defended it."[35]

Hubley reflected a broader transformation among Lancaster's German-speaking Whigs, who found themselves drawn into a larger enterprise overriding customary patterns of association. After Lexington and Concord, hundreds of the town's Germans had openly embraced the American rebellion. Only two years later, however, provincial and Continental officials bemoaned their flagging enthusiasm. In January 1777, the Board of War complained that many of the county's "Germans have fallen off from that patriotism and commendable zeal for the preservation of the liberties of this

country, for which they were distinguished in the outset of the dispute."
Pennsylvania's Militia Act and Test Acts soon furnished additional grounds
for dissent. The state's new draft system resembled the compulsory military
service they or their forebears had cast off upon departing for Penn's province, while many naturalized Germans hesitated to contravene their oath to
the king. Most Germans who sympathized with the resistance also ran up
against Pennsylvania's familiar language barrier. During early 1778, Lancaster's Reverend Helfenstein petitioned state officials for a local German-
language newspaper, stressing that most of his parishioners "cannot read
English, and some don't understand it."[36]

To rally their German neighbors, Whig printers redoubled their efforts to
reach them in their own language, employing conventional media to transmit
unconventional messages. The *Pennsylvanische Zeitungs-Blat*, a new German-
language newspaper published in Lancaster during the final months of the
Philadelphia occupation, provided provincial news, updates on the war's
progress, and weekly summaries of congressional proceedings. Before the
war with Britain, the opening pages of Lancaster's lone German-language
almanac had noted such seminal historical moments as the launching of the
Protestant Reformation and Columbus's landing in America. After 1776,
however, two newly published almanacs, Francis Bailey's *Der Gantz Neue
Verbesserte nord-americanische Calender* and Matthias Bartgis's *Der Hinckend-und
stolpernd-doch eilfertig-fliegend-und laufende americanische Reichs-Bott*, highlighted
such noteworthy occasions as the repeal of the Stamp Act, the convening of
the first Continental Congress, the British evacuation of Boston, the declaration of independence, and the Hessians' capture at Trenton. Lancaster's German speakers also celebrated their Virginian commander in chief, George
Washington. The front page of the *Pennsylvanische Zeitungs-Blat* featured
weekly orders from the general, while an imprint in the 1778 edition of *Der
Gantz neue Verbesserte nord-americanishe Calender* dubbed Washington "Landes
Vater," or father of the newly sovereign American states. Continuing a familiar provincial practice, German publishers also privileged English words with
a peculiar resonance over their German equivalents. Theophilus Cossart's ap-
propriately titled almanac *Der Republikanische Calender*, for instance, boasted
the piece "Gedancken über die Independence." As local printers diligently
promoted the resistance, their new publications both reflected and reinforced
revolutionary commitments.[37]

After 1777, America's domestic struggle assumed global dimensions as
the revolutionaries acquired transatlantic allies and the contest spilled over
into foreign waters and terrain, transcending the regional and national. In
early spring 1778, Lancaster's Whigs rejoiced at rumors that the French,

Spanish, Prussian, and Polish courts had endorsed American independence. Almost a year later, Jasper Yeates spread the word that a "combined Fleet of France & Spain will be on the American Coast next month in order to protect our Trade." The Whigs proved especially grateful for the assistance of "our friends the French army." A British prisoner sourly noted in spring 1780 that his hosts stood "in great spirits, as they say several thousand French are coming to join Washington's Army—sent across the Atlantic by their great and good ally to assist them." Locals gleefully embraced news of British defeats across the globe as the conflict unfolded on an international stage. In October 1778, Yeates celebrated a report that the Spanish had "blocked up Gibraltar," telling his father-in-law that a general European war "seems inevitable." Such assistance from foreign powers further eroded Americans' attachments to Great Britain while reinforcing novel commitments to the sovereign United States.[38]

The escalating war furnished residents with unexpected opportunities to affirm their ties with their new foreign allies. Indeed, now more than ever before, Lancaster became an international crossroads embracing even more diverse peoples with conflicting traditions and allegiances. During the summer of 1780, at the request of the marquis de Lafayette, residents supplied over two hundred horses to the French army. The summer before, Whigs had somberly turned out for the funeral of a visiting French colonel buried "with all the honors of war." The officers of Count Casimir Pulaski's famed multinational legion recruited in the borough through mid-1778, offering dramatic testimony of their commitment to America's independence. Yet the revolutionaries' interactions with foreign troops also underscored the divisions between Old World and New, reaffirming locals' inflated perception of themselves as distinctly American and invested with peculiar freedoms. When Pulaski's corps returned a year later, his men clashed with Georgia light horsemen stationed in Lancaster for the winter. After residents criticized the high-handedness of Pulaski's officers, the Board of War issued the count a mild reproof, underlining the "necessity of European officers divesting themselves of European Ideas, while they serve in America," for "the Inhabitants of these States are unused to the severe exactions of Military power," explained the board, and "expect protection, and not violence and oppression from troops raised and supported at their own expense."[39]

Our Boasted Liberty

Lancaster's revolutionaries cultivated their wartime alliances in the streets, celebrating independence, military victories, and French intervention with parades, music, militia musters, and *feux de joie*. Whigs showed their support for cause and country by attending bonfires, ringing church bells, illuminating their windows, and joining in elaborate patriotic toasts. Revolutionary rites and festivities bound residents separated by language and custom into a shared patriotic enterprise. Amidst great unease and uncertainty, patriotic performances enabled Whigs to assert their revolutionary identity, solidify their ranks, and rally support for the war. Participating in patriotic rituals helped revolutionaries renew their commitments to a cause transcending narrow cultural and communal interests, to think beyond their ethnicity and locale and imagine a broader Continental experience. Through their increasingly elaborate public ceremonies, Whigs celebrated their ties with near and distant revolutionary brethren, with newly independent citizens freed from the constraints imposed by their former colonial status within the British Empire. By reaffirming their break with Britain and proclaiming their allegiance to the new United States, local patriots contributed to a nascent sense of American nationhood.[40]

Patriotic rituals of assent afforded Lancaster's militants the opportunity to distinguish themselves from their enemies and showcase their solidarity as they refined their ranks and marginalized the opposition. Moments after toasting their revolutionary brethren on July 4, 1779, Whigs damned the "foes of America, slaves to tyranny." The revolutionaries' festivities quickly degenerated into raucous affairs, which dissenters came to dread. In a ritualistic policing of the fold, militants seized upon celebrations to humble and harass the opposition, unleashing years of pent-up frustration on the disaffected. Residents who failed to honor festive occasions reaped violent reprisals from their furious neighbors. Dissenters routinely had "their windows smashed in and their goods spoiled" for neglecting to illuminate their homes. Pacifists, whose faith and principles precluded their participation in the patriotic proceedings, proved especially vulnerable. During the boisterous celebrations of Burgoyne's surrender in October 1777, militants besieged the home of Thomas Poultney, a prominent Quaker and respected craftsman. Poultney had resided in Lancaster since the 1740s and was counted among the community's more prosperous inhabitants. Increasingly alienated from his radical neighbors, he packed up his large family in 1780 and relocated to the friendlier environs of Philadelphia.[41]

While rallying militants, aggressive patriotic displays often aggravated the long-simmering tensions between Lancaster's competing revolutionary factions, who continued to vie for influence within their embattled community. Fearing a descent into anarchy, many moderates recoiled from the reckless violence that endangered their well-ordered society. Jasper Yeates, for instance, privately sympathized with Poultney, complaining that his property was "terribly handled." Writing confidentially to a friend, Yeates observed, "He is really an inoffensive man" who "thinks very properly of the present contest," but "rejoicings of this kind . . . are diametrically contrary to the Quaker system." For conservative-leaning Whigs like Yeates, who valued traditions of deference and respect for property, the radicals' spiteful persecution of the community's respectable inhabitants was a vile expression of the rebellion's democratic excesses.[42]

Occasionally, Whigs incorporated their captives into patriotic displays. During their celebration of the victory at Saratoga, revolutionaries subversively draped the Hessian banners seized at Trenton on their courthouse wall to signify their military prowess and humiliate their enemies. By displaying the flags alongside several American standards, local patriots claimed the Hessians as their own, symbolically integrating their captives into the solemn rites of nationhood. Lancaster's revolutionaries drew inspiration from Philadelphia's well-publicized 1777 Fourth of July celebration, where the patriots' captured Hessian band performed and a well-drilled corps of British deserters fired successive volleys skyward. Vividly recounted in the pages of the *Pennsylvania Gazette*, the celebration offered local patriots a model worthy of emulation.[43]

Lancaster's Whigs exhibited a peculiar fascination with their captives, often measuring American military success by the number of prisoners seized in a particular engagement. Yet the steady accumulation of captives simultaneously fueled apprehensions within, as thousands of prisoners taken in faraway engagements soon found their way into the borough, so that dread and triumphalism fed on each other in almost dialectical alternation. Only two weeks after locals celebrated the surrender of the British fortress at Stony Point, over twenty of the garrison's freshly paroled British officers were stalking the streets of Lancaster. Similarly, within three months of their victory at Cowpens, deep in the Carolinas, Whigs nervously watched more than 350 of the battle's rank-and-file prisoners pour into their dangerously overcrowded barracks. Fearing that winter weather would detain the prisoners indefinitely, residents were relieved to see Burgoyne's army continue west across the Susquehanna after it passed through Lancaster en route to Virginia in December 1778. They were surely displeased when several hundred of the captives returned two years later. The number of prisoners destined for Lancaster typically depended on the location of their capture, the space available in the barracks, and the current proximity of British lines. By war's end, however, the borough had hosted captives from every major victory in the field.[44]

The revolutionaries' continued accumulation of captives ultimately bolstered faith in the cause. In late summer 1779, Jasper Yeates spread word from the east that "Philadelphia's new jail is filled with British prisoners, and the town swarms with their officers." In short, he concluded, "Every thing looks well." More than a year earlier, after the Battle of Saratoga, where General Horatio Gates claimed over five thousand prisoners, locals had seized the opportunity to gloat and to disparage their enemies, knowing that the loss of such a substantial force dealt a severe blow to British arms. Judging the victory "by far the most considerable thing done in the course of the war," Yeates reflected, "How humiliating must it be to Burgoyne," a man "whose pompous stile assured certain conquest and laurels to his followers!" The recently relocated eastern refugee James Milligan shared his neighbors' joy in their triumph, observing, "History Records but few equal to it." Milligan felt that Burgoyne's defeat would provide Whigs the momentum to liberate Philadelphia, "especially if the Victorious Yankees under Genl. Gates joins Genl. Washington."[45]

Three months after the battle, another resident proudly recounted how a friend had christened his newborn son Washington Gates "that his name might witness the noble achievements effected by our arms at the instant of his birth." A widely circulated sermon enthused that Saratoga would "raise the dignity and importance of our embassadors in Europe, and make us more and more respectable in the eyes of the world," serving as "a happy prelude," the minister noted optimistically, to "victory over all our enemies in America." In their exuberance, Whigs even created a new dance called "Burgoyne's Surrender," and reveled in a host of songs penned in honor of the victory, such as "The Battle of Saratoga" and "A Song, on the Surrender of General Burgoyne." Another song composed in Lancaster, titled "The New Recruit, or, Gallant Volunteers," brashly defied the enemy, promising to "make them all Burgoynes." Through their songs, sermons, and celebrations, Whigs registered their contempt for their adversaries and their enormous pride in their own military achievements.[46]

Whigs understood the value of their captives and paraded them in elaborate displays to celebrate their successes and boost sagging morale. A Philadelphia loyalist who witnessed the parading of the captured Hessians after the Battle of Trenton remarked bitterly, "This was rebel generosity, of which they made such a brag during the whole of the war." Another loyalist dismissed the spectacle as a crude propaganda ploy, convinced that the captives were actually "German-Americans brought by Congress from Lancaster County to deceive the people." In Lancaster, curious spectators eagerly watched the prisoners file in and out of their borough. The deflated troops occasionally conjured up pathetic scenes that elicited locals' sympathy. Often ragged and exhausted from the strains of battle and captivity, poorly provisioned and shuffled from one detention site to the next, the prisoners straggled into town under heavy guard, occasionally in the dead of winter or with frightened family members in tow. In January 1780, a resident noted the departure of the British captured at Stony Point, "among them women and little children, who suffered much from the cold." In early 1781, Christopher Marshall recorded the arrival of several hundred British and Tory prisoners "whose appearance," he observed, "was the picture of human poverty and want, both in clothes, flesh, and meager looks."[47]

At the same time, seeing their much-vaunted foes humbled in defeat and marched into captivity fired Whigs' enthusiasm, renewing their confidence in their cause. As their prisoners grew in number, locals evinced a boastful pride and sense of mastery over their enemies. Newly captured British prisoners increasingly suffered the scorn of the town's angry militants. Even the more favored German captives sometimes arrived to the insults of resentful inhabitants. After passing through Lancaster in early 1779, a captured Brunswick officer complained that he and his colleagues were "ashamed of being Germans, because we had never encountered so much meanness in one place as here from our compatriots." The 1778 edition of *The Lancaster Almanack* featured "A New Liberty Song," which boldly taunted the enemy: "Our children rout your armies, our boats destroy your fleet; And to compleat the dire disgrace, coop'd up within our town, You live the scorn of all our host, the slaves of Washington." Adding insult to injury, Whigs set their derisive lyrics to the familiar tune of "The British Grenadier."[48]

The rituals of captivity weighed heavily on the prisoners. When the remnants of Burgoyne's army arrived in Lancaster during the summer of 1781, their American escort dutifully separated the officers from the enlisted men. "Distressing and humiliating as the scene was, when we commanded our men to pile up their arms and abandon them on the plains of Saratoga," recalled Lieutenant Thomas Anburey, "still much greater was the separation of the officers from the men at Lancaster." After the prisoners were paraded outside the barracks, a Continental regiment, "forming a square around the British soldiers, conducted them to the prison." The scene "effected that which the united force of inclement seasons, hunger and thirst, incessant barbarity, adverse fortune, and American insults heaped together, could never have effected–it drew tears from the eyes of veterans, who would rather have shed their blood," wrote Anburey. "To behold so many men, who had bravely fought by our side—who in all their sufferings looked up to us for protection, forced from us into a prison," he concluded, was "too deeply affecting, and we hastened from the spot."[49]

The Whigs' prisoners routinely arrived under the escort of Continental troops or militia detachments from neighboring states. Alternating as a detention, provisioning, and administrative center, Lancaster quickly became a bustling hive of military activity, with thousands of troops from across the country passing through the community en route to camp or to distant military engagements. Just as they gathered to inspect their prisoners, curious spectators avidly turned out to scrutinize their neighbors in arms. As Washington and Howe vied for control of Pennsylvania in early 1778, Christopher Marshall and friends enthusiastically welcomed the "New England troops" bound for American headquarters. Weeks earlier, Edward Shippen had informed a friend, "We have here a large Number of Light Horse in fine order," who have been "well trained to their business." Most of them, he noted, could "leap over any common fence or 5 rail fence." In May 1779, Marshall joined a "great number of spectators" during the exercises of a

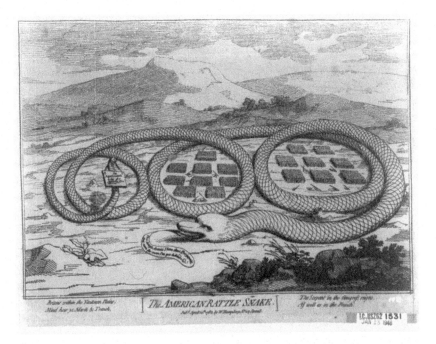

FIGURE 3. "The American Rattle Snake" by the British artist James Gillray, London, April 12, 1782, depicting the revolutionaries' capture of the two British armies at Saratoga and Yorktown. The surrender of the two armies fed patriots' growing sense of mastery over their enemies. Courtesy Library of Congress, Prints and Photographs Division.

visiting troop of Georgia light horse. As the war progressed, the assembled American forces provided a stark contrast to the town's disarmed and disheveled prisoners. Late in the conflict, when 450 Continentals marched through Lancaster for the Carolinas, even the paroled British officer Thomas Hughes grudgingly conceded that they possessed "good clothing, were well arm'd and show'd more of the military in their appearance than I ever conceived American troops had yet attain'd."[50]

Whether Virginia riflemen or Continental dragoons, in moments of doubt, passing troops reassured locals that they possessed determined allies willing to take the fight to their enemies. Their interactions with visiting troops helped the town's revolutionaries transcend their locale and identify with a cause larger than their own by nurturing ties to distant friends who brought their own perspectives and priorities to the contest. By fraternizing with their revolutionary brethren, locals could situate their struggle within a Continental context and envision themselves as part of a broader American fold defined by diverse, competing interests. Along with news of military developments, visiting American troops reminded locals of the degree to which their own fate hinged on the contributions of anonymous patriots engaged in remote battles across the new United States, even if some longtime residents, habitually suspicious of outsiders, preferred distant, imagined allies to the presence of armed strangers.

Like the steady influx of prisoners, the continuing arrival of troops from neighboring states occasionally taxed locals' hospitality and strained civil and military relations. Even these tensions, however, could rally Lancaster's diverse revolutionaries by mitigating long-standing ethnic divisions and reaffirming connections to a larger American community. During the spring of 1777, Lancaster's English- and German-speaking Whigs closed ranks following a violent clash with a visiting Continental regiment, consisting largely of Canadian refugees unaccustomed to the dizzying diversity of Pennsylvania's interior. On the morning of March 17, members of Colonel Moses Hazen's Second Canadian Regiment took to Lancaster's streets for a riotous Saint Patrick's Day celebration. Before retiring to their quarters, the revelers fatally assaulted the German resident Matthias Schneider. Hours later, after furious residents traded ethnic barbs with one of the visiting soldiers, a small regimental detachment commanded by a Canadian, Ensign Edmond Minyier, arrived on the scene to restore order. In the ensuing commotion, Minyier ordered his men to fire on a fleeing resident, mortally wounding the German associator Jacob Gross.[51]

As the presiding civil authority, Lancaster's ethnically integrated committee demanded that Minyier be committed to the county jail pending trial. When

Minyier's commanding officer refused to comply, the committee appealed to Congress, declaring that the "People will deem themselves miserable indeed when the Military shall rise superior to the Civil Power, and prevent offenders from being brought to Justice." The committee demanded that Minyier and his regimental accomplices be made to answer to both the "Laws of the Land and the Articles of War," lest "our boasted Liberty" become a "Sound and Nothing more." Finally, committee members condemned the inflaming of "national Prejudices," insisting that "such Distinctions as arise from the Places where our Cradles were rocked, should be wholly swallowed up under the general Designation of Americans." During a grim and unpredictable war, Lancaster's motley revolutionaries labored to overcome their differences and cooperate amidst successive crises. Ultimately, they met with a surprising degree of success. Indeed, when the British officer Thomas Anburey passed through Lancaster a year after his capture at Saratoga, he marveled at the Whigs' "diversity of religions, nations, and languages." The curious prisoner, however, found the "harmony they live in no less edifying."[52]

The rhythmic American troop movements through Lancaster quickened during late summer 1781, as Washington marshaled his forces for the decisive confrontation at Yorktown. Receiving word of the stunning American victory in late October, locals wasted no time in launching their hastily improvised celebrations. One resident giddily described the day's festivities: "On the news of taking Lord Cornwallis our Town looked Beautiful with the illuminations the colours flying canon & small arms fireing & the young fillows of the Town parading the streets with Lawrel in their hats." In keeping with custom, militants singled out their enemies during the proceedings, shattering the windows of dissenters who had neglected to illuminate their homes in honor of the occasion. After learning the details of the engagement, most Whigs grasped the implications. "The Surrender of Lord Cornwallis affords me the Dawn of a Peace," wrote Jasper Yeates. "This Idea is more pleasing to me than any other Circumstance," he concluded, "tho' I feel much Satisfaction at the rising Glories of America." Less pleasing to locals in the months ahead was the arrival of the British Yorktown prisoners, as Continental authorities struggled to bring their disorderly captives to heel in a nation still at war.[53]

The first arrival of British prisoners in December 1775 brought the war to Lancaster's doorstep, and in fundamental ways, the conflict persisted until their final departure in May 1783. The demands and vicissitudes of war fostered internal division and insecurity, leaving Lancaster's committed Whigs peculiarly invested in military success. The revolutionaries' lingering vulnerability solidified their ranks by hardening resentments toward shared adversaries both within and beyond their community. With the fates of cause and community inextricably linked, the contest gradually bound Lancaster's diverse insurgents into a common enterprise as battle and ideological lines overrode familiar patterns of association and allegiance. Immersed in an ongoing exchange with their revolutionary brethren and in a continuing dialogue with Continental developments, local Whigs gave tentative expression to an emerging national consciousness. In ritual and rhetoric, Lancaster's revolutionaries affirmed themselves and marginalized their enemies through an aggressively defiant patriotism.

CHAPTER 6

"The Country Is Full of Prisoners of War"

Nationalism, Resistance, and Assimilation

As the Revolutionary War shifted theaters, gradually moving from north to south, and British operations became more unpredictable, deviating with successive changes of command, Continental officials shuffled their captives among multiplying detention sites, and Lancaster remained the central hub through which most of the prisoners eventually flowed. By the time Cornwallis's surrendering troops emerged from their entrenchments amid the smoldering debris of the Yorktown plain, Lancaster had been joined by more than a half-dozen related host communities in an expanding Continental detention network stretching from the Pennsylvania interior to the Virginia backcountry. As the revolutionaries' leading detention center, Lancaster became the proving ground for early Continental policy, establishing enduring patterns in Americans' wartime relations with their British and German prisoners. These patterns resonated over time and space, echoing across state boundaries through the revolutionaries' associated detention facilities as the war progressed. By 1781, the interior's diverse host communities shared Lancaster's anxieties, sympathies, and antipathies. Most of the British and German prisoners, in turn, were approaching their enemies in more predictable ways.

Like Lancaster, a mostly German-speaking market community nestled deep in the grain-producing American interior, Frederick, Maryland, had long operated as a key detention center for enemy prisoners. On April 22,

1783, Frederick's patriots learned of the formal declaration of peace ending the war with Great Britain and acknowledging Americans' hard-won
independence. The town's ecstatic Whigs celebrated the news by parading
through the streets to the sound of fifes and drums, organizing an elaborate
fireworks display, and proudly toasting Congress, General Washington, and
liberty. The following evening, the community's leading patriots hosted a
dance, where a small band played for the assembled guests. In most respects,
Frederick's celebration was a conventional affair. During the War for Independence, avid revolutionaries routinely celebrated their military victories
with such elaborate patriotic displays. Upon learning of the peace, supporters
of the revolutionary resistance in cities, towns, and villages across the United
States staged similar performances.

Frederick's festivities, however, involved a slight twist. The fireworks for
the locals' celebration were fashioned by Hessian artillerymen. A Hessian
band supplied the music for the Whigs' formal fête, where Hessian officers
eagerly joined in the festivities, drinking, dining, and dancing with local patriots. Like the Hessians who'd strolled the streets of Lancaster years before,
these Germans were prisoners of war, part of the more than five thousand
auxiliaries seized as captives during the conflict with Britain. The German
prisoners had arrived in Frederick over a year earlier, after surrendering to
American forces at Yorktown with several thousand of their British and loyalist allies. In spring 1783, they were approaching the end of a long captivity.[1]

Home to a committed revolutionary resistance, safely removed from the
hostilities, and equipped with facilities for the captives' confinement, Frederick had begun detaining small numbers of loyalists as early as 1776, followed
by more substantial detachments of British prisoners just two years later. As
in Lancaster, Frederick's mostly German-speaking inhabitants and increasingly disgruntled British prisoners made for a combustible combination.
One of the town's first British prisoners complained that the county's "rude
unfeeling German ruffians, fit for assassinations, murder, and death, treated
us with great ignominy and insult." In late December 1777, Frederick's British prisoners reportedly set their jail on fire in a failed bid to escape. After-
wards, when the prisoners grew "very Clamorous," Charles Beatty, the town
major, threatened "sacrificing them all if they were not quiet." Exaggerated
reports of the uprising soon spread as far as Lancaster, where the borough's
jailed British prisoners swapped stories of enraged Frederick militia cruelly
bayonetting the helpless captives. That same December, when state officials
informed Beatty that an even larger contingent of British prisoners was en
route to Frederick, he replied, "If they are as great villains as part of those
here already I know not what to do with them."[2]

Frederick's militants also fretted about their British prisoners' potentially subversive ties with local loyalists. After Maryland state officials convicted three loyalists of treason for hatching a scheme to capture Frederick's powder magazine before liberating and arming the town's prisoners, they condemned the conspirators to be hanged, drawn, and quartered—"dreadful Examples" of revolutionaries' hatred for their internal enemies. As with Lancaster's German captives, however, many of Frederick's auxiliary prisoners fared noticeably better than their British allies, eagerly interacting with their predominantly German-speaking hosts. By 1782, the German prisoners' poor accommodations and provisions encouraged growing numbers to abandon the town's overcrowded barracks to labor among the inhabitants. Unlike their British comrades, within a year and a half of surrendering at Yorktown, many of Frederick's German captives had become both visible and valuable contributors to the community's daily life.[3]

During their stay in Frederick, the relatively well behaved Germans made a comparatively favorable impression on the town's inhabitants. For many of Frederick's German captives, the feeling was mutual, with some even opting to start a new life among their captors by deserting their ranks and beginning the long process of assimilation. The town's German prisoners curiously recounted the tale of an Ensign Spangenberg, a recently promoted officer seized at Yorktown who had deserted his corps en route to Frederick. Rumors now placed the former captive in Virginia, where the enterprising deserter had reportedly married into a local family, sworn the oath of allegiance, and begun offering Latin lessons to his grateful neighbors. Revolutionary authorities, both civil and military, avidly encouraged German prisoners to desert, posting broadsides throughout the town promising captives who remained in the United States land and all the rights and privileges of citizenship. Frederick's Whigs thus welcomed the auxiliaries' participation in their patriotic celebrations because they no longer considered them enemies—not simply because peace had brought a formal end to the hostilities, but because some of the captives were now becoming Americans. The Germans' privileged status in captivity and relentless Continental propaganda had gradually transformed them from alien invaders into ideological kin and potentially welcome members of the American fold. Thus, years after venturing to North America to thwart the rebellious colonies' struggle for national liberation, many of Frederick's German captives had paradoxically become active and enthusiastic participants in the embryonic rites of American nationalism.[4]

By contrast, conspicuously absent from Frederick's celebrations were the town's British prisoners, who had been relocated four months earlier to more secure detention sites in Pennsylvania following a rash of escapes. British captives proved more inclined to flee than their German allies wherever they were held, but their detention sites surely influenced their decision. If few British prisoners felt any sympathy for the revolutionary resistance, fewer still ever came to terms with their captivity in largely German-speaking host communities. While some German captives took comfort in the sights and sounds of their surroundings, their British counterparts found them all the more disturbingly alien. That they generally fared worse in captivity than German prisoners also gave them reason to escape.[5]

Following Cornwallis's surrender at Yorktown, the revolutionaries held the unprecedented sum of more than ten thousand enemy prisoners. Frustratingly for Continental authorities, however, the more prisoners they captured, the more pressure on their overtaxed detention facilities and the greater the number of escapes. With locals newly confident of victory and eager to resume routines free of the constraints, pressures, and uncertainties of war, the Continentals' thinly stretched detention network threatened to unravel almost as soon as it emerged full-blown. As Continental officials struggled to control their captives, hundreds of British prisoners continued to defy their American hosts and exploit locals' negligence to make their escape. The resistance of the British confirmed their growing pattern of misbehavior and reinforced the revolutionaries' long-standing enmity toward their former kinsmen. Emboldened by their victory at Yorktown and driven by a resurgent patriotism, the revolutionaries answered their prisoners' defiance with heightened coercion.

After a long and costly war marked by considerable sacrifice, the revolutionaries displayed little tolerance for their inveterate enemies, abusing their recalcitrant captives with renewed vigor. By 1783, wayward German prisoners fared as poorly as their British allies. When several German prisoners unwisely cheered King George during Frederick's celebration of the peace, the local officer of the guard ordered the offenders arrested and beaten. As in years past, depending on the particular circumstances, the revolutionaries alternated between being merciful hosts and vengeful custodians. As patriots began slowly reconstituting their war-weary but newly independent communities, penitent, compliant captives could still hope to find a home and protector in the United States, while irredeemable enemies only invited redoubled abuse. Provided that they cooperated with their captors, non-English-speaking Germans faced better prospects in captivity and made better candidates for citizenship than the Britons, who, until 1776, had been a kindred people. From colonial subjects defined by birth and residence, the Americans had become republican citizens defined by ideological choice.[6]

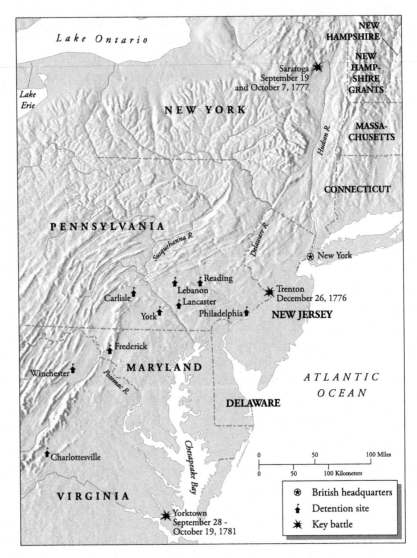

MAP 2. A sample of key Continental detention sites for British and German prisoners, circa 1780. Drawn by Alice Thiede. Revolutionaries claimed the majority of their captives—over thirteen thousand—at the battles of Trenton, Saratoga, and Yorktown.

Dangerous Guests

In late December 1781, Brigadier General Moses Hazen's Second Canadian Regiment took up quarters in Lancaster for the second time in four years. Continental authorities ordered the regiment to Lancaster to guard the British prisoners and reduce the number of escapes. The removal of the British

Convention troops to neighboring York five months before had relieved pressure on the barracks, but the borough still contained more than six hundred prisoners, and escapes remained a problem, having increased steadily since 1779, as Lancaster's accumulating British captives broke out of jail or fled the barracks, often with the aid of loyalists eager to spirit the fugitives to safety. Thus, from British headquarters in August 1781, Major Frederick Mackenzie welcomed the arrival of twenty-five "British Soldiers who were prisoners at Lancaster." Nineteen of the fugitives "came off together," Mackenzie reported, after being "conducted the whole way by one man." By 1781, Lancaster's prisoners had access to an elaborate escape network consisting of loyalist guides and scattered safe houses stretching from Pennsylvania to New York. Meanwhile, the county's under-strength and poorly disciplined militia proved an inadequate guard.[7]

The escapes in Lancaster reflected broader trends. From the makeshift detention centers now dispersed across the American interior, alarming numbers of British prisoners fled their captivity. Between July 1780 and June 1781 alone, more than two hundred British fugitives reported to British headquarters. To the dismay of Continental officials, the more prisoners they acquired, the more they were likely to lose. Since Horatio Gates's capture of over five thousand British and German prisoners at the Battle of Saratoga in October 1777, escapes had become increasingly common. General Gates had granted Burgoyne generous surrender terms, agreeing that the prisoners could march to Massachusetts and sail for Britain on the condition that they refrain from engaging in the North American hostilities. Congress and Washington objected to the Convention's terms, however, fearing that once the prisoners returned to England, they would relieve British garrisons and free up troops for North American service. Instead, Continental officials postponed the prisoners' return, hoping to use their new captives as leverage in negotiations designed to secure British recognition of American sovereignty. With each of the belligerents soon accusing the other of violating the Convention, the prisoners remained under American control, taxing revolutionary resources for the duration of the war.[8]

A continuing scarcity of men and matériel left the Americans constantly scrambling to secure adequate guards and accommodations for their captives. Sent south from Cambridge, Massachusetts, to Charlottesville, Virginia, in the winter of 1778 and 1779, and back north to York, Pennsylvania, in the summer of 1781, Burgoyne's Convention Army, as the captives taken at Saratoga became known, had begun to disintegrate within months of surrendering in New York. In Massachusetts alone, between November 1777 and November 1778, Burgoyne's army suffered more than seven hundred escapes and desertions, a reduction of almost 15 percent. Nearly a thousand more Convention captives escaped during the sixteen months that followed their relocation to Virginia in January 1779, with most of the fugitives desperately seeking the safety of British lines. Aided by loyalists, many of the fugitives successfully eluded their American captors and doggedly made their way to British headquarters.[9]

In July 1779, William Atlee complained to Continental officials of the British Convention prisoners who regularly passed through Lancaster County to "join the Army under Genl. Clinton." Anticipating that most of the fugitives were headed north to British headquarters, Washington posted guards at ferries and crossroads to intercept them. In mid-1779 he reported, "We are every day apprehending these People in their attempts to get into New York." After the British invasion of southern Virginia in late 1780, a few British Convention prisoners even dared return to captivity after successfully reaching their own lines, presumably with orders and intelligence for their detained colleagues. Washington found the machinations of the British Convention troops especially exasperating, cursing the "dangerous guests" lurking in the "bowels of our Country." From Virginia, Governor Thomas Jefferson agreed, observing in November 1780: "Our apprehensions as to desertion to the enemy and corresponding with the disaffected arise from the British altogether. We have no fear of either from the Germans." As long as British prisoners enjoyed the prospect of fleeing to their own lines, Jefferson added, "nothing less than stone walls" could prevent their escape. Hard numbers bore out the revolutionaries' misgivings. The continuing escapes and desertions reduced Burgoyne's army from some five thousand men in late 1777 to fewer than three thousand in 1782.[10]

Continental authorities faced even graver difficulties following the surrender of more than six thousand British and German troops at the Battle of Yorktown in October 1781. The Whigs' victory brought their total number of prisoners to upwards of ten thousand, severely taxing their already strained resources. By 1782, after their stunning triumph in Virginia, the war-weary inhabitants of the Continentals' major host communities had also become less vigilant, confident that the capture of Cornwallis's army signaled the end of Britain's prospects of reclaiming its rebellious colonies. With the hostilities finally drawing to a close, locals considered their captives less a threat than a regrettable nuisance or an exploitable resource. In late October, the victorious American troops escorted their new Yorktown prisoners from the Chesapeake tidewater to long-established detention sites deep in the Virginia and Maryland interior. During and after their relocation, the defiant captives made the most of the Americans' negligence by fleeing in unprecedented numbers. An estimated nine hundred of the poorly superintended prisoners fled their ranks within a few weeks of surrendering at Yorktown. On the heels of what had promised to prove their decisive blow to British arms, the Continentals' brittle detention network began to buckle under a volatile combination of local carelessness and an unmanageable number of prisoners.[11]

In Winchester, Virginia, for example, where Continental officials placed some two thousand of their new British and German prisoners, pressures quickly built to a crisis. Like Lancaster and Frederick an ethnically diverse community comfortably removed from the hostilities and situated at a well-traveled crossroads, Winchester had hosted smaller detachments of prisoners earlier in the war, including several hundred British and German captives evacuated from Pennsylvania during Howe's invasion of the province in late 1777. With a smaller population and more meager facilities than either Lancaster or Frederick, however, the community proved poorly prepared for the sudden influx of a few thousand enemy captives. In early November 1781, an American officer reported that because of the town's inadequate accommodations, more than a thousand of the captives remained "oblig'd to camp out." Carelessly attended by the militia and scattered throughout the settlement, the British seized every opportunity to escape, often crossing the "Potomack in hunting Shirts and other Dresses of Disguise" with the help of local loyalists. By November 25, the local commandant complained that he could muster no more than eight hundred of the prisoners. In early January 1782, an American colonel sent to Winchester to investigate informed Secretary at War Benjamin Lincoln that the "Abuses here Committed are beyond Anything I can possibly describe." The officer noted that the "Prisoners are suffered to go almost at Liberty" and the "Whole Country within twenty miles of this place is swarming with Read Coats." Ongoing efforts to secure the captives were thwarted by locals eager to hire their labor. Estimating that half the prisoners were now "dispersed thro this and the Neighbouring Countys," the officer recommended closing the post.[12]

The mounting local abuses created new worries for Continental officials. Just months after Cornwallis's surrender promised to seal Britain's fate, the authorities began to fear they were losing control of their prisoners, as locals' negligence kept threatening to squander the precious advantage won at Yorktown. With victory now in their grasp, Continental officials wished to keep their captives properly secured to curb disorder, hasten the peace, and facilitate a final prisoner exchange. In January, Secretary Lincoln ordered the newly taken British prisoners relocated to York and Lancaster, "where they could be better secured in Picketted Barracks" and "guarded by a Continental Regiment." Conversely, Washington proposed that the German prisoners, "who are more tractable," remain in the "Frontier Towns." Lincoln ordered Hazen's regiment to guard the prisoners detained at York and Lancaster. The British captives' arrival in late January brought Lancaster's prisoner population to more than fourteen hundred. Following the prisoners' relocation, a concerned Congress urged state authorities to pass laws to minimize escapes. In April 1782, Pennsylvania's assembly offered an eight dollar bounty for every fugitive returned to confinement. Residents convicted of the "base and treacherous practice of aiding, abetting, concealing or assisting" the escaped prisoners now faced the prospect of thirty-nine lashes or a £50 fine.[13]

Yet throughout the Pennsylvania interior the escapes continued, as careless local authorities violated the order to confine their captives by hiring out their labor. Continental officials had experimented with the hiring of captives' labor as early as 1776, with decidedly mixed results. The revolutionaries reaped notable dividends from the employment of their German prisoners, who proved mostly eager and reliable laborers. But Whig officials had become more reluctant to hire out their British captives owing to their greater tendency to escape. In October 1779, Timothy Pickering on behalf of the Board of War assured Congress that the "fidelity of the Hessians may be relied on without scruple," but, he said, "We have been cautious in letting out the British unless recommended as trusty men." In late summer 1781, William Atlee warned Thomas Bradford, Philadelphia's deputy commissary of prisoners, to remain on the lookout for a fugitive named Warrington. One of the prisoners from the Battle of Cowpens, Warrington had hired out in Lancaster but "behaved so ill" he was returned to the barracks. After hiring out a second time, the "cunning fellow" made his escape. Several months later, Atlee asked Bradford to send him a few Hessian laborers, who had been in relative short supply throughout the county since the Trenton prisoners' exchange in mid-1778. Given their British prisoners' reputation for misbehavior, whenever possible, Continental officials still preferred to keep them confined under close guard. By 1782, however, with a long-awaited peace in the offing, the British captives found their labor in great demand.[14]

After six anxiety-filled years of monitoring enemy prisoners, the residents of Pennsylvania's host towns now hoped to move on from the disruptive pressures and uncertainties of war to the more predictable routines of a peacetime community. Since 1776, some enterprising locals had looked to turn their prisoners to advantage, approaching them as an exploitable resource and harnessing their labor whenever permitted. With the end of the hostilities in sight and with security consequently a less pressing concern,

many Lancaster County residents again sought to capitalize on their prisoners' presence by appropriating their labor, placing local interests before the
more patriotic, self-sacrificing imperatives of Continental officials. Though
locals harbored lingering suspicions and resentments of their British captives,
they also faced a nagging labor shortage, particularly during their cyclical
harvest. Always keen to relieve pressure on the borough, Lancaster officials
yielded to outlying labor demands by releasing growing numbers of their
British prisoners to work for the farmers in the country. Once freed from
the confines of Lancaster's barracks, many of the prisoners gladly seized the
opportunity to escape. More than forty British fugitives made their way to
their New York headquarters from early May to June 1782. By September,
more than seventy others had followed. Yet despite a June 7 congressional
order prohibiting the hiring of British captives, residents continued to exploit
them.[15]

Determined to secure the captives and rein in local abuses, Hazen sought
Continental intervention. In June 1782, Hazen alerted Secretary Lincoln
that Pennsylvania's deputy commissaries were exercising an "independent,
uncontroulable power, . . . not subject to my restraint." As a result of their
reckless management, Hazen added, the "country is full of prisoners of war,"
while "every loss of prisoners however unjust is charged on the Regiment."
On July 3, Congress authorized Hazen to arrest and to commence court-
martial proceedings against the offending commissaries for "disobedience
of orders and neglect of duty, in suffering the escape of prisoners." Congress
asked Secretary Lincoln to appoint replacements. Since 1777, the Whigs'
prisoners had fallen under the supervision of civilian commissaries, operating under the oversight of a commissary general of prisoners. On July 24,
Congress repealed all resolutions and appointments approved by the commissary general and placed the prisoners under the authority of the secretary at
war. A few days earlier, Congress had ordered anew that "no permission be
granted to British Prisoners on any conditions whatever to go out to work
with the Inhabitants," great numbers "having already been lost to the United
States by such indulgencies."[16]

With the British still refusing to provision the Convention troops, Congress's uncompromising policy led critics to counter that hiring out would
considerably reduce the Continental expense of supplying the prisoners. In
early 1782, Robert Morris, the superintendent of finance, put the price of
supporting the Saratoga and Yorktown prisoners at $1,000 per day. Calculat-
ing the costs, Congress proposed a compromise. In December 1782, it approved the hiring of British prisoners on the condition that their American
employers post a sizable £100 penal bond as security for each laborer's safe

return. Congress also instructed Secretary Lincoln to deny further provisions to the British captives' wives and children and to send the families who refused to support themselves to New York. As an additional cost-cutting measure, Congress considered reducing the prisoners' rations.[17]

Meanwhile, in Lancaster, Hazen orchestrated an elaborate sting operation designed to tighten security and neutralize the local escape network by employing agents to pose as fugitives and roam the countryside soliciting aid from potential conspirators. Despite the risks, loyalists, British deserters, and fellow captives generously volunteered to assist the fleeing prisoners. The loyalist George Weidell, for example, "advanced considerable Sums of Money" to Lancaster's prisoners to "enable them to effect their Escape within the British Lines." Sergeant Roger Lamb and several of his British comrades fled Pennsylvania in early 1782 with the aid of a former prisoner who had deserted from the Royal Welch Fusiliers. Edward Miller of the British Twentieth Regiment testified from New York in late summer 1782 to helping one unnamed Pennsylvania loyalist liberate over thirty of Lancaster's prisoners. Operating from Lancaster in conjunction with local loyalists, the Yorktown captive John McDonald reportedly supplied both funds and guides to facilitate the "escape of above 200 British Soldiers."[18]

Escape posed grave dangers for both the prisoners and their accomplices. Fleeing captives not only discarded their uniforms to masquerade as Americans in "poor country clothing," but also hid in the woods through the day and moved at night, under cover of darkness, for weeks on end, avoiding well-traveled roads, across more than 150 miles of enemy territory. Fugitives might have to elude their pursuers for months before finally reaching the security of British lines. Assisting the fugitives likewise proved a perilous enterprise. While fleeing Pennsylvania, Lamb's party took refuge among several of the "king's friends," one of whom stressed the "great hazard" involved in providing safe haven to fugitives. After reaching British headquarters in New York, Lamb learned that his unfortunate guide had subsequently been apprehended and executed by revolutionary authorities.[19]

By war's end, Pennsylvania had prosecuted over forty suspects for promoting escapes, eventually convicting more than thirty offenders. During 1782 and 1783, the Court of Oyer and Terminer presided over eleven escape-related cases in Lancaster County. Lancaster's John Maguire, a devoted loyalist, was "discovered, imprisoned," and "ruined" for furnishing guides to the fugitives. Even when fortunate enough to escape the clutches of revolutionary authorities, conspirators paid a price for aiding the enemy. In late 1783, George Weidell's wife, Ann, informed British headquarters that assisting the fugitives had left her and her family "much reduced in their

circumstances." The Lancaster loyalist William Tanner, one of Maguire's accomplices who avoided detection, was "reduc'd to pinching penury" after
assisting in the escape of nearly twenty prisoners. Under Hazen's supervision,
locals also tracked fugitives for state-sponsored bounties. In August 1782,
for instance, three Lebanon residents sought compensation after seizing a
"Number of Prisoners of War who were Secreted in different Parts of the
Country." Four months later, William Henry, Lancaster County treasurer,
paid out £241 in bounties for returned fugitives.[20]

With the assistance of provincial authorities, Hazen gradually curbed the
number of escapes. When Hazen's regiment finally left Lancaster in November 1782, the borough's residents thanked him for his "faithful & steady
Attention as Superintendent of the Prisoners of War" and for his "Spirited
Conduct . . . in Promoting the Public Weal." But even though Hazen had
restored a measure of order to local affairs by curbing the worst abuses, Lancaster's several hundred British captives remained a problem. Many of the
borough's captives, weary of confinement and eager to rejoin their forces,
looked to flee at their first opportunity. In December, Hazen's successor,
Colonel Richard Butler, informed Washington that the "number of prisoners here are considerable & troublesome," but he hoped he would "manage
them." In January 1783, William Henry issued thirty-three "certificates for
apprehending prisoners with receipts for the reward paid." Between late
February and early April 1783, at least seventeen British fugitives reported
to British headquarters.[21]

New Germany

If hiring out provided a convenient means of escape for many British prisoners, it offered a gradual means of assimilation for hundreds of German
captives. Although Whigs eventually curtailed their hiring of the British,
the hiring of Germans proceeded apace from early 1777 through the duration of the war. Promised generous wages and freedom from confinement,
thousands of Germans leaped at the opportunity to work for American employers, proving dependable and industrious laborers. More than two-thirds
of the Trenton prisoners—the first sizable German contingent seized during
the hostilities—hired out only months after their capture. When the Hessian officer Lieutenant Jakob Piel passed through Lancaster in April 1778
en route to British-occupied Philadelphia for his exchange, he found most
of the German prisoners at work in the town or the surrounding countryside. The majority of Germans who hired out to the Americans were
merely attempting to make the best of their unenviable situation as prisoners

of war. Many, however, soon grew attached to their new surroundings and looked to capitalize on the favorable economic prospects in the vast American interior.[22]

Forging ties among the local German speakers, earning better wages than most could ever hope to earn at home, and enticed by Americans' persistent promises of land and citizenship, growing numbers of the captives chose to desert their ranks and settle in the United States, with many taking up residence near their sites of detention. Years before the surrender at Yorktown, still leery of their American hosts and eager to return to Germany, most of the Trenton prisoners had patiently awaited their exchange. A handful had even dared to escape, venturing, in some cases, as much as 120 miles with the "help of kindly hearted inhabitants" before reaching the safety of British lines during Howe's occupation of Philadelphia. Others who had initially contemplated deserting had hesitated and returned to their ranks for fear of punishment if captured by the British Army; Hessian deserters fortunate enough to escape execution still faced a grim punishment in the form of lashings or a running of the gauntlet. By 1781, however, as the Whigs' military prospects improved, as the auxiliaries became better acquainted with their enemies, and as more and more Germans entered captivity, desertions increased dramatically. Once it became evident that the Americans could actually win the war and seal their independence, deserting carried less risk and greater appeal for the Germans.[23]

The duration of the war had also compromised the quality of newly arriving German recruits. As German princes labored to replace their American losses and maintain the troop quotas mandated by their subsidy treaties with Britain, recruiting practices steadily deteriorated, producing less reliable soldiers. Because the German suppliers often recruited from neighboring principalities, growing numbers of the auxiliaries felt little loyalty to their regiments or to the sovereigns who contracted their services. Thus in Lancaster, for instance, one of the Trenton captives indignantly complained to his American hosts that though not "a Hessian by birth," he had been "forced to go into this country." Disaffected auxiliaries responded accordingly, deserting in droves either as captives or as active-duty soldiers. During 1776, fewer than one hundred of the Hessen-Kassel troops deserted, compared to more than four hundred in 1778 and upwards of three hundred in 1779. During 1781, with the war slowly turning against the British, close to five hundred Hessen-Kassel troops joined the Americans.[24]

Typically, the German captives who hired out labored in war-related industries or on the flourishing farms dotting the Pennsylvania, Maryland, and Virginia countryside. But resourceful American employers found a variety of uses for their prisoners, learning to exploit their particular skills. Among the prisoners taken at Trenton was a small Hessian band; soon after the prisoners' arrival, residents of Lancaster began paying the musicians £15 a night to perform at their neighborhood gatherings. In June 1778, Francis Bailey, the Scots Irish publisher of the Lancaster-based *Pennsylvanische Zeitungs Blat*, employed a Hessian printer. Several of Lancaster's leading Whigs retained Hessians as servants. The more faithful and diligent the auxiliaries' service in American employ, the stronger the bond formed with their grateful hosts. Indeed, while many of Lancaster's English and German speakers learned to rue the arrival of British prisoners, they came to regret the departure of their German captives. In January 1779, William Atlee notified Thomas Bradford, Philadelphia's deputy commissary of prisoners, that he wished to keep some of the Hessians in Lancaster, claiming, "We cannot do without them here."[25]

Although many of Lancaster's German prisoners gladly forged new ties in captivity, a few rekindled old bonds. In early 1777, when the Middletown resident Christian Spaat learned that his brother-in-law numbered among the Hessians recently sent to Lancaster, Lancaster's committee generously granted the prisoner permission to reside with "his family for some little time." In July 1778, August Wille, a German Jaeger captured at the Second Battle of Trenton, formally appealed to Congress for permission to remain in the United States. Sent to Lancaster in January 1777, Wille was surprised to discover that he had relatives in the neighborhood. Insisting that he had been coerced into the Hessian service, he now welcomed his captivity among the Americans and hired on as a laborer with William Atlee. Confident that he could earn a good living in Pennsylvania, Wille announced his determination to "become a good Subject to the United States of America."[26]

Throughout the war, the combatants negotiated formal cartels to exchange their prisoners. These prisoner exchanges posed a growing dilemma for Continental officials, who wished to maximize Hessian desertions while ensuring the safe and timely return of as many American prisoners as possible. To maintain good faith in their exchanges with the enemy, Whigs dutifully returned their German captives, hoping that scores would desert after rejoining the British. Officials reasoned that the Germans' good treatment while in American hands would induce many to leave British employ and rejoin their former captors. During the early summer of 1778, Whigs began exchanging their Trenton prisoners. James Beatty, the new commissary general of prisoners, instructed Atlee to remind the German captives in his care of the "favourable ideas they already entertain of our Country" and that "we shall be glad to see them return." Observing that the Hessians "go very reluctantly," Atlee predicted that they "will try to get back to this part of the world, which they call 'New Germany' if they can." Beatty echoed Atlee's optimism, noting that General Washington "has great expectations from these Hessians," whose "attachment to this Country is amazing." A Lebanon resident recalled the "confusion and disquiet" attending the prisoners' departure, adding that "many bade us a cordial farewell and wept much." Before returning another detachment of German captives in December 1780, Atlee forecast that if "their Friends don't take good care of them," the community would "see many of them with us again." Some of Lancaster's German prisoners had even married local women by the time of their exchange and had no intention of returning to active service.[27]

Just as American officials had anticipated, many of the prisoners forwarded for exchange did eventually desert. After the summer 1778 exchange, an annoyed General Wilhelm Knyphausen, commander of the Hessen-Kassel troops, complained to his sovereign that 132 of the 739 captives had chosen to remain with the enemy. According to Knyphausen, the newly exchanged prisoners returned with "glowing descriptions of the country," recounting "how well they were treated" and inciting new defections among their comrades. Sent to Lancaster in January 1777, Conrad Aubel never left the state, deserting en route to his exchange. After taking Pennsylvania's new oath of allegiance in July 1778, Aubel married and settled in Northumberland County, some fifty to sixty miles north of his former place of detention. A few German prisoners made a more perilous and circuitous return to Pennsylvania. Following his arrival in Lancaster in early 1777, the Trenton captive Johann Conrad Dietz hired out in neighboring Heidelberg Township. Exchanged during the summer of 1778, Dietz returned to the British service in Manhattan. In September 1779, he was retaken aboard a British transport bound for Quebec. Sent to Philadelphia, Dietz eventually deserted and moved west to Upper Paxton Township, where his new neighbors included several former auxiliaries.[28]

Despite the rise in German desertions, some of Pennsylvania's most zealous patriots, embittered by the war, stubbornly refused to warm to the captive auxiliaries. Early Whig propaganda and tales from the front reviling the mercenaries had sealed these revolutionaries' deep-seated hatred of the German hirelings. Indeed, for such ardent patriots, loath to forgive or forget their revolution's costs, wartime enmities lingered long after Cornwallis's capitulation at Yorktown. Even the relations between the captive auxiliaries and local German speakers showed the strains of older regional divisions newly exacerbated by war. For generations of Pennsylvania Germans, "Hessen" remained a disparaging term recalling the invaders' peculiar Old World origins and wartime affiliations.[29]

By 1778, however, many of the interior's German speakers were giving their newly captured German prisoners a more enthusiastic reception.
When the Convention Army passed through Lancaster in December 1778,
for example, one resident noted that a "great many of the Dutch" flocked
to "wait upon the German prisoners." Lieutenant Thomas Anburey observed that, "seeing in what a comfortable manner their countrymen live,"
the Germans deserted in great numbers. After deserting, Atlee reported, the
Germans "remained among the Inhabitants, as Labourers and Tradesmen."
By the time Burgoyne's army reached Virginia in January 1779, more than
four hundred Germans had deserted, mostly in Pennsylvania. A Brunswick
officer complained that the locals "used all possible persuasion to make our
men stay behind," with "the German girls" doing "their best to get them
for husbands." Even officers "were not safe from such proposals," he added;
several received tempting offers of marriage to "girls worth three to four
thousand pounds." General Friedrich Adolph von Riedesel, commander of
the Brunswick troops under Burgoyne, would eventually lament that the
"country now abounds with deserters." Frederick Valentine Melsheimer, for
example, chaplain to a regiment of Brunswick dragoons, deserted in Pennsylvania and went on to serve as pastor to several Lutheran congregations before
marrying and settling in Lancaster County's Manheim Township, just north
of Lancaster, in 1784.[30]

Throughout the war, Whigs continued to offer generous inducements to
German deserters. In April 1778, Congress devised fresh incentives for the
auxiliaries, insisting that they had a vested interest in ensuring a revolutionary
victory. Congress cleverly cast the war with Britain as a universal struggle for
liberty, destined to "establish perfect freedom in this new world, for those
who are borne down by the oppression and tyranny of the old." Accordingly,
the revolutionaries invited the Germans—as their ideological kin—to enjoy
the "privileges of free and independent states," promising them that "large
and fertile tracts of country . . . will amply reward your industry." To their
August 1776 offer of fifty acres of land for German rank-and-file deserters,
the Whigs added an ox, a cow, and three hogs. Noncommissioned officers
could now expect to receive two hundred acres plus livestock, and officers
an impressive eight hundred acres. As proof of their sincerity, the Whigs
pointed to their charitable dealings with their German captives, who, from
the "moment they were disarmed," had been treated "more like citizens than
prisoners of war." Congress assured the Germans, "We are willing to receive
you with open arms into the bosom of our country."[31]

Prospective deserters occasionally received encouragement from within
their own ranks. In December 1778, Ensigns Karl Führer and Karl Kleinschmidt,

two of the exchanged Trenton captives who later defected to the Americans, boldly justified their desertion in the pages of the *Pennsylvania Packet*. "Whenever a Prince undertakes to sell his subjects to a foreign power for infamous and wicked purposes, without their knowledge or consent," the officers proclaimed, "we are of the opinion, such subjects have a right to vacate the contract as soon as opportunity offers. This doctrine we conceive to be authorized by the law of nations, by reason and by common sense." As thanks for the kind treatment they received in captivity, the pair offered to help the revolutionaries raise a corps of Hessian deserters.[32]

Shortly after Trenton, a handful of German prisoners willingly joined the American service. In Lancaster, more than a dozen Waldeckers enlisted as early as March 1777. Later that year, the Trenton captive William Pine asked Pennsylvania officials for permission to "Work in the Country for my Living, Which I would rather do, than Join the Hessian Battallion again." Pine expressed his desire to "take the Oath of Alligiance" and become a "true & faithfull Subject to the United States." To "serve the Country," he ultimately enlisted in a passing Georgia battalion. During the spring of 1778, the Polish Count Casimir Pulaski's legion actively recruited among Lancaster's Hessian prisoners. Two years later, when the French Colonel Charles-Armand Tuffin's regiment of light horse visited the bustling host town of Reading, the Hessian captive Andreas Wiederholdt reported that the unit consisted entirely of German deserters.[33]

Although Continental officials generally opposed the recruitment of both their British and German prisoners during the early years of the war, they modified their position over the course of the hostilities. As with their British prisoners, Washington and the Congress initially resisted the temptation to bolster their enrollments with German recruits. Afraid that the practice would legitimize Britain's continued enlisting of American prisoners, Continental authorities preferred to keep their captives readily available for exchange. Despite the fact that some captives were clearly eager to enlist, officials also worried that the new recruits would prove unreliable in battle, not wishing to fall into the hands of their former employers. As a dubious member of Congress reckoned in June 1778, the soldiers' "fear of the halter in case of their being made prisoners would induce them to seek safety in flight."[34]

By 1782, however, the mounting costs of provisioning the prisoners and the pronounced decline in American enlistments prompted Congress to reconsider. In June 1782, Congress offered three-year terms of enlistment to the German prisoners, with each recruit promised an eight-dollar bounty and one hundred acres of land. Throughout the summer, Continental recruiting parties made the rounds at the various detention centers, exhorting their captured enemies to enlist. In Winchester, for example, with many of the revolutionaries' former German prisoners now in arms for the United States and among the recruiters urging their newly taken captives to join their ranks, Armand's corps enlisted over forty of the auxiliaries. In Frederick, determined recruiters enrolled some fifty German prisoners during the month of September alone. By late 1782, Armand's freshly enlisted auxiliaries were escorting their former British comrades to their new sites of detention.[35]

With the hostilities drawing to a close in the months following the British surrender at Yorktown, many German captives eagerly embraced the generosity of their American hosts. In Pennsylvania, Germans like the Brunswick captive Christian Heiman now affixed their signatures to formal oaths of allegiance, swearing fealty to the United States in anticipation of a fresh start in their newly adopted country. Only several years before, Lancaster's Reformed minister had delivered a stinging sermon to the town's Hessian prisoners, rebuking the auxiliaries for taking up arms against the American rebels. Having descended on American shores as minions of violence, the auxiliaries, their liberators promised, could now reap the blessings and bounty of a fertile land among free peoples—both English and German speakers—of manifest prosperity. Drummed into foreign service, committed to a faraway conflict few understood, and lacking a true nation of their own, the German captives could escape the clutches of tyranny and enjoy the freedoms of a liberal, voluntaristic society by embracing the Americans' bold new republican experiment and claiming formal membership in the new United States. Even Germans immune to the enticements of republican citizenship could appreciate the wealth and abundance on display in the cities, towns, and villages of Britain's rebellious colonies.[36]

Enemies Holding No Faith

While eventually encouraging the enlistment of their German prisoners, Continental officials continued to oppose the recruitment of their British captives. In early 1776, still confident of winning converts among their imperial antagonists, Continental authorities briefly entertained the prospect of recruiting British prisoners. As late as November 1776, the Board of War argued, "The enemy have inlisted great numbers of our people, who were prisoners, and it is but justice that we should retaliate." Washington, however, considered the prisoners' enlistment "neither consistent with the rules of war, nor politick," dismissing his new British captives as unreliable and potentially subversive recruits. By late 1776, Congress had proscribed the enlistment of enemy prisoners, ordering the British captives who had recently joined American units in Lancaster returned to their royal regiments.[37]

Eager to bolster their enrollments, however, ambitious recruiters frequently violated recruiting procedure, to the continuing frustration of Continental officials. In 1778, for example, Washington reprimanded Massachusetts officials for enlisting Convention prisoners as substitutes for state residents, stressing the "danger of substituting as Soldiers, men who have given a glaring proof of a treacherous disposition, and who are bound to us by no motives of attachment," for "Citizens, in whom the ties of Country, kindred, and some times property, are so many securities for their fidelity." Predicting the speedy "defection of every British Soldier," he concluded that "Mr. Burgoyne could hardly, if he were consulted, suggest a more effectual plan for plundering us of so much Money" and "reinforcing Mr. Howe with so many Men." On top of this, he foresaw "additional losses which may be dreaded, in desertions among the native Soldiers, from the contagion of ill example, and the arts of seduction." After the Convention troops relocated to Virginia, Washington advised a state official, "Above all things, suffer them not to engage in your service as Soldiers, for sure as they do, so sure do they rob you of your bounty and arms, and more than probably carry a man or two along with them to the enemy."[38]

Painful experience had taught Continental authorities that their British prisoners viewed enlistment in American units as the quickest way to return to their own ranks by deserting at the earliest and most convenient opportunity. The escapades of the British Convention prisoner William Beattie exemplify the Continentals' grounds for concern. Taken at Saratoga, Beattie accompanied the Convention Army to Cambridge, Massachusetts, where he enlisted in spring 1778 with Moses Hazen's regiment, which was then recruiting among the British prisoners. Seven months later, Beattie deserted his new regiment and fled to Long Island, where he joined the Queen's Rangers. His luck took a turn for the worse when he was recaptured years later at Yorktown and sent to Lancaster, where, by a remarkable coincidence, Hazen's regiment had just arrived to guard the British captives. Soon recognized by his guards, he was promptly returned to service in Hazen's regiment. Amazingly, he appears to have escaped serious punishment by his captors. Beattie repaid the Americans' generosity by serving for several months before deserting again and making his way to British-held New York City in late 1782. Seeking compensation for his troubles, he immediately filed a claim at British headquarters for moneys owed. Beattie's case paradoxically demonstrates both the continuing fluidity between British and American lines and the enduring ties binding British regulars to their own ranks.[39]

Despite the repeated warnings of Continental officials and the failure of earlier efforts to win the support of British captives, some local authorities initially encouraged the defection of Convention troops in order to weaken British arms and reduce the costs of provisioning the prisoners. In Virginia, for instance, deserters who swore an oath of allegiance before state magistrates received passes allowing them to move about the country in search of employment. Many deserters, however, conveniently used the passes to make their way back to British lines. To avoid suspicion, some of the fugitives concealed their regimentals in knapsacks and traveled in disguise. In July 1779, a Pennsylvanian residing near Wright's Ferry on the Susquehanna complained of the continuing flood of escaped prisoners streaming through the interior en route to New York. He cautioned that the "Enemy may soon Recrut an Army if they are permited to Pass through the Cuntry in such numbers." In March 1781, Congress angrily accused the British of violating the Convention of Saratoga by returning the fugitives to active duty against the United States. As the fugitives made every effort to "evade the most solemn stipulations," Congress proclaimed that they be "treated as Enemies holding no faith." To prevent continued escapes, Continental officials insisted that the British enlisted men and noncommissioned officers of Burgoyne's army remain "closely confined and effectually guarded."[40]

To maintain discipline in captivity and to prevent desertions to the enemy, Convention Army officers initially discouraged escapes by their enlisted men. Escaped prisoners fortunate enough to reach their own lines found themselves assigned to new regiments if their own units remained in captivity. Because British officers bore much of the expense for their regimental recruiting, escapes frequently amounted to a personal financial loss, since the fugitives would eventually have to be replaced to maintain the unit's integrity. Yet by 1779, frustrated by Congress's failure to liberate the Convention prisoners in accordance with the terms of their capitulation, the British command actively encouraged escapes. According to one fugitive, General Burgoyne distinguished between desertions to the enemy and "honorable desertions," involving "soldiers, who, through every difficulty, made their way to, and joined, his majesty's forces."[41]

To reward successful escapes, British headquarters paid one to two guineas to each British or German soldier who fled captivity to return to active service. Thus, during the seven months between June 1780 and February 1781, the British high command awarded 194 prisoners a total of £203.14 upon reporting to New York. After reaching British lines, the fugitives could also file claims for their pay in arrears. Soldiers who had suffered confinement received compensation, while those who had enlisted with or hired out to the enemy frequently had their claims denied. As an additional inducement to escape, headquarters amply compensated the prisoners' guides. Between May 6 and June 9, 1782, British officials awarded nine guides, including Ninas, "A Negro," over 140 guineas for safely delivering forty-seven prisoners. The obvious risks notwithstanding, aiding the prisoners' flight to freedom could prove a lucrative enterprise. Jesse Smith and Isaac Curser left British headquarters nearly one hundred guineas richer after escorting twenty-two fugitives to New York. When one loyalist collected payment for returning several Hessen-Hanau prisoners, their grateful commanding officer promised him an extra half guinea for each of their comrades he delivered to safety.[42]

But even if the Germans occasionally fled captivity, they proved model prisoners compared to their British allies. Of the nearly three hundred fugitives compensated for reaching New York between July 1780 and June 1781, only thirty-four belonged to German units. By contrast, a full 213, or roughly 72 percent, belonged to British regiments, while the remaining forty-eight numbered among the king's provincial forces. According to the British Convention prisoner Lieutenant Thomas Anburey, the Germans fared so well in captivity that most were content to remain under American supervision until exchanged, often hiring out and collecting wages from local employers into the bargain. Conversely, the British prisoners, animated by what Anburey termed "*amor patriae*," defied their captors at every turn, with hundreds determined to run grave risks in order to return to active duty and avenge American slights. Repeatedly recaptured following his escapes from detention sites in Virginia, Maryland, and Pennsylvania, John Clayton of the Twentieth Regiment of Foot reached New York in late summer 1781, two years after initially fleeing from Charlottesville. Cornelius O'Brien of the Twenty-fourth Regiment fled Lancaster in June 1781, only to be retaken by an American privateer upon attempting to hire a boat at New Jersey's Egg Harbor. The fast-talking fugitive promptly reclaimed his freedom by passing for a native New Yorker.[43]

Unlike their German allies, many British veterans felt both an emotional attachment to the king's forces and a patriotic pride nurtured during their nation's eighteenth-century wars with France. A French witness to Cornwallis's surrender at Yorktown contrasted the surprisingly compliant demeanor of the German auxiliaries with the seething "arrogance and ill-humor" of their British comrades, who "affected great contempt for the Americans." For the British soldier, service within a particular regiment typically implied a broader duty to king and country. Thus, early in the war, the British high command praised fifteen recalcitrant prisoners for defying their American captors, who had "tried to seduce them to take arms against their king and fight against their brother soldiers." Similarly, when the Americans invited a captive British sergeant to desert near war's end, the grizzled veteran spurned their advances, recalling later that he had been "determined to die rather than serve any state hostile to Great Britain." After fleeing to New York, he angrily derided his compatriots who languished in captivity instead of making their escape, charging that "they had lost that animation which ought to possess the breast of the soldier."[44]

Crown officers articulated a more refined, if still somewhat nebulous, vision of British nationhood than the lower ranks they commanded in the field. For British officers, patriotism entailed pride in their monarch as a symbol of rational liberty, Protestant prosperity, and imperial supremacy. In 1780, when Whig officials threatened to jail several of Lancaster's paroled British officers for singing "God Save the King," the incorrigible offenders swore to "sing it whenever we choose in defiance of all the gaols and rebels in America." After breaking his parole and fleeing from Lancaster County with several of his fellow officers in 1776, one British captain testified that it was the "earnest desire of taking an active part in the Service of their Country" that drove him and the others to "make their escape." Such, of course, was the very sort of language the imperial high command wished to hear from British fugitives, but for crown officers—career soldiers invested in the royal service—the sentiment was heartfelt. When a paroled British lieutenant died in early 1782, William Atlee offered to have him buried on the grounds of Lancaster's Anglican church. Instead, Major James Gordon, the commander of Lancaster's prisoners, insisted that the deceased be buried among the British dead within the stockade, reasoning that "officers and soldiers should not be separated," thus preserving the war's battle lines even in death.[45]

From the start, the Americans' rebel status poisoned their relations with British prisoners. No longer content with their inferior status as colonial subjects, Whigs defied the empire from within, repudiating both king and country. Once fellow citizens of the British, the revolutionaries now aspired to sovereign nationhood, free of their former imperial entanglements and obligations. Fiery British nationalists promptly damned the American rebels' subversive aspirations as the most vile form of treason. By 1778, the rebels' new alliance with Britain's inveterate enemies the French had alienated even hitherto sympathetic Britons. For Britons of all stripes, the revolutionaries' self-righteous paeans to liberty stank of hypocrisy, given their opportunistic marriage of convenience to the papist and despotic French. During the summer of 1781, Thomas Anburey scornfully noted how the Continental forces had taken to wearing black-and-white cockades as a "compliment to, and a symbol of affection for, their generous and magnanimous allies the French." A Continental officer who watched the king's vanquished forces ground their arms at Yorktown observed that it was upon surrendering to his American conquerors that the "spirit and pride of the British soldier was put to the severest test." Many of the soldiers "manifested a *sullen temper*," he noted, "throwing their arms on the pile with violence, as if determined to render them useless." Despite their shared language and culture, seven years of brutal warfare had left the combatants the most irreconcilable of adversaries. Indeed, the very closeness of their connection, their long-standing bonds of culture and kinship, made the rupture between Britons and Americans all the more bitter.[46]

The emotional distance between the former brethren became increasingly obvious as the war progressed, not merely on the fields of battle but also at the sites of detention, where the Americans answered their rebellious British captives with threats, coercion, and abuse. Weary of the hostilities but still saddled with thousands of resentful prisoners, local militants unleashed years of accumulated rage. Recaptured and sent to Lancaster after fleeing captivity in Virginia, the Convention prisoner John Rhoads soon tried to escape from the barracks, only to be apprehended, clapped in irons, and tossed into a dungeon, where he languished for three months. One British soldier taken in early 1781 during Cornwallis's campaign through the South complained of the conditions in Winchester, where he and his comrades suffered "all manner of ill treatment, insult and abuse." After American guards escorted his detachment to Lancaster, he described their cruelty as "shameful and altogether incompatible with the profession of either soldiers or christians," for "they drove us like so many bullocks to the slaughter." He noted how the captain of the guard "broke his broad sword by cutting and slashing the prisoners, who were too much weakened by hunger and former ill treatment to keep up in the march."[47]

Scorned by virulent enemies, resentful revolutionaries now brandished their own militant patriotism at the point of their bayonets. The Yorktown prisoner Sergeant Roger Lamb escaped from Frederick, Maryland, in November 1781, only weeks after surrendering in Virginia. Caught several miles from town and returned to Frederick, Lamb was roughly paraded through the streets and thrown into the blockhouse, where he suffered daily torments from his guards. Once, after spitefully setting the straw in his cell ablaze, Lamb's guards mocked his panicked efforts to extinguish the flames. "I found that I could obtain no mercy from these savages," he later recalled. "Every day I was worse used than on the preceding." Like Lamb, the most zealous patriots had no sympathy for their enemies. After an unruly group of

British enlisted prisoners taunted members of Frederick's militia as "Rogues" and "Rebels" in late 1781, the Americans brutally assaulted the captives in their cells, putting a few to "the bayonet," as their terrified comrades watched in horror.[48]

As the revolutionaries gave vent to years of simmering animus, even superior rank and status afforded the prisoners no assurances of protection. Thomas Anburey reported that he and his fellow officers feared for their safety in Frederick after a Whig official lost his son at Camden and appeared "extremely anxious to be revenged upon us." In April 1781, Anburey had a dispute with his patriot landlord, who flew into a "violent passion," threatening the officer with imprisonment. "We have so long been accustomed to ill language and insolence from the inferior sort," Anburey observed, "that we really pay no more attention to it, than . . . we should to the cackling of so many geese." Even women occasionally cast off their customary deference to belittle their prisoners. Reveling in Britain's misfortune, a Virginia matron boasted to a newly taken Yorktown prisoner, Captain Samuel Graham, that one of her two sons was "at the catching of Johnny Burgoyne" and the other at the bagging of Cornwallis. "Next year," she crowed, both would "catch Clinton at New York." In the months after Yorktown, following heated arguments in Lancaster and Frederick, local militants dispensed public beatings to crown officers. Following their hosts' violent assault, Frederick's captive officers petitioned state officials, complaining of the "most outrageous & atrocious insults and abuse offered to our persons and property." From Lancaster, Major James Gordon, commander of the prisoners, notified General Sir Guy Carleton in New York of the "very illiberal treatment the British Officers have met with at this Post, both from the civil Inhabitants, & Continental Officers." Ever defiant, Gordon assured his commander that he would "treat the opinion of the Americans and their ill usage to me with that contempt it deserves."[49]

Over the course of the war, the Americans won occasional British converts, as some captives willingly deserted their ranks to join their transatlantic cousins. From Philadelphia, deputy commissary of prisoners Thomas Bradford reported numerous cases of British captives petitioning to take the oath of allegiance and remain in the United States. Late in the war, as local controls continued to break down, Lieutenant Anburey noticed a disturbing rise in defections to the enemy among the British Convention troops. Captain Graham later echoed the concern from Lancaster, where desertions were taking a toll on the Convention Army. Desertion was commonplace among eighteenth-century armies, and like their German allies, some British regulars found the prospect of a new life in North America too appealing to resist. Private John Robert Shaw of the Thirty-third Regiment, for example, arrived in Lancaster in the summer of 1781 following his capture in North Carolina. Shaw joined his British comrades in several escape attempts before finally deserting and taking odd jobs among the locals to survive. "Determined against having any further connection with the English army," he soon returned to Lancaster, where he enlisted with an American recruiting party in hopes of earning his freedom at war's end. After enlisting, he married a domestic servant from Carlisle. Choosing to remain in the United States after the cessation of hostilities, Shaw eventually headed west, settling in Kentucky. Decades after embarking for the colonies to subdue the rebellion, he recalled that it was his "very good fortune" to fall into American hands.[50]

But in his determination to join and remain among the rebels, Shaw proved an exception to the rule. Indeed, for every Shaw, there were many who, like Beattie, Rhoads, and Lamb, stubbornly defied the Americans. Lamb's experience remains especially well documented, as he produced two memoirs following his return to Britain. Lamb fled his American captors at great personal risk on three separate occasions. First taken while serving with the Ninth Regiment of Foot at Saratoga, he eventually fled Massachusetts for New York in late 1778. Upon reaching British headquarters, he volunteered for active duty and joined the Twenty-third Regiment of Foot, Royal Welch Fusiliers. Recaptured with Cornwallis's army several years later, he escaped from York, Pennsylvania, for his second trip to British headquarters in March 1782, just three months after his failed escape from Maryland. Lamb spurned the prospect of a future among his former captors as a "dereliction of loyal duty and his relationship with the old world, where he fondly hoped to cultivate the society of his early acquaintance."[51]

With the approach of peace, many Americans remained equally disdainful of their British captives. Even the British regulars who eagerly deserted to the Americans remained occasional targets of resentment and suspicion. One British deserter quickly came to rue his decision after "finding himself universally despised" by Pennsylvania's Whigs. Although Pennsylvanians had long grown accustomed to the sight of Hessian laborers roaming the interior, the deserter reckoned that a group of British prisoners would "soon spread an alarm through the country." Locals' caution was hardly surprising, given the British captives' reputation for misbehavior. Within a year of their victory at Yorktown, many revolutionaries, still stinging from the costs of war, dismissed their British enemies as completely unassimilable and thus unwelcome candidates for membership in the new nation. In October 1782,

Congress resolved that for the duration of the war, no British subjects would be "permitted to become citizens of the United States."[52]

Most Wretched and Most Miserable Men

If the Whigs had grown accustomed to British resistance, they had also come to expect German compliance. By 1781, efforts to seduce the auxiliaries had yielded encouraging results, with many Germans now eager to join the Americans in their fields, workshops, and battalions. The Germans' increasingly favorable disposition earned them markedly better treatment than the revolutionaries' British captives, along with a claim to membership in the new United States. But owing to the Germans' lingering military obligations or familial and cultural ties, only a portion of the captives yielded to America's charms. Unable or unwilling to adjust to the alien American environment, hundreds longed to return to their homes in Europe. To many patriots, however, their prisoners' dogged resistance smacked of ingratitude.

By mid-1782, largely because of the mounting costs of maintaining the prisoners, German captives who refused to cooperate with the Americans came under increasing pressure from Continental authorities. Their enemies soundly defeated, the revolutionaries no longer felt a compelling need to undermine British military operations by seducing their German prisoners, alternating more freely between coercion and reward. By showcasing their commitment to the new nation as laborers, soldiers, or citizens, compliant prisoners exhibited the makings of virtuous republicans and would thus find a friend and protector in the United States. But unrepentant captives who spurned republican generosity by stubbornly remaining under the oppressive yoke of Old World tyranny would be dealt with as inveterate enemies of the United States. In early July 1782, Congress invited all German captives who took an oath of allegiance and paid $80 for their maintenance while prisoners of war to become free citizens of the United States. Prisoners who wished to become citizens but lacked the sum required to obtain their freedom could sign three-year indentures, in which case their new local employers would pay their discharge fees. On July 30, a German American clergyman conveyed Congress's proposal to several hundred German Convention troops assembled at Pennsylvania's Reading barracks.[53]

The predominantly German-speaking seat of Berks County, located more than forty miles northwest of Philadelphia and fifty miles east of the Susquehanna in Pennsylvania's lush Delaware Valley, Reading, like Lancaster some thirty miles to the southwest, had hosted large detachments of enemy prisoners since early 1776. Like their compatriots in Lancaster and Frederick,

Reading's diverse inhabitants had registered immediate fears over the potentially hostile intentions of their British enlisted prisoners, advocating their close confinement. As recently as January 1781, over fifty of the town's British prisoners had orchestrated a failed jailbreak. The town's paroled British officers fed additional resentments. In October 1777, a few of the officers exploited the panic accompanying Howe's invasion as an opportunity to bully their hosts, who, they cautioned, should "make Intrest with them, in order to be favoured when the Regulars would come." For one American officer stationed in Reading through the Philadelphia occupation, the offending parolees embodied the "*scoundrel in red.*" Repeated complaints led Elias Boudinot, the newly appointed commissary general of prisoners, to damn the offenders as a "set of supercilious & haughty People" who "scarcely deserve the Treatment due to Gentlemen." From headquarters, Boudinot insisted that the officers remain under a strict curfew, warning that "by no means" should they be "allowed to go about at Night." The prisoners' provocations ignited the fury of local militants, who eventually thrashed one of the officers in the street before tossing him into the town jail. By contrast, locals reported fewer troubles with their German captives, who, as late as spring 1782, fared notably better than their British allies, often hiring out in town or the surrounding countryside. A Hessen-Hanau officer assured his prince from New York in May 1782 that the situation of Reading's German prisoners was "not so very bad." Indeed, he reported, the recently relocated Convention prisoners "work in the country and meet once monthly in the barracks, where roll is called, and then each one goes back to his work again."[54]

Now, mere weeks later, after informing the freshly assembled German prisoners that the king of Great Britain was refusing to pay for their subsistence, the community's minister encouraged them to consider Congress's proposal for becoming American citizens. Following the minister's address, the patriot Captain Thomas Bartholomew Bowen presented the prisoners with an additional option for assimilating into the United States, urging them to enlist with the Americans in return for generous Continental bounties. As Bowen explained, rather than purchasing their freedom or signing three-year indentures, the Germans could instead join the ranks of America's citizen soldiers "under the Banners of that Magnanimous Commander General Washington, defending the cause of Liberty and the Rights of Humanity." Upon completing their terms of enlistment, Bowen assured the prospective inductees, "you may enjoy yourselves, with your offspring, under your own Vine and Fig Tree, saying I have deserted the services of a Tyrannical King for those of a Free and Rising State." Such an offer, the captain assured the Germans, amounted to a "liberty not known to other Prisoners of War."[55]

A week later, an impatient General Hazen delivered a sterner address to Reading's prisoners. He announced that because the king was refusing to provision or exchange the prisoners, and the Americans could afford to provide only for their own troops, the Germans would no longer receive supplies. Consequently, either the captives must repay their maintenance, indenture themselves, or enlist in the American service. The prisoners who refused would remain closely confined. While pondering their options, the Germans requested permission to send two of their sergeants to New York to confer with their superior officers before making their final decision. Then, in early September, two of the German noncommissioned officers escaped from Reading's barracks.[56]

Frustrated by their prisoners' intransigence, American officials removed approximately 350 of the Germans from the comfort of their barracks, depositing sixty in jail and the remainder in the open jail yard. During mid-September, the authorities transferred most of the Germans to Lancaster for close confinement, making the prisoners pay the cost of their transportation. Those who refused to pay suffered a miserable imprisonment in Lancaster's dungeon. Officials placed the remaining German prisoners in jail, where, as one observer later reported, they were "so crowded, they could neither sit, nor lay down." The prisoners received scanty and spoiled provisions, along with frequent visits from relentless American recruiters. Ironically, those German captives who had enlisted under coercion at home now faced growing pressure to enlist with their enemies abroad.[57]

After enduring these conditions for more than a month, many of the Germans reluctantly chose to enlist or sign indentures. In Lancaster, Justus Groh of the Knyphausen Regiment signed a three-year indenture with Emmanuel Carpenter, a former county associator and state assemblyman. Roughly eighty Germans joined Hazen's regiment in Lancaster. Fifty others enlisted for six months as marines aboard the frigate *South Carolina*. The ship's captain offered no bounty but promised the prisoners that once their enlistments expired, they would be "at liberty to go to any part of the country they pleased." Yet, in a surprising twist of fate, a British warship captured the vessel in December 1782 and promptly carried the Germans to New York to resume their duties in the king's service. Assuring their commanders that they had enlisted with the rebels only "in hopes of freeing themselves from a miserable captivity," the prisoners were returned to active duty.[58]

At considerable cost, other Germans doggedly resisted American demands. In the face of mounting abuse from their captors, a group of Hessians confined in Philadelphia complained to their superiors in New York that they were being "treated not like prisoners of war to a Christian Nation, but like wretches fallen into the hands of Barbarians." Under increasing pressure to indenture themselves to American employers, the captives indignantly declared that they "were not transported to this country as Malefactors to be punished for their Crimes, and to be sold for slaves." Instead, they came as soldiers, "sent upon a different service." Rather than submitting to "so scandalous a transaction," the Germans stubbornly vowed to "end our days in patient resignation to our adverse fate."[59]

Like many of their British allies before them, some German captives cleverly duped the Americans by enlisting or indenturing themselves with the express design of escaping to New York. For instance, two newly indentured Hessen-Hanau privates by the names of Pohl and Rueffer straggled into British headquarters in May 1783 after absconding from their employers. Over a dozen of their comrades had beaten them to New York following their desertion from Moses Hazen's regiment. Seven of the recently enlisted deserters had reached British lines with the assistance of "well-intentioned farmers," who, at the urging of Hessian officers, promised to return with additional fugitives.[60]

During late fall 1782, more than a dozen of Reading's German prisoners escaped to New York, where they immediately complained of their "hard treatment" and "great sufferings" in captivity. A despairing Hessen-Hanau captain notified his prince from British headquarters that many of his troops had "taken service with the Americans and still others" had "indentured themselves" after months of coercion. In early December, General Sir Guy Carleton, commander of British forces in North America, demanded that Washington investigate the alleged abuse. Within a week, American officials released most of the Germans from jail but confined them to their barracks. In late December, Secretary Lincoln denied the accusations of coercion, instead indicating that some of the Germans had "in compliance with their own solicitation been indulged the privilege of becoming citizens of America and what ever contract they have made with the Inhabitants has been their own voluntary act." The German Convention prisoner Johann Bense offered a sharply contrasting view of events, later recalling that "in the last year of our captivity," he and his comrades were the "most wretched and most miserable men."[61]

A Very Long and Disagreeable Confinement

Following the declaration of peace formally concluding the hostilities in early 1783, the Whigs sorted out their remaining captives, permitting decided or potential converts to remain in the United States while compelling their irredeemable enemies to depart for foreign shores. Through their evolving prisoner policy, Continental officials defiantly asserted and defended their nation's newly won sovereignty. Deemed the lawful property of American citizens, prisoners who had recently contracted their labor were now prevented from returning to their regiments before satisfying their obligations to their new employers. Emboldened by victory, Continental officials justified their uncompromising policy toward their captives as the legitimate and long-overdue retribution for Britain's well-documented abuse of American prisoners.

In late March 1783, Continental officials received news of the peace ending the war with Great Britain. On April 11, Congress proclaimed a formal cessation of hostilities. Article 7 of the provisional peace treaty called for the liberation of all prisoners of war. In mid-April, Washington and Secretary Lincoln ordered their British and German prisoners freed and sent to New York as soon as possible. On April 21, Washington informed British headquarters that the captives would be conducted from their places of detention in early May in incremental detachments of five hundred. The return of the revolutionaries' British prisoners highlighted the bitter divisions separating the former kinsmen.[62]

Fearful that spiteful British captives would seek revenge against their triumphant hosts, Continental officials took precautions to ensure American security. Washington recommended that British officers superintend the prisoners' march to "prevent any Irregularities, that disorderly persons may be disposed to commit." On May 5, Secretary Lincoln cautioned Brigadier General Alured Clarke, the British officer supervising the prisoners' evacuation, to "maintain that order and discipline among the Troops, while on their March, which the safety and interest of our Citizens may require," further informing him that in order "to render the exertions of your officers efficient, by enabling them to arrest and punish Delinquents," an "Escort of American Troops" would "march with each division." Lancaster's British prisoners left the borough in three divisions on May 9, 10, and 11. On May 8, Major James Gordon, the senior officer of Lancaster's British prisoners, gratefully welcomed the end of a "very long & disagreeable confinement."[63]

Upon learning of the peace, some of the German captives were eager to rejoin their regiments but remained under lengthy indentures. At Mount Hope, New Jersey, for example, more than thirty Hessians labored at the furnace of the ironmaster John Jacob Faesch. Given the option to enlist, hire out, or remain closely confined, the prisoners had signed indentures in early March 1783, just weeks before receiving news of the peace. The soldiers later testified that they had no knowledge of the duration of their contracts.

When they sought to return to their regiments, Faesch informed them that they were bound by three-year indentures. Worried that the prisoners would try to flee, Faesch promised a $10 reward for the safe return of any laborer apprehended without a written pass more than three miles from his Mount Hope works. In late March, the prisoners appealed to the Hessian high command, claiming that they had indentured themselves under coercion and now wished to return to their units. General Carleton asked Secretary Lincoln to investigate the prisoners' complaint and adhere to the "true spirit of the Treaty" formally ending the hostilities.[64]

Lincoln dismissed the allegations, countering that the Germans had voluntarily contracted their labor. If the prisoners now wished to rejoin their regiments, they must first reimburse their new employers for their discharge fees. After also rejecting the Germans' claims of coercion, General Hazen contrasted their more favorable circumstances with the deplorable conditions endured by American prisoners, proclaiming it a "virtue" to allow a "mercenary soldier and a prisoner of war to become at his own election a free citizen in the State to which he owes his existence." In a testy exchange with the Hessian high command, Elias Boudinot, now president of Congress, sourly suggested that any perceived Continental mistreatment of prisoners served as fitting retaliation for Britain's flagrantly callous treatment of American captives. For Boudinot and other Continental officials solicitous of both their fellow citizens and their national sovereignty, Whig prisoner policy had become the vehicle of an assertive American nationalism.[65]

With a few thousand German captives still dispersed throughout the American interior, their increasingly skeptical commanders began calculating the likelihood of their return. In early spring 1783, Lieutenant General Friedrich von Lossberg, the new ranking commander of the Hessen-Kassel forces, wrote his sovereign from New York to say that although "a good number" of the troops sent to Lancaster and Reading remained in prison, the "majority had either accepted military service or gone into the country among the farmers." Months before, Captain Christian von Eschwege of Hessen-Hanau reported home from headquarters that most of the Reading detainees had "sold themselves as servants." Eschwege worried that the newly indentured would be the least likely to "get away" because their masters "keep a very close watch over them." Weeks later, the captain predicted that few prisoners from his sovereign's Leib Company would return, since "some of them have already married." With negotiations over the release of the indentured prisoners stalled, von Lossberg obtained royal permission to purchase their freedom, eventually securing the release of twenty-two of the Mount Hope detainees. When he learned that some earlier deserters now wished to rejoin their regiments but feared reprisals, he promised pardons to any who returned before the British evacuation. Discouraged by the stragglers' hesitation, he braced his monarch for the worst, speculating that "in all likelihood many of the prisoners will remain behind."[66]

In mid-summer 1783, Adjutant General Major Carl Baurmeister, one of the Hessian officers assigned to round up the remaining captives in American hands, confirmed headquarters' worst fears. As Baurmeister explained, while many German captives eagerly awaited returning to the security of their own lines and to the comforts of their own homes, hundreds of others—"scattered over the country from Philadelphia to Lancaster and Reading"—hoped to make the most of their new circumstances by settling permanently in the United States. Just weeks earlier, as his detachment prepared to sail from New York, a disheartened Eschwege reported that some of the remaining Hessen-Hanau prisoners had "told their comrades, who have returned, that they have no desire to return to Germany," preferring to "seek their fortune in America." Only recently dispatched to North America, hundreds of the former auxiliaries had now become virtually indistinguishable from many of the long-settled German immigrants who had preceded them to Britain's former colonies. According to Baurmeister, since surrendering at Saratoga, many of the former captives had "married and settled on their own land."[67]

Equally disconcerting, of the approximately seventeen hundred foreign auxiliaries taken with Cornwallis in October 1781, more than an estimated eight hundred had chosen to desert. In late spring 1783, von Lossberg conceded that both the Bose and Hereditary Prince regiments had documented "many desertions" stemming from "American promises of land and such," adding that "among the Ansbach troops," the "desertions were even more plentiful." The two Hessen-Kassel battalions captured at Yorktown suffered desertion rates of nearly 40 percent, while more than five hundred of the Ansbach-Bayreuth prisoners abandoned their corps after 1781. Private Johann Conrad Döhla, one of the Bayreuth prisoners, speculated that 69 of the 102 men in his unit had decided to remain in North America. When Döhla passed through Lancaster en route to New York, he encountered deserters from his corps who had earlier enlisted with an American regiment now stationed in Pennsylvania. Some of these soldiers had married into local families and had no intention of leaving their new homes, opting instead for a fresh start in the new republic. Like their patriot hosts, these erstwhile captives now aspired to their own version of American independence. In this sense, they constituted a very distinctive set of immigrants.[68]

Even some of the Germans who had endured a more rigorous captivity with the Americans tried their luck in the new nation. Several of John Jacob Faesch's thirty-some servants, for instance, chose to remain in New Jersey after finally securing their freedom. Meanwhile, across the Delaware in Pennsylvania, the private Heinrich Hennecke numbered among the eighty or so Convention prisoners who had enlisted in General Hazen's regiment during the fall of 1782. Hennecke married a local widow the day he enlisted and served faithfully for the remaining months of the war. Following his discharge, he settled in York, Pennsylvania, where he raised a family. In 1828, six years after his death, Hennecke's family was awarded one hundred acres for his welcome service in the Continental Army. Over the course of the Revolutionary War, upwards of thirty-five thousand German auxiliaries fought alongside the British. An estimated five to six thousand ultimately chose to remain in North America, in many cases after a lengthy captivity among the very rebels whom they had been sent to subdue.[69]

In late November 1783, as the last of the British and German troops prepared to sail from New York, Captain Johann Ewald, a Hessian Jaeger, surveyed the scene, describing the Whigs' jubilation as they celebrated their enemies' departure: "On all corners one saw the flag of thirteen stripes flying, cannon salutes were fired, and all the bells rang. The shores were crowded with people who threw their hats in the air, screaming and boisterous with joy, and wished us a pleasant voyage with white handkerchiefs." The Americans' exuberant patriotic display contrasted sharply with the somber mood prevailing aboard the departing British transports. "On the ships, which lay at anchor with the troops," Ewald noted, "a deep stillness prevailed as if everyone were mourning the loss of the thirteen beautiful provinces."[70]

The departing British and German troops had cause to mourn. Although most longed to leave the United States and return to their homes, the soldiers carried bitter memories of their stunning collapse. In losing the colonies to independence, the king's forces had participated in a spectacular failure. Tens of thousands had taken up the fight as seasoned veterans with years of experience in the wars of Europe or America or both, but they had been humbled by what many had contemptuously dismissed as a ragtag band of shopkeepers, farmers, artisans, and laborers, hastily assembled and trained citizen soldiers drawn to arms by the promise of adventure, the threat to their liberty and property, or the lure of an enlistment bounty. In the process, the invaders had lost many of their own, some to graves near the battlefields where they had fallen, others to American farms and workshops, where the former soldiers now hoped to make the most of New World opportunities alongside their recent adversaries. Lacking a nation of their own, thousands of German auxiliaries eagerly joined America's new experiment, enticed by promises of civil and religious freedom or, more often, by its fertile, abundant lands. By surrendering their arms, renouncing their Old World commitments, and affirming revolutionary ideals, erstwhile enemies could become welcome members of the American fold and wager their futures on the new republic.

That the Whigs embraced so many of their onetime enemies underscores the Revolution's universalistic ideals. That they so spitefully scorned their more defiant adversaries—both British and German—reveals an emerging strain of American exceptionalism. Engaged in a revolutionary process of nation building, zealous Continental officials hoped to remove potential contaminants from their budding republic, lest they endanger the American experiment. Ultimately, the revolutionaries' interactions with their enemies demonstrate both the inclusive and exclusive dimensions of America's aggressive, if fleeting, wartime nationalism. As the waning patriotic commitments of the early 1780s indicate, however, the development of American nationalism remained an ongoing and deeply contested process.[71]

Like their southern brethren in Frederick, on April 22, 1783, Lancaster's diverse revolutionaries joyously celebrated the peace. After assembling at the courthouse for a public reading of Congress's armistice proclamation, local patriots tolled the town bells and fired a thirteen-gun salute. With their enemies finally defeated and bound for distant shores, patriots had cause to rejoice. After eight years of warfare, they had won their independence and forged a new nation. The Whigs' dealings with their enemies, at home and on the field, had contributed to the formation of a distinct revolutionary identity by nurturing a new conception of citizenship rooted in shared republican commitment. Within the new United States, American citizenship provided diverse Americans with a common if continually contested identity that could potentially subsume or temporarily supersede the more parochial ethnic and regional identities that had long divided the peoples of prerevolutionary America.[72]

The year and a half following Britain's defeat at the Battle of Yorktown complicated the process of national identity formation fed earlier by war. United against common enemies during a bitter contest that had endangered their cause and community, Lancaster's insurgents proved eager to attend to more familiar concerns once the wartime crisis had passed. By 1782, with victory in hand and their enemies defeated, many revolutionaries gladly relaxed their Continental commitments. Residents' sporadic bursts of patriotism had always been colored and compromised by a more deeply ingrained parochialism that placed local and individual interests ahead of any broader Continental agenda. Their victory at Yorktown swelled the pride of locals in the achievements of their newly independent nation, but gradually their full attention returned to narrower provincial and individual concerns. Nurtured during the war, locals' patriotism withered during the peace, demonstrating how national commitments could never fully transcend the pursuit of individual or communal interests, and making the process of national identity formation a continuing project for future generations. Indeed, the resurgent parochialism of the early 1780s boded ill for the future, as diverse Americans began contesting the meanings of their Revolution before it was even complete, foreshadowing the bitter social and political divisions of the late 1780s and 1790s.

Epilogue

The Empty Barracks

By the late 1780s, the Lancaster barracks which had loomed so large in locals' wartime imagination had sunk into disrepair. Stripped of its purpose, the hulking edifice that had only a few years before housed thousands of enemy prisoners now stood a silent, empty shell. Overgrown with weeds from years of neglect, the building's adjacent graveyard, permanent home to the British and German prisoners who had perished in captivity, merged indistinguishably with the surrounding landscape. The decaying grounds eloquently symbolized residents' determination to exchange the unwelcome intrusions of war for the more predictable rhythms of their once flourishing market community. As the last of Lancaster's remaining prisoners filed out of their barracks to depart for New York in spring 1783, residents gratefully entered a postwar world free of the anxieties that had colored their relations for nearly a decade. When the British and German prisoners had arrived in Lancaster, the war had inevitably followed. With the captives came new fears and resentments. These pressures brought the community together in new ways, encouraging locals to forge alliances they would never have formed outside of war. Transcending their more particular divisions and attachments, residents cultivated in the course of their wartime interactions a shared American identity. Without the threats that had nurtured locals' patriotic bonds, Lancaster's postwar divisions emerged in sharp relief.[1]

War's end found the people of Lancaster with unresolved differences. The remaining disaffected few refused to forgive their rough treatment during the hostilities, while militants still simmered over their neighbors' defiance. The revolutionaries' factional divide stretched into peacetime, as the community's moderates and radicals pursued their competing visions of the nation's future. Radicals embraced the Revolution's promise of greater freedom and opportunity for the individual, while their more conservative-leaning rivals envisioned a strong centralized government with a national-izing agenda. Haunted by the violence, disorder, and unrestrained radicalism of the Revolution, the increasingly conservative Jasper Yeates now longed for the return of material security and deference to authority. In the summer of 1783, the future Federalist opined that Congress ought to have "much fuller and more energetic authority than what they at present are possessed of." Privately he confessed: "I cannot for my own part see how the machine of government throughout this continent can be conducted as matters stand at present. Local interests as well as prejudices will always clog the wheels, and I don't believe, (when the common danger which has united us thus long is past,) that the best informed and directed plans of the Angel Gabriel himself, would meet with the common concurrence." Thus, "odious as the word is," Yeates concluded, "a little more monarchy must be mixed with our democracy." Given his community's many sacrifices in the struggle against imperial power, Yeates's musings would have sent his more radical neighbors into paroxysms of rage.[2]

Shifting postwar demographics magnified local divisions. A decade after the first skirmish at Lexington Green, Lancaster County had become—in striking ways—more audibly and visibly German. The county's Anglo popu-lation underwent a proportional decline, with Germans now outnumbering their English-speaking neighbors by more than two to one. As the borough's population climbed to nearly four thousand inhabitants by 1790, Germans maintained their majority, still constituting above 60 percent of residents. By the mid-1780s, casual observers described Lancaster as "almost entirely German," with "not more than 50 English families," and assorted German dialects continued to resound in both the public and private spheres. Nearly a decade of revolution had failed to dispel long-established patterns of preju-dice and parochialism, with familiar forms of ethnic separation and discrimi-nation persisting through the 1780s. Although the war had reinforced what they held in common, Lancaster's revolutionaries never shed their diverse ethnic identities, remaining fully conscious of their differences. In a letter celebrating the capture of Cornwallis, for example, a Lancaster County cor-respondent mocked his German neighbors' poor English in referring to their

hope that "de ging will luce de goondry." Even long-settled residents accustomed to dealing with their diverse neighbors betrayed hints of intolerance.
Edward Burd Jr.'s family rebuked him for sullying the family line by marrying a "Low-bred Dutch girl," while Lancaster's new Lutheran pastor Gotthilf
Mühlenberg discouraged interethnic unions as a threat to his German parishioners' heritage. Just as before the war, most locals still preferred to marry
within their particular ethnicities and denominations, determined to preserve
their languages and cultures and to bolster their churches and communities.[3]

Amid Lancaster's lingering divisions, community leaders cast about for
ways to harmonize local and national interests. Hoping to serve both community and nation, in 1787 Anglo and German promoters assisted in the
founding of Lancaster's interdenominational Franklin College. Designed for
German speakers, the college aimed to preserve the nation's "present republican system of government" by cultivating informed and virtuous citizens.
Envisioning the institution as a means of instilling in German Americans
a "more accurate and general knowledge of the English language," Lancaster's Anglican minister stressed the urgency of its mission. "Whatever
impediments you throw in the course of spreading this language in its true
pronunciation and elegance among your children," the reverend advised his
German neighbors, "will be so many obstructions to their future interest
in private and public life," to "their future eminence in the public councils
of America," and to "that national union with their fellow citizens of the
United States." Two years later, at the urging of Pennsylvania's delegates
to Congress, borough officials launched a failed bid to make Lancaster the
nation's permanent capital. Mindful that the designated site would need to
meet the "general National Interests," local petitioners spelled out the borough's attractions in painstaking detail, assuring Congress that Lancaster's
citizens were "federal and strongly attached to the new System of Government." Given the competing provincial interests at stake, a friend in Congress
warned local promoters—in language reminiscent of their Revolution—that
the success of Lancaster's campaign hinged on the support of fellow Pennsylvanians, for "divided we fall."[4]

Indeed, for the residents who remained keen to reconcile local differences, nothing unified the community so well as shared memories of war and
revolution. Revisiting the Revolutionary War awakened the community's
national consciousness, reminding townsfolk of their broader commitments
beyond ethnicity and locale. Relieved of the unifying presence of their wartime enemies, locals staged artificial, representational displays of unity, symbolically reviving the Revolution in Lancaster through the ceremonial rites
of nationhood. For the residents who had borne arms or suffered for the

cause, these postwar rites carried real emotional power, rekindling memories of wartime sacrifice across the healing distance of time. By recalling locals' overarching commitments and commonalities, national celebrations evoked a spirit of unity amid division. Since 1777, townsfolk had gathered every Fourth of July to commemorate their nation's independence. During the war, these moments had provided welcome opportunities to endorse the united American resistance. But the most spectacular of Lancaster's celebrations occurred in July 1791. Joining residents that summer at the invitation of Lancaster officials was George Washington, hero of the Revolution and the nation's first chief executive. Offering a tangible connection to the nation's revolutionary origins, Washington's visit contributed a vital ingredient to the town's eagerly anticipated commemoration.[5]

Many residents, both English and German speakers, shared a long-standing fascination with their new president, who had come to embody their revolutionary ideal of patriotic self-sacrifice for the common good. Amid the successive toasts offered during Lancaster's wartime commemorations of independence, the celebrants invariably raised their glasses in honor of "His Excellency, Gen. Washington," whom many already considered the nation's principal founder. The longtime Washington admirer Edward Shippen never lived to see the general's greatest triumph, the stunning victory at Yorktown which crushed British hopes of reclaiming the rebellious colonies, quietly expiring at his Lancaster home only days before Cornwallis's surrender. Years earlier, Shippen had lauded "our magnanimous general" for earning the "admiration of the Thirteen United States" and becoming the "Idol of his Army," declaring that "the very sight of that great Patriot" must warm the "Hearts of all the well affected people in the Metropolis of America." Small wonder, he concluded, that even "some of the British Officers should revere so worthy a Character." Similarly, in the wake of General Gates's decisive victory at Saratoga, the Lancaster native Adam Hubley forecast even greater conquests for the army under "our brave Hero Washington." Hubley's younger brother Bernard Junior, a Continental officer in the German Regiment, later drew on Washington's military correspondence to pen one of the earliest histories of the Revolutionary War.[6]

The bitterly contested struggle with Britain had filled Germans like the Hubleys with an abiding respect for their wartime commander in chief. By the early 1780s, some of Lancaster County's Germans not only embraced Washington as their new *Landes Vater* but also showcased their newfound admiration in vivid iconographic imagery. During the Revolution, an unnamed local painter, known to us only as the Sussel-Washington artist, began featuring the general in bold, brightly colored European-inspired paintings in the

German *fraktur* tradition. In highly stylized portraits, Washington appeared in assorted poses—alongside his faithful wife, Martha, or astride a noble mount as the great man on horseback. By infusing Old World forms with New World content, the artist merged the German past and the American present. Germans' affection for Washington and the nation he led was the work of their Revolution.[7]

FIGURE 4. The Sussel-Washington artist's rendering of the revolutionaries' commander in chief. Applying American content to European forms, the painting fuses Old World and New. *Fraktur: Equestrian George Washington by Sussel-Washington Artist, circa 1780–1790.* Courtesy Independence National Historical Park.

On July 4, 1791, Lancaster's Germans enthusiastically took to the streets in the company of their Anglo neighbors, as they had every year since their formal declaration of independence. Now joined by their nation's president, locals celebrated their Revolution, affirming their shared wartime sacrifices and republican commitments. Washington and his entourage had arrived in Lancaster the previous evening to the cheers of roaring crowds. Milling about among the town's bustling throngs were many of the local veterans who had fought under the general during the hostilities. For the eager celebrants, the day's festivities boasted all of the now customary sights and sounds, with the flying of banners, tolling of bells, rattling of drums, thundering of cannons, and parading of militia. With wartime passions no longer dictating residents' interactions, the day was happily spared the violent destruction of property. In most ways, however, the celebratory scenes mirrored the elaborately staged proceedings of a decade before.[8]

That evening, Washington feasted with local notables in the courthouse, where borough officials presented a formal address on behalf of the inhabitants. Welcoming their distinguished guest "with no less grateful respect than their fellow-citizens of the East and South," residents celebrated his "transcendent love of country," which united Americans "by the great political bond of one common interest." Washington, in reply, graciously attributed the nation's peace and prosperity to the selfless "patriotic exertions" of his fellow citizens. By personally honoring the Revolution's most celebrated icon on the anniversary of their independence, locals reaffirmed their collective commitment to the nation they had helped to create. Among the evening's more memorable toasts was a stirring tribute to the "Patriots and Heroes who fought and fell in the Glorious cause of American Liberty." Although such encomiums had become standard fare by 1791, with memories of the war still fresh in the community's collective consciousness, the sentiment was genuine.[9]

To the uncritical observer caught up in the spectacle, the day's celebrations gave the superficial impression of a unified, nationally invested community. For local organizers, that was the point—to bring residents together in remembrance of their shared national bond. Like the wartime rites they sought to replicate, however, the carefully orchestrated proceedings masked deeper, lingering divisions. Lancaster's festivities were refracted differently through different parts of the community, as diverse residents experienced the day's events from their own unique perspectives. Devout sectarians, no more inclined to attend postwar rites than they were to join in the wartime celebrations of a decade before, skipped the ceremonies altogether, to the eternal frustration of their churchgoing neighbors. The town's moderate leadership enjoyed the spectacle from a position of privilege. Returned to their seat of authority sixteen years after the dislocations of war had elevated new political rivals in Lancaster's radicals, they provided the president's formal escort into town and later dined with him at the courthouse. Conversely, their more radical neighbors, mostly relegated to the crowds, took in the proceedings from the streets. The dizzying cacophony of the day's festivities, meanwhile, muffled the divergent languages and dialects emanating from the motley participants.[10]

Most telling of all, the single published account of the occasion appeared in Lancaster's only newspaper, the *Neue Unparthyesche Lancasteresche Zeitung und Anzeigs-Nachrichter*. Forty years earlier, the community's first short-lived newspaper, the *Lancastersche Zeitung*, featured corresponding English and German sections. Lancaster's new weekly, by contrast, appeared almost exclusively in German, proving of limited value to most Anglo residents and perpetuating the local linguistic divide. Even in locals' tributes to unity, traces of division remained, testifying to the still embryonic state of American national identity. Yet, during the waking hours of July 5, in the unscripted conclusion to Washington's visit, men and women, young and old, English and German speakers, lined Lancaster's streets to bid their president good fortune and an affectionate farewell as he embarked for Philadelphia to attend to the affairs of nationhood, equal testimony to their enduring commitment to their revolutionary legacy.[11]

Notes

Source Abbreviations

AA	Force, American Archives
APS	American Philosophical Society
BHP	Records of British Army Headquarters in America, 1775–1783
CR	Hazard, The Colonial Records of Pennsylvania
DLAR	David Library of the American Revolution
HSP	Historical Society of Pennsylvania
JCC	Ford, Journals of the Continental Congress, 1774–1789
LOC	Library of Congress
PA	Hazard, The Pennsylvania Archives
PCC	Papers of the Continental Congress
PLCHS	Papers Read before the Lancaster County Historical Society
PMHB	Pennsylvania Magazine of History and Biography
PRG	Records of Pennsylvania's Revolutionary Governments, 1775–1790
WMQ	The William and Mary Quarterly

Prologue

1. Thomas Anburey, *Travels through the Interior Parts of America*, 2 vols. (1789; repr., New York, 1969), 2:284. For early Lancaster, see Jerome Wood Jr., *Conestoga Crossroads: Lancaster, Pennsylvania, 1730–1790* (Harrisburg, 1979); and Mark Häberlein, *The Practice of Pluralism: Congregational Life and Religious Diversity in Lancaster, Pennsylvania, 1730–1820* (University Park, 2009).

2. George Washington to Benjamin Harrison, May 5, 1779, in *The Writings of George Washington, from the Original Manuscript Sources, 1775–1799*, ed. John C. Fitzpatrick, 39 vols. (Washington, D.C., 1931–1944), 15:9.

3. For prisoners during the Revolutionary War, see Caroline Cox, *A Proper Sense of Honor: Service and Sacrifice in George Washington's Army* (Chapel Hill, 2004), 199–236; Francis Cogliano, *American Maritime Prisoners in the Revolutionary War: The Captivity of William Russell* (Annapolis, 2001); Edwin Burrows, *Forgotten Patriots: The Untold Story of American Prisoners during the Revolutionary War* (New York, 2008); Linda Colley, *Captives: Britain, Empire, and the World, 1600–1850* (New York, 2002), 203–40; Robert Doyle, *The Enemy in Our Hands: America's Treatment of Prisoners of War from the Revolution to the War on Terror* (Lexington, 2010), 11–48; and Paul Springer, *America's Captives: Treatment of POWs from the Revolution to the War on Terror* (Lawrence, 2010),

13–41. For a close, well-researched study of the dealings between the revolutionaries and their German captives, see Daniel Krebs, *A Generous and Merciful Enemy: Life for German Prisoners of War during the American Revolution* (Norman, 2013).

4. For early American identity formation, see David Waldstreicher, *In the Midst of Perpetual Fetes: The Making of American Nationalism, 1776–1820* (Chapel Hill, 1997); Simon P. Newman, *Parades and the Politics of the Street: Festive Culture in the Early American Republic* (Philadelphia, 1997); and Carroll Smith-Rosenberg, *This Violent Empire: The Birth of an American National Identity* (Chapel Hill, 2010). For Pennsylvania and the mid-Atlantic, see Gregory Knouff, *The Soldiers' Revolution: Pennsylvanians in Arms and the Forging of Early American Identity* (University Park, 2004); Liam Riordan, *Many Identities, One Nation: The Revolution and Its Legacy in the Mid-Atlantic* (Philadelphia, 2007); and Peter Silver, *Our Savage Neighbors: How Indian War Transformed Early America* (New York, 2008).

1. "A Colony of Aliens"

1. Wood, *Conestoga Crossroads*, 1–20; Jerome Wood, "The Town Proprietors of Lancaster, 1730–1790," *The Pennsylvania Magazine of History and Biography* (hereafter *PMHB*) 96 (July 1972): 346–68; Wayne L. Bockelman, "Continuity and Change in Revolutionary Pennsylvania: A Study of County Government and Officeholders" (Ph.D. diss., Northwestern University, 1969), 142–50. See also Franklin Ellis and Samuel Evans, *History of Lancaster County, Pennsylvania, with Biographical Sketches of Many of Its Pioneers and Prominent Men* (Philadelphia, 1883); Daniel Rupp, *History of Lancaster and York Counties* (Lancaster, 1845); Jacob Isidor Mombert, *An Authentic History of Lancaster County, in the State of Pennsylvania* (Lancaster, 1869); James T. Lemon, *The Best Poor Man's Country: A Geographical Study of Early Southeastern Pennsylvania* (New York, 1976); and Roger C. Henderson, *Community Development and the Revolutionary Transition in Eighteenth-Century Lancaster County, Pennsylvania* (Binghamton, 1983).

2. Wood, "The Town Proprietors of Lancaster," 346–68; Lemon, *Best Poor Man's Country*, 118–49; Kevin Kenny, *Peaceable Kingdom Lost: The Paxton Boys and the Destruction of William Penn's Holy Experiment* (New York, 2009), 34–36. For the role of county seats in Pennsylvania's urban geography, see Judith Ridner, *A Town In-Between: Carlisle, Pennsylvania, and the Early Mid-Atlantic Interior* (Philadelphia, 2010).

3. Wood, *Conestoga Crossroads*, 5–8, 11–17, 51, 93–94; Lemon, *Best Poor Man's Country*, 46–47, 62–63, 149.

4. Quoted in Wood, *Conestoga Crossroads*, 47, 93; Witham Marshe, *Journal of the Treaty at Lancaster in 1744, with the Six Nations* (Lancaster, 1884), 11; M. Luther Heisey, "How Lancaster Grew, and What People Thought of It," *Papers Read before the Lancaster County Historical Society* (hereafter *PLCHS*) 45 (1941): 90–91; Elizabeth Clarke Kieffer, "Social Life in Lancaster Borough," *PLCHS* 45 (1941): 106–7; Lemon, *Best Poor Man's Country*, 8; Wood, "The Town Proprietors of Lancaster," 356. See also Wood, *Conestoga Crossroads*, 16–19.

5. Quoted in Wood, *Conestoga Crossroads*, 69; Patrick Griffin, "The People with No Name: Ulster's Migrants and Identity Formation in Eighteenth-Century

Pennsylvania," *The William and Mary Quarterly* (hereafter *WMQ*) 58 (July 2001): 587–614, esp. 604. See also, Wood, *Conestoga Crossroads*, 11–12, 93–120, 139–80.

6. Heisey, "How Lancaster Grew," 93–94; Wood, *Conestoga Crossroads*, 11–12, 93–120.

7. Häberlein, *Practice of Pluralism*, 67–68, 166–70; Wood, *Conestoga Crossroads*, 29, 98–99, 172, 174; *The Pennsylvania Archives* (hereafter *PA*), ed. Samuel Hazard et al., 9 ser., 119 vols. (Philadelphia and Harrisburg, 1852–1949), 3rd ser., 17:3–15.

8. Wood, *Conestoga Crossroads*, 121–37, esp. 124–25.

9. Wood, *Conestoga Crossroads*, 98–99, 124, 126, 133, 142; Häberlein, *Practice of Pluralism*, 43, 48; *PA*, 3rd ser., 17:3–15.

10. Quoted in Wood, *Conestoga Crossroads*, 170; see also 159–79, esp. 168–69; Häberlein, *Practice of Pluralism*, 2; Lemon, *Best Poor Man's Country*, 12.

11. Häberlein, *Practice of Pluralism*, 125–28; Wood, *Conestoga Crossroads*, 163–66, 175–76.

12. Quoted in Häberlein, *Practice of Pluralism*, 121; see also 42–43, 127–28; Wood, *Conestoga Crossroads*, 163, 167, 172–74.

13. Wood, *Conestoga Crossroads*, 1, 7–9, 47–49, 69, 159; Henderson, *Community Development and the Revolutionary Transition*, 47; Bockelman, "Continuity and Change in Revolutionary Pennsylvania," 142–50; Lemon, *Best Poor Man's Country*, 19, 47, 69; Häberlein, *Practice of Pluralism*, 79, 106–7; Aaron Spencer Fogleman, *Hopeful Journeys: German Immigration, Settlement, and Political Culture in Colonial America, 1717–1775* (Philadelphia, 1996), 1–65; Alan Taylor, *American Colonies* (New York, 2001), 320–21. See also Marianne Wokeck, *Trade in Strangers: The Beginnings of Mass Migration to North America* (University Park, 1999). In 1761, Thomas Barton placed the county's population at approximately twenty-four thousand; see Häberlein, *Practice of Pluralism*, 138.

14. Quoted in Griffin, "The People with No Name," 593; Heinrich Mühlenberg, *The Journals of Henry Melchior Mühlenberg*, trans. and ed. Theodore G. Tappert and John W. Doberstein, 3 vols. (Philadelphia, 1942–1957), 1:260; Lemon, *Best Poor Man's Country*, 43–49, 62–63, 69, 78–83; Bockelman, "Continuity and Change in Revolutionary Pennsylvania," 144–50; Kenny, *Peaceable Kingdom Lost*, 34–35.

15. Marshe, *Journal of the Treaty at Lancaster*, 10; Wood, *Conestoga Crossroads*, 7–9, 13–15, 159, 181–215; Heisey, "How Lancaster Grew," 90; Häberlein, *Practice of Pluralism*, 1–13, 129–36, 138–80; Lemon, *Best Poor Man's Country*, 14.

16. Quoted in Wood, *Conestoga Crossroads*, 94; William Moraley, *The Infortunate: The Voyage and Adventures of William Moraley, an Indentured Servant*, ed. Susan E. Klepp and Billy G. Smith (University Park, 1992), 71. See also Wood, *Conestoga Crossroads*, 7–9, 27, 29–30, 49, 63, 205–15. For ethnic interactions in eighteenth-century Pennsylvania, see Dietmar Rothermund, "The German Problem of Colonial Pennsylvania," *PMHB* 84 (Jan. 1960): 3–21; Dietmar Rothermund, *The Layman's Progress: Religious and Political Experience in Colonial Pennsylvania, 1740–1770* (Philadelphia, 1962), 113–31; Alan Tully, "Englishmen and Germans: National-Group Contact in Colonial Pennsylvania, 1700–1755," *Pennsylvania History* 45 (July 1978): 237–56; Alan Tully, "Ethnicity, Religion, and Politics in Early America," *PMHB* 107 (Oct. 1983): 491–536; Laura L. Becker, "Diversity and Its Significance in an Eighteenth-Century Pennsylvania Town," in *Friends and Neighbors: Group Life in America's First Plural Society*, ed. Michael Zuckerman (Philadelphia, 1982), 196–221; Sally Schwartz,

"A Mixed Multitude": The Struggle for Toleration in Colonial Pennsylvania (New York, 1987); Marianne S. Wokeck, "German Settlements in the British North American Colonies: A Patchwork of Cultural Assimilation and Persistence," in *In Search of Peace and Prosperity: New German Settlements in Eighteenth-Century Europe and America*, ed. Hartmut Lehmann et al. (University Park, 2000), 191–216; Fogleman, *Hopeful Journeys*; and Häberlein, *Practice of Pluralism*.

17. Quoted in Kenny, *Peaceable Kingdom Lost*, 24–26; quoted in Rothermund, "The German Problem of Colonial Pennsylvania," 9; see in addition 3–21; Taylor, *American Colonies*, 320–21; Schwartz, *"A Mixed Multitude,"* 159–204.

18. Benjamin Franklin to Peter Collinson, May 9, 1753, in *The Papers of Benjamin Franklin*, ed. Leonard W. Labaree et al. 40 vols. (New Haven, 1959–2011), 4:483–85.

19. Benjamin Franklin to Peter Collinson, May 9, 1753, in Labaree, *Papers of Benjamin Franklin*, 4:483–85; Benjamin Franklin, *Observations concerning the Increase of Mankind, Peopling of Countries, &c.* (Boston, 1755), 10; William Smith, *A Brief State of the Province of Pennsylvania* (London, 1755), 19, 40; "English versus Germans," *PMHB* 16 (Apr. 1892): 120.

20. Quoted in Schwartz, *"A Mixed Multitude,"* 189, 237; see also 187; Lemon, *Best Poor Man's Country*, 45; Häberlein, *Practice of Pluralism*, 160; Silver, *Our Savage Neighbors*, 192–93.

21. Heisey, "How Lancaster Grew," 91; Wood, *Conestoga Crossroads*, 18–19, 23–25, 27–32, 39, 43; Häberlein, *Practice of Pluralism*, 106–7, 172–73; Ellis and Evans, *History of Lancaster County*, 373. For Lancaster's borough charter, see Mombert, *An Authentic History of Lancaster County*, 141–46.

22. Heisey, "How Lancaster Grew," 91; quoted in Wood, *Conestoga Crossroads*, 27, 29; Jasper Yeates to Sam Carsan, Dec. 22, 1764, Burd-Shippen Family Collection, reel 2, film 707, David Library of the American Revolution (hereafter DLAR); Jasper Yeates to Sam Carsan, June 25, 1765, Burd-Shippen Family Collection, reel 2; Mühlenberg, *Journals*, 2:423–24.

23. Quoted in Häberlein, *Practice of Pluralism*, 138. For the significance of ethnocultural distinctions in colonial Pennsylvania, see Rothermund, "The German Problem of Colonial Pennsylvania"; Wood, *Conestoga Crossroads*, 7–8, 13–15, 159, 181–215; Tully, "Ethnicity, Religion, and Politics in Early America," 495–96, 500, 503–4; Schwartz, *"A Mixed Multitude"*; Becker, "Diversity and Its Significance in an Eighteenth-Century Pennsylvania Town"; Wokeck, "German Settlements in the British North American Colonies"; Fogleman, *Hopeful Journeys*, 80–82, 99; Kenny, *Peaceable Kingdom Lost*, 25–27; and Häberlein, *Practice of Pluralism*.

24. My treatment of Lancaster's early religious history relies heavily on Häberlein's deeply researched, *Practice of Pluralism*. See 4–13, 33, 39, 106–8, 115, 136; and also Wood, *Conestoga Crossroads*, 13–15, 181–203.

25. Griffin, "The People with No Name," 599; Häberlein, *Practice of Pluralism*, 9–10, 28–29, 39, 56–57; Wood, *Conestoga Crossroads*, 15, 19, 217–19; Ellis and Evans, *History of Lancaster County*, 403.

26. Häberlein, *Practice of Pluralism*, 37, 54–55, 102, 108, 118; Mühlenberg, *Journals*, 1:94; Wood, *Conestoga Crossroads*, 187–89.

27. Quoted in Häberlein, *Practice of Pluralism*, 109; Mühlenberg, *Journals*, 1:115, 268–69, 261, 271; Heinrich Mühlenberg, *The Correspondence of Heinrich Melchior*

Mühlenberg, trans. and ed. John W. Kleiner et al., 3 vols. (Camden, 1993–2009), 3:177, 83, 105–6, 219; Mühlenberg, *Correspondence*, 2:173, 123, 184. See also Wood, *Conestoga Crossroads*, 184–94; Häberlein, *Practice of Pluralism*, 15, 78.

28. Mühlenberg, *Correspondence*, 1:180–81; Mühlenberg, *Journals*, 1:195, 111, 115; Mühlenberg, *Journals*, 2:339; Wood, *Conestoga Crossroads*, 184–88; Häberlein, *Practice of Pluralism*, 5, 61–70, 98–99.

29. Quoted in Silver, *Our Savage Neighbors*, 29; Mühlenberg, *Journals*, 1:109, 90; Mühlenberg, *Correspondence*, 1:85–86, 248; Mühlenberg, *Journals*, 2:424–25; Häberlein, *Practice of Pluralism*, 61–66, 69–70.

30. Silver, *Our Savage Neighbors*, xix; Häberlein, *Practice of Pluralism*, 12, 179; Griffin, "The People with No Name"; Becker, "Diversity and Its Significance in an Eighteenth-Century Pennsylvania Town"; Wokeck, "German Settlements in the British North American Colonies."

31. Quoted in Wood, *Conestoga Crossroads*, 195; see also 13–15; Häberlein, *Practice of Pluralism*, 12, 17, 30, 58, 93, 138–66.

32. Mühlenberg, *Correspondence*, 3:184; Wood, *Conestoga Crossroads*, 60, 176, 202; Häberlein, *Practice of Pluralism*, 30, 58, 125–28, 138–66.

33. Häberlein, *Practice of Pluralism*, 148–54; Wood, *Conestoga Crossroads*, 8–9, 205, 213–15, 226, 240; Lemon, *Best Poor Man's Country*, 14–15.

34. Andrew Burnaby, *Travels through the Middle Settlements in North-America, in the Years 1759 and 1760, with Observations upon the State of the Colonies* (Dublin, 1775), 201. For ethnocultural politics in colonial Pennsylvania, see Wayne L. Bockelman and Owen S. Ireland, "The Internal Revolution in Pennsylvania: An Ethnic-Religious Interpretation," *Pennsylvania History* 41 (Apr. 1974): 125–59; Tully, "Ethnicity, Religion, and Politics in Early America"; Alan Tully, *Forming American Politics: Ideals, Interests, and Institutions in Colonial New York and Pennsylvania* (Baltimore, 1994); Schwartz, *"A Mixed Multitude,"* esp. 159–204; Becker, "Diversity and Its Significance in an Eighteenth-Century Pennsylvania Town"; and Taylor, *American Colonies*, 271–72, 320–22.

35. Bockelman and Ireland, "The Internal Revolution in Pennsylvania," 127–34, 137–41; Tully, "Englishmen and Germans," 242–44; Tully, "Ethnicity, Religion, and Politics in Early America," 497–503, 506, 511–13; Tully, *Forming American Politics*, 146–49, 197, 285–309, 407–15; Schwartz, *"A Mixed Multitude,"* 159–204; Richard K. MacMaster, *Land, Piety, Peoplehood: The Establishment of Mennonite Communities in America, 1683–1790* (Scottdale, 1985), 230, 232; Fogleman, *Hopeful Journeys*, 135–42, 148, 152; Lemon, *Best Poor Man's Country*, 86–87.

36. Wood, *Conestoga Crossroads*, 29–32, 39, 175, 206; Häberlein, *Practice of Pluralism*, 125–26, 133; Bockelman, "Continuity and Change in Revolutionary Pennsylvania," 165–66; Ellis and Evans, *History of Lancaster County*, 213–17, 373. Replacing Worrall as Lancaster's most politically influential Friend was the Quaker James Webb.

37. Mombert, *An Authentic History of Lancaster County*, 142; quoted in Wood, *Conestoga Crossroads*, 28; see also 19, 23, 26–27, 41–44; Häberlein, *Practice of Pluralism*, 4–5. See in addition Bockelman and Ireland, "The Internal Revolution in Pennsylvania," 139; Wokeck, "German Settlements in the British North American Colonies," 192, 199, 211–12.

38. Wood, *Conestoga Crossroads*, 24–25, 28–32, 39–40, 159, 175; Ellis and Evans, *History of Lancaster County*, 373–74; Häberlein, *Practice of Pluralism*, 42, 110–11.

39. Quoted in Bockelman and Ireland, "The Internal Revolution in Pennsylvania," 137–38; Ellis and Evans, *History of Lancaster County*, 213–17; Bockelman, "Continuity and Change in Revolutionary Pennsylvania," 65–67, 142–209; Wayne L. Bockelman, "Local Politics in Pre-Revolutionary Lancaster County," *PMHB* 97 (Jan. 1973): 45–74; Tully, "Ethnicity, Religion, and Politics in Early America," 507. For the evolving role of the Germans and Scots Irish in Pennsylvania politics, see especially Bockelman and Ireland, "The Internal Revolution in Pennsylvania."

40. Silver, *Our Savage Neighbors*, esp. 110–14; Rothermund, "The German Problem of Colonial Pennsylvania," 17; Tully, "Ethnicity, Religion, and Politics in Early America," 504–13; Schwartz, *"A Mixed Multitude,"* 205–56; Bockelman, "Continuity and Change in Revolutionary Pennsylvania," 43.

41. Quoted in James H. Merrell, *Into the American Woods: Negotiators on the Pennsylvania Frontier* (New York, 1999), 247; see also 34–38; Silver, *Our Savage Neighbors*, xxv–xxvi, 8–11; Kenny, *Peaceable Kingdom Lost*, 2, 11–61. For the Seven Years' War, see also Fred Anderson, *Crucible of War: The Seven Years' War and the Fate of Empire in British North America, 1754–1766* (New York, 2000).

42. Quoted in Kenny, *Peaceable Kingdom Lost*, 54; see also 69–71; Wood, *Conestoga Crossroads*, 2, 71–73, 118; Silver, *Our Savage Neighbors*, 195.

43. Edward Shippen to Robert Morris, Nov. 6, 1755, Burd-Shippen Family Collection, reel 2; Kenny, *Peaceable Kingdom Lost*, 71–75; Silver, *Our Savage Neighbors*, 49; Krista Camenzind, "Violence, Race, and the Paxton Boys," in *Friends and Enemies in Penn's Woods: Indians, Colonists, and the Racial Construction of Pennsylvania*, ed. William Pencak and Daniel Richter (University Park, 2004), 201–20, esp. 210; Edward Shippen to William Allen, June 30, 1755, Burd-Shippen Family Collection, reel 2; Edward Shippen to James Burd, July 8, 1755, Burd-Shippen Family Collection, reel 2.

44. Edward Shippen to Alex Champion, Dec. 15, 1755, Burd-Shippen Family Collection, reel 2; Kenny, *Peaceable Kingdom Lost*, 72–74; Wood, *Conestoga Crossroads*, 74–75.

45. Quoted in Wood, *Conestoga Crossroads*, 75–76; Heisey, "How Lancaster Grew," 93; Edward Shippen to Robert Morris, Nov. 4, 1755, Burd-Shippen Family Collection, reel 2; Rupp, *History of Lancaster and York Counties*, 336–37.

46. Quoted in Kenny, *Peaceable Kingdom Lost*, 73–74; Edward Shippen to Robert Morris, June 17, 1755, Burd-Shippen Family Collection, reel 2; Silver, *Our Savage Neighbors*, 110–14.

47. Edward Shippen to Robert Morris, Feb. 17, 1756, Burd-Shippen Family Collection, reel 2; Wood, *Conestoga Crossroads*, 74–79, 141–42; Häberlein, *Practice of Pluralism*, 27–28, 40, 167, 169.

48. Edward Shippen to Robert Morris, Nov. 6, 1755, Burd-Shippen Family Collection, reel 2; Edward Shippen to James Burd, June 16, 1757, Burd-Shippen Family Collection, reel 2; Edward Shippen to Joseph Shippen, Aug. 5, 1756, Burd-Shippen Family Collection, reel 2; Edward Shippen to William Denny, May 11, 1758, Burd-Shippen Family Collection, reel 2; *Letters and Papers Relating Chiefly to the Provincial History of Pennsylvania, with Some Notices of the Writers*, ed. Thomas Balch (Philadelphia, 1855), 82–83; Kenny, *Peaceable Kingdom Lost*, 79, 90–91; Wood, *Conestoga Crossroads*, 77, 202; Schwartz, *"A Mixed Multitude,"* 238, 255.

49. James Burd to Edward Burd, Dec. 28, 1756, Burd-Shippen Family Collection, reel 2; Edward Shippen to James Burd, Mar. 24, 1756, Burd-Shippen Family Collection, reel 2; Edward Shippen to Joseph Shippen, Sept. 5, 1756, Burd-Shippen Family Collection, reel 2; Bockelman, "Continuity and Change in Revolutionary Pennsylvania," 148; Kenny, *Peaceable Kingdom Lost*, 86–87; Camenzind, "Violence, Race, and the Paxton Boys," 209–10; Silver, *Our Savage Neighbors*, 40–53.

50. Edward Shippen to Joseph Shippen, Aug. 31, 1756, Burd-Shippen Family Collection, reel 2; Edward Shippen to Joseph Shippen, May 9, 1757, Burd-Shippen Family Collection, reel 2; Edward Shippen to James Burd, May 22, 1757, Burd-Shippen Family Collection, reel 2; Rupp, *History of Lancaster and York Counties*, 337.

51. Balch, *Letters and Papers*, 98; Tully, "Ethnicity, Religion, and Politics in Early America," 504–13, 518; Tully, *Forming American Politics*, 149–51, 156–58; Schwartz, "*A Mixed Multitude*," 205–56, esp. 207–15, 223–25; Fogleman, *Hopeful Journeys*, 140–41; MacMaster, *Land, Piety, Peoplehood*, 239–42; Kenny, *Peaceable Kingdom Lost*, 77–84; Camenzind, "Violence, Race, and the Paxton Boys," 215; Silver, *Our Savage Neighbors*, 28, 100, 108.

52. Balch, *Letters and Papers*, 78; quoted in Wood, *Conestoga Crossroads*, 73, 76; William Smith, *A Brief View of the Conduct of Pennsylvania, for the Year 1755* (London, 1756), 88; Rupp, *History of Lancaster and York Counties*, 338; Wayland F. Dunaway, *The Scotch-Irish of Colonial Pennsylvania* (Chapel Hill, 1944), 130–31; Tully, "Ethnicity, Religion, and Politics in Early America," 505–13; Tully, *Forming American Politics*, 157; Schwartz, "*A Mixed Multitude*," 214; Fogleman, *Hopeful Journeys*, 140–41; Kenny, *Peaceable Kingdom Lost*, 80–82, 93; Silver, *Our Savage Neighbors*, 75–78.

53. Kenny, *Peaceable Kingdom Lost*, 111–22; Silver, *Our Savage Neighbors*, 141; Tully, "Ethnicity, Religion, and Politics in Early America," 513–19; Tully, *Forming American Politics*, 182–93; Schwartz, "*A Mixed Multitude*," 225–29.

54. Kenny, *Peaceable Kingdom Lost*, 119–39; Silver, *Our Savage Neighbors*, 163–79.

55. Quoted in Camenzind, "Violence, Race, and the Paxton Boys," 201; Edward Shippen to John Penn, Dec. 14, 1763, Burd-Shippen Family Collection, reel 2; Edward Shippen to John Penn, Dec. 27, 1763, Burd-Shippen Family Collection, reel 2; Edward Shippen to Joseph Shippen, Jan. 5, 1764, Burd-Shippen Family Collection, reel 2; Wood, *Conestoga Crossroads*, 76; Kenny, *Peaceable Kingdom Lost*, 130–46; Silver, *Our Savage Neighbors*, 177–81.

56. Kenny, *Peaceable Kingdom Lost*, 147–55, 159–70; Silver, *Our Savage Neighbors*, 181–90; Fogleman, *Hopeful Journeys*, 143.

57. Thomas Barton, *The Conduct of the Paxton-Men, Impartially Represented* (Philadelphia, 1764), Early American Imprints, ser. 1: Evans, 1639–1800, no. 9594, 6, 30; Silver, *Our Savage Neighbors*, 207, 372; Kenny, *Peaceable Kingdom Lost*, 40, 172, 174–78, 181; Häberlein, *Practice of Pluralism*, 122.

58. Quoted in Silver, *Our Savage Neighbors*, 179; see also 164–65, 167.

59. Tully, "Ethnicity, Religion, and Politics in Early America," 515–30; Tully, *Forming American Politics*, 191–99; Schwartz, "*A Mixed Multitude*," 229–36.

60. Tully, "Ethnicity, Religion, and Politics in Early America," 505–11; Tully, *Forming American Politics*, 157, 305; Schwartz, "*A Mixed Multitude*," 211–12, 215.

61. Edward Shippen Jr. to Edward Shippen, Sept. 14, 1756, Burd-Shippen Family Collection, reel 2; quoted in Schwartz, "*A Mixed Multitude*," 232–33; see also 236;

Rothermund, "The German Problem of Colonial Pennsylvania," 18–19; Bockel-man, "Local Politics in Pre-Revolutionary Lancaster County," 50–51, 71–73; Tully, "Ethnicity, Religion, and Politics in Early America," 527–29; Tully, *Forming American Politics*, 305, 411–12.

62. Balch, *Letters and Papers*, 205, 210–211; Jasper Yeates to James Burd, Sept. 17, 1769, Burd-Shippen Family Collection, reel 2; Tully, "Ethnicity, Religion, and Poli-tics in Early America," 529; Silver, *Our Savage Neighbors*, 223–24; Bockelman, "Con-tinuity and Change in Revolutionary Pennsylvania," 173–75; Bockelman, "Local Politics in Pre-Revolutionary Lancaster County," 50–51, 71–73; Wood, *Conestoga Crossroads*, 29, 31.

63. Balch, *Letters and Papers*, 211–12; Jasper Yeates to James Burd, Sept. 8, 1768, Burd-Shippen Family Collection, reel 2; quoted in Bockelman, "Local Politics in Pre-Revolutionary Lancaster County," 51; Jasper Yeates to Duncan Campbell, Mar. 15, 1768, Burd-Shippen Family Collection, reel 2; Jasper Yeates to Duncan Camp-bell, Sept. 24, 1770, Burd-Shippen Family Collection, reel 2.

64. Wood, *Conestoga Crossroads*, 205–15; Schwartz, *"A Mixed Multitude,"* 193.

65. Heisey, "How Lancaster Grew," 93, 104; Lemon, *Best Poor Man's Country*, 137–38; Wood, *Conestoga Crossroads*, 59–62, 96–98, 205–8, 211–13; Häberlein, *Practice of Pluralism*, 126, 151–52; Jasper Yeates to Sam Carsan, Oct. 16, 1765, Burd-Shippen Family Collection, reel 2; Jasper Yeates to Duncan Campbell, Dec. 9, 1769, Burd-Shippen Family Collection, reel 2; Jasper Yeates to Duncan Campbell, Aug. 10, 1770, Burd-Shippen Family Collection, reel 2; Jasper Yeates to Duncan Campbell, Jan. 2, 1771, Burd-Shippen Family Collection, reel 2.

66. Balch, *Letters and Papers*, 225; Edward Shippen to Edward Shippen Jr., Dec. 21, 1772, Burd-Shippen Family Collection, reel 2; quoted in Wood, *Conestoga Cross-roads*, 135; Jasper Yeates to Sam Carsan, Jan. 8, 1766, Burd-Shippen Family Col-lection, reel 2; Jasper Yeates to Sam Carsan, Sept. 17, 1771, Burd-Shippen Family Collection, reel 2; Jasper Yeates to Joseph Swift, Dec. 1, 1771, Burd-Shippen Fam-ily Collection, reel 2; Edward Burd to James Burd, Apr. 26, 1772, Burd-Shippen Family Collection, reel 2. See also Wood, *Conestoga Crossroads*, 205, 212–14.

67. Quoted in Häberlein, *Practice of Pluralism*, 139; see also 85, 112, 138–66; Müh-lenberg, *Journals*, 1:223; Mühlenberg, *Journals*, 2:299, 510.

68. Wood, *Conestoga Crossroads*, 100–101, 174, 212–13; Häberlein, *Practice of Plu-ralism*, 151–52.

69. Wood, *Conestoga Crossroads*, 195, 205, 212–13, 215; Häberlein, *Practice of Plu-ralism*, 148–53. For the persistence of German identity, see Fogleman, *Hopeful Jour-neys*, 149–53; and Steven M. Nolt, *Foreigners in Their Own Land: Pennsylvania Germans in the Early Republic* (University Park, 2002).

70. Mühlenberg, *Correspondence*, 3:194–95; Häberlein, *Practice of Pluralism*, 36, 95–96, 98–99, 122; Wood, *Conestoga Crossroads*, 164, 217–21.

71. Jasper Yeates to Sam Carsan, June 25, 1765, Burd-Shippen Family Collec-tion, reel 2; Jasper Yeates to Nicholas van Dike, May 19, 1765, Burd-Shippen Family Collection, reel 2; Jasper Yeates to Richard Peters, Jan. 28, 1766, Burd-Shippen Fam-ily Collection, reel 2. For Lancaster marriages and church membership, Häberlein's *Practice of Pluralism* is especially valuable; see, for example, 10–11, 139–40, 148–53, 180. For Yeates, see Häberlein, 126; and Wood, *Conestoga Crossroads*, 176–77.

72. Edward Shippen to Joseph Shippen, Aug. 5, 1756; Edward Shippen to Joseph Shippen, Mar. 11, 1757; Edward Shippen to Colonel Alford, Apr. 25, 1757; Edward Shippen to James Burd, Aug. 23, 1757; Edward Shippen to James Burd, June 16, 1757; and Edward Shippen to James Burd, Mar. 24, 1757, all in Burd-Shippen Family Collection, reel 2.

2. "Divided We Must Inevitably Fall"

1. Knouff, *The Soldiers' Revolution*, 33. For the Revolution in Lancaster, see Ellis and Evans, *History of Lancaster County*, 33–69; Mombert, *An Authentic History of Lancaster County*, 199–306; Wood, *Conestoga Crossroads*, 79–89; and Charles H. Kessler, *Lancaster in the Revolution* (Lititz, 1975).

2. Lancaster County Committee of Safety Records, June 15, 1774, Peter Force Papers, ser. 7E, reel 16, film 559, DLAR; Mombert, *An Authentic History of Lancaster County*, 199–201; Lancaster County Committee of Safety Records, July 2, 1774, Peter Force Papers.

3. Lancaster County Committee of Safety Records, July 9, 1774, Peter Force Papers; Draft of an intended address to the people, July 9, 1774, Yeates Papers, Jasper Yeates Correspondence, 1762–1786, no. 740, Historical Society of Pennsylvania (hereafter HSP).

4. Lancaster County Committee of Safety Records, July 9, 1774, and Sept. 9, 1774, Peter Force Papers.

5. Alexander Harris, *A Biographical History of Lancaster County: Being a History of Early Settlers and Eminent Men of the County* (Baltimore, 1997), 502–8, 524–25. For a brief profile of Shippen's public career, see Wood, *Conestoga Crossroads*, 175–76. For a profile of Lancaster's leading Whigs, see G. Terry Madonna, *The Revolutionary Leadership* (Lititz, 1976).

6. Draft of an intended address to the people, July 9, 1774; Lancaster County Committee of Safety Records, July 9, 1774.

7. For German Americans during the Revolution, see Henry Melchior Mühlenberg Richards, *The Pennsylvania-German in the Revolutionary War, 1775–1783* (Lancaster, 1908); Arthur D. Graeff, *The Relations between the Pennsylvania Germans and the British Authorities, 1750–1776* (Norristown, 1939), 221–52; Schwartz, *"A Mixed Multitude,"* 257–91; A. G. Roeber, *Palatines, Liberty, and Property: German Lutherans in Colonial British America* (Baltimore, 1993), 283–310; Charles Patrick Neimeyer, *America Goes to War: A Social History of the Continental Army* (New York, 1996), 44–52, 63–64. For the Revolution's impact on ethnically diverse communities, see Liam Riordan, "Identity and Revolution: Everyday Life and Crisis in Three Delaware River Towns," *Pennsylvania History* 64 (Winter 1997): 56–101; Riordan, *Many Identities, One Nation*; John B. Frantz and William Pencak, ed., *Beyond Philadelphia: The American Revolution in the Pennsylvania Hinterland* (University Park, 1998); and Häberlein, *Practice of Pluralism*, 181–215.

8. For the Revolution in Pennsylvania, see, for example, David Freeman Hawke, *In the Midst of a Revolution* (Philadelphia, 1961); Richard Alan Ryerson, *The Revolution Is Now Begun: The Radical Committees of Philadelphia, 1765–1776* (Philadelphia, 1978); Steven Rosswurm, *Arms, Country, and Class: The Philadelphia Militia and "Lower*

Sort" during the American Revolution, 1775–1783 (New Brunswick, 1988); Frantz and Pencak, *Beyond Philadelphia*; and Knouff, *The Soldiers' Revolution*.

9. Jasper Yeates to Lindsay Coats, Apr. 21, 1765, Burd-Shippen Family Collection, reel 2; Jasper Yeates to Richard Peters, May 14, 1765, Burd-Shippen Family Collection, reel 2; Jasper Yeates to Sam Carsan, May 25, 1766, Burd-Shippen Family Collection, reel 2; Graeff, *Relations between the Pennsylvania Germans and the British Authorities*, 221–37; Schwartz, *"A Mixed Multitude,"* 267–69; Fogleman, *Hopeful Journeys*, 145–46; Wood, *Conestoga Crossroads*, 207; Jasper Yeates to Richard Peters, Apr. 2, 1766, Burd-Shippen Family Collection, reel 2.

10. Jasper Yeates to Duncan Campbell, Feb. 13, 1769, Burd-Shippen Family Collection, reel 2; *Pennsylvania Gazette* (Philadelphia), May 12, 1768, and June 28, 1770.

11. *Ein Lied von dem gegenwartigen Zustand in America* (Lancaster, 1774), Early American Imprints, ser. 1: Evans, 1639–1800, no. 49265; Balch, *Letters and Papers*, 237.

12. Lancaster County Committee of Safety Records, Apr. 27, 1775, and May 1, 1775, Peter Force Papers.

13. John Carmichael, *A Self-defensive War Lawful, Proved in a Sermon, Preached at Lancaster, before Captain Ross's Company of Militia, in the Presbyterian Church, on Sabbath Morning, June 4th, 1775* (Philadelphia, 1775), Early American Imprints, ser. 1: Evans, 1639–1800, no. 13862, 14–15, 30. See also Balch, *Letters and Papers*, 244.

14. "The Hubley Family," *Notes and Queries, Historical, Biographical, and Genealogical, Relating Chiefly to Interior Pennsylvania*, ed. William Henry Egle, annual vol. (1897): 202; *Lancaster County Committee of Observation, February 10, 1776* (Lancaster, 1776), Early American Imprints, ser. 1: Evans, 1639–1800, no. 14817; Jasper Yeates to Duncan Campbell, Aug. 10, 1770, Burd-Shippen Family Collection, reel 2; Lancaster County Committee of Safety Records, May 1, 1775, May 4, 1775, and May 5, 1775, Peter Force Papers; Wood, *Conestoga Crossroads*, 126, 147–48; John W. W. Loose, *The Military Market Basket* (Lititz, 1976); Lancaster County Committee of Safety Records, May 23, 1775, Peter Force Papers; Samuel E. Dyke, *The Pennsylvania Rifle* (Lititz, 1974); Lancaster County Committee of Safety Records, Nov. 9, 1775, Peter Force Papers; Lemon, *Best Poor Man's Country*, 139; *PA*, 2nd ser., 13:520.

15. *Letters from America, 1776–1779: Being Letters of Brunswick, Hessian, and Waldeck Officers with the British Armies during the Revolution*, trans. and ed. Ray W. Pettengill (Boston, 1924), 239; Lancaster County Committee of Safety Records, May 1, 1775; "Items from Letters," *PLCHS* 27 (1923): 96. For the participation of marginal figures, see Schwartz, *"A Mixed Multitude,"* 279; Knouff, *The Soldiers' Revolution*, 35–76; and Neimeyer, *America Goes to War*.

16. During the summer of 1776, the county furnished over three hundred men to the Flying Camp. *Pennsylvania Gazette*, Aug. 14, 1776; Lancaster Committee of Safety Records, June 20, 1775, and July 24, 1775, Peter Force Papers; Lancaster Committee to the Continental Congress, July 10, 1775, Peter Force Collection, ser. 9, reel 101, Library of Congress (hereafter LOC); Lancaster Committee to the Continental Congress, July 22, 1775, Peter Force Collection, ser. 9, reel 101; Ellis and Evans, *History of Lancaster County*, 38–39; "Lancaster Borough Return of All Males between 16 and 50," 1776, Revolutionary War Collection, Lancaster County Historical Society; Henry C. Peden Jr., *Revolutionary Patriots of Lancaster County, Pennsylvania, 1775–1783* (Westminster, 2002). For the assimilation of Lancaster units

into the Pennsylvania Line, see Ellis and Evans, *History of Lancaster County*, 44, 48–50, 56–57, 59. For the German Regiment and the Marechausee Corps, see Ellis and Evans, *History of Lancaster County*, 56; Charles F. Stein, "The German Battalion of the American Revolution," *The Report: A Journal of German-American History* 36 (1975): 26–50; Henry J. Retzer, *The German Regiment of Maryland and Pennsylvania in the Continental Army, 1776–1781* (Westminster, 1991); John B. B. Trussell Jr., *The Pennsylvania Line: Regimental Organization and Operations, 1776–1783* (Harrisburg, 1977), 222–26, 229–31; and Neimeyer, *America Goes to War*, 49–51.

17. Madonna, *The Revolutionary Leadership*, 22–24, 32–34; Peden, *Revolutionary Patriots of Lancaster County*, 14, 271; Edward Shippen to Council of Safety, Nov. 8, 1776, *American Archives, Consisting of a Collection of Authetick Records, State Papers, Debates, and Letters and Other Notices of Public Affairs* (hereafter *AA*), ed. Peter Force, 2 ser., 9 vols. (Washington, D.C., 1837–1853), 5th ser., 3:749; Sebastian Graff to Jasper Yeates, Nov. 26, 1776, *AA*, 5th ser., 3:749; Officers of Colonel Slough's Battalion to the Colonel, Oct. 21, 1775, Yeates Papers; Stein, "The German Battalion," 31–43; Richards, *The Pennsylvania-German in the Revolutionary War*, 197, 229, 417–18; Revolutionary War Pension and Bounty-Land-Warrant Application Files, files W8117, W3199, R234, National Archives. For new political opportunities created by the Revolution, see Bockelman, "Continuity and Change in Revolutionary Pennsylvania," 142–209.

18. Lancaster County Committee of Safety Records, June 15, 1774, Dec. 15, 1774, Nov. 8, 1775, Nov. 9, 1775, and Jan. 14, 1775, Peter Force Papers. For lists of civil officeholders in prerevolutionary Lancaster County, see Ellis and Evans, *History of Lancaster County*, 213–18, 373–74. See also Madonna, *The Revolutionary Leadership*.

19. Pettengill, *Letters from America*, 239; Schwartz, *"A Mixed Multitude,"* 279; Knouff, *The Soldiers' Revolution*, 30.

20. Mühlenberg, *Journals*, 2:699, 701. For German American political culture, see Fogleman, *Hopeful Journeys*, 127–53. For German notions of liberty and property, see Roeber, *Palatines, Liberty, and Property*.

21. Alexander Graydon, *Memoirs of His Own Time, with Reminiscences of the Men and Events of the Revolution* (Philadelphia, 1846), 121–22; Mühlenberg, *Journals*, 2:700; *Ein Lied von dem gegenwartigen Zustand in America*.

22. "Hubley Family," 200–203; Harris, *Biographical History of Lancaster County*, 321–23; Ellis and Evans, *History of Lancaster County*, 216, 373; Häberlein, *Practice of Pluralism*, 86–87, 95; Wood, *Conestoga Crossroads*, 29, 32, 148; Richards, *The Pennsylvania-German in the Revolutionary War*, 127, 185, 196, 212, 215, 289, 305, 411–14, 418, 422, 424; Revolutionary War Pension and Bounty-Land-Warrant Application Files, files W2850 and S39750; Bernard Hubley, *The History of the American Revolution* (Northumberland, 1805).

23. Slough belonged to both the Lutheran and Anglican churches. Ellis and Evans, *History of Lancaster County*, 214; Lancaster County Committee of Safety Records, May 5, 1775; Wood, *Conestoga Crossroads*, 174. For brief profiles of Reigart and Slough, see Madonna, *The Revolutionary Leadership*, 5–8, 28, 32–34; for similar cases, see the profiles of Wilhelm Bausman, John Hubley, and Casper Shaffner, 22–24, 25–26, 30–31.

24. Graeff, *Relations between the Pennsylvania Germans and the British Authorities*, 227–31; Schwartz, *"A Mixed Multitude,"* 279. For the nationalizing influence of the German-language press, see Willi Paul Adams, "The Colonial German-Language

Press and the American Revolution," in *The Press and the American Revolution*, ed. Bernard Bailyn et al. (Worcester, 1980), 151–228.

25. Quoted in Adams, "The Colonial German-Language Press," 180, 187, 189; see also 183, 188; Schwartz, *"A Mixed Multitude,"* 267–68; Graeff, *Relations between the Pennsylvania Germans and the British Authorities*, 227–31.

26. "Was ist wohl schöners anzuschau'n, Als wenn ein Stämpler hängt am Baum." *Der Wochentliche Philadelphische Staatsbote* (Philadelphia), Sept. 9, 1765; quoted in Adams, "The Colonial German-Language Press," 185; see also 190, 194–96, 203; Graeff, *Relations between the Pennsylvania Germans and the British Authorities*, 229; and *Staatsbote*, Nov. 25, 1765, and Feb. 24, 1766.

27. Quoted in Adams, "The Colonial German-Language Press," 194, 204, 195. "Durch Zusammenhalten stehen wir, Durch Trennung fallen wir." *Staatsbote*, May 30, 1769; Graeff, *Relations between the Pennsylvania Germans and the British Authorities*, 231; see also Adams, "The Colonial German-Language Press," 185–87, 193.

28. Quoted in Adams, "The Colonial German-Language Press," 207; Edward Burd to James Burd, Mar. 15, 1776, Shippen Family Papers, no. 595A, 7, HSP; Thomas Paine, *The Selected Works of Tom Paine*, ed. Howard Fast (New York, 1945), 20; see also Adams, "The Colonial German-Language Press," 151–54, 183, 192, 204–5, 212, 217–19; Schwartz, *"A Mixed Multitude,"* 279; Neimeyer, *America Goes to War*, 48–49; Roeber, *Palatines, Liberty, and Property*, 283–84.

29. Quoted in William T. Parsons, *The Pennsylvania Dutch: A Persistent Minority* (Boston, 1976), 150; Neimeyer, *America Goes to War*, 49–52, 64; Graeff, *Relations between the Pennsylvania Germans and the British Authorities*, 252; Frantz and Pencak, *Beyond Philadelphia*, xx.

30. Quoted in Schwartz, *"A Mixed Multitude,"* 280–82.

31. Ryerson, *The Revolution Is Now Begun*, 162–63, 165, 229, 231–34; Schwartz, *"A Mixed Multitude,"* 280–82.

32. *The Alarm: or, An Address to the People of Pennsylvania* (Philadelphia, 1776), Early American Imprints, ser. 1: Evans, 1639–1800, no. 14642; for the German translation, see *Der Alarm: oder, Einer Erweckungs-Zuschrift an das Volk von Pennsylvanien* (Philadelphia, 1776), Early American Imprints, ser. 1: Evans, 1639–1800, no. 14643; Pettengill, *Letters from America*, 240; Schwartz, *"A Mixed Multitude,"* 267, 279; Neimeyer, *America Goes to War*, 50–51. For the muster rolls of Lancaster County's rifle companies, see *Pennsylvania in the War of the Revolution: Battalions and Line, 1775–1783*, ed. John Blair Linn and William Henry Egle, 2 vols. (Harrisburg, 1880), 1:37–42. See the muster rolls of Lancaster County's militia battalions in *PA*, 3rd ser., 23. See the muster rolls of the German Regiment in Stein, "The German Battalion," 44–49.

33. Confronting an unprecedented crisis, Pennsylvania's diverse Whigs achieved new levels of cooperation, particularly through the summer of 1776, when the colonial rebellion became a war for independence, inaugurating a process of nation building involving the formulation of a distinct American identity. For Lancaster County during the Seven Years' War, see Wood, *Conestoga Crossroads*, 74–79; Silver, *Our Savage Neighbors*; Kenny, *Peaceable Kingdom Lost*.

34. Carmichael, *A Self-defensive War Lawful*, 5, 34; Lancaster County Committee of Safety Records, July 24, 1775; Lancaster Committee to the Continental Congress, July 10, 1775, and July 22, 1775, Peter Force Collection, ser. 9, reel 101; Ellis and Evans, *History of Lancaster County*, 38–40.

35. Remonstrance of Private Associators, Colonel Feree's Battalion, Sept. 1775, Records of Pennsylvania's Revolutionary Governments, 1775–1790 (hereafter PRG), reel 10, film 24, DLAR; see also Knouff, *The Soldiers' Revolution*, 79.

36. Carmichael, *A Self-defensive War Lawful*, 28–29; *The Colonial Records of Pennsylvania* (hereafter *CR*), ed. Samuel Hazard, 16 vols. (Philadelphia, 1838–1853), 10:320.

37. *Pennsylvania Packet* (Philadelphia), Aug. 28, 1775; *March to Quebec: Journals of the Members of Arnold's Expedition*, ed. Kenneth Roberts (New York, 1938), 301. For the experiences of the riflemen, see Henry J. Young, "The Spirit of 1775: A Letter of Robert Magaw, Major of the Continental Riflemen to the Gentlemen of the Committee of Correspondence in the Town of Carlisle, dated at Cambridge, 13 August 1775, with an Essay on the Background and the Sequel," *John and Mary's Journal* 1 (Mar. 1975): 1–60.

38. Young, "The Spirit of 1775," 7; quoted in Knouff, *The Soldiers' Revolution*, 85; Christopher French Journal, Mar. 20, 1776, reel 1, film 398, DLAR.

39. *PA*, 5th ser., 2:5; James Thacher, *Military Journal of the American Revolution* (Hartford, 1862), 31; Christopher French Journal, Mar. 22, 1776; Young, "The Spirit of 1775," 1–60; *PA*, 2nd ser., 10:8–10.

40. *PA*, 2nd ser., 10:7.

41. "God in his great goodness grant, in the future vicissitudes of the world," Henry concluded, "that our countrymen, whenever their essential rights shall be attacked, will divest themselves of all party prejudice, and devote their lives and properties in defence of the sacred liberties of their country." See Roberts, *March to Quebec*, 301, 383. For the prisoners seized at Quebec, see Ellis and Evans, *History of Lancaster County*, 42–43; J. Samuel Walker, *The Perils of Patriotism: John Joseph Henry and the American Attack on Quebec, 1775* (Lititz, 1975). See also *Pennsylvania Gazette*, July 10, 1776.

42. Pettengill, *Letters from America*, 240.

43. *The Association, agreed upon by the grand American Continental Congress* (Boston, 1774), Early American Imprints, ser. 1: Evans, 1639–1800, no. 42724; Lancaster County Committee of Safety Records, Nov. 10, 1775, Nov. 22, 1774, Dec. 15, 1774, Dec. 1774, Aug. 11, 1774, Mar. 13, 1775, Mar. 16, 1776, and Nov. 9, 1775, all in Peter Force Papers; Ellis and Evans, *History of Lancaster County*, 36.

44. Lancaster Committee to Alexander McKee, Jan. 15, 1776, Peter Force Collection, ser. 9, reel 102; Lancaster County Committee of Safety Records, June 8, 1776, Peter Force Papers; Lancaster Committee to George Ross, Jan. 15, 1776, Peter Force Collection, ser. 9, reel 102.

45. Quoted in MacMaster, *Land, Piety, Peoplehood*, 229, 235–36; see also 230–80. For Pennsylvania pacifists during the Seven Years' War, see Schwartz, *"A Mixed Multitude,"* 206–21. For initial disagreements between patriots and pacifists, see Anne M. Ousterhout, *A State Divided: Opposition in Pennsylvania to the American Revolution* (Westport, 1987), 103–44; and Schwartz, *"A Mixed Multitude,"* 272–78.

46. "The Hebron Church Diary," *Notes and Queries*, 4th ser. (1895), 2:332; "Items from Letters," 96.

47. Lancaster Committee to Manheim and Rapho Committees, May 29, 1775, Yeates Papers; Lancaster Committee to Pennsylvania Delegates in Congress, June 3, 1775, Yeates Papers. For other accounts of the controversy, see Ousterhout, *A State Divided*, 110–11; and Schwartz, *"A Mixed Multitude,"* 275–76.

48. Lancaster County Committee of Safety Records, May 29, 1775, Peter Force Papers; Carmichael, *A Self-defensive War Lawful*, 20; Lancaster Committee to Pennsylvania Delegates in Congress, June 3, 1775, Yeates Papers.

49. Lancaster Committee to Pennsylvania Delegates in Congress, June 3, 1775, Yeates Papers; Lancaster County Committee of Safety Records, June 2, 1775, and June 10, 1775, Peter Force Papers; "Items from Letters," 96.

50. "Items from Letters," 96; Matthias Slough to Jasper Yeates, June 26, 1775, Society Miscellaneous Collection, no. 425, HSP; Balch, *Letters and Papers*, 242; Edward Burd to Jasper Yeates, June 7, 1775, Yeates Papers; Lancaster County Committee of Safety Records, June 2, 1775, and June 16, and 17, 1775, Peter Force Papers.

51. *PA*, 8th ser., 8:7249; *CR*, 10:293; "Items from Letters," 96; Officers of Lancaster County Associators to Lancaster Committee, Mar. 29, 1776, Peter Force Collection, ser. 9, reel 102; Officers of Donegal Associators to Lancaster Committee, June 15, 1775, Peter Force Collection, ser. 9, reel 101; Company of Mount Joy Township to Lancaster Committee, June 16, 1775, Peter Force Collection, ser. 9, reel 101; Lancaster County Committee of Safety Records, Aug. 3, 1775, Peter Force Papers. See also Schwartz, *"A Mixed Multitude,"* 276.

52. *PA*, 8th ser., 8:7262, 7382, 7487, 7505–6. See also Ousterhout, *A State Divided*, 114–16, 128, 130; and Schwartz, *"A Mixed Multitude,"* 277–78.

53. For Lancaster County officeholding, see Bockelman, "Continuity and Change in Revolutionary Pennsylvania." For broader Pennsylvania trends, see Hawke, *In the Midst of a Revolution*, 165–79; Ryerson, *The Revolution Is Now Begun*; and Rosswurm, *Arms, Country, and Class*.

54. Edward Shippen to Joseph Shippen, May 13, 1775, Shippen Papers, BSh62, American Philosophical Society (hereafter APS); Edward Shippen to Joseph Shippen, Apr. 1776, Shippen Papers, BSh62, APS; Edward Shippen to Joseph Shippen, June 8, 1776, Shippen Papers, BSh62, APS; *Pennsylvania Gazette*, June 19, 1776; William F. Ayars, *Lancaster Diary, 1776: Excerpts from Diaries, Day-Books, Journals, Newspapers, and Court Records of the Daily Life of Lancaster County, Pennsylvania, in the Year 1776* (Lancaster, 1976), 36; Lancaster County Committee of Safety Records, July 2, 1774, and Dec. 15, 1774, Peter Force Papers; Edward Shippen to Joseph Shippen, Aug. 20, 1774, Shippen Family Papers, 10, HSP; Edward Shippen to Joseph Shippen, July 27, 1774, Balch-Shippen Papers, no. 25, 2, HSP; Edward Shippen to Joseph Shippen, Jan. 19, 1776, Shippen Family Papers, 10, HSP; Hawke, *In the Midst of a Revolution*, 172; Harris, *Biographical History of Lancaster County*, 375–81.

55. Quoted in Ousterhout, *A State Divided*, 111; quoted in Hawke, *In the Midst of a Revolution*, 141–42. See in addition, Jasper Yeates to James Burd, Mar. 7, 1776, Shippen Family Papers, 7, HSP; Jasper Yeates to James Burd, Mar. 29, 1777, Shippen Family Papers, 8, HSP; Balch, *Letters and Papers*, 244–45.

56. William Shippen to Edward Shippen, July 27, 1776, Burd-Shippen Family Collection, reel 2. See also Ryerson, *The Revolution Is Now Begun*.

57. Ayars, *Lancaster Diary*, 41, 43; Kessler, *Lancaster in the Revolution*, 48–49.

58. An Officer of the New York Forces, Nov. 3, 1775, *AA*, 4th ser., 3:1343; Continental Congress, Nov. 17, 1775, *AA*, 4th ser., 3:1921; An Officer at La Prairie, Nov. 3, 1775, *AA*, 4th ser., 3:1342; Colonel Bedel to New Hampshire Committee of Safety, Oct. 27, 1775, *AA*, 4th ser., 3:1207; An Officer at Fort St. Johns, Nov. 3, 1775, *AA*, 4th ser., 3:1344, Extracts of Letters Received in England from Quebec,

Nov. 9, 1775, *AA*, 4th ser., 3:1418; Richard Henry Lee to Catherine Macaulay, Nov. 29, 1775, in *Letters of Delegates to Congress, 1774–1789*, ed. Paul H. Smith et al., 25 vols. (Washington, D.C., 1976–2000), 2:405–6; General Montgomery to General Schuyler, Oct. 20, 1775, *AA*, 4th ser., 3:1132; Don Higginbotham, *The War of American Independence: Military Attitudes, Policies, and Practice, 1763–1789* (New York, 1971), 106–12. For Continental prisoner policy, see Charles H. Metzger, *The Prisoner in the American Revolution* (Chicago, 1971); Martha W. Dixon, "Divided Authority: The American Management of Prisoners in the Revolutionary War, 1775–1783" (Ph.D. diss., University of Utah, 1977); Doyle, *The Enemy in Our Hands*, 11–31; Springer, *America's Captives*, 13–41; and Krebs, *A Generous and Merciful Enemy*.

59. *Journals of the Continental Congress, 1774–1789* (hereafter *JCC*), ed. Worthington C. Ford et al., 34 vols. (Washington, D.C., 1904–1937), 4:361; Doyle, *The Enemy in Our Hands*, 11–12; Springer, *America's Captives*, 9–12; Daniel Krebs, "Approaching the Enemy: German Captives in the American War of Independence, 1776–1783" (Ph.D. diss., Emory University, 2007), 191–93; Ian K. Steele, "When Worlds Collide: The Fate of Canadian and French Prisoners Taken at Fort Niagara, 1759," *Journal of Canadian Studies* 39 (Fall 2005): 9–39.

60. Dixon, "Divided Authority," 3–4; Colley, *Captives*, 203–38. For British treatment of American prisoners, see Cox, *A Proper Sense of Honor*, 199–235; and Burrows, *Forgotten Patriots*.

61. Continental Congress, Nov. 17, 1775, *AA*, 4th ser., 3:1921; *JCC*, 3:358, 404; George Washington to President of Congress, Nov. 8, 1775, in Fitzpatrick, *Writings of George Washington*, 4:73; Dixon, "Divided Authority," 115–37.

62. Jasper Yeates to Joseph Swift, Jan. 30, 1768, Burd-Shippen Family Collection, reel 2; Silver, *Our Savage Neighbors*; Kenny, *Peaceable Kingdom Lost*; Colin Calloway, *The American Revolution in Indian Country: Crisis and Diversity in Native American Communities* (New York, 1995).

3. "A Dangerous Set of People"

1. Lancaster County Committee of Safety Records, Dec. 9, 1775, Peter Force Papers; Continental Congress, Nov. 17, 1775, *AA*, 4th ser., 3:1921; *JCC*, 3:358, 404; "Notes from Letters of Judge Yeates, December 9, 1775," *Notes and Queries*, 1st and 2nd ser. (1894–1895), 2:382; "Extracts from Moravian Diaries at Bethlehem," *PLCHS* 27 (1923): 91; *PA*, 2nd ser., 1:440–48; "List of the Officers Taken at St. Johns," *Notes and Queries*, annual vol. (1900): 171–72.

2. *JCC*, 3:359, 398–99, 434, 435; Lancaster County Committee of Safety Records, Dec. 9, 1775; "Notes from Letters of Judge Yeates," 382.

3. Lancaster County Committee of Safety Records, Dec. 27, 1775, Peter Force Papers; Lancaster Committee to President of Congress, Jan. 10, 1776, *AA*, 4th ser., 4:619; Lancaster Committee to President of Congress, Dec. 21, 1775, Papers of the Continental Congress (hereafter PCC), reel 83, National Archives; "Notes from Letters of Judge Yeates," 382.

4. Lancaster Committee to President of Congress, Jan. 10, 1776, *AA*, 4th ser., 4:619; British Officers to Continental Congress, Jan. 20, 1776, *AA*, 4th ser., 4:801–2; President of Congress to Lancaster Committee, Jan. 18, 1776, *AA*, 4th ser., 4:761–63; *JCC*, 4:21.

5. George Washington to Thomas Gage, Aug. 11, 1775, *AA*, 4th ser., 3:245; Roberts, *March to Quebec*, 591; Thomas Gage to George Washington, Aug. 13, 1775, *AA*, 4th ser., 3:246; Larry Bowman, *Captive Americans: Prisoners during the American Revolution* (Athens, 1976); Cogliano, *American Maritime Prisoners in the Revolutionary War*; Cox, *A Proper Sense of Honor*, 199–235; Burrows, *Forgotten Patriots*. The British eventually placed most captured American officers under parole.

6. George Washington to Major Christopher French, Sept. 26, 1775, *AA*, 4th ser., 3:810–11; George Washington to Hartford Committee, Sept. 26, 1775, *AA*, 4th ser., 3:810. See also Robert Harrison to Springfield Committee, Feb. 9, 1776, *AA*, 4th ser., 4:973; Joseph Reed to Major Christopher French, Sept. 3, 1775, *AA*, 4th ser., 3:639; Joseph Reed to Hartford Committee, Sept. 3, 1775, *AA*, 4th ser., 3:639–40.

7. Michael Zuckerman, "Identity in British America: Unease in Eden," in *Colonial Identity in the Atlantic World, 1500–1800*, ed. Nicholas Canny and Anthony Pagden (Princeton, 1987), 115–57; John Murrin, "A Roof without Walls: The Dilemma of American National Identity," in *Beyond Confederation: Origins of the Constitution and American National Identity*, ed. Richard Beeman et al. (Chapel Hill, 1987), 333–48; T. H. Breen, "Ideology and Nationalism on the Eve of the American Revolution: Revisions *Once More* in Need of Revising," *Journal of American History* 84 (June 1997): 13–39; Smith-Rosenberg, *This Violent Empire*, 1–18; Stephen Conway, "From Fellow-Nationals to Foreigners: British Perceptions of the Americans, circa 1739–1783," *WMQ* 59 (Jan. 2002): 65–100; Colley, *Captives*, 203–38.

8. Philip Schuyler to Captain Hulbert, Nov. 1, 1775, *AA*, 4th ser., 4:816; George Washington to General Thomas Gage, Aug. 19, 1775, *AA*, 4th ser., 3:246–47; President of Congress to Lancaster Committee, Jan. 18, 1776, *AA*, 4th ser., 4:761–63. See also Edward Shippen to James Burd, Apr. 11, 1774, Shippen Family Papers, 7, HSP; James Burd to Edward Shippen, Dec. 4, 1774, Shippen Family Papers, 7, HSP; Edward Shippen to Joseph Shippen, May 13, 1775, Shippen Family Papers, BSh6lf.1, APS; "Lancaster Committee to York Committee, March 19, 1776," *Notes and Queries*, 1st and 2nd ser., 1:428; "Eberhart Michael to John André, April 26, 1776," *PLCHS* 18 (1914): 134–35.

9. Unknown British Officer, Nov. 19, 1775, *AA*, 4th ser., 3:1608.

10. Edward Shippen to Joseph Shippen, May 13, 1775, Shippen Family Papers, BSh6lf.1, APS; "Eberhart Michael to John André," 134–35; Wood, *Conestoga Crossroads*, 141, 175–76; Häberlein, *Practice of Pluralism*, 45, 48, 125–26.

11. According to Linda Colley, the War for Independence was "always about different and shifting constructions of identity." See Colley, *Captives*, 203–38, esp. 233. For other examples of the Revolution's dislocating effects on preexisting identities and attachments, see Riordan, "Identity and Revolution," 56–101; Wayne Bodle, *The Valley Forge Winter: Civilians and Soldiers in War* (University Park, 2002); Knouff, *The Soldiers' Revolution*; Smith-Rosenberg, *This Violent Empire*, 1–18. For the condition of the British Army at the beginning of the War for Independence, see J. A. Houlding, *Fit for Service: The Training of the British Army, 1715–1795* (Oxford, 1981).

12. The historiography of revolutionary Pennsylvania has emphasized the ways in which the Revolution exacerbated social differences. See, for example, Hawke, *In the Midst of a Revolution*; Ryerson, *The Revolution Is Now Begun*; Rosswurm, *Arms, Country, and Class*; Ousterhout, *A State Divided*; Frantz and Pencak, *Beyond Philadelphia*; Francis Fox, *Sweet Land of Liberty: The Ordeal of the American Revolution in*

Northampton County, Pennsylvania (University Park, 2000); and Riordan, *Many Identities, One Nation*, 43–81. For examples of American identity formation during the Revolution, see Charles Royster, *A Revolutionary People at War: The Continental Army and American Character, 1775–1783* (Chapel Hill, 1979); Waldstreicher, *In the Midst of Perpetual Fetes*, 17–52; Colley, *Captives*, 203–38; Knouff, *The Soldiers' Revolution*; and Smith-Rosenberg, *This Violent Empire*, 1–54.

13. Lancaster County Committee of Safety Records, Dec. 9, 1775; "Notes from Letters of Judge Yeates," 382; President of Congress to Lancaster Committee, Jan. 18, 1776, *AA*, 4th ser., 4:761–63; *JCC*, 4:22; George Ross to President of Congress, July 7, 1776, *AA*, 5th ser., 1:103–4; *JCC*, 3:359, 398–99, 434, 435. For the improvised nature of and tensions associated with Continental prisoner policy, see Dixon, "Divided Authority"; and Springer, *America's Captives*, 13–41.

14. *PA*, 2nd ser., 13:510; Colonel Arthur St. Clair to President of Congress, Jan. 27, 1776, *AA*, 4th ser., 4:867; Continental Congress, Jan. 31, 1776, *AA*, 4th ser., 4:1660; Board of War to George Washington, Nov. 19, 1776, *AA*, 5th ser., 3:762; George Washington to Board of War, Nov. 30, 1776, *AA*, 5th ser., 3:920. Subsequent developments suggested that British rank-and-file prisoners often enlisted in American ranks with the intention of escaping to British lines.

15. Thomas Hughes, *A Journal by Thos Hughes, for His Amusement and Designed Only for His Perusal by the Time He Attains the Age of 50, If He Lives So Long* (Cambridge, 1947), 19–20, 31, 37, 71, 75; Anburey, *Travels through the Interior Parts of America*, 2:313; Alexander Campbell, "A Narrative of the Loss of the Ship Glasgow Packet, July 22–31, 1776," Sir Henry Clinton Papers, 17:39, William Clements Library; Lord George Germaine to Major General Howe, Feb. 1, 1776, *AA*, 4th ser., 4:902–3. See also Matthew H. Spring, *With Zeal and With Bayonets Only: The British Army on Campaign in North America* (Norman, 2008), 124–37; Richard Archer, *As If an Enemy's Country: The British Occupation of Boston and the Origins of Revolution* (New York, 2010).

16. Wood, *Conestoga Crossroads*, 77–79; Kenny, *Peaceable Kingdom Lost*, 140; John Shy, *Toward Lexington: The Role of the British Army in the Coming of the American Revolution* (Princeton, 1965), 207–9. See also Archer, *As If an Enemy's Country*.

17. "Captain Home's Narrative of His Treatment When Prisoner," n.d., Sir Guy Carleton Papers, Records of British Army Headquarters in America, 1775–1783 (hereafter BHP), reel 3, film 57, DLAR; Philip Greenwalt to Lancaster Committee, June 16, 1776, Yeates Papers; Frederic Shriver Klein, *Fighting the Battles* (Lititz, 1975); Walker, *The Perils of Patriotism*; Ellis and Evans, *History of Lancaster County*, 42–43; Howard Peckham, ed., *The Toll of Independence: Engagements and Battle Casualties of the American Revolution* (Chicago, 1974), 11.

18. For Woodhull, see Häberlein, *Practice of Pluralism*, 130–31, 181. For the region's ethnocultural diversity, see Wood, *Conestoga Crossroads*, 1–20, 181–215; Zuckerman, *Friends and Neighbors*; Schwartz, *"A Mixed Multitude"*; Tully, *Forming American Politics*; Häberlein, *Practice of Pluralism*; A. G. Roeber, "The Origin of Whatever Is Not English among Us: The Dutch-Speaking and the German-Speaking Peoples of Colonial British America," in *Strangers within the Realm: Cultural Margins of the First British Empire*, ed. Bernard Bailyn and Philip D. Morgan (Chapel Hill, 1991), 220–283; Fogleman, *Hopeful Journeys*; Lehmann et al., *In Search of Peace and Prosperity*; David Doyle, *Ireland, Irishmen, and Revolutionary America, 1760–1820* (Cork, 1981);

Maldwyn Jones, "The Scotch-Irish in British America," in Bailyn and Morgan, *Strangers within the Realm*, 284–313; Patrick Griffin, *The People with No Name: Ireland's Ulster Scots, America's Scots Irish, and the Creation of a British Atlantic World, 1689–1764* (Princeton, 2001); and Peden, *Revolutionary Patriots of Lancaster County*.

19. Carmichael, *A Self-defensive War Lawful*, 23; quoted in Robert McConnell Hatch, *Major John André: A Gallant in Spy's Clothing* (Boston, 1986), 60.

20. Lancaster Committee to President of Congress, Dec. 21, 1775, PCC, reel 83; Lancaster Committee to President of Congress, Jan. 22, 1776, *AA*, 4th ser., 4:801; British Officers to Continental Congress, Jan. 20, 1776, *AA*, 4th ser., 4:801–2.

21. President of Congress to Lancaster Committee, Jan. 18, 1776, *AA*, 4th ser., 4:761–63; Congress to Lancaster Committee, Jan. 20, 1776, *AA*, 4th ser., 4:801; Jasper Yeates to Colonel Wilson, Jan. 20, 1776, Simon Gratz Manuscripts, case 2, box 13, Supreme Court of Pennsylvania, HSP; Lancaster Committee to President of Congress, Jan. 22, 1776, *AA*, 4th ser., 4:801.

22. "Items from Letters," 96; Wood, *Conestoga Crossroads*, 139–80; Lancaster Committee to President of Congress, Jan. 3, 1776, *AA*, 4th ser., 4:561; *PA*, 2nd ser., 1:440–48; Samuel Miller Sener, *The Lancaster Barracks: Where the British and Hessian Prisoners were Detained during the Revolution* (Harrisburg, 1895), 20; John Wilson to Lancaster Committee, Feb. 24, 1776, Sol Feinstone Collection, 1685, reel 3, film 1, DLAR.

23. Pennsylvania Council of Safety to President of Congress, Feb. 20, 1776, *AA*, 4th ser., 4:1213–14; Pennsylvania Council of Safety, Feb. 20, 1776, *AA*, 4th ser., 4:1573.

24. *PA*, 2nd ser., 13:512–15; Continental Congress, Feb. 26, 1776, *AA*, 4th ser., 4:1690; Pennsylvania Committee of Safety, Mar. 2, 1776, *AA*, 4th ser., 5:718; *CR*, 10:515; Lancaster County Committee of Safety Records, Mar. 19, 1776, Peter Force Papers; Edward Shippen to Joseph Shippen, Mar. 23, 1776, Shippen Family Papers, 10, HSP.

25. British Officers to President of Congress, July 12, 1776, *AA*, 5th ser., 1:222–23; quoted in Hatch, *Major John André*, 67. For officers and assumptions of honor, see Cox, *A Proper Sense of Honor*, 199–235; and Burrows, *Forgotten Patriots*, 27–28, 45.

26. *PA*, 2nd ser., 13:525–26; "Lancaster Committee to York and Cumberland Committees, June 16, 1776," *Notes and Queries*, 1st and 2nd ser., 2:380–81; *PA*, 2nd ser., 13:520, 522–23; *CR*, 10:546; *PA*, 2nd ser., 1:477; Philip Greenwalt to Lancaster Committee, June 16, 1776, Yeates Papers; Lebanon Committee to Lancaster Committee, July 16, 1776, Peter Force Collection, ser. 9, reel 102.

27. Examination of William Poor, July 26, 1776, *AA*, 5th ser., 1:596–97; Examination of John White, July 26, 1776, *AA*, 5th ser., 1:597–99; George Ross to President of Congress, July 7, 1776, *AA*, 5th ser., 1:103–4. See also Cumberland Committee to President of Congress, July 14, 1776, *AA*, 5th ser., 1:328; List of Prisoners in Gaol, Nov. 14, 1776, Peter Force Collection, ser. 9, reel 103.

28. For the blurred lines separating the combatants, see also Colley, *Captives*, 203–38.

29. George Ross to President of Congress, July 7, 1776, *AA*, 5th ser., 1:103–4; Young, "The Spirit of 1775"; *Pennsylvania Packet*, Aug. 28, 1775; Royster, *A Revolutionary People at War*, 33–35; Knouff, *The Soldiers' Revolution*, 135–36; Linda Baumgarten,

What Clothes Reveal: The Language of Clothing in Colonial and Federal America (New Haven, 2002), 18, 20, 66, 69, 72, 74.

30. Balch, *Letters and Papers*, 238–39; Edward Shippen to James Burd, Mar. 4, 1776, Shippen Family Papers, 7, HSP; Lancaster Committee to Alexander McKee, Jan. 15, 1776, Peter Force Collection, ser. 9, reel 102; Lancaster Committee to George Ross, Jan. 15, 1776, Peter Force Collection, ser. 9, reel 102.

31. James Read to Edward Shippen, May 18, 1776, Shippen Family Papers, 7, HSP.

32. For Pennsylvania's growing divisions, see Ousterhout, *A State Divided*; Ryerson, *The Revolution Is Now Begun*; Knouff, *The Soldiers' Revolution*, 195–231; and Frantz and Pencak, *Beyond Philadelphia*.

33. *JCC*, 3:402; Cumberland Committee to President of Congress, July 14, 1776, *AA*, 5th ser., 1:328; *PA*, 1st ser., 4:789; *PA*, 2nd ser., 1:593–95; Lebanon Committee to Lancaster Committee, July 24, 1776, Peter Force Collection, ser. 9, reel 102.

34. Edward Burd to Jasper Yeates, Apr. 15, 1776, Yeates Papers; Lancaster County Committee of Safety Records, Dec. 27, 1775, and Mar. 25, 1776, Peter Force Papers; Jasper Yeates to Colonel Wilson, Jan. 20, 1776, Simon Gratz Manuscripts; Hatch, *Major John André*, 67; Examination of William Poor, July 26, 1776; Examination of John White, July 26, 1776; Petition of James White, Oct. 9, 1777, PRG, Clemency Files, reel 36; Petition of John White, Oct. 16, 1777, PRG, Clemency Files, reel 36; Lancaster Committee to Captain John Henry, June 6, 1776, Yeates Papers.

35. Continental Congress, Feb. 28, 1776, *AA*, 4th ser., 4:1689–90; Continental Congress, Apr. 12, 1776, *AA*, 4th ser., 5:1670–71; Pennsylvania Council of Safety, Apr. 13, 1776, *AA*, 4th ser., 5:738–39; Continental Congress, Apr. 9, 1776, *AA*, 4th ser., 5:1662; Continental Congress, May 21, 1776, *AA*, 4th ser., 6:1675–77; Pennsylvania Assembly, May 30, 1776, *AA*, 4th ser., 6:854–55. See also George Washington to President of Congress, May 11, 1776, *AA*, 4th ser., 6:423–25; "Minutes Respecting the Mode of Treating Prisoners in England," *AA*, 4th ser., 6:425–26.

36. George Ross to President of Congress, July 7, 1776, *AA*, 5th ser., 1:103–4; "Extracts from Moravian Diaries," 91–92.

37. George Ross to President of Congress, July 7, 1776, *AA*, 5th ser., 1:103–4.

38. Sarah Yeates to Jasper Yeates, July 15, 1776, Yeates Papers; Continental Congress, July 10, 1776, *AA*, 5th ser., 1:1571; President of Congress to Lancaster Committee, July 12, 1776, *AA*, 5th ser., 1:219; Lancaster Committee to Committee Members and Militia Officers, Lancaster County, July 14, 1776, *AA*, 5th ser., 1:327; Lancaster Committee, July 11, 1776, *AA*, 5th ser., 1:188; William Atlee to President of Congress, July 13, 1776, *AA*, 5th ser., 1:255; "Extracts from Moravian Diaries," 91–92; *PA*, 2nd ser., 13:349–50; Matthias Slough to Jasper Yeates, Aug. 22, 1776, Society Miscellaneous Collection, HSP; James Ewing to Lancaster Committee, 1776, Peter Force Collection, ser. 9, reel 103; William Atlee to George Ross, Mar. 12, 1777, reel 74, PCC; *JCC*, 6:184, 190.

39. Inhabitants of Reading to Pennsylvania Assembly, Mar. 6, 1776, *AA*, 4th ser., 5:675; Sarah Yeates to Jasper Yeates, July 15, 1776, Yeates Papers; Continental Congress, July 10, 1776, *AA*, 5th ser., 1:1571; President of Congress to Lancaster Committee, July 12, 1776, *AA*, 5th ser., 1:219; Henry Haller to President of Congress,

July 13, 1776, *AA*, 5th ser., 1:254; Lancaster Committee to Council of Safety, July 18, 1776, *AA*, 5th ser., 1:411; "Extracts from Moravian Diaries," 92; Lancaster Committee, July 23, 1776, *AA*, 5th ser., 1:533; William Atlee to Board of War, July 23, 1776, *AA*, 5th ser., 1:535; James Burd to Edward Shippen, July 15, 1776, Shippen Family Papers, 7, HSP; Lancaster Committee, Aug. 24, 1776, *AA*, 5th ser., 1:1135; Lancaster Committee, Sept. 17, 1776, *AA*, 5th ser., 2:365.

40. Council of Safety to Lancaster Committee, Mar. 6, 1776, Peter Force Collection, ser. 9, reel 102; Lancaster County Committee of Safety Records, Apr. 10, 1776, Peter Force Papers; Lancaster County Committee of Safety Records, Apr. 12, 1776, Peter Force Papers; "Report of Subcommittee respecting Tradesmen among the Prisoners," Apr. 11, 1776, Peter Force Collection, ser. 9, reel 102. For hiring out during the Seven Years' War, see Steele, "When Worlds Collide," 9–39.

41. *PA*, 2nd ser., 13:536; British Soldiers Permitted to Work List, July 15, 1776, Peter Force Collection, ser. 9, reel 102; Lancaster Committee, July 23, 1776, *AA*, 5th ser., 1:534; Lancaster Committee, July 25, 1776, *AA*, 5th ser., 1:572–73; Lancaster Committee, July 26, 1776, *AA*, 5th ser., 1:596; *PA*, 2nd ser., 1:486; Council of Safety to Lancaster Committee, July 29, 1776, Peter Force Collection, ser. 9, reel 102; Lancaster Committee, July 30, 1776, *AA*, 5th ser., 1:673; Examination of Peter Schoecker, Aug. 2, 1776, *AA*, 5th ser., 1:760–61; Lancaster Committee, Aug. 5, 1776, *AA*, 5th ser., 1:760; Lancaster Committee, Aug. 16, 1776, *AA*, 5th ser., 1:947–48; Lancaster Committee, Aug. 19, 1776, *AA*, 5th ser., 1:1062; Lancaster Committee, Aug. 24, 1776, *AA*, 5th ser., 1:1135; Lancaster Committee, Sept. 11, 1776, *AA*, 5th ser., 2:287; Lancaster Committee, Sept. 17, 1776, *AA*, 5th ser., 2:365; Lancaster Committee, Oct. 12, 1776, *AA*, 5th ser., 2:1008; "Captain George Musser's Orderly Book, October 1776," *Notes and Queries*, annual vol. (1900): 128; Sarah Yeates to Jasper Yeates, July 15, 1776, Yeates Papers.

42. Council of Safety to President of Congress, Feb. 20, 1776, *AA*, 4th ser., 4:1213–14.

43. James Work to William Atlee, Aug. 26, 1776, Peter Force Collection, ser. 9, reel 102; Robert Treat Paine to Peter Grubb, Sept. 18, 1776, in Smith, *Letters of Delegates to Congress*, 5:197; Sam Boyd to Adam Reigart, Sept. 23, 1776, Peter Force Collection, ser. 9, reel 102; James Moore to Lancaster Committee, Sept. 23, 1776, Peter Force Collection, ser. 9, reel 102; Lancaster Committee, Oct. 12, 1776, *AA*, 5th ser., 2:1008; "Captain George Musser's Orderly Book," 128; Captain Christopher Crawford's Book, Lancaster County, Pennsylvania Papers, 1724–1816, Petitions for Lebanon, 1772–1816, HSP; List of Prisoners in Gaol, Nov. 14, 1776, Peter Force Collection, ser. 9, reel 103; List of Regulars in Gaol, Nov. 15, 1776, Peter Force Collection, ser. 9, reel 103; Prisoners' Names, Nov. 15, 1776, Peter Force Collection, ser. 9, reel 103.

44. Captain Christopher Crawford's Book; Northumberland Committee to Paxton Committee, Sept. 5, 1776, Peter Force Collection, ser. 9, reel 102; "Captain George Musser's Orderly Book," 128; Colonel James Burd to William Atlee, Sept. 9, 1776, Peter Force Collection, ser. 9, reel 102; John Harris to George Fry, Sept. 9, 1776, Peter Force Collection, ser. 9, reel 102; Lancaster Committee, Sept. 11, 1776, *AA*, 5th ser., 2:287.

45. Lancaster Committee, Sept. 24, 1776, *AA*, 5th ser., 2:491; Lancaster Committee, Sept. 26, 1776, *AA*, 5th ser., 2:546. For another example, see Sarah Yeates to Jasper Yeates, July 15, 1776, Yeates Papers.

46. Captain Christopher Crawford's Book; *Pennsylvania Gazette*, Oct. 30, 1776; Edward Shippen to William Atlee, Aug. 30, 1776, Burd-Shippen Collection, reel 2; "Captain George Musser's Orderly Book," 128; Sarah Yeates to Jasper Yeates, July 15, 1776, Yeates Papers; List of Prisoners, Aug. 27, 1776, Peter Force Collection, ser. 9, reel 102; John Harris to George Fry, Sept. 9, 1776, Peter Force Collection, ser. 9, reel 102; Lancaster Committee, Sept. 11, 1776, *AA*, 5th ser., 2:287; James Moore to Lancaster Committee, Sept. 23, 1776, Peter Force Collection, ser. 9, reel 102; Sam Boyd to Adam Reigart, Sept. 23, 1776, Peter Force Collection, ser. 9, reel 102; List of Prisoners in Gaol, Nov. 14, 1776, Peter Force Collection, ser. 9, reel 103; List of Regulars in Gaol, Nov. 15, 1776, Peter Force Collection, ser. 9, reel 103; Prisoners' Names, Nov. 15, 1776, Peter Force Collection, ser. 9, reel 103.

47. Houlding, *Fit for Service*; Sylvia Frey, *The British Soldier in America: A Social History of Military Life in the Revolutionary Period* (Austin, 1981); Stephen Brumwell, *Redcoats: The British Soldier and War in the Americas, 1755–1763* (Cambridge, 2001); Spring, *With Zeal and With Bayonets Only*.

48. Board of War to Lancaster Committee, Nov. 15, 1776, Peter Force Collection, ser. 9, reel 103; Lancaster Committee, Sept. 24, 1776, *AA*, 5th ser., 2:491; Continental Congress, Oct. 7, 1776, *AA*, 5th ser., 2:1389; Continental Congress, Oct. 22, 1776, Peter Force Collection, ser. 9, reel 102; Council of Safety to Lancaster Committee, Nov. 2, 1776, Peter Force Collection, ser. 9, reel 103.

49. Council of Safety, July 3, 1776, *AA*, 4th ser., 6:1298; Ousterhout, *A State Divided*, 229–78; Knouff, *The Soldiers' Revolution*, 155–231; Silver, *Our Savage Neighbors*, 227–60.

50. Council of Safety to Lancaster Committee, Mar. 19, 1776, Yeates Papers; "Edward Shippen to Joseph Shippen, July 13, 1776," *PLCHS* 11 (1906–1907): 18. See also James Read to Edward Shippen, May 18, 1776, Shippen Family Papers, 7, HSP; Council of Safety to Colonels, Lancaster County, Nov. 11, 1776, Grubb Collection, Colonel Peter Grubb, Revolutionary War Papers, 1775–1777, HSP; Council of Safety to Colonels, Lancaster County, Dec. 8, 1776, Peter Force Collection, ser. 9, reel 103; George Ross, Circular to Lancaster County Associators, Dec. 18, 1776, *AA*, 5th ser., 3:1273.

51. Peter Grubb Jr. to Peter Grubb Sr., Sept. 16, 1776, Grubb Collection, Peter Grubb Correspondence, 1765–1779; *PA*, 2nd ser., 10:312–17; Klein, *Fighting the Battles*; *PA*, 2nd ser., 1:509–22; Edward Shippen to William Shippen, Sept. 14, 1776, Shippen Papers, BSh62, APS; Sarah Yeates to Jasper Yeates, Oct. 17, 1776, Simon Gratz Manuscripts, case 2, box 13, Supreme Court of Pennsylvania; Edward Shippen to Joseph Shippen, Nov. 30, 1776, Shippen Papers, BSh62, APS.

52. Edward Shippen to Jasper Yeates, Jan. 9, 1777, Yeates Papers; Christopher Marshall to Children, Feb. 6, 1778, Christopher Marshall Letterbook, HSP; Christopher Marshall, *Extracts from the Diary of Christopher Marshall, 1774–1781* (1877; repr., New York, 1969), 200–201; Sarah Yeates to Jasper Yeates, Oct. 17, 1776, Simon Gratz Manuscripts; Lancaster Committee, Dec. 17, 1776, *AA*, 5th ser., 3:1257. For the British prison ships, see Metzger, *The Prisoner in the American Revolution*, 281–91; Bowman, *Captive Americans*, 42–49; Burrows, *Forgotten Patriots*, 12–14, 53–57, 92–93, 197–200.

53. Quoted in Hatch, *Major John André*, 67.

54. Lancaster Committee, Aug. 5, 1776, *AA*, 5th ser., 1:759–60. For the culture of violence in Pennsylvania's backcountry, see Silver, *Our Savage Neighbors*; and Kenny, *Peaceable Kingdom Lost*.

55. Lancaster Committee to Colonels, Lancaster County, May 28, 1776, Yeates Papers; Edward Shippen to Joseph Shippen, Apr. 1776, Shippen Papers, BSh62, APS; *PA*, 2nd ser., 13:531; Council of Safety to Colonels, Lancaster County, Nov. 11, 1776, Grubb Collection; William Atlee to Peter Grubb, Nov. 14, 1776, Grubb Collection, Colonel Peter Grubb, Revolutionary War Papers; Board of War to George Washington, Nov. 19, 1776, *AA*, 5th ser., 3:762; Board of War to Council of Safety, Nov. 19, 1776, *AA*, 5th ser., 3:778; Council of Safety to Lancaster Committee, Nov. 20, 1776, *AA*, 5th ser., 3:777–78; Board of War to George Washington, Nov. 23, 1776, *AA*, 5th ser., 3:820; George Washington to Board of War, Dec. 4, 1776, *AA*, 5th ser., 3:1070.

56. Lancaster Committee, Nov. 22, 1776, Peter Force Collection, ser. 9, reel 103; Lancaster Committee, Nov. 27, 1776, *AA*, 5th ser., 3:869; Council of Safety to Lancaster Committee, Nov. 30, 1776, Peter Force Collection, ser. 9, reel 103; Lancaster Committee, Nov. 30, 1776, *AA*, 5th ser., 3:918–19; Lancaster Committee to William Atlee, Dec. 16, 1776, Peter Force Collection, ser. 9, reel 103; "Extracts from Moravian Diaries," 92; George Washington to Board of War, Dec. 4, 1776, *AA*, 5th ser., 3:1070; *PA*, 2nd ser., 13:530–31.

57. For related dynamics, see Silver, *Our Savage Neighbors.*

58. "Captain George Musser's Orderly Book," 128; Peden, *Revolutionary Patriots of Lancaster County.*

59. Lancaster Committee, Nov. 22, 1776, Peter Force Collection, ser. 9, reel 103.

60. George Ross to James Wilson, Nov. 26, 1776, in Smith, *Letters of Delegates to Congress,* 5:547.

61. Balch, *Letters and Papers,* 258; Ousterhout, *A State Divided;* Ryerson, *The Revolution Is Now Begun,* 207–46; Knouff, *The Soldiers' Revolution,* 195–231; Council of Safety to Lancaster Committee, Dec. 8, 1776, Peter Force Collection, ser. 9, reel 103; Council of Safety to George Washington, Dec. 13, 1776, *AA*, 5th ser., 3:1199; "Extracts from Moravian Diaries," 92.

62. Edward Shippen to James Burd, Dec. 30, 1776, Shippen Family Papers, 7, HSP; Pennsylvania Council of Safety to Lancaster Committee, Dec. 31, 1776, *AA*, 5th ser., 3:1511.

4. "'Tis Britain Alone That Is Our Enemy"

1. Edward Shippen to James Burd, Dec. 30, 1776, Shippen Family Papers, 7, HSP; Continental Congress to George Washington, Dec. 28, 1776, *AA*, 5th ser., 3:1458–59; *PA*, 1st ser., 5:146–47; George Washington to Robert Morris, George Clymer, and George Walton, Jan. 1, 1777, in Fitzpatrick, *Writings of George Washington,* 6:464; Council of Safety to Lancaster Committee, Dec. 31, 1776, *AA*, 5th ser., 3:1511. For the Hessians, see Rodney Atwood, *The Hessians: Mercenaries from Hessen-Kassel in the American Revolution* (Cambridge, 1980); Elliott Hoffman, "The German Soldiers in the American Revolution" (Ph.D. diss., University of New Hampshire, 1982); Melodie Andrews, "'Myrmidons from Abroad': The Role of the German Mercenary in the Coming of American Independence" (Ph.D. diss., University of Houston, 1986); and especially Krebs, *A Generous and Merciful Enemy.* For the Battle of Trenton, see Atwood, *The Hessians,* 84–116; and David Hackett Fischer, *Washington's Crossing* (New York, 2004).

2. The Continental campaign to subvert Britain's German auxiliaries has been well-documented by historians of the American Revolution; see Lyman H. Butterfield, "Psychological Warfare in 1776: The Jefferson-Franklin Plan to Cause Hessian Desertions," *Proceedings of the American Philosophical Society* 94 (June 1950): 233–41; Carl Berger, *Broadsides and Bayonets: The Propaganda War of the American Revolution* (Philadelphia, 1961), 119–38; Atwood, *The Hessians*, 184–206; Andrews, "Myrmidons from Abroad," 338–45; and Neimeyer, *America Goes to War*, 52–63. For Continentals' dealings with their German prisoners, see Krebs, *A Generous and Merciful Enemy*.

3. See Atwood, *The Hessians*, 58–83, 171–83; Krebs, *A Generous and Merciful Enemy*, 143–66. For the auxiliaries' connections to Americans' declaration of independence, see especially Andrews, "Myrmidons from Abroad."

4. Atwood, *The Hessians*, 7–21, 23; Hoffman, "German Soldiers in the American Revolution," 27, 36–40; Andrews, "Myrmidons from Abroad," 42, 57–59.

5. Atwood, *The Hessians*, 22–57; Hoffman, "German Soldiers in the American Revolution," 26–28, 41–42, 79, 82; Andrews, "Myrmidons from Abroad," 38–61, 66–67, 70–72.

6. Atwood, *The Hessians*, 22–57, 144–45, 207; Hoffman, "German Soldiers in the American Revolution," 49–50, 74–86, 94, 114–20, 408–9; Andrews, "Myrmidons from Abroad," 57–58. For the auxiliary treaties and German recruitment, see also Krebs, *A Generous and Merciful Enemy*, 19–55.

7. Motion by Lord North, Feb. 29, 1776, *AA*, 4th ser., 6:283; Berger, *Broadsides and Bayonets*, 119–20; Butterfield, "Psychological Warfare in 1776," 233; Atwood, *The Hessians*, 24, 32, 59.

8. Extract of a Letter from Germany, Aug. 10, 1775, *AA*, 4th ser., 3:74; Letter from Arthur Lee, Apr. 15, 1776, *AA*, 4th ser., 5:941. I am indebted to the findings of earlier historians for my treatment of the Whigs' 1776 campaign to subvert the auxiliaries. See especially Butterfield, "Psychological Warfare in 1776"; Berger, *Broadsides and Bayonets*, 119–38; Atwood, *The Hessians*, 184–206; and Andrews, "Myrmidons from Abroad," 338–45.

9. George Washington to Continental Congress, May 11, 1776, *AA*, 4th ser., 6:423–24; Continental Congress, Aug. 9, 1776, *AA*, 5th ser., 1:1602; Committee on Letters from General Washington, with Treaties for the Employment of Germans and Hessians against America, May 21, 1776, *AA*, 4th ser., 6:1675.

10. Continental Congress, Aug. 14, 1776, *AA*, 5th ser., 1:1607–8.

11. Continental Congress, Aug. 14, 1776.

12. James Wilson to Continental Congress, Aug. 22, 1776, *AA*, 5th ser., 1:1110; George Washington to Continental Congress, Aug. 18, 1776, *AA*, 5th ser., 1:1025; George Washington to Continental Congress, Aug. 19, 1776, *AA*, 5th ser., 1:1065–66; George Washington to Continental Congress, Aug. 26, 1776, *AA*, 5th ser., 1:1158; Benjamin Franklin to Horatio Gates, Aug. 28, 1776, *AA*, 5th ser., 1:1193; Charles Witt to New York Convention, Oct. 24, 1776, *AA*, 5th ser., 2:1222; Butterfield, "Psychological Warfare in 1776," 236–38; Berger, *Broadsides and Bayonets*, 122–24; Atwood, *The Hessians*, 186–88.

13. Atwood, *The Hessians*, 46–47, 60, 157, 159–64, 189, 195–96; Hoffman, "German Soldiers in the American Revolution," 417–18, 440–41; Andrews, "Myrmidons from Abroad," 77.

14. Ernst Kipping, *The Hessian View of America, 1776–1783* (Monmouth Beach, 1971), 13–14.

15. Mühlenberg, *Journals*, 2:757; Atwood, *The Hessians*, 38–45, 66, 204–5, 207–15; Neimeyer, *America Goes to War*, 54–55. For the recruitment and social composition of the German troops, see also Krebs, *A Generous and Merciful Enemy*, 36–74.

16. Atwood, *The Hessians*, 38–39, 155–57, 185–86, 190, 195–96; Berger, *Broadsides and Bayonets*, 124–25.

17. Mühlenberg, *Journals*, 2:757; Letter from General Gates to General Schuyler: Enclosing Examination and Capitulation of Anthony Hasselaband, Sept. 5, 1776, *AA*, 5th ser., 2:203–4; Information Given by a Hessian Deserter, Sept. 5, 1776, *AA*, 5th ser., 2:708; London, Sept. 2, 1776, *AA*, 5th ser., 1:626; Examination of Two Canadian Captains, Aug. 1776, *AA*, 5th ser., 1:798–800; Extract of a Letter to Williamsburg, Aug. 20, 1776, *AA*, 5th ser., 1:1077–78; Extract of a Letter from an Officer in General Frazier's Battalion, Sept. 3, 1776, *AA*, 5th ser., 1:1259–60; James Thacher, *A Military Journal during the American Revolutionary War, from 1775 to 1783* (2nd ed., Boston, 1827), 67; Butterfield, "Psychological Warfare in 1776," 240; Berger, *Broadsides and Bayonets*, 124–26; Atwood, *The Hessians*, 51–52, 60, 187–90, 192–93; Andrews, "Myrmidons from Abroad," 301–2.

18. Atwood, *The Hessians*, 68–81, 189; Thacher, *Military Journal*, 67.

19. Berger, *Broadsides and Bayonets*, 126; Atwood, *The Hessians*, 190. For a detailed treatment of Trenton, see Fischer, *Washington's Crossing*.

20. Continental Congress to George Washington, Dec. 28, 1776, *AA*, 5th ser., 3:1458–59; George Washington to Robert Morris, George Clymer, and George Walton, Jan. 1, 1777, in Fitzpatrick, *Writings of George Washington*, 6:464; *PA*, 1st ser., 5:146; "Diary of Lieutenant Jakob Piel, from 1776 to 1783," trans. Bruce E. Burgoyne, *Journal of the Johannes Schwalm Historical Association* 4 (1989): 15.

21. *PA*, 1st ser., 5:146–47; Council of Safety to Lancaster Committee, Dec. 31, 1776, *AA*, 5th ser., 3:1511.

22. For anti-German sentiment, see Rothermund, "The German Problem of Colonial Pennsylvania"; Schwartz, *"A Mixed Multitude,"* 159–204; Liam Riordan, "'The Complexion of My Country': The German as 'Other' in Colonial Pennsylvania," in *Germans and Indians: Fantasies, Encounters, Projections*, ed. Colin G. Calloway et al. (Lincoln, 2002), 97–119; Jon Butler, *Becoming America: The Revolution before 1776* (Cambridge, 2000), 31–32. See also Andrews, "Myrmidons from Abroad," 281–93.

23. President of Congress to Governments of New Hampshire, Massachusetts, Connecticut, New York, New Jersey, Delaware, and Maryland, June 4, 1776, *AA*, 4th ser., 6:707; *New-York Journal* (New York), May 30, 1776; "Revolutionary War Letters of Colonel William Douglas," *The New-York Historical Society Quarterly Bulletin* 13 (July 1929): 79; Extract of a Letter from an English Officer, Dec. 3, 1776, *AA*, 5th ser., 3:1059; Andrews, "Myrmidons from Abroad," 70, 130, 199–203, 263.

24. Ambrose Serle, *The American Journal of Ambrose Serle, Secretary to Lord Howe, 1776–1778* (San Marino, 1940), 77. See also Andrews, "Myrmidons from Abroad," 152–241.

25. Joseph Shippen to Edward Shippen, Jan. 15, 1776, Shippen Family Papers, 7, HSP; *The New-York Gazette and the Weekly Mercury* (New York), May 13, 1776; Edward Shippen Jr. to Jasper Yeates, Jan. 19, 1776, Shippen Family Papers, 7, HSP; *Pennsylvania Gazette*, May 22, 1776; Andrews, "Myrmidons from Abroad," 209–15;

Hawke, *In the Midst of a Revolution*, 92–94; Ryerson, *The Revolution Is Now Begun*, 171, 208, 222, 228. The reference was to George Whitefield, Great Awakening evangelist.

26. Ben Franklin to Lord Howe, July 21, 1776, *AA*, 5th ser., 1:482–83; *Pennsylvania Gazette*, Oct. 16, 1776. See also George Washington to Massachusetts Assembly, July 11, 1776, *AA*, 5th ser., 1:192–93.

27. "An Address to General Arthur St. Clair's Brigade, 1776," *PMHB* 23 (1899): 250; Ebenezer Hazard to General Gates, Oct. 11, 1776, *AA*, 5th ser., 2:995; Council of Safety to Colonels, Lancaster County, Nov. 11, 1776, Grubb Collection; Andrews, "Myrmidons from Abroad," 207; *PA*, 2nd ser., 10:307; Extract of a Letter from an Officer in General Frazier's Battalion, Sept. 3, 1776, *AA*, 5th ser., 1:1259–60; Edward J. Lowell, *The Hessians and the Other German Auxiliaries of Great Britain in the Revolutionary War* (New York, 1884), 65; Atwood, *The Hessians*, 68, 71; Extract of a Letter from an Officer at Harlem, Sept. 25, 1776, *AA*, 5th ser., 2:524; Tench Tilghman to William Duer, Oct. 8, 1776, *AA*, 5th ser., 2:948; Robert Morris to Commissioners in France, Dec. 21, 1776, *AA*, 5th ser., 3:1334; Extract of a Letter from Headquarters to Virginia, Nov. 8, 1776, *AA*, 5th ser., 3:603; Jasper Yeates to Edward Shippen, Dec. 7, 1776, Shippen Family Papers, 12, HSP.

28. *Pennsylvania Packet*, Dec. 18, 1776, Dec. 27, 1776, and Jan. 4, 1777; Robert Morris to Commissioners in France, Dec. 21, 1776, *AA*, 5th ser., 3:1334.

29. James Wilson to Jasper Yeates, Sept. 14, 1776, in Smith, *Letters of Delegates to Congress*, 5:171; *PA*, 2nd ser., 10:310; Journal of the Transaction of August 27, 1776, upon Long-Island, by Colonel Samuel Atlee, Aug. 27, 1776, *AA*, 5th ser., 1:1251–55, esp. 1254.

30. For German Americans see, for example, Wokeck, "German Settlements in the British North American Colonies"; Roeber, *Palatines, Liberty, and Property*; and Fogleman, *Hopeful Journeys*. For Lancaster's German speakers see Wood, *Conestoga Crossroads*, 7–9, 205–15. In addition, see Hoffman, "German Soldiers in the American Revolution," 54, 415, 434; and Andrews, "Myrmidons from Abroad," 281–93.

31. Johann Ewald, *Diary of the American War: A Hessian Journal*, trans. and ed. Joseph P. Tustin (New Haven, 1979), 91; Mühlenberg, *Journals*, 2:757.

32. John Hubley to William Atlee, Aug. 13, 1776, *AA*, 5th ser., 1:931; quoted in Roeber, *Palatines, Liberty, and Property*, 306–7; Ernst Kipping, *The Hessian View of America*, 24; *PA*, 2nd ser., 10:203. See also "Diary of Lieutenant Jakob Piel," 14, 16; "Anton Adolf Heinrich Du Roi's Diary of the Convention Army's March from Massachusetts to Virginia," trans. Gerhard K. Friesen, *Journal of the Johannes Schwalm Historical Association* 7 (2001): 23, 24.

33. Mühlenberg, *Journals*, 2:771–72; Committee for Transacting Continental Business to President of Congress, Dec. 30, 1776, *AA*, 5th ser., 3:1484; "Johannes Reuber's Diary," trans. Herbert N. Freund, *Journal of the Johannes Schwalm Historical Association* 1 (1979): 8; "Diary of Lieutenant Jakob Piel," 14.

34. *PA*, 1st ser., 5:146–47. For the German translation see the *Staatsbote*, Jan. 8, 1777. See also Andrews, "Myrmidons from Abroad," 340.

35. *Pennsylvania Journal* (Philadelphia), Mar. 5, 1777; Anonymous to Thomas Bradford, Mar. 6, 1777, Thomas Bradford Papers, British Army Prisoners, 1, HSP; Andrews, "Myrmidons from Abroad," 341–42.

36. Board of War to Lancaster Committee, Jan. 31, 1777, Peter Force Collection, ser. 9, reel 103; Council of Safety to Lancaster Committee, Dec. 31, 1776, *AA*, 5th

ser., 3:1511; Council of Safety to Lancaster Committee, Jan. 5, 1777, Peter Force Collection, ser. 9, reel 103; Lancaster County Committee of Safety Records, Feb. 18, 1777, Peter Force Papers.

37. Council of Safety to Lancaster Committee, Jan. 5, 1777, Peter Force Collection, ser. 9, reel 103; Lancaster Committee Address to Hessian Prisoners, Jan. 10, 1777, Peter Force Collection, ser. 9, reel 103; *PA*, 2nd ser., 13:540, 535–36, 539; Lancaster County Committee of Safety Records, Jan. 3, 1777, Peter Force Papers; "Extracts from Moravian Diaries," 92; "Johannes Reuber's Diary," 9.

38. *PA*, 2nd ser., 13:540, 536; Lancaster Committee to Board of War, Jan. 1777, Peter Force Collection, ser. 9, reel 103; Joseph Simon to David Franks, Mar. 21, 1777, McAllister Mss., HSP; Return of Prisoners in Barracks, Feb. 10, 1777, Peter Force Collection, ser. 9, reel 103; "Items from Letters," 97; Tradesmen among the Hessian Prisoners at Lancaster, Jan. 10, 1777, PRG, reel 11; Hessian Lists and Returns, with Professions, Jan. 1777, Peter Force Collection, ser. 9, reel 103; Board of War to Lancaster Committee, Jan. 31, 1777, Peter Force Collection, ser. 9, reel 103; Lancaster County Committee of Safety Records, Feb. 18, 1777.

39. *PA*, 2nd ser., 13:536; Lancaster Committee to Board of War, Feb. 1777, Peter Force Collection, ser. 9, reel 103.

40. Christopher Ludwick to Continental Congress, Mar. 8, 1777, PCC, reel 50. See also William Ward Condit, "Christopher Ludwick, the Patriotic Gingerbread Baker," *PMHB* 81 (Oct. 1957): 365–90.

41. Council of Safety to Lancaster Committee, Mar. 3, 1777, Peter Force Collection, ser. 9, reel 103; Pennsylvania War Office to Lancaster Committee, May 29, 1777, Peter Force Collection, ser. 9, reel 103; Council of Safety to Lancaster Committee, Mar. 4, 1777, Peter Force Collection, ser. 9, reel 103; "Johannes Reuber's Diary," 9; Berger, *Broadsides and Bayonets*, 128; Resolves, Council of Safety, Jan. 11, 1777, Peter Force Collection, ser. 9, reel 103.

42. Edward Burd to James Burd, May 26, 1777, Shippen Family Papers, 8, HSP; Joseph Simon to David Franks, Apr. 20, 1777, McAllister Mss.; Council of Safety to Lancaster Committee, Mar. 4, 1777, Peter Force Collection, ser. 9, reel 103; Council of Safety to Lancaster Committee, Mar. 31, 1777, Peter Force Collection, ser. 9, reel 103; "Hessian Laborers at Lancaster, Pennsylvania, 1777," *National Genealogical Society Quarterly* 59 (Sept. 1971): 188; Hessian Prisoners, Occupation or Trade, Employers, Apr. 1777, Peter Force Collection, ser. 9, reel 103; Charles Lukens to Lancaster Committee, May 27, 1777, Peter Force Collection, ser. 9, reel 103; Pennsylvania War Office to Lancaster Committee, May 29, 1777, Peter Force Collection, ser. 9, reel 103; E. Wood to Lancaster Committee, June 2, 1777, Peter Force Collection, ser. 9, reel 103; Valentine Eckert to Lancaster Committee, June 6, 1777, Peter Force Collection, ser. 9, reel 103; William Atlee to Elias Boudinot, Sept. 8, 1777, Peter Force Collection, ser. 9, reel 104; "Johannes Reuber's Diary," 9; Atwood, *The Hessians*, 185–86; Kipping, *The Hessian View of America*, 43–46; Gladys Bucher Sowers, *Hessian Prisoners and Their Employers in the Lebanon Township Area* (Lebanon, 2002); Joseph Simon to David Franks, Apr. 6, 1777, McAllister Mss.

43. Board of War to Lancaster Committee, May 10, 1777, Peter Force Collection, ser. 9, reel 103; Board of War to Lancaster Committee, May 26, 1777, Peter Force Collection, ser. 9, reel 103; Resolves, Council of Safety, Jan. 11, 1777, Peter Force Collection, ser. 9, reel 103; "Hessian Laborers at Lancaster, Pennsylvania,

1777," 188; Council of Safety to Lancaster Committee, Mar. 4, 1777, Peter Force Collection, ser. 9, reel 103; Board of War to Lancaster Committee, Apr. 2, 1777, Peter Force Collection, ser. 9, reel 103; Benjamin Flower to Lancaster Committee, Apr. 11, 1777, Peter Force Collection, ser. 9, reel 103; Board of War to Lancaster Committee, May 5, 1777, Peter Force Collection, ser. 9, reel 103; Pennsylvania War Office to Lancaster Committee, May 29, 1777, Peter Force Collection, ser. 9, reel 103; Board of War to Lancaster Committee, June 23, 1777, Peter Force Collection, ser. 9, reel 103; Kipping, *The Hessian View of America*, 24; Sowers, *Hessian Prisoners and Their Employers*, 12–14, 68.

44. Edward Burd to James Burd, May 26, 1777, Shippen Family Papers, 8, HSP; James Burd to Jasper Yeates, July 22, 1777, Yeates Papers; "Johannes Reuber's Diary," 9; Atwood, *The Hessians*, 198–99; Neimeyer, *America Goes to War*, 56; Krebs, *A Generous and Merciful Enemy*, 147–48.

45. Sowers, *Hessian Prisoners and Their Employers*, 32, 33, 59, 67; Kipping, *The Hessian View of America*, 43–46.

46. Board of War to William Atlee, Sept. 16, 1777, Peter Force Collection, ser. 9, reel 104; Thomas Hartley to William Atlee, Feb. 11, 1777, Peter Force Collection, ser. 9, reel 103; Kipping, *The Hessian View of America*, 43–45; *PA*, 2nd ser., 10:258; Sowers, *Hessian Prisoners and Their Employers*, 56; Thomas Hartley to Jasper Yeates, Feb. 10, 1777, Peter Force Collection, ser. 9, reel 103.

47. Kipping, *The Hessian View of America*, 43–45; Sowers, *Hessian Prisoners and Their Employers*, 25, 56, 62, 67.

48. Board of War to Lancaster Committee, Apr. 17, 1777, Peter Force Collection, ser. 9, reel 103; Levy Andrew Levy to Patrick Rice, Apr. 25, 1777, McAllister Mss.; Joseph Simon to David Franks, Apr. 20, 1777, McAllister Mss.; Town Major to Lancaster Committee, Apr. 26, 1777, Peter Force Collection, ser. 9, reel 103; Board of War to Lancaster Committee, Jan. 21, 1777, Peter Force Collection, ser. 9, reel 103; Joseph Simon to Patrick Rice, Jan. 24, 1777, McAllister Mss.; Lancaster County Committee of Safety Records, Feb. 18, 1777, Peter Force Papers; Levy Andrew Levy to Patrick Rice, May 14, 1777, McAllister Mss.; Town Major to Lancaster Committee, May 22, 1777, Peter Force Collection, ser. 9, reel 103; Levy Andrew Levy to Patrick Rice, July 4, 1777, McAllister Mss.; Joseph Lee Boyle, *"Their Distress is almost intolerable": The Elias Boudinot Letterbook, 1777–1778* (Bowie, 2002), 14; List of Naval Prisoners in the Lancaster Gaol, July 14, 1777, Peter Force Collection, ser. 9, reel 104; List of 42nd and 71st Regiments, Aug. 15–16, 1777, Peter Force Collection, ser. 9, reel 104.

49. British Prisoners to Lancaster Committee, May 3, 1777, Peter Force Collection, ser. 9, reel 103; James Mercer to Lancaster Committee, May 18, 1777, Peter Force Collection, ser. 9, reel 103; Board of War to Lancaster Committee, Apr. 17, 1777, Peter Force Collection, ser. 9, reel 103; Joseph Simon to David Franks, Apr. 20, 1777, McAllister Mss.; Lancaster Committee to Board of War, Jan. 1777, Peter Force Collection, ser. 9, reel 103; Prisoners' Petition to Lancaster Committee, June 28, 1776, Peter Force Collection, ser. 9, reel 103; Joseph Simon to Patrick Rice, May 19, 1776, McAllister Mss.; Joseph Simon to Patrick Rice, May 23, 1777, McAllister Mss.

50. "Extracts from Moravian Diaries," 92; "Johannes Reuber's Diary," 9; Account of the North American War, 1776–1778, 129–30, Morristown National Historical Park, Hessian Documents of the American Revolution, 1776–1783, fiche 5–11,

DLAR; Lancaster County Committee, June 5, 1777, Peter Force Collection, ser. 8D, reel 48, LOC; British Prisoners' Petition, June 19, 1777, Peter Force Collection, ser. 9, reel 103; Prisoners' Petition to Lancaster Committee, June 28, 1777, Peter Force Collection, ser. 9, reel 103; Grand Jury to Lancaster Committee, Aug. 8, 1777, Peter Force Collection, ser. 9, reel 104.

51. *CR*, 11:236; Lancaster County Committee, June 5, 1777, Peter Force Collection, ser. 8D, reel 48; *PA*, 1st ser., 5:376; Levy Andrew Levy to Patrick Rice, June 15, 1777, McAllister Mss.; Levy Andrew Levy to Patrick Rice, July 16, 1777, McAllister Mss.

52. Richard Peters to Elias Boudinot, Apr. 29, 1777, Elias Boudinot Papers, LOC; Boyle, *"Their Distress is almost intolerable,"* 14; Richard Peters to Elias Boudinot, July 17, 1777, Elias Boudinot Papers; Elias Boudinot to William Atlee, Aug. 11, 1777, Peter Force Collection, ser. 9, reel 104.

53. Elias Boudinot to William Atlee, Aug. 11, 1777, Peter Force Collection, ser. 9, reel 104; Marshall, *Diary*, 123–24; Supreme Executive Council to Bartram Galbraith, Aug. 20, 1777, PRG, reel 12.

54. William Atlee to Elias Boudinot, Sept. 8, 1777, Peter Force Collection, ser. 9, reel 104; Marshall, *Diary*, 123; Richard Peters to William Atlee, Sept. 14, 1777, Peter Force Collection, ser. 9, reel 104; Christopher Marshall to Children, Aug. 24, 1777, Christopher Marshall Letterbook; Hessian Prisoners Sent to Lebanon, Aug. 25, 1777, Peter Force Collection, ser. 9, reel 104; Levy Andrew Levy to Patrick Rice, Aug. 27, 1777, McAllister Mss.; Bartram Galbraith to Thomas Wharton, Sept. 2, 1777, PRG, reel 12; Isaac Zane, Sept. 20, 1777, Peter Force Collection, ser. 9, reel 104; "Diary of Lieutenant Jakob Piel," 16; "Johannes Reuber's Diary," 9–10; Board of War to William Atlee, Sept. 16, 1777, Peter Force Collection, ser. 9, reel 104; List of the Hessian Prisoners and Their Employers, Sept.–Nov. 1777, Peter Force Collection, ser. 9, reel 104; Kipping, *The Hessian View of America*, 43–46; Sowers, *Hessian Prisoners and Their Employers*, 22–68.

55. Richard Peters to William Atlee, Oct. 4, 1777, Peter Force Collection, ser. 9, reel 104.

56. William Atlee to Elias Boudinot, Dec. 13, 1777, Elias Boudinot Papers; Richard Peters to William Atlee, Oct. 4, 1777, Peter Force Collection, ser. 9, reel 104; List of the Hessian Prisoners and Their Employers, Sept.–Nov. 1777, Peter Force Collection, ser. 9, reel 104; Joseph Simon to Patrick Rice, Sept. 29, 1777, McAllister Mss.; Kipping, *The Hessian View of America*, 43–46; Sowers, *Hessian Prisoners and Their Employers*, 22–68; Deposition of Thomas Wileman, Feb. 18, 1778, BHP, reel 3A.

57. Edward Shippen to James Burd, Aug. 29, 1777, Shippen Family Papers, 8, HSP; Marshall, *Diary*, 124, 170; "Johannes Reuber's Diary," 9–10.

58. "Piramids of Hessian puddings," to be precise, "some of them full as long as a Childs legg, & measured seven inches around, & as black as a sweep chimneys face." Anonymous to Thomas Bradford, Mar. 6, 1777, Thomas Bradford Papers, British Army Prisoners, 1. For the Battle of Redbank, see Atwood, *The Hessians*, 117–30.

59. For locals' hiring of Hessian laborers, see Kipping, *The Hessian View of America*, 43–45; and Sowers, *Hessian Prisoners and Their Employers*, 22–68.

60. Mühlenberg, *Journals*, 2:757. See also Atwood, *The Hessians*, 98, 128–29.

61. "Johannes Reuber's Diary," 9–10.

62. Atwood, *The Hessians*, 99, 188; Hoffman, "German Soldiers in the American Revolution," 483; Neimeyer, *America Goes to War*, 53–58.

63. Atwood, *The Hessians*, 129–30, 193–97; Hoffman, "German Soldiers in the American Revolution," 487–89; Neimeyer, *America Goes to War*, 58–64. For the British and German prisoners taken at Saratoga see George W. Knepper, "The Convention Army, 1777–1783" (Ph.D. diss., University of Michigan, 1954); William M. Dabney, *After Saratoga: The Story of the Convention Army* (Albuquerque, 1955).

5. "Enemies of Our Peace"

1. Jasper Yeates to Joseph Shippen, Sept. 10, 1777, Shippen Family Papers, BSh6lf.1, APS; Christopher Marshall to Children, Aug. 24, 1777, Christopher Marshall Letterbook; "Extracts from Moravian Diaries," 92; Edward Shippen to Joseph Shippen, Sept. 10, 1777, Shippen Family Papers, BSh6lf.1, APS; Marshall, *Diary*, 126; Levy Andrew Levy to Patrick Rice, Sept. 12, 1777, William Henry Papers, 1759–1812, 2, HSP. For the war in Pennsylvania, see Bodle, *Valley Forge Winter*; and Knouff, *The Soldiers' Revolution*.

2. Residents filed a petition that, according to one signatory, urged the assembly to "call out the whole force of this State . . . in order to attack Gen. Howe . . . ruin his army, and rid the Colonies of such cruel monsters." Howe, for his part, was content to remain in Philadelphia, where his army settled in for the winter, launching occasional raids into the interior. See Marshall, *Diary*, 153; also 130–31, 150, 159, 163, 171–73.

3. Christopher Marshall to Sons, Apr. 2, 1778, Christopher Marshall Letterbook; Knouff, *The Soldiers' Revolution*, 54–60, 107, 195–231; Ousterhout, *A State Divided*, 145–228.

4. For loyalists, see Wallace Brown, *The King's Friends: The Composition and Motives of the American Loyalist Claimants* (Providence, 1965); Wallace Brown, *The Good Americans: The Loyalists in the American Revolution* (New York, 1969); Robert M. Calhoon, *The Loyalists in Revolutionary America, 1760–1781* (New York, 1973); Joseph S. Tiedemann, Eugene R. Fingerhut, and Robert W. Venables, ed., *The Other Loyalists: Ordinary People, Royalism, and the Revolution in the Middle Colonies, 1763–1787* (Albany, 2009); Ruma Chopra, *Unnatural Rebellion: Loyalists in New York City during the Revolution* (Charlottesville, 2011). For Lancaster and Pennsylvania loyalists, see Wilbur H. Siebert, *The Loyalists of Pennsylvania* (Columbus, 1920); Henry J. Young, "The Treatment of the Loyalists in Pennsylvania" (Ph.D. diss., Johns Hopkins University, 1955); Ousterhout, *A State Divided*; and Rollin C. Steinmetz, *Loyalists, Pacifists, and Prisoners* (Lititz, 1976). For loyalists and the problem of identity, see Judith van Buskirk, *Generous Enemies: Patriots and Loyalists in Revolutionary New York* (Philadelphia, 2002); Bodle, *Valley Forge Winter*, 75–102; Knouff, *The Soldiers' Revolution*, 195–231; and Riordan, "Identity and Revolution."

5. Robert L. Brunhouse, *The Counter-Revolution in Pennsylvania, 1776–1790* (Harrisburg, 1942), 38–40; Knouff, *The Soldiers' Revolution*, 201; Peden, *Revolutionary Patriots of Lancaster County*.

6. Bartram Galbraith to Supreme Executive Council, Aug. 5, 1777, PRG, reel 12; Council of Safety to Lancaster Committee, July 14, 1776, Grubb Collection;

Captains Martin and Adams to Lancaster Committee, July 30, 1776, *AA*, 5th ser., 1:673; Sarah Yeates to Jasper Yeates, Sept. 14, 1776, Yeates Papers; Bartram Galbraith to Supreme Executive Council, June 2, 1777, PRG, reel 12; Knouff, *The Soldiers' Revolution*, 71.

7. John Hubley to Supreme Executive Council, July 14, 1777, PRG, reel 12; Marshall, *Diary*, 120–21; Brunhouse, *Counter-Revolution*, 41; Ousterhout, *A State Divided*, 155–56, 160–62, 164–67, 191–94, 205, 283–89.

8. Jasper Yeates to James Burd, Sept. 4, 1777, Shippen Family Papers, 8, HSP; Christopher Marshall to Children, Aug. 24, 1777, Christopher Marshall Letterbook; Edward Burd to Jasper Yeates, Sept. 16, 1777, Yeates Papers; Christopher Marshall to Children, Mar. 27, 1778, Christopher Marshall Letterbook; Christopher Marshall to Children, Apr. 1, 1778, Christopher Marshall Letterbook; Edward Shippen to Joseph Shippen, May 19, 1778, Shippen Family Papers, BSh6lf.1, APS. For similar developments in Northampton County, see Fox, *Sweet Land of Liberty*.

9. "Hebron Church Diary," 358; "Extracts from Moravian Diaries," 91–93. See also "Hebron Church Diary," 357, 359–63. For the Whigs' troubles with pacifists, see Young, "Treatment of the Loyalists in Pennsylvania"; Steinmetz, *Loyalists, Pacifists, and Prisoners*; Schwartz, *"A Mixed Multitude,"* 257–91; MacMaster, *Land, Piety, Peoplehood*, 249–80; Knouff, *The Soldiers' Revolution*, 201–4; Fox, *Sweet Land of Liberty*; and Ousterhout, *A State Divided*, esp. 110–11, 113–16, 128, 130, 147, 160–62, 192–94.

10. Ousterhout, *A State Divided*, 8, 39, 111–12, 125, 145, 304–17; Knouff, *The Soldiers' Revolution*, 52–54, 57–61, 195–207, 209, 214–16, 219–20, 228–31, 266–70.

11. Ayars, *Lancaster Diary*, 71; "Toryism at Middletown, 1776," *Notes and Queries*, 3rd ser. (1887), 1:237–39; Thomas Barton's Petition, May 29, 1778, PRG, Clemency Files, reel 36; Hughes, *A Journal*, 67; Knouff, *The Soldiers' Revolution*, 52–54, 58, 195–207; Ousterhout, *A State Divided*, 112, 139, 145–83; Häberlein, *Practice of Pluralism*, 182–83.

12. Quoted in Knouff, *The Soldiers' Revolution*, 58–59; *Pennsylvania Evening Post* (Philadelphia), Mar. 18, 1778; Ousterhout, *A State Divided*, 145–83. See also Knouff, *The Soldiers' Revolution*, 54–57, 60, 107, 207.

13. Marshall, *Diary*, 132, 143, 161–62, 138–39, 141–42.

14. "Hebron Church Diary," 332–33; Marshall, *Diary*, 123; *Pennsylvania Packet*, May 6, 1778; quoted in Knouff, *The Soldiers' Revolution*, 218; Lancaster Committee to Alexander McKee, Jan. 15, 1776, Peter Force Collection, ser. 9, reel 102; Lancaster Committee to George Ross, Jan. 15, 1776, Peter Force Collection, ser. 9, reel 102. See also "Hebron Church Diary," 334, 359–60; Marshall, *Diary*, 122, 192; *Pennsylvania Gazette*, July 16, 1777, Aug. 6, 1777, and May 19, 1779; *Pennsylvania Packet*, July 25, 1778, July 30, 1778, and Aug. 13, 1778; Mühlenberg, *Journals*, 3:175; Ousterhout, *A State Divided*, 229–78. For the racialization of loyalists, see Knouff, *The Soldiers' Revolution*, 216–20.

15. Marshall, *Diary*, 123; Mittimus for John Brown, Nov. 21, 1777, PRG, reel 12. See also Marshall, *Diary*, 144, 146–47, 164, 172–73. For earlier and later examples, see Lancaster County Committee of Safety Records, June 8, 1776, Peter Force Papers; Peter Gotshalk, Sept. 24, 1780, PRG, Clemency Files, reel 36; *Pennsylvania Gazette*, Mar. 21, 1778, and May 23, 1781; Court of Oyer and Terminer, May 1781, Records of the Supreme Court, Courts of Oyer and Terminer, Court Papers, 1780–1781, Lancaster County, RG-33, Supreme Court, Eastern District, Courts of Oyer and Terminer, Court Papers, 1757–1787, reel 3, Lancaster County Historical Society; An Examination

of Abraham Beam, Jan. 19, 1781, Records of the Supreme Court, Courts of Oyer and Terminer, Court Papers, 1780–1781, Lancaster County, RG-33, Supreme Court, Eastern District, Courts of Oyer and Terminer, Court Papers, 1757–1787, reel 3.

16. Colonel Burd to Lancaster Committee, July 3, 1776, *AA*, 5th ser., 1:4–5; Edward Burd to Jasper Yeates, Sept. 8, 1777, Yeates Papers; *PA*, 1st ser., 5:628–29; Regulations for the Main Guard at Lancaster, Jan. 20, 1778, PRG, reel 13; Marshall, *Diary*, 128, 131; "Extracts from Moravian Diaries," 93. Ultimately, ten other conspirators were implicated in the plot. York County resident James Rankin, the alleged leader of the cabal, escaped and went on to fight for the British. For the conspiracy, see Ousterhout, *A State Divided*, 136–37, 169.

17. The county militia often proved short of arms. Some militiamen also balked at performing guard duty during the harvest. Lancaster Committee to John Henry and Edward Cowan, June 6, 1776, Yeates Papers; List of Prisoners, Aug. 27, 1776, Peter Force Collection, ser. 9, reel 102; James Burd to Lancaster Committee, July 18, 1776, Peter Force Collection, ser. 9, reel 102; John Thome to Lancaster Committee, July 24, 1776, Peter Force Collection, ser. 9, reel 102; Marshall, *Diary*, 272, 260; William Atlee, Notice of Broken Parole, May 9, 1778, Peter Force Collection, ser. 9, reel 104; William Atlee to Timothy Pickering, May 14, 1778, Peter Force Collection, ser. 9, reel 104; Charles Hall to Joseph Reed, July 17, 1780, PRG, Forfeited Estates File, County Files, Lancaster County, 1779–1780, reel 43; B. Ball to William Atlee, Jan. 17, 1780, Peter Force Collection, ser. 9, reel 106; Joseph Smith to William Atlee, List of Prisoners, Mar. 11, 1780, Peter Force Collection, ser. 9, reel 106; Hughes, *A Journal*, 72, 79, 92, 93; Adam Hubley to Joseph Reed, May 21, 1781, PRG, reel 18; Adam Hubley to Joseph Reed, June 17, 1781, PRG, reel 18; Adam Hubley to Joseph Reed, Aug. 6, 1781, PRG, reel 18; "Items from Letters," 97.

18. James Mercer to Lancaster Committee, May 18, 1777, Peter Force Collection, ser. 9, reel 103; William Atlee to Board of War, Aug. 27, 1780, Peter Force Collection, ser. 9, reel 106; *PA*, 1st ser., 9:335; James Burd to Lancaster Committee, July 18, 1776, Peter Force Collection, ser. 9, reel 102; John Thome to Lancaster Committee, July 24, 1776, Peter Force Collection, ser. 9, reel 102; List of Prisoners, Aug. 27, 1776, Peter Force Collection, ser. 9, reel 102; Petition of Michael Immel, Nov. 5, 1777, PRG, Clemency Files, reel 36; Petition of Caleb Johnson, Nov. 5, 1777, PRG, Clemency Files, reel 36; James Jacks to William Atlee, July 27, 1778, Peter Force Collection, ser. 9, reel 105; Charles Hall to Joseph Reed, July 17, 1780, PRG, Forfeited Estates File, County Files, Lancaster County, 1779–1780, reel 43; John Thompson, Certificate of Conviction, May 14, 1781, PRG, Clemency Files, reel 37; Marshall, *Diary*, 131–32, 152, 275.

19. *PA*, 1st ser., 8:755–56; Marshall, *Diary*, 270.

20. John Robert Shaw, *An Autobiography of Thirty Years, 1777–1807*, ed. Oressa M. Teagarden (Athens, 1992), 48–49; *PA*, 1st ser., 9:156–58; Adam Hubley to Joseph Reed, June 23, 1781, PRG, reel 18; Adam Hubley to Joseph Reed, July 13, 1781, PRG, reel 18; "A Revolutionary Letter," *PLCHS* 31 (1927): 8–10. During the summer of 1781, Dr. Henry Norris, a loyalist, conferred with British officials about supplying Lancaster's prisoners with arms and ammunition to facilitate their escape; see Knepper, "The Convention Army," 254.

21. Adam Hubley to Joseph Reed, Aug. 12, 1781, PRG, reel 18; *PA*, 2nd ser., 3:433–34; "Extracts from the Papers of General William Irvine," *PMHB* 5 (1881): 263; Joseph Reed to Lieutenants of Lancaster and York Counties, Aug. 6, 1781, PRG,

reel 18; William Scott to Joseph Reed, Aug. 8, 1781, PRG, reel 18; William Atlee to Joseph Reed, Aug. 9, 1781, Simon Gratz Manuscripts, case 3, box 19, High Court of Errors and Appeals of Pennsylvania; Marshall, *Diary*, 279–80; Benjamin Lincoln to Continental Congress, Dec. 6, 1781, PCC, reel 162. See also Richard Peters to Elias Boudinot, July 24, 1777, Elias Boudinot Papers.

22. Albert Helfenstein to the President and Supreme Executive Council, Nov. 17, 1777, PRG, reel 13; Ayars, *Lancaster Diary*, 71; Thomas Barton's Petition, May 29, 1778, PRG, Clemency Files, reel 36; Marshall, *Diary*, 182, 184–85; Mühlenberg, *Journals*, 3:160; Hughes, *A Journal*, 67; William Henry to Joseph Reed, Nov. 27, 1779, William Henry Papers, 2; Häberlein, *Practice of Pluralism*, 182–83; Knouff, *The Soldiers' Revolution*, 52–54, 57–60, 195–207. For the politicization of identities, see esp. Riordan, "Identity and Revolution."

23. Quoted in Henry J. Young, "Treason and Its Punishment in Revolutionary Pennsylvania," *PMHB* 90 (July 1966): 287–313, see 288; *Pennsylvania Packet* (Lancaster), Apr. 8, 1778. See also Young, "Treason and Its Punishment in Revolutionary Pennsylvania," 290–91, 293–95, 303–7; Ousterhout, *A State Divided*, 147–48, 160, 170–73, 192, 285–89.

24. Elizabeth Voght, Petition to Supreme Executive Council, Jan. 3, 1780, PRG, Application for Passes, 1776–1790, reel 30; William Atlee to Joseph Reed, Dec. 19, 1778, Simon Gratz Manuscripts, case 3, box 19, High Court of Errors and Appeals of Pennsylvania; Inventory of the Effects of Christian Vought of Lancaster, Nov. 6, 1778, PRG, Forfeited Estates File, Christian Vought, Lancaster, 1779–1782, reel 43; Certificate to George Graff for Christian Vought's Estate, Lancaster County, Jan. 15, 1782, PRG, Forfeited Estates File, Christian Vought, Lancaster, 1779–1782, reel 43; Michael Witman, Warrant to Arrest, Aug. 13, 1778, Peter Force Collection, ser. 9, reel 105; List of Persons to Be Tried for High Treason, July 6, 1779, PRG, reel 15; John Hubley to Joseph Reed, Jan. 10, 1780, PRG, reel 15; Peter Gotshalk, Sept. 24, 1780, PRG, Clemency Files, reel 36; George Weidel, Sept. 24, 1780, PRG, Clemency Files, reel 37; Conviction of Jacob Barkman, Oct. 3, 1781, PRG, Clemency Files, reel 37; Conviction of Abraham Beam, Oct. 3, 1781, PRG, Clemency Files, reel 37; Petition of Abraham Beam and Jacob Barkman, Oct. 3, 1781, PRG, Clemency Files, reel 37; John Thompson, Certificate of Conviction, May 14, 1781, PRG, Clemency Files, reel 37; Marshall, *Diary*, 275; *Pennsylvania Gazette*, May 23, 1781. See also Ousterhout, *A State Divided*, 207–10, 216, 287–88.

25. Philip Marsteller to Lancaster Committee, Feb. 10, 1777, Peter Force Collection, ser. 9, reel 103; Memorial of John Maguire, n.d., BHP, reel 23; Ayars, *Lancaster Diary*, 39, 38; Warrant for Commitment of Matthew McHugh, Dec. 16, 1776, *AA*, 5th ser., 3:1241; Matthew McHugh to Matthias Slough, Jan. 1, 1777, Peter Force Collection, ser. 9, reel 103; McHugh Testimony, Jan. 29, 1777, Peter Force Collection, ser. 9, reel 103; Petition of James White, Oct. 9, 1777, PRG, Clemency Files, reel 36; Petition of John White, October 16, 1777, PRG, Clemency Files, reel 36. For another reference to Maguire, see Colley, *Captives*, 213. See also Ousterhout, *A State Divided*, 213, 286, 291–92.

26. Hughes, *A Journal*, 18; Anburey, *Travels through the Interior Parts of America*, 2:299; "Anton Adolf Heinrich Du Roi's Diary," 23.

27. Thomas P. Cope, *Philadelphia Merchant: The Diary of Thomas P. Cope, 1800–1851* (South Bend, 1978), 142–43; Hughes, *A Journal*, 81; Marshall, *Diary*, 271, 273–74; Wood, *Conestoga Crossroads*, 83; Häberlein, *Practice of Pluralism*, 135.

28. Hughes, *A Journal*, 68. See also Edward Burd to Jasper Yeates, Apr. 15, 1776, Yeates Papers; Marshall, *Diary*, 229.

29. Edward Burd to Jasper Yeates, Sept. 8, 1777, Yeates Papers; Marshall, *Diary*, 150, 152; Hughes, *A Journal*, 74. Find additional examples in Hughes, *A Journal*, 69, 70, 75–76, 98–99; Marshall, *Diary*, 123, 125–28, 130, 132–40, 170, 194, 227, 229, 242, 268–69, 271; Jasper Yeates to James Burd, June 6, 1779, and Apr. 10, 1781, Shippen Family Papers, 8, HSP.

30. Peter Grubb Jr. to Peter Grubb Sr., Sept. 16, 1776, Grubb Collection; Thomas Hartley to William Atlee and Paul Zantzinger, Sept. 18, 1777, Peter Force Papers.

31. Adam Hubley to William Atlee and Paul Zantzinger, Sept. 15, 1777, Peter Force Collection, ser. 9, reel 104; Adam Hubley to William Atlee, Paul Zantzinger, and John Hubley, Sept. 26, 1777, Peter Force Collection, ser. 9, reel 104; Thomas McKean to William Atlee, June 12, 1780, Peter Force Transcripts, ser. 7E, Correspondence and Papers of William Atlee, reel 6, LOC; Thomas Hartley to William Atlee and Paul Zantzinger, Sept. 23, 1777, Peter Force Collection, ser. 9, reel 104.

32. Adam Hubley to William Atlee, Paul Zantzinger, and John Hubley, Oct. 14, 1777, Peter Force Papers; Hughes, *A Journal*, 70; James Milligan to Edward Hand, Nov. 2, 1777, Edward Hand Papers, 1777–1778, reel 1, film 705, DLAR; "Original Revolutionary Letter," *The Historical Magazine, and Notes and Queries concerning the Antiquities, History, and Biography of America* 4 (1860): 138; Marshall, *Diary*, 177.

33. Marshall, *Diary*, 127–28, 182, 115, 153, 150–51, 156; Christopher Marshall to Children, Apr. 1, 1778, Christopher Marshall Letterbook; Christopher Marshall to Sons, Apr. 2, 1778, Christopher Marshall Letterbook; Christopher Marshall to Anonymous, Jan. 13, 1778, Christopher Marshall Letterbook.

34. Israel Evans, *A Discourse, delivered, on the 18th Day of December, 1777, the Day of Public Thanksgiving, Appointed by the Honourable Continental Congress* (Lancaster, 1778), Early American Imprints, ser. 1: Evans, 1639–1800, no. 15791, 15; Marshall, *Diary*, 223; Edward Shippen to Richard Cary, July 20, 1778, Shippen Papers, BSh62, APS; Jasper Yeates to James Burd, June 29, 1780, Shippen Family Papers, 8, HSP. See also Marshall, *Diary*, 126–28, 134, 143, 162, 174–75, 178, 234.

35. Adam Hubley to William Atlee, Paul Zantzinger, and John Hubley, Sept. 21, 1777, Peter Force Papers; Adam Hubley to William Atlee and Paul Zantzinger, Sept. 15, 1777, Peter Force Collection, ser. 9, reel 104; Adam Hubley to William Atlee, Paul Zantzinger, and John Hubley, Sept. 23, 1777, Peter Force Papers.

36. Board of War to Lancaster Committee, Jan. 31, 1777, Peter Force Collection, ser. 9, reel 103; *PA*, 2nd ser., 3:141–42; "Items from Letters," 96; Pettengill, *Letters from America*, 239; *Minutes and Letters of the Coetus of the German Reformed Congregations in Pennsylvania, 1747–1792*, William Hinke, ed. (Philadelphia, 1903), 366–67; Andrews, "Myrmidons from Abroad," 285–92; Neimeyer, *America Goes to War*, 44–52, 63–64.

37. This appears to be the first reference to Washington as the father of the country. My thanks to Aaron Fogleman for the citation. *Der Gantz Neue Verbesserte nord-americanische Calender* (Lancaster, 1778), Early American Imprints, ser. 1: Evans, 1639–1800, no. 16053; *Der Republikanische Calender* (Lancaster, 1781), Early American Imprints, ser. 1: Evans, 1639–1800, no. 17326. See the 1772 to 1775 editions, nos. 12417, 12810, 13332, and 14119, of *Der Hoch-deutsche-americanische Calender*, the 1777 edition, no. 15236, of *Der Hinckend-und stolpernd-doch eilfertig-fliegend-und laufende americanische Reichs-Bott*, and the 1777 to 1781 editions, nos. 15578, 16053,

16503, 16978, and 17353, of *Der Gantz Neue Verbesserte nord-americanische Calender* in Early American Imprints, ser. 1: Evans, 1639–1800. See, for example, the *Pennsylvanische Zeitungs-Blat* (Lancaster), Feb. 4 to 25, 1778.

38. Jasper Yeates to James Burd, Feb. 19, 1779, Shippen Family Papers, 8, HSP; Marshall, *Diary*, 256; Hughes, *A Journal*, 86; Balch, *Letters and Papers*, 267. See also Marshall, *Diary*, 175, 178–79, 182–84, 193–94, 196, 200, 206, 213–14, 227–32, 234, 238, 242–43, 254, 257, 270–73; William Atlee to Esther Atlee, Dec. 3, 1779, Peter Force Collection, ser. 9, reel 105; Edward Shippen to James Burd, July 15, 1778, Shippen Family Papers, 8, HSP; Edward Burd to James Burd, Aug. 6, 1779, Shippen Family Papers, 8, HSP; William Atlee to James Burd, Aug. 7, 1779, Shippen Family Papers, 8, HSP; Jasper Yeates to James Burd, Aug. 31, 1779, Shippen Family Papers, 8, HSP; Jasper Yeates to James Burd, June 11, 1780, Shippen Family Papers, 8, HSP; Jasper Yeates to James Burd, June 29, 1780, Shippen Family Papers, 8, HSP; Jasper Yeates to James Burd, Feb. 26, 1781, Shippen Family Papers, 8, HSP; Jasper Yeates to James Burd, Sept. 18, 1781, Shippen Family Papers, 8, HSP; "Extracts from Moravian Diaries," 93; "Items from Letters," 97. When Americans defied their imperial kinsmen by embracing their inveterate enemy, the French, they crossed an important threshold, just as had been the case when they declared their independence. Previously a bitter adversary in the wars for empire, France now paradoxically offered its American allies the hope of liberation from imperial bondage. For the importance of the French alliance in rupturing the bond between Britons and Americans, see Conway, "From Fellow-Nationals to Foreigners."

39. Rachel Gratz to Barnard Gratz, Aug. 3, 1779, Sol Feinstone Collection, 399, reel 1; Mombert, *An Authentic History of Lancaster County*, 275–77; Jasper Yeates to James Burd, June 11, 1780, Shippen Family Papers, 8, HSP; Marshall, *Diary*, 213, 254; Thomas McKean to William Atlee, June 5, 1778, Peter Force Collection, ser. 9, reel 104; Timothy Pickering to William Atlee, June 5, 1778, Peter Force Collection, ser. 9, reel 104.

40. Marshall, *Diary*, 138, 181, 222–24, 264, 269, 282; Hughes, *A Journal*, 69, 90, 98–99; Jasper Yeates to Edward Hand, Oct. 23, 1777, Society Small Collection, Yeates, HSP; "Extracts from Moravian Diaries," 93–95; "Items from Letters," 97; "Ebenezer Hazard in Pennsylvania, 1777," *PMHB* 81 (Jan. 1957), 84–85. War and revolution inspired Americans to new heights of ritual activity. For the relationship between patriotic rituals and nationalism, see Peter Shaw, *American Patriots and the Rituals of Revolution* (Cambridge, 1981); Waldstreicher, *In the Midst of Perpetual Fetes*; Newman, *Parades and the Politics of the Street*; and Len Travers, *Celebrating the Fourth: Independence Day and the Rites of Nationalism in the Early Republic* (Amherst, 1997).

41. Marshall, *Diary*, 223; "Extracts from Moravian Diaries," 93, 95; Jasper Yeates to Edward Hand, Oct. 23, 1777, Society Small Collection; "Ebenezer Hazard in Pennsylvania, 1777," 84–85. For Poultney, see Häberlein, *Practice of Pluralism*, 133–35.

42. Jasper Yeates to Edward Hand, Oct. 23, 1777, Society Small Collection.

43. "Ebenezer Hazard in Pennsylvania, 1777," 84–85; *Pennsylvania Gazette*, July 9, 1777. For an example in Frederick, Maryland, see Johann Conrad Döhla, *A Hessian Diary of the American Revolution*, trans. and ed. Bruce E. Burgoyne (Bowie, 1994), 220–21; Johann Ernst Prechtel, *A Hessian Officer's Diary of the American Revolution*, trans. and ed. Bruce E. Burgoyne (Bowie, 1994), 251–52.

44. Marshall, *Diary*, 135–42, 148, 227, 242, 268–69, 273; Jasper Yeates to James Burd, June 6, 1779, Shippen Family Papers, 8, HSP; Edward Burd to James Burd, Aug. 6, 1779, Shippen Family Papers, 8, HSP; Jasper Yeates to James Burd, Aug. 31, 1779, Shippen Family Papers, 8, HSP; Abraham Skinner to William Atlee, July 22, 1779, Peter Force Collection, ser. 9, reel 105; Return of the Officers Taken at Stony Point, July 22, 1779, Peter Force Collection, ser. 9, reel 105; List of the British Prisoners of Warr brought to Lancaster from the Southward, April 1781, Peter Force Collection, ser. 9, reel 106; William Henry to William Atlee, Apr. 12, 1781, William Henry Papers, 1; William Henry to William Atlee, Apr. 26, 1781, William Henry Papers, 1; Hughes, *A Journal*, 70; Edward Shippen to James Burd, Jan. 2, 1779, Shippen Family Papers, 8, HSP.

45. Jasper Yeates to James Burd, Aug. 31, 1779, Burd-Shippen Family Collection, reel 2; Jasper Yeates to Edward Hand, Oct. 23, 1777, Society Small Collection; James Milligan to Edward Hand, Nov. 2, 1777, Edward Hand Papers; Marshall, *Diary*, 135–40.

46. *Pennsylvania Ledger* (Philadelphia), Feb. 11, 1778; Evans, "A Discourse," 14; Graydon, *Memoirs of His Own Time*, 305; *Pennsylvania Packet*, Apr. 8, 1778; *A Song, on the Surrendery of General Burgoyne* (Massachusetts, 1777), Early American Imprints, ser. 1: Evans, 1639–1800, no. 16529.

47. Quoted in Andrews, "Myrmidons from Abroad," 340, 339; "Extracts from Moravian Diaries," 94; Marshall, *Diary*, 273; see also 123, 131, 133, 138, 148, 172, 207–9, 234, 269; Committee for Transacting Continental Business, Dec. 30, 1776, *AA*, 5th ser., 3:1484; "Johannes Reuber's Diary," 8; Hughes, *A Journal*, 78; Anburey, *Travels through the Interior Parts of America*, 2:278, 308–9; Edward Shippen to James Burd, Jan. 2, 1779, Shippen Family Papers, 8, HSP.

48. "Anton Adolf Heinrich Du Roi's Diary," 23; *The Lancaster Almanack, for the Year of Our Lord, 1778* (Lancaster, 1777), Evans, no. 15579. Paroled British officers met with growing verbal and physical abuse from their captors. See, for example, Hughes, *A Journal*, 88, 92, 99.

49. Anburey, *Travels through the Interior Parts of America*, 2:507–9.

50. Marshall, *Diary*, 174, 216; Edward Shippen to James Read, Feb. 15, 1778, Burd-Shippen Family Collection, reel 2; Hughes, *A Journal*, 79; also 80–81, 85, 99. In addition, see Marshall, *Diary*, 131–33, 142–43, 145, 160–61, 164, 176–77, 183, 192, 205, 208, 212, 235–36, 265, 269; Jasper Yeates to James Burd, Oct. 3, 1777, Shippen Family Papers, 8, HSP; "Extracts from Moravian Diaries," 92–94.

51. Lancaster Committee to Pennsylvania Delegates in Congress, Mar. 20, 1777, PCC, State Papers, Pennsylvania, vol. 1, 335–38, National Archives; Lancaster County Committee, Examination into the Death of Jacob Gross, Mar. 18, 1777, PCC, State Papers, Pennsylvania, vol. 1, 339–46; Lancaster County Coroner and Jury Inquisition into the Death of Matthias Schneider, Mar. 19, 1777, PCC, State Papers, Pennsylvania, vol. 1, 347–48; Lancaster County Coroner and Jury Inquisition into the Death of Jacob Gross, Mar. 19, 1777, PCC, State Papers, Pennsylvania, vol. 1, 351–52; "Hebron Church Diary," 333; Mühlenberg, *Journals*, 3:26. For another example, see Marshall, *Diary*, 275–76.

52. Lancaster Committee to Pennsylvania Delegates in Congress, Mar. 20, 1777, PCC; Anburey, *Travels through the Interior Parts of America*, 2:284.

53. Sarah Yeates to Jasper Yeates, Oct. 29, 1781; Jasper Yeates to Sarah Yeates, Oct. 27, 1781; and Sarah Yeates to Jasper Yeates, Oct. 25, 1781, all in Yeates Papers.

6. "The Country Is Full of Prisoners of War"

1. Döhla, *A Hessian Diary*, 220–21; Prechtel, *A Hessian Officer's Diary*, 251–52. For nationalist rites and celebrations, see Shaw, *American Patriots and the Rituals of Revolution*; Waldstreicher, *In the Midst of Perpetual Fetes*; Newman, *Parades and the Politics of the Street*; and Travers, *Celebrating the Fourth*.

2. John Ferdinand Smyth Stuart, *A Tour in the United States of America*, 2 vols. (London, 1784), 2:252–53; Maryland State Papers: Red Books, S989–25, fol. 01, Maryland State Archives; Deposition of Thomas Wileman, Feb. 18, 1778. For early Frederick, see Elizabeth Augusta Kessel, "Germans on the Maryland Frontier: A Social History of Frederick County, Maryland, 1730–1800" (Ph.D. diss., Rice University, 1981). For Frederick during the War for Independence, see Andrew Krug, "'Such a Banditty You Never See Collected!': Frederick Town and the American Revolution," *Maryland Historical Magazine* 95 (2000): 5–28; John Thomas Scharf, *The History Of Western Maryland: Being a History of Frederick, Montgomery, Carroll, Washington, Allegany, and Garrett Counties, from the Earliest Period to the Present Day*, 2 vols. (Philadelphia, 1882), 1:121–45. For Frederick as a host site for enemy prisoners, consult Lucy Leigh Bowie, *The Ancient Barracks at Fredericktown, Where Hessian Prisoners were Quartered during the Revolutionary War* (Frederick, 1939); Lucy Leigh Bowie, "German Prisoners in the American Revolution," *Maryland Historical Magazine* 40 (1945): 185–200; Lion G. Miles, "Prisoners of War in Frederick County, Maryland, during the American Revolution," *The Rainbow: Journal of the Pennsylvania German Society* 23 (1989): 41–43.

3. Alexander Hanson to Thomas Sim Lee, Sept. 9, 1781, Frederick County Treason Papers, 1777–1781, file C, Maryland Historical Society; Krug, "'Such a Banditty You Never See Collected!,'" 19–22; Dorothy MacKay Quynn, "The Loyalist Plot in Frederick," *Maryland Historical Magazine* 40 (1945): 201–10; Scharf, *History of Western Maryland*, 1:142–43.

4. Reports of the North American War under the Commanding General von Lossberg, 1782–1784, 17–18, Hessian Documents of the American Revolution, fiche 336–43; Journal of the Regiment von Bose, 1776–1783, 90, Hessian Documents of the American Revolution, fiche 295–98. For particular examples of Hessian assimilation, see Lion G. Miles, *The Hessians of Lewis Miller* (Millville, 1983).

5. Döhla, *A Hessian Diary*, 215; Dixon, "Divided Authority," 178–200.

6. Döhla, *A Hessian Diary*, 221. For the evolution of American citizenship, see James H. Kettner, *The Development of American Citizenship, 1608–1870* (Chapel Hill, 1978).

7. Frederick Mackenzie, *The Diary of Frederick Mackenzie: Giving a Daily Narrative of His Military Service as an Officer of the Regiment of Royal Welch Fusiliers during the Years 1775–1781 in Massachusetts, Rhode Island, and New York*, 2 vols. (Cambridge, 1930), 2:586; George Washington to Moses Hazen, Dec. 6, 1781, in Fitzpatrick, *Writings of George Washington*, 23:374; Benjamin Lincoln to George Washington, Oct. 4, 1782, Returns, George Washington Papers, 1741–1799, ser. 4, General Correspondence, 1697–1799, LOC; Allan S. Everest, *Moses Hazen and the Canadian Refugees in the American Revolution* (Syracuse, 1976), 96–101; Dixon, "Divided Authority,"

236–37. For escapes in Pennsylvania, see Young, "Treatment of the Loyalists in Pennsylvania," 131–33; Ousterhout, *A State Divided*, 291–92; and Richard Sampson, *Escape in America: The British Convention Prisoners, 1777–1783* (Chippenham, 1995), 147–60.

8. June 27, 1780 to May 18, 1781, Return of Escaped Prisoners, Mackenzie Papers, Great Britain, Army in America, Prisoners of the Americans, William Clements Library. For the Convention Army, see Dabney, *After Saratoga*; Knepper, "The Convention Army"; Dixon, "Divided Authority," 201–43; and Springer, *America's Captives*, 21–22.

9. Dabney, *After Saratoga*, 40, 65; Dixon, "Divided Authority," 201–43. George Knepper suggests that more prisoners escaped in Massachusetts; see "The Convention Army," 197.

10. William Atlee to John Jay, July 23, 1779, PCC, reel 90; George Washington to Benjamin Harrison, May 5, 1779, in Fitzpatrick, *Writings of George Washington*, 15:8–10; Thomas Jefferson to James Wood, Nov. 3, and Nov. 7, 1780, in *The Papers of Thomas Jefferson*, ed. Julian P. Boyd et al., 39 vols. (Princeton, 1950–2012), 4:95, 101; Thomas Jefferson to Samuel Huntington, Nov. 10, 1780, in Boyd, *Papers of Thomas Jefferson*, 4:110; Dabney, *After Saratoga*, 65. See also *Pennsylvania Gazette*, July 28, 1779; *JCC*, 19:299–302.

11. Benjamin Lincoln to George Washington, Oct. 4, 1782, Returns, George Washington Papers; George Washington to Abraham Skinner, Oct. 25, 1781, George Washington Papers; Dixon, "Divided Authority," 178–81.

12. Quoted in Lion G. Miles, "The Winchester Hessian Barracks," *Winchester-Frederick County Historical Society Journal* 3 (1988): 19–63; see 42; Daniel Morgan to George Washington, Nov. 25, 1781, George Washington Papers; Caleb North to Benjamin Lincoln, Jan. 6, 1782, PCC, reel 162; James Wood to Benjamin Lincoln, Jan. 5, 1782, PCC, reel 162; Dixon, "Divided Authority," 181–87. See also Miles, "The Winchester Hessian Barracks," 41–49. For early Winchester, see Christopher Hendricks, *The Backcountry Towns of Colonial Virginia* (Knoxville, 2006).

13. George Washington to Moses Rawlings, Dec. 12, 1781, in Fitzpatrick, *Writings of George Washington*, 23:383–84; Benjamin Lincoln to Congress, Jan. 16, 1782, PCC, reel 162; George Washington to Moses Hazen, Dec. 6, 1781, in Fitzpatrick, *Writings of George Washington*, 23:374; Benjamin Lincoln to George Washington, Oct. 4, 1782, Return, George Washington Papers; *Pennsylvania Gazette*, Apr. 24, 1782, and June 12, 1782. Pennsylvania's assembly first considered offering a bounty for fugitives in late 1781; see *Pennsylvania Gazette*, Dec. 5, 1781. Congress proposed reimbursing the states; see *JCC*, 22:154–56. Everest cites returns that put the number of British prisoners in Lancaster at just over thirteen hundred; see *Moses Hazen and the Canadian Refugees*, 99.

14. Timothy Pickering to President of Congress, Oct. 12, 1779, PCC, reel 157; William Atlee to Thomas Bradford, Sept. 12, 1781, Thomas Bradford Papers, British Army Prisoners, 4; *Pennsylvania Gazette*, June 5, 1776; *Pennsylvania Packet*, Jan. 28, 1778; Frey, *The British Soldier in America*, 131; William Atlee to Thomas Bradford, Feb. 6, 1782, Thomas Bradford Papers, British Army Prisoners, 4; *JCC*, 22:321.

15. May 6 to June 9, 1782, Return of Escaped Prisoners, with an Account of Payments to Guides, Mackenzie Papers, Great Britain, Army in America, Prisoners of the Americans; Abstract of Bounty Money Paid by Order of His Excellency General Sir Guy Carleton, July 20 to Sept. 3, 1782, BHP, reel 15; *JCC*, 22:321, 403. For

wartime tensions between locals and Continental authorities, see Dixon, "Divided Authority," 115–243.

16. Moses Hazen to Benjamin Lincoln, June 1782, Sol Feinstone Collection, 531, reel 1; *JCC*, 22:372–73, 403, 413–14; Moses Hazen to Benjamin Lincoln, July 1782, PCC, reel 162; Benjamin Lincoln to Congress, July 3, 1782, PCC, reel 162; Dixon, "Divided Authority," 76–113.

17. *JCC*, 22:323–24, 335, 343–44, 382; *JCC*, 23:660–61, 785; *The Papers of Robert Morris, 1781–1784*, ed. E. James Ferguson and John Catanzariti, 6 vols. (Pittsburgh, 1973–1980), 4:439–41; *Papers of Robert Morris*, 5:91–93.

18. Ann Weidell Petition, Aug. 2, 1783, BHP, reel 22; John McDonald Petition, Aug. 31, 1783, BHP, reel 23; Roger Lamb, *An Original and Authentic Journal of Occurrences during the Late American War from Its Commencement to the Year 1783* (Dublin, 1809), 399–413; Board of Enquiry, Jan. 20, 1783, BHP, reel 18. For details of Hazen's sting operation, see Ousterhout, *A State Divided*, 292; and Sampson, *Escape in America*, 175–76.

19. Journal and Reports of Colonel Lenz, 1777–1784, 27, Hessian Documents of the American Revolution, fiche 360–62; Lamb, *Journal*, 402, 405; Letters and Reports from Hesse-Hanau Officers, 1776–1780, 76, Hessian Documents of the American Revolution, fiche 355–59.

20. Quoted in Colley, *Captives*, 213; Ann Weidell Petition, Aug. 2, 1783; Petition of William Tanner, n.d., BHP, reel 24; Alexander Montgomery, Peter Harter, Henry Slotterbeck Petition, Aug. 19, 1782, PRG, reel 19; Richard McAlester and Archibald McClean to William Atlee, July 30, 1782, Peter Force Transcripts, ser. 7E, Correspondence and Papers of William Atlee, reel 6; William Henry to David Rittenhouse, Dec. 23, 1782, William Henry Papers, 1. See also *CR*, 13:457, 516, 526, 535, 544; *CR*, 14:34; Sampson, *Escape in America*, 151, 175. For figures concerning the prosecution of Pennsylvania loyalists, see Young, "Treatment of the Loyalists in Pennsylvania," 131–33; and Ousterhout, *A State Divided*, 291–92.

21. Meetings of Burgesses and Assistants of Borough, Nov. 2, 1782, Lancaster Corporation Book Minutes, 1742–1818, Lancaster County Historical Society; Richard Butler to George Washington, Dec. 7, 1782, George Washington Papers; William Henry, Bounties Paid, Jan. 9, 1783, William Henry Papers, 2; Abstract of Bounty Money Paid by Order of His Excellency General Sir Guy Carleton, Feb. 26 to Mar. 26, 1783, BHP, reel 19; Abstract of Bounty Money Paid by Order of His Excellency General Sir Guy Carleton, Mar. 29 to Apr. 10, 1783, BHP, reel 19.

22. "Diary of Lieutenant Jakob Piel, from 1776 to 1783, Part 2," trans. Bruce E. Burgoyne, *Journal of the Johannes Schwalm Historical Association* 4 (1990): 23; Kipping, *The Hessian View of America*, 9–11, 43–46; Atwood, *The Hessians*, 190–205; Neimeyer, *America Goes to War*, 52–64.

23. Correspondence of General von Knyphausen, 1776–September 1779, 221, Hessian Documents of the American Revolution, fiche 47–60; Atwood, *The Hessians*, 184–206; Neimeyer, *America Goes to War*, 53–63.

24. Petition from August Wille, a Jager, July 3, 1778, PCC, reel 56. For German recruiting, see Atwood, *The Hessians*, 207–15; and esp. Krebs, *A Generous and Merciful Enemy*, 36–55. The rise in prisoners' desertions mirrored an overall increase in Hessian desertions. I am indebted to Charles Neimeyer for the figures concerning Hessen-Kassel desertions; see *America Goes to War*, 53–63, particularly 56.

25. William Atlee to Thomas Bradford, Jan. 29, 1779, Thomas Bradford Papers, British Army Prisoners, 2; Marshall, *Diary*, 170; Timothy Pickering to William Atlee, June 8, 1778, Peter Force Collection, ser. 9, reel 104; Joseph Nourse to William Atlee, June 22, 1778, Peter Force Collection, ser. 9, reel 105; William Atlee to Thomas Bradford, July 16, 1781, Thomas Bradford Papers, British Naval Prisoners, 2; List of Hessians and Employers, July 15, 1778, Peter Force Collection, ser. 9, reel 105; William Atlee to Esther Atlee, Oct. 15, 1779, Peter Force Collection, ser. 9, reel 105; William Atlee to Thomas Bradford, Aug. 14, 1778, Thomas Bradford Papers, British Army Prisoners, 1; William Atlee to Thomas Bradford, Dec. 8, 1780, Thomas Bradford Papers, British Army Prisoners, 3.

26. Lancaster County Committee, Mar. 29, 1777, Peter Force Collection, ser. 8D, reel 48; Petition from August Wille, July 3, 1778; List of the Grenadiers and Yagers and their Employers, Sept. to Nov. 1777, Peter Force Collection, ser. 9, reel 104.

27. James Beatty to William Atlee, June 30, 1778, Peter Force Collection, ser. 9, reel 105; William Atlee to Thomas Bradford, Aug. 14, 1778, Thomas Bradford Papers, British Army Prisoners, 1; "Hebron Church Diary," 350; William Atlee to Thomas Bradford, Dec. 8, 1780, Thomas Bradford Papers, British Army Prisoners, 3; William Atlee to Michael App, June 18, 1778, Peter Force Collection, ser. 9, reel 105; James Beatty to Thomas Bradford, June 30, 1778, Thomas Bradford Papers, British Army Prisoners, 1; Neimeyer, *America Goes to War*, 57. For prisoner exchanges, see Dixon, "Divided Authority," 245–91; and Betsy Knight, "Prisoner Exchange and Parole in the American Revolution," *WMQ* 48 (Apr. 1991): 201–22.

28. Correspondence of General von Knyphausen, 286–87, 299, 375; "Profiles," *Journal of the Johannes Schwalm Historical Association* 3 (1987): 41–44; Atwood, *The Hessians*, 191; Neimeyer, *America Goes to War*, 57.

29. Laura Becker, "Prisoners of War in the American Revolution: A Community Perspective," *Military Affairs* 46 (Dec. 1982): 169–73. See, for example, "Anton Adolf Heinrich Du Roi's Diary," 23–24. For the postwar assimilation of former German auxiliaries, see Miles, *The Hessians of Lewis Miller*.

30. Marshall, *Diary*, 208; Anburey, *Travels through the Interior Parts of America*, 2:309; William Atlee to John Jay, July 23, 1779, PCC, reel 90; "Anton Adolf Heinrich Du Roi's Diary," 26; quoted in Neimeyer, *America Goes to War*, 59; Charles Glatfelter, *Pastors and People: German Lutheran and Reformed Churches in the Pennsylvania Field, 1717–1793*, 2 vols. (Breinigsville, 1980), 1:87–88.

31. *JCC*, 10:405–10. See also Atwood, *The Hessians*, 191–92, 196.

32. *Pennsylvania Packet* (Philadelphia), Dec. 24, 1778; Atwood, *The Hessians*, 184, 201–2; Neimeyer, *America Goes to War*, 57–58.

33. William Pine to Thomas Wharton, Oct. 8, 1777, Clemency Files, PRG, reel 36; William Pine to Thomas Wharton, Oct. 13, 1777, Clemency Files, PRG, reel 36; A Return of the Prisoners in Barrick at Lancaster, Feb. 10, 1777, Peter Force Collection, ser. 9, reel 103; Prisoners–Agreements of Exchange, with Lists, 1777–1783, Peter Force Collection, ser. 9, reel 104; William Pine to Supreme Executive Council, Dec. 11, 1777, Clemency Files, PRG, reel 36; William Atlee to Thomas Bradford, Jan. 29, 1779, Thomas Bradford Papers, British Army Prisoners, 2; Neimeyer, *America Goes to War*, 60–61.

34. Thomas McKean to William Atlee, June 5, 1778, Peter Force Collection, ser. 9, reel 104; Lancaster County Committee of Safety Records, Feb. 18, 1777, Peter

Force Papers; Timothy Pickering to William Atlee, May 27, 1778, PCC, reel 90; William Atlee to Henry Laurens, June 2, 1778, PCC, reel 90; Timothy Pickering to William Atlee, June 5, 1778, Peter Force Collection, ser. 9, reel 104; Neimeyer, *America Goes to War*, 57–63.

35. *JCC*, 22:274–76, 316–18; Miles, "The Winchester Hessian Barracks," 50; Prechtel, *A Hessian Officer's Diary*, 242–46; Döhla, *A Hessian Diary*, 192, 194, 210–15.

36. Christian Heiman, Oath of Allegiance, Oct. 10, 1782, William Henry Papers, 1; Wood, *Conestoga Crossroads*, 195; "A Brunswick Grenadier with Burgoyne: The Journal of Johann Bense, 1776–1783," trans. Helga B. Doblin, *New York History* 66 (Oct. 1985): 420–44, esp. 438; Kipping, *The Hessian View of America*, 13–18; Atwood, *The Hessians*, 167–68, 194–95; Neimeyer, *America Goes to War*, 63.

37. Board of War to General Washington, Nov. 19, 1776, *AA*, 5th ser., 3:762; George Washington to Board of War, Nov. 30, 1776, *AA*, 5th ser., 3:920; Further Report from the Committee of Conference, May 31, 1776, *AA*, 4th ser., 6:1692; *Pennsylvania Gazette*, June 5, 1776.

38. George Washington to James Bowdoin, Mar. 17, 1778, in Fitzpatrick, *Writings of George Washington*, 11:98–99; George Washington to Benjamin Harrison, May 5, 1779, in Fitzpatrick, *Writings of George Washington*, 15:8–10; Recruiting Instructions, Jan. 13, 1777, in Fitzpatrick, *Writings of George Washington*, 7:7.

39. Board of Enquiry, Jan. 20, 1783.

40. Samuel Boyd to Charles Hall, July 23, 1779, Peter Force Collection, ser. 9, reel 105; *JCC*, 19:299–302; Lamb, *Journal*, 253–54; George Washington to Benjamin Harrison, May 5, 1779, in Fitzpatrick, *Writings of George Washington*, 15:8–10; *Pennsylvania Gazette*, July 28, 1779; William Atlee to John Jay, July 23, 1779, PCC, reel 90.

41. Lamb, *Journal*, 263; see also 253–54, 262, 398–99, 413; Anburey, *Travels through the Interior Parts of America*, 2:438–39.

42. May 6 to June 9, 1782, Return of Escaped Prisoners, with an Account of Payments to Guides, Mackenzie Papers; June 27, 1780 to January 24, 1781, List of Men who were Paid a Bounty for Escaping from the Americans, Mackenzie Papers, Great Britain, Army in America, Prisoners of the Americans; Board of Enquiry, Jan. 20, 1783; Dabney, *After Saratoga*, 65; Journal and Reports of Colonel Lenz, 27–28.

43. Anburey, *Travels through the Interior Parts of America*, 2:438–42; June 27, 1780 to May 18, 1781, Return of Escaped Prisoners, Mackenzie Papers; Board of Enquiry, Jan. 20, 1783; Dabney, *After Saratoga*, 65.

44. Quoted in Spring, *With Zeal and With Bayonets Only*, 130–31; quoted in Frey, *The British Soldier in America*, 131; Lamb, *Journal*, 390–91, 398. See also Frey, *The British Soldier in America*, 129–30, 132; Spring, *With Zeal and With Bayonets Only*, 103–37; Linda Colley, *Britons: Forging the Nation, 1707–1837* (New Haven, 1992); and Colley, *Captives*, 203–38.

45. Hughes, *A Journal*, 84; "Captain Home's Narrative of His Treatment When Prisoner," n.d.; "An English Officer's Account of His Services in America, 1779–1781," *The Historical Magazine, and Notes and Queries concerning the Antiquities, History, and Biography of America* 9 (1865): 304.

46. Anburey, *Travels through the Interior Parts of America*, 2:499–500; quoted in Spring, *With Zeal and With Bayonets Only*, 130. See Conway, "From Fellow-Nationals to Foreigners"; Colley, *Captives*, 203–38.

47. Shaw, *An Autobiography of Thirty Years*, 45–46; Board of Enquiry, Jan. 20, 1783.

48. Lamb, *Journal*, 392–95; Moses Rawlings to George Washington, Dec. 2, 1781, George Washington Papers.

49. Anburey, *Travels through the Interior Parts of America*, 2:500, 490–91; "An English Officer's Account of His Services in America," 302; "Unpublished Letters," *Maryland Historical Magazine* 23 (1928): 249–51; James Gordon to Guy Carleton, Mar. 17, 1783, BHP, reel 18.

50. Shaw, *An Autobiography of Thirty Years*, 55, 42; see in addition 44–59; Thomas Bracknell to Thomas Bradford, n.d., Thomas Bradford Papers, British Army Prisoners, 1; Hugh Wier to Thomas Bradford, n.d., Thomas Bradford Papers, British Army Prisoners, 1; Joseph Ball to Thomas Bradford, Nov. 22, 1779, Thomas Bradford Papers, British Army Prisoners, 2; *JCC*, 18:913; *JCC*, 23:571–72; Anburey, *Travels through the Interior Parts of America*, 2:492–93; "An English Officer's Account of His Services in America," 304; Dabney, *After Saratoga*, 65; Frey, *The British Soldier in America*, 73.

51. Roger Lamb, *Memoir of His Own Life* (Dublin, 1811), 270. For the details of Lamb's escapes, see esp. Lamb, *Journal*.

52. Lamb, *Journal*, 399–400; *JCC*, 23:639. Congress also feared that Britain would refuse to release American captives if British prisoners received American citizenship; see, for example, *JCC*, 18:913.

53. *JCC*, 22:316–18; German Troops, Depositions before a Board of Enquiry, Jan. 1783, BHP, reel 17; Extracts from the Minister of Finance and the Secretary of the Board of War of the United States, July 11, 1782, BHP, reel 14; An Account of the Treatment Shewn the Troops of Hesse Hanau and Brunswick, Detained Prisoners at Reading in Pennsylvania, n.d., BHP, reel 14; Extracts of a Memorandum Book of a Brunswick Sergeant, Who Made His Escape from Reading to New York, n.d., BHP, reel 24; Substance of the Depositions upon Oath of Fifty Men, n.d., BHP, reel 24; "A Brunswick Grenadier with Burgoyne," 442.

54. Henry Haller to William Atlee, Oct. 7, 1777, Peter Force Collection, ser. 9, reel 104; Graydon, *Memoirs of His Own Time*, 304–6; Elias Boudinot to William Atlee, Aug. 11, 1777, Peter Force Collection, ser. 9, reel 104; Journal and Reports of Colonel Lenz, 25; Inhabitants of Reading to Pennsylvania Assembly, Mar. 6, 1776, *AA*, 4th ser., 5:675; Henry Haller to William Atlee, Jan. 5, 1781, Peter Force Collection, ser. 9, reel 106. For Reading during the War for Independence, see Laura Becker, "The American Revolution as a Community Experience: A Case Study of Reading, Pennsylvania" (Ph.D. diss., University of Pennsylvania, 1978); Karen Guenther, "Berks County," in Frantz and Pencak, *Beyond Philadelphia*, 67–84.

55. Address of Captain Bowen, to the Brunswick and Hesse Hanau Prisoners of War, Reading, July 30, 1782, BHP, reel 14; German Troops, Depositions before a Board of Enquiry, Jan. 1783.

56. German Troops, Depositions before a Board of Enquiry, Jan. 1783; An Account of the Treatment Shewn the Troops of Hesse Hanau and Brunswick, n.d.; Substance of the Depositions upon Oath of Fifty Men, n.d.

57. German Troops, Depositions before a Board of Enquiry, Jan. 1783; An Account of the Treatment Shewn the Troops of Hesse Hanau and Brunswick, n.d.; A Few Particular Circumstances Respecting the Treatment Shewen the Brunswick

Troops Included in the Convention of Saratoga Now Prisoners in Pennsylvania, 1782, BHP, reel 14; Substance of the Depositions upon Oath of Fifty Men, n.d.; Extracts of a Memorandum Book of a Brunswick Sergeant, n.d.; "A Brunswick Grenadier with Burgoyne," 442–43.

58. German Troops, Depositions before a Board of Enquiry, Jan. 1783; Sowers, *Hessian Prisoners and Their Employers*, 11–12; Substance of the Depositions upon Oath of Fifty Men, n.d.; Prisoners, Certificate by Capt. A Gillon, Oct. 16, 1782, BHP, reel 16; *JCC*, 23:632; Lion Miles, "Johann Leibheit and the Convention Army," *Journal of the Johannes Schwalm Historical Association* 2 (1981): 31–44.

59. Translation of a Letter from the Hessian Prisoners of War of the Regt. De Knyphausen in the Gaol at Philadelphia, July 28, 1782, BHP, reel 24.

60. Letters and Reports from Hesse-Hanau Officers, 73–75, 88.

61. Carl Reinking to Guy Carleton, Dec. 10, 1782, BHP, reel 17; Letters and Reports from Hesse-Hanau Officers, 74; Benjamin Lincoln to George Washington, Dec. 22, 1782, George Washington Papers; "A Brunswick Grenadier with Burgoyne," 443; Captain de Eschwege to Major Mackenzy, Dec. 10, 1782, BHP, reel 17; Guy Carleton to George Washington, Dec. 11, 1782, George Washington Papers; George Washington to Benjamin Lincoln, Dec. 16, 1782, in Fitzpatrick, *Writings of George Washington*, 25:436.

62. George Washington to Governor Clinton, Apr. 21, 1783, BHP, reel 19; Dixon, "Divided Authority," 301–10.

63. George Washington to Governor Clinton, Apr. 21, 1783, BHP, reel 19; Benjamin Lincoln to Alured Clarke, May 5, 1783, BHP, reel 19; James Gordon to Guy Carleton, May 8, 1783, BHP, reel 20.

64. Guy Carleton to Benjamin Lincoln, June 29, 1783, BHP, reel 21; Abstract of a Letter from Thirty Five Hessian Prisoners of War to His Excellency Lieutenant General de Lossberg, Mar. 20, 1783, BHP, reel 18; Reports of the North American War under the Commanding General von Lossberg, 112; Alured Clarke to Benjamin Lincoln, May 25, 1783, BHP, reel 20; Substance of a Letter from the Hessian Prisoners of War with John Jacob Faesch at Mount Hope, May 25, 1783, BHP, reel 24; Alured Clarke to Benjamin Lincoln, May 27, 1783, BHP, reel 20; General Lossberg to Guy Carleton, June 19, 1783, BHP, reel 21; Extract of a Letter from the Hessian Prisoners at Mount Hope, to His Excellency Lieutenant General de Lossberg, June 22, 1783, BHP, reel 21; Deposition of Jacob Peter, June 27, 1783, BHP, reel 21; Carl Baurmeister to Guy Carleton, July 18, 1783, BHP, reel 21; Atwood, *The Hessians*, 199–200.

65. Moses Hazen to Benjamin Lincoln, June 7, 1783, BHP, reel 20; Benjamin Lincoln to Alured Clarke, May 26, 1783, BHP, reel 20; Carl Baurmeister to Guy Carleton, July 18, 1783, BHP, reel 21; Carl Leopold Baurmeister, *Revolution in America: Confidential Letters and Journals 1776–1784 of Adjutant General Major Baurmeister of the Hessian Forces*, trans. and ed. Bernhard A. Uhlendorf (New Brunswick, 1957), 573; Atwood, *The Hessians*, 200–201.

66. Reports of the North American War under the Commanding General von Lossberg, 98, 151, 119, 128, 152, 158, 167–68; Letters and Reports from Hesse-Hanau Officers, 75, 78–79; Journals and Reports of the Campaign in America, 1778–1783, 111, Hessian Documents of the American Revolution, fiche 344–48.

67. Carl Baurmeister to Guy Carleton, July 18, 1783, BHP, reel 21; Letters and Reports from Hesse-Hanau Officers, 85–86, 90; Baurmeister, *Revolution in America*, 574–75; Reports of the North American War under the Commanding General von Lossberg, 151. See also Miles, *The Hessians of Lewis Miller*.

68. Journals and Reports of the Campaign in America, 104–5; Reports of the North American War under the Commanding General von Lossberg, 159–60; Miles, "Prisoners of War in Frederick County, Maryland," 41–43; Atwood, *The Hessians*, 194; Döhla, *A Hessian Diary*, 211, 221–22, 225, 228; Neimeyer, *America Goes to War*, 61–63; Krebs, *A Generous and Merciful Enemy*, 97.

69. Atwood, *The Hessians*, 201; Miles, "Johann Leibheit and the Convention Army," 35; Miles, *The Hessians of Lewis Miller*, 24. Charles Neimeyer speculates that nearly 25 percent of the auxiliaries settled in North America; see *America Goes to War*, 61. For more recent data concerning auxiliaries who remained in North America, see Krebs, *A Generous and Merciful Enemy*, 242–60.

70. Ewald, *Diary of the American War*, 360.

71. For the continuing development of American nationalism, see esp. Waldstreicher, *In the Midst of Perpetual Fetes*; Newman, *Parades and the Politics of the Street*; and Travers, *Celebrating the Fourth*.

72. "Extracts from Moravian Diaries," 95.

Epilogue

1. Heisey, "How Lancaster Grew," 97.

2. Jasper Yeates to Edward Hand, July 4, 1783, Society Small Collection.

3. Quoted in Wood, *Conestoga Crossroads*, 241; Johann David Schöpf, *Travels in the Confederation, 1783–1784*, trans. and ed. Alfred J. Morrison, 2 vols. (1911; repr., New York, 1968), 2:11; *Freeman's Journal* (Philadelphia), Nov. 14, 1781; quoted in Häberlein, *Practice of Pluralism*, 150. See also Lemon, *Best Poor Man's Country*, 77–80; Wood, *Conestoga Crossroads*, 47, 159, 213, 215; and Häberlein, *Practice of Pluralism*, 153. See in addition the postwar marriage records of Lancaster's Reformed and Anglican congregations in *Lancaster County, Pennsylvania, Church Records of the Eighteenth Century*, ed. F. Edward Wright and Robert L. Hess, 5 vols. (Westminster, 1994), 2:176–87 and 3:123–25.

4. Quoted in Wood, *Conestoga Crossroads*, 222–24, 214–15, 249–53; Joseph Hutchins, *A Sermon, preached in the Lutheran Church, on the opening of Franklin College, in the borough of Lancaster, Pennsylvania, July 17, 1787* (Philadelphia, 1806), Early American Imprints, Ser. 2: Shaw-Shoemaker, 1801–1819, no. 10602, 14–15; S. M. Sener, "Lancaster's Bid for the National Capital," *PLCHS* 2 (1897–1898): 243.

5. F. R. Diffenderffer, "Washington at Lancaster," *PLCHS* 10 (1905–1906): 100–105; William Frederic Worner, "Washington's First Visit to Lancaster and the Observance of His Death," *PLCHS* 26 (1922): 209–13.

6. Marshall, *Diary*, 223; Edward Shippen to James Read, Feb. 15, 1778, Burd-Shippen Family Collection, reel 2; Adam Hubley to William Atlee, Paul Zantzinger, and John Hubley, Oct. 14, 1777, Peter Force Papers; Hubley, *History of the American Revolution*.

7. Corinne Earnest and Russell Earnest, *Fraktur: Folk Art and Family* (Atglen, 1999), 26–27, 81–83; Corinne Earnest and Russell Earnest, *To the Latest Posterity: Pennsylvania-German Family Registers in the Fraktur Tradition* (University Park, 2003), xvii–xxi, 15–24.

8. Diffenderffer, "Washington at Lancaster," 102–3; Worner, "Washington's First Visit to Lancaster," 211–13.

9. Diffenderffer, "Washington at Lancaster," 103–5; Worner, "Washington's First Visit to Lancaster," 212–13.

10. Diffenderffer, "Washington at Lancaster," 103–5; Worner, "Washington's First Visit to Lancaster," 211–13.

11. Worner, "Washington's First Visit to Lancaster," 212–13; Wood, *Conestoga Crossroads*, 230, 240–41.

INDEX

Note: Italic page numbers refer to maps and figures.

Allen, Daniel, 87
Allen, John, 89
American exceptionalism, 185
American patriotism: British captives' effect on, 76; and declaration of peace, 153; defining of, 64; in Frederick, Maryland, 153–54; in Lancaster's rites and festivities, 4, 5, 7, 127, 138, 143–51, 185–86, 189–90, 192–93; loyalists on, 146–47; and national identity, 186, 228n40; and Whigs, 144, 145–47, 153
Amish, 9, 60
Anburey, Thomas: on Americans, 173–74; as British captive, 1–2, 3, 147–48, 150, 175; on German captives, 172; on German desertions, 167; on Lancaster, 1–2; on loyalists, 137
André, John, 75, 79, 81, 91–92, 137
Anglicans: denominational ties of, 19–20, 22, 37; and English speakers, 38; and German speakers, 52; in Lancaster, 15, 19, 20, 22; as loyalists, 130; political support of Quakers, 23
App, Michael, 49
Armand Tuffin, Charles, 168, 169
Arnold, Benedict, 59
assimilation: of German captives, 154, 163–69, 177, 178, 183–85, 237n69; German speakers' reluctance to assimilate, 16, 179–80
Atlee, Samuel, 91, 108, 116
Atlee, William: and accounts of military actions, 139; and British captives, 118, 119, 120, 133, 158, 160, 173; brother captured by British, 91; and German captives, 113–14, 118, 119, 120, 165–66, 167
Aubel, Conrad, 166

Bailey, Francis, 142, 165
Bartgis, Matthias, 142

Barton, Thomas, 13, 19, 33, 37, 38, 130, 135, 197n13
Battle of Fort Washington, 103
Battle of Germantown, 126
Battle of Long Island, 91, 103, 105, 107, 108, 110, 139
Battle of Paoli, 141
Battle of Princeton, 103
Battle of Redbank, 121, 122
Battle of Saratoga, 1, 2, 123, 134–35, 141, 145–46, 157, 161, 183
Battle of Trenton, 6, 94, 96, 103, 116, 120, 122–24, 146, 160, 163–68
Baurmeister, Carl, 183
Bausman, Wilhelm, 13, 24, 49, 116
Beattie, William, 170, 176
Beatty, Charles, 153
Beatty, James, 165–66
Bense, Johann, 180
Berks County, Pennsylvania, 30
Bethlehem, Pennsylvania, 19
Beyer, Susanna, 22
Bird, Mark, 116, 120
Boston Port Bill, 41
Boston Tea Party, 41
Boudinot, Elias, 118, 119, 178, 182
Bowen, Thomas Bartholomew, 178
Braddock, Edward, 26, 27
Bradford, Thomas, 160, 165, 175
Britain: American prisoners of, 73, 74, 77, 78, 84, 85, 91, 92, 168, 181, 182, 235n52; and Americans' belligerent status, 69, 73; British captives' loyalty to, 172–73, 176; colonial empire of, 144; Hessians hired by, 98–100, 105–7, 124; and imperial crisis, 41–47; prisoner policy, 5; and Seven Years' War, 25–31, 39, 78
British Army: desertions of, 140, 158, 162; and loyalists, 132; and occupation of Philadelphia, 6–7, 120, 121, 123, 125–26, 130–31, 132, 133, 136, 138, 223n2

239